The Truman Merry-Go-Round

The Truman
MERRY-GO-ROUND

by Robert S. Allen
Co-author of "The Washington Merry-Go-Round"
and William V. Shannon

New York
The Vanguard Press, Inc.

CONTENTS

The Truman Merry-Go-Round

THE MAKING OF A PRESIDENT

> "Are those really Congressmen?
> are those the great Judges?
> is that the President?
> Then I will sleep awhile yet—
> for I see that
> These States sleep."
>   —WALT WHITMAN

THE presidency made Harry Truman a man. That is the story of his first administration.

But it did not make him a great man. That is the story of his second administration.

When Franklin Roosevelt died in 1945 and Harry Truman took his place, it was as if the star of the show had left and his role had been taken by a spear carrier from the mob scene. Nobody had the heart to criticize his early performance. For a while, everyone hoped that if he just kept ad-libbing along, the supporting cast and the impressive scenery would somehow carry him through. And everybody—from the stagehands to the professional critics—was eager to applaud enthusiastically.

In the five years that have followed, Harry Truman has received across the footlights everything from vociferous applause and hearty words of encouragement to dead cats and coarse suggestions that he go back to wherever it was he came from.

The most fabulous accident in American political history, Truman is the greatest American success story any writer could hope to dream up. He who had never held an important executive position in his life was suddenly thrust into the toughest and most exacting executive job in the world. A man who had never been on intimate terms with

3

a cabinet member or an ambassador was now called upon to form his own cabinet and pick his own ambassadors.

What happens in such a case is a thrilling human tale that can be told only in terms of the man himself. What he was, what happened to him, what he became, and how what he became affected the world around him! But it is almost impossible to keep the outlines of this human story clear, because everyone tends to see the holders of great office not as they are but as they look—reflected, distorted, and magnified in the mirror of the power and glory that is theirs. They are looked at in this mirror because of the deep instinctive human need for leaders and the strong tendency, when the man is inferior, to make him fit our preconceived mental image of what he ought to be. As a wise Frenchman once remarked, "Certain men gain the highest places; it is not that their merits put them there, but that it is absolutely necessary that the places be filled."

Already the Truman myth makers are at work, glorifying here, touching up there, and busily digging up signs of "early promise" and pretentious preparations for later greatness. These conjurers, staggered by the sheer, incredible fact that Harry Truman is President of these United States, unconsciously feel they cannot accept the bald reality as a freak of chance; instead, they must justify and rationalize to make it seem not only natural and understandable but right and desirable as well.

They find it difficult to concede that a man of mediocre mind, ordinary personality, little comprehension, and second-rate talents should be President. Unable to grasp the fact that this dull, ordinary man should somehow muddle through the greatest job in the world and muddle through fairly creditably, they struggle to find significance which does not exist, exalt what is commonplace, and acclaim words that are platitudinous and deeds that are vacant expedients. When all else fails, these pundits lock themselves in the impenetrable fortress of paradox and call him "a great average man."

There is no need to justify Truman or to debunk him. The facts of his career are a matter of public record. There is need to sum up and evaluate his record as it has developed so far.

In assessing Truman's performance, it is necessary to discard the antonymy of "weak" and "strong." Neither word fits him. He is not a soft, jelly-boned character, as some of our Presidents have been. Also, he has considerably more brains and industry than did either Coolidge or Harding. On the other hand, he does not have a big, sure grasp of great affairs or any passionate convictions on the great issues.

"Limited" is the word for Harry Truman. He has a limited perception of the problems at hand, a limited imagination, and a sharply limited sense of personal initiative.

He brought all these limitations into the White House in 1945, and he brought with them a king-sized inferiority complex. The latter was not immediately apparent beneath his bright, chipper, quick-striding manner. But all his life he had been a backbencher, a background figure.

As a boy, Harry Truman was shy, quiet, studious. But not uncomfortably brilliant. Since he was not the top-ranking student in his class, he did not arouse any unpleasant bitterness or jealous envy. He learned to play the piano not because of any personal zeal for music but to placate his strong-willed mother. As a boy he was always an outsider. Harry A. Bundschu, now federal referee in bankruptcy in Kansas City and a boyhood friend of the President, described the latter's childhood in an article approved by Truman and published in the *Kansas City Star* (March 1, 1949):

"Vivian Truman and I played and hunted together. We both had dogs and guns and used to roam through the woods and along the streams near the Missouri River. Harry was older. I first remember him as a quiet boy in short pants wearing heavy spectacles. He usually had a music roll in one hand and a lot of books under the other arm. He attended to his own business and seemed to do whatever his mother told him. He practiced on the piano and studied his lessons, and didn't take part in the games and rough play of the older boys. However, I have distinct recollections of one Saturday afternoon.

"We wanted to play ball in Bryant's pasture across the street from the Truman house on West Waldo, but didn't have enough boys to make up a game. Finally Vivian said, 'I'll get Harry to play with us.'

"My reaction, like a lot of the others, was to the effect that in the first place Harry wouldn't be interested, and in the second place a ball game would be a little too rough on him. But Harry quit his practicing on the piano and joined us on the lot. He took his place at first base, and it wasn't but a few minutes before we found out that he could holler louder, throw the ball harder, and play just as rough as any kid on the lot."

Truman frankly does not recall this incident. If it occurred, it must have been an isolated event. He does recall not being able to play ball because he was so nearsighted. Instead, he had to be content with being umpire once in a while and filling in as pinch hitter in an emergency.

In 1901, Truman graduated from Independence High School. He tried his hand at various jobs. He worked as mail boy for the *Kansas City Star,* as timekeeper for a railroad contractor, and as clerk in a bank. None of these jobs seemed to lead anywhere in particular, and soon he returned to the shelter of life on the family farm. Throughout his twenties, he lived at home as a bachelor and worked as his father's helper.

When Truman was thirty-two, his father died, and he succeeded him in the management of the farm and as a road overseer for Jackson County. That was 1916, the year of Pershing's expedition into Mexico in pursuit of Pancho Villa. Truman, mostly for reasons of sociability, had earlier joined the National Guard, but when this crisis came up, he followed the obvious and entirely common-sense policy of staying home and taking care of the farm. When war came, the next year, he went overseas and served honorably as an artillery officer at the front.

The war was a heaven-sent release for Truman. For the first time in his life, he—the "mother's boy," the shy, bespectacled wallflower— was freed from the dominating supervision of his mother, from the dreary round of farm and household chores, as well as from all the normal inhibitions of civilian life. Rather than putting him in a military strait jacket, the war gave him a great adventure in self-expression. It was a splash of color in a world of drab routine.

The experience opened up several pleasant prospects. First, it thrust a new invigorating responsibility on his shoulders. While in training at Fort Sill, Oklahoma, he and Eddie Jacobson, an old friend, were put in charge of the camp canteen. Canteens were notorious money-losers, but the two rookies not only broke even but made a $15,000 profit for the government.

As soon as peace was restored, Truman returned to Missouri, mar-

ried Bess Wallace, a boyhood acquaintance, and went into partnership
with Jacobson in a men's shop in Kansas City. He was never to return
to farming again.

The haberdashery was short-lived. It has since become in retrospect
probably the world's most famous store, but at that time business was
something less than flourishing, and the depression of 1921-22 soon
wiped it out. Once again, as after his high-school graduation, Truman
appeared to have failed in an attempt to lead a more independent life.
At thirty-eight, there seemed nothing to do but go back to the farm.

At this point, a fat, long-eared, solemn-faced politician entered to
play the ethereal role of Cinderella's godmother.

Tom Pendergast, saloon keeper, cement dealer, and boss of the unsavory Kansas City political machine, heard through his nephew Jim
and his brother Mike that Harry Truman, Jim's hard-up ex-battery
commander, would be very glad to get the Jackson County judgeship
if it came his way. Pendergast, having no other candidate immediately
in mind to oppose the Republican incumbent, gave his relatives the
okay to do something for their friend. Truman had previously heard
that this nomination was open and hopefully inquired about it. When
the gods—and Tom Pendergast—threw it his way, he grasped it
ardently.

Truman was elected in 1922, suffered a defeat at the next election,
but came back in 1926 to win a four-year term as presiding judge.
(During the two-year interim, Truman worked for the Missouri
Automobile Club.) His office was not a judicial post. Truman's work
as "judge" consisted of supervising road building and the maintenance
of county institutions, which in other states is performed by the county
commissioner.

This first easy victory in 1922 sent another temporary shot of life
into the withered roots of Truman's ambition. Following his election,
he began to attend the Kansas City Law School. But after two years
of night study, Truman gave up the course without taking a degree or
trying the bar exams. From then on, he settled into a quiet, comfortable rut. He worked conscientiously at the everyday duties of his office
and built up a record as a safe, reliable member of the Pendergast
machine. With a strong local background, an unimpeachable record
as a veteran and an officeholder, and a pleasant, unoffending person-

ality, he made no enemies and many well-wishers. The "organization" in these years pulled off some malodorous tricks, but Truman was not forced to participate in them.

As has been true much of his life, Harry Truman was with them but not of them.

He worked moderately hard, played the piano once in a while, gambled modestly at poker, drank bourbon, went to church on Sunday except when he felt like sleeping late, enjoyed brief vacations, spoiled daughter Margaret, his only child, and, like millions of others, just took life as it came.

In 1934, Truman was hoping that perhaps Pendergast would promote him to the congressional seat newly created under the redistricting of that year. Instead, the old man, in need of a good rural candidate to strengthen his Kansas City faction, chose Truman as his candidate for the Democratic nomination for the U.S. Senate. Truman was thus plucked out of complete obscurity to be a useful pawn in a bigger game. It was to become a familiar role.

In the primary, Truman made a respectable run upstate, but he came into Kansas City apparently decisively behind. In the opinion of his backers, however, this was surely the time for all good cemeteries to come to the aid of the party. The dead and the missing did not betray their high trust. Truman carried Ward 1 in Kansas City by a vote of 17,485 to 49 for his opponent, Ward 2 by 15,145 to 24, and Ward 3 by 8,182 to 34. These three wards alone gave Truman a majority of 40,000. Truman won the nomination by 40,000.

After the Kilkenny fight within the party, the regular election was a cinch.

Two years later, interesting returns similar to those of the 1934 primary prompted federal attorney Maurice Milligan to make an investigation. He eventually secured 283 convictions for vote frauds and revealed that 86,000 phony names had been added to the registration rolls. Concerning these scandals, Truman remarked, "Those things were due to the overzealousness of Tom's boys. They were too anxious to make a good showing for the boss, and they took the easiest way. Tom didn't know anything about it—he was never involved in that sort of thing."

Milligan soon proved that the sort of thing Tom was personally involved in was equally fraudulent. Pendergast was bundled off to Leavenworth for taking a bribe in an insurance-settlement case. Truman had no taste for such persistent bad manners. One of his first acts as President was to fire the snoopy Mr. Milligan.

This background as a Pendergast servitor has come up in later years to harass Truman, but he always clings to it with stubborn defiance and endless rationalization. His two favorite excuses are that everyone else was playing along with the machine (which is not true), and that, in any event, Pendergast's private charities ought to be allowed to overshadow his political sins.

During the 1944 campaign, when he was running for Vice-President, it was suggested that he might be in a vulnerable position because of the Kansas City machine hookup. He replied, "I am not! Why am I in a weak position? There was nothing wrong with my relations with the Pendergast machine. Since about 1920, that machine had a majority of about 100,000 votes it could deliver in a Democratic primary, and every politician, including myself, went to Tom Pendergast for support."

This convenient reinterpretation gives Truman the entirely erroneous position of a free operator of independent weight bidding for Pendergast support. Actually, of course, he took orders and did what he was told, like everyone else in the organization.

Truman, continuing his defense, declared, "Pendergast is a fine gentleman. Why, if you read the *Kansas City Star* you get the idea he had horns. Nothing of the kind. Tom Pendergast did a great deal of good. He was always helping people, even people who did nothing for him. He gave away huge amounts to charity. You could trust him. His word was his bond."

Once the well-bonded Mr. Truman arrived in the Senate, he followed a passive role.

In his maiden speech, he promised his senior colleagues that he would sit back and keep his mouth shut until he learned the ropes. This asinine custom of "silent freshmen" is more honored in the breach than the observance and ought to be breached even more. But Truman honored it faithfully throughout his first term in the Senate.

He never introduced a major bill, made an important speech, or played an important part in committee proceedings. It was not until 1939 that he began to assume an even moderately active part in committee work. He was definitely classed among the Senatorial Mutes. During his first session, the savagely fought Wheeler-Rayburn holding company bill came before the Senate. One day, after listening to a long and dramatic debate over the bill, Truman and the late Lewis Schwellenbach walked from the chamber together. "Exciting debate, wasn't it?" Schwellenbach remarked. "Yes, it was," Truman replied, and then added a little wistfully, "I wish I had understood it all."

Truman's private political views were not liberal. They were the stock agglomeration of opinions and prejudices of the moderately well-to-do, rural, border-state Democrat. He stood for economy, was suspicious of both organized labor and Wall Street, believed in legal rights for Negroes but not in social equality, and favored as little government action as possible. As a consequence, Truman often felt rather uneasy in the Democratic Party as Franklin Roosevelt was running it.

In 1936, two years after he became a senator, Truman wrote a revealing private letter to a college student in New York who had written asking him (along with many others) why he was a Democrat.

"This is a matter," Truman replied, "of history and policy more than anything else. . . . The Republican Party has always stood for a strong centralized government, and the Democratic Party has stood for strong state and local governments. However, under the present administration, that situation seems to be somewhat reversed, because the Republicans are now asking for strong state government and the Democrats have been working for a strong centralized government, under the emergency.

"However, the general principles of the Democratic Party are for as little government as possible, and for that government to be as close to the people as it is possible to put it. That is the principal reason I am a Democrat. Another good reason is that I was raised one. My mother and my grandmother and all the rest of my family have all been good Democrats. That is about the best reason, I think."

But, whatever Truman may have thought privately in his senatorial days about the virtues of small government, he realized there was only one thing Pendergast was interested in, and that was federal patronage. Truman knew only one way to get patronage. It was by becoming an extremely loyal administration man. Therefore, what he lacked in constructive support he fully made up in steadfastness.

He went firmly down the line on every New Deal measure, including the Supreme Court "packing" bill. Only rarely did his political shirt show signs of tattletale gray. In 1936, he voted against the Wagner bill, which would have established a permanent low-cost housing program. In January, 1939, he voted for a cut in the relief appropriation bill, and Roosevelt lost by one vote. Truman voted for the Wagner Labor Act, but he announced that he would like to amend it and make it less compulsory.

He said, in a speech to the Senate, "The time has come when labor unions, cooperatives, and similar organizations which have grown to such vast proportions . . . are going to be required to make an accounting of their funds and of what they do with them, for the benefit of the public and in the public interest. . . . There is no difference between a labor leader with too much money to spend and Mark Hanna with too much money to spend on an election."

In 1937, the administration was anxious to have the Senate Democrats choose Alben Barkley as Majority Floor Leader rather than Pat Harrison, the veteran Mississippi Tory. Truman had pledged his vote to Harrison, but Roosevelt lieutenants attempted to get him to switch. Pendergast was phoned in Kansas City in an effort to put the pressure on, but Truman told the boss he had pledged his word and must remain loyal. Pendergast gave up. Loyalty was the one claim whose validity no machine politician could deny. The administration found its extra vote somewhere else.

In 1940, it was this loyalty which re-elected Truman to the Senate. Pendergast was by that time in jail, but Truman stuck with the organization. (It is sometimes forgotten that he could not have done anything else, even if he had wanted to. He scarcely had any place else to go.)

Truman rallied all his latent aggressiveness and his inherent instinct for self-preservation during the 1940 campaign. He stumped the State intensively. If there was a county clambake he missed, it was no fault of his. This desperate beating of the bushes paid off in a razor-thin primary victory. Once nominated, he was carried back to office on Roosevelt's capacious coattails.

Truman in his first term was little more than an extra vote in Alben Barkley's hip pocket. He was a less useful and constructive member of the Senate than Lew Schwellenbach of Washington and Lister Hill of Alabama, and less stridently loyal to the administration than "Shay" Minton of Indiana and Josh Lee of Oklahoma. He was back among senators like Bulow of South Dakota, Schwartz of Wyoming, Smathers of New Jersey, and Herring of Iowa, all of whom were equally loyal and equally undistinguished figures in the New Deal Congresses of the 1930's. This quartet of backbenchers, like many of Truman's other colleagues, have long since died or retired to obscurity.

Upon the opening of his second term in the Senate, Truman showed a flash of initiative.

The same much-repressed instinct for aggressive independent action which, after high school, had prompted him to try his luck briefly away from the farm, which had stirred again a decade and a half later when he made his unhappy haberdashery venture, and which had caused him hopefully to take up the study of law when he was almost forty, once more broke through the thick crust of vacuous docility and submissive conventionality. Early in 1941, he sponsored and became the first chairman of what was to become famous as the Defense, and later the Truman War Investigating Committee. It was a master stroke.

For the first time in his whole life, initiative paid off for Harry Truman. The Senate War Investigating Committee made him famous and made him President.

Organizing and presiding over this Committee was a task peculiarly suited to Truman. Essentially, the job of the Committee permitted no real conflict. There were no confusing ideological issues and no unpleasant struggles between labor and management or farmer and consumer. There could not be two points of view when the matter at hand was whether the government in wartime should get full value in return for the money it expended. Truman, therefore, had no necessity to "take sides" or make any basic policy decisions. He was in the safe and enviable position of being a critic of efficiency and not purpose.

All witnesses were treated courteously, and there were no flare-ups between Committee members. Truman was so obviously mild and self-effacing that he anesthetized the potential jealous envy of hotheads like Brewster of Maine. All Committee reports were unanimous. Truman was a regular Democrat with whom the people in the executive offices could readily cooperate, but at the same time he could safely criticize the administration on grounds of war efficiency without seeming to attack the President or incurring his wrath. As a result, Truman made no lasting enemies in wartime Washington.

He was a diligent and attentive member of his Committee, but little of the actual planning or investigating was done by him personally. Unlike Tom Walsh of Montana, who spent eighteen months in lonely study and patient digging before he called his first witness and began to crack the Teapot Dome scandal, and unlike Hugo Black, who personally planned and supervised every minute detail that went into his excoriating exposé of the utility lobby, Harry Truman left the fundamental investigating, as well as the drafting of reports, in the hands of the anonymous Committee staff. He was not cut out to be a prosecuting attorney, and he never undertook that role.

The story of Truman's nomination for the vice-presidency has been told many times. But the full story will never be known. One myth connected with it, however, should certainly be dispelled.

This is the fiction that Truman received the nomination with no effort on his part and that, indeed, he took it with considerable reluctance and regret. Actually, he battled for it furiously and, in his way, very effectively.

The myth about his nomination is silly, because deep down Truman has always been an extremely ambitious man. This is shown by the way he has fought like a tiger to hold any office that anyone ever tried to take away from him. This was true of his Jackson County judgeship, his Senate fight in 1940, and of his presidential melee in 1948. All he ever lacked was the initial guts really to go after the prizes he wanted, and the self-confidence to believe that if he did fight for them, the big jobs could really and truly be his.

When Tom Pendergast offered him the senatorship on a silver platter in 1934, he could scarcely believe it. Similarly, ten years later, when those delicious rumors began to float around that Roosevelt and the big bosses were considering him for the vice-presidency, it took Truman some time to adjust his ego to the staggering reality. For several weeks, he went around mumbling, as if it were a magic formula, the stock opinion of his fellow border-state and Southern conservatives that "Sam Rayburn or Jimmy Byrnes would make a fine Vice-President." But all the while he knew that with the right kind of breaks it might readily come to him, and his mind raced in wild anticipation.

By the time he got to the convention at Chicago, his true feelings had struggled to the surface, and he was candidly admitting, with, of course, an apologetic and self-deprecating smile, that he would be very glad to take the nomination. Sam Rayburn was completely forgotten, and, as for Jimmy Byrnes, Truman had managed to drop the conventional pose of admiration and liking for the pride of Spartanburg, South Carolina, at least sufficiently to join heartily in slitting Byrnes's throat.

Truman was feverishly active on the floor of the convention, backstage, in hotel lobbies, and elsewhere, buttonholing and cajoling political bosses, cabinet officers, and just plain delegates for their votes. When the nomination came to him, Harry Truman was a very proud, happy, and self-satisfied man.

As a vice-presidential candidate, he laid one egg after another from coast to coast.

He read his ghostwritten speeches slowly and mechanically, as if he were translating them from Hindustani as he went along. When he ad-libbed, he swung wildly and ineffectively. Again and again, in delicate local situations, he opened his mouth only to put his feet into it. Finally, in desperation, Roosevelt dispatched handy-andy George Allen to Truman's campaign train with the injunction to "stop him from making all those damn fool statements."

Allen did his best, told his funniest stories, and encouraged his bush-league candidate to do the best he could in his debut in the big time. Truman still managed to pull some "beauts," however.

When he visited Massachusetts, he made a ringing attack on isolationists and urged Dewey to repudiate those in his party. A reporter asked Truman what about Democratic isolationists like Massachusetts' aged Senator David I. Walsh? Without thinking for a moment, Truman came right back, "Oh, his term has two more years to go. Maybe we can reform him."

Walsh and his supporters were so burned up that you could see the smoke from Cape Cod to the Vermont border.

When Roosevelt came to Boston a few days later, he had to invoke the sacred memory of Al Smith and practically sing "Wrap the Green Flag Round Me, Boys" to repair the damage of that howler.

But Tom Dewey had Bricker on his hands, so Roosevelt managed to stagger through to victory, Truman notwithstanding.

To want to be Vice-President was one thing. To want to be the PRESIDENT was quite another. At least, that was the initial reaction of Harry Truman on April 12, 1945.

On that fateful day and for several months thereafter, he became painfully aware of his size or, rather, of the size of the office he had inherited. He was like a small boy with a very big club; he was always being surprised at the far-off things he hit when he swung it.

The most overworked word used to describe Truman's attitude in those early weeks was "humble." But this was correct for only one side of the coin. From the beginning, though quite awed by his vast powers, Truman actually had some very strong and set notions about how he could improve on Roosevelt's performance. He set out to do so in three different ways.

First, he had long before fallen for the ancient conservative decoy that there was nothing wrong with the New Deal policies except the people who administered them. Those New Dealers were tactless and cantankerous and just liked to stir up animosity for the hell of it. The first order of business was not to scrap the program but to scrap its makers. Truman felt he could not touch the heads of the War and Navy Departments as long as the war was on; Ickes had to be kept because he was so notably honest and efficient; and Wallace couldn't be fired because that would make a lot of people angry. But as for the rest . . . off with their heads!

Truman fired Francis Biddle, Claude Wickard, Frank Walker, Henry Morgenthau, Frances Perkins, and scores of others within three months after taking office.

"My God, the way they've cleaned house here, you'd think they were

Republicans," a White House secretary remarked bitterly as she cleaned out her desk. It was, indeed, a purge. In several instances, Truman had nothing against the incumbent and no clear idea as to whom he wanted to replace him with. The selection of Clinton Anderson as Secretary of Agriculture is a graphic case in point.

It was due almost solely to the fact that in June, 1945, there was a periodic uproar in Congress about rationing and food shortages, and Anderson happened to be chairman of the House committee making the noisy investigation. What better way to buy off opposition—or, as Truman conceived it, what better way to end friction and create "harmony"—than to give the Agriculture job to one of the critics?

A second Truman aim in those early weeks was more efficiency. It was tacitly understood that the new President's first recommendation to Congress would be promptly honored as a token of congressional cooperation. Truman's request, of all things, was for a modest grant of power to reorganize the executive departments. The requested legislation was soon passed.

It was characteristic of Truman, and revealing of his true political mentality, for him to feel, in the midst of grave crises in foreign affairs and serious reconversion problems looming at home, that the most important thing he had to do was to tidy up the administrative housekeeping.

Truman's third chief idea in his early months in office was that Roosevelt had aroused a lot of bad feeling on Capitol Hill and had gotten nothing out of Congress because of his driving, aggressive tactics. Truman was convinced that the fellows were really well intentioned and good-natured. They could be persuaded to go along with a liberal program, just as he himself had always been persuaded to go along, if they were approached in the right way.

So Leslie Biffle, the slick, soft-spoken Senate Secretary, became the congressional fixer and a White House fixture. Midnight poker sessions and private congressional luncheons became the order of the day for the President. Under Truman's jolly ministrations, bourbon and bonhomie would usher in a new era of good feeling and make Roosevelt look like a piker.

That neither sonorous paper schemes for government reorganization nor the creation of an atmosphere of specious good fellowship would produce any results was clear to almost every experienced observer. But most of them chalked it up as evidence of Truman's good intentions and inexperience. In fact, however, it was much more serious and significant than that.

Both policies were stupid. No amount of gizzard-tingling Kentucky bourbon and droll Southern stories could soften up hard-shelled reactionaries like George and Byrd, any more than they could sway genuine liberals. Truman was dealing with strong-willed men who were their own bosses and who had not spent twenty-five years as rubber stamps registering other men's convictions. Similarly, Truman fell for a blatant newspaper dodge when he thought that conservatives really believed in the "basic principles" of the Wagner Act or the AAA or the reclamation program, and only disagreed with the way they were administered.

From the very first, the Old Guarders were out to meat-ax these policies and to get as far back toward 1929 as they could. Only a man of Truman's pacific nature and deeply ingrained submissiveness could have entertained the idea that he could successfully administer the biggest job in the world by skirting conflict and cheerfully appealing to the better nature of hard-bitten politicos.

Old Justice Oliver Wendell Holmes once said, "Conflict is the core of life." It was to take Harry Truman three long years to find that out and to make up his mind as to which side he was on in the basic struggles of our day.

However, at the same time that Truman was trying to handshake and pussyfoot his way through the perils of power, he was also grievously aware of his own limitations. Never was a man in the White House so filled with a sense of his own inadequacy and so weighted down with a crushing sense of guilt.

It was as if a boy had somehow usurped the place of his strong, wise, reliable, and omniscient father. Roosevelt had been the Great White Father for so long: leading the way, making the tough decisions, arbitrating the disputes, reassuring the doubtful, assigning to each his role. In the preceding presidential campaign, there were home-made signs reading "Humanity Needs Roosevelt." How could Truman feel it was right and just for him to be here in Roosevelt's place?

He could scarcely imagine anyone putting up a sign reading "Humanity Needs Harry Truman."

Truman did not crack under the strain because all the time, deep down inside him, was the strong, cocky belief that he was a pretty smart and competent guy. And there is nothing to compare with the presidency as an ego builder. So he kept staggering forward in the only way he knew, which, for the time being, meant a continuation of old habits of "reasonableness" and genial backslapping. But, should that cocky self-confidence break through and take command, he would be a very different man.

Meanwhile, however, there was that gnawing sense of guilt and inadequacy which found expression in numerous odd ways. He sadly explained to White House visitors that he had never wanted the job, that he had been pushed into it, that he wished somehow it were possible to turn the job over to someone else. (None of which he fundamentally believed.) To strong, ambitious men like Jim Farley and Jimmy Byrnes, he seemed almost to apologize that he, and not they, had gotten the presidency. On the slightest pretext, he sent flowers to be laid on Roosevelt's grave at Hyde Park. Mrs. Roosevelt he put on a pedestal and deferred to almost obsequiously. In public, he frequently admitted that "the President" and "Harry Truman" were not synonymous in his mind.

In 1945, he was best man for ex-Senator Bennett Champ Clark at the latter's wedding. Afterward, he was heard to remark, "Sometimes I forget I'm President of the United States." One cynical reporter commented, "Well, that's really getting it from the horse's mouth."

The clearest manifestation of his insecurity was the ready manner in which he responded to forceful suggestions from the press. If newspapers suggested that Herbert Hoover's great talents as an "elder statesman" should be made use of, Truman obligingly dug the battered great engineer out of moth balls and sent him around the world on a food survey. If newspapers raised a clamor that a Republican be put on the Supreme Court to keep it "balanced," Truman obediently appointed Republican Senator Harold Burton. It was as if Truman, uncertain in his own mind what his course should be, looked to the newspapers for guidance and was reassured by their plaudits.

Meanwhile, Truman seemed to take great pleasure in the increased affluence of his personal position.

Until public concern for his safety became angrily vocal, he was fond of making extensive jaunts in the presidential plane, even in dangerous winter weather. His new yacht, the USS "Williamsburg," formerly the plaything of a wealthy New Yorker, provided much-cherished moments of relaxation. Week ends on the Potomac became the rule. He acquired a Cadillac convertible and took great relish in driving it personally. It was clear that the frugal mode of living he had formerly followed had been due to the meagerness of a senator's salary rather than to any love of the simple life for its own sake.

Truman showed a similar scorn for simplicity in the matter of military dress.

Roosevelt had given a provisional order that a new uniform was to be designed which would eliminate most of the braid and the insignia and reduce the distinction between officers and enlisted men. Truman, however, like many average men, does not really like the equalitarian side of democracy. As a Legionnaire, a Shriner, and a former National Guard officer, Truman likes gold braid and colorful dress on his soldiers. The officers are still wearing their fancy uniforms.

But perhaps for these very reasons, Mr. Truman was popular in the opening months of his first administration. He was "John Q. Public come to Washington," the average man's Average Man.

But with the coming of peace, Truman and his associates had to face the awesome problems of peacemaking and the ugly and irritating problems of domestic reconversion. The honeymoon was over.

The year that followed was a horrible one for Mr. Truman and an even worse one for America.

Slammed in the face with one smashing crisis after another, Truman was capable of responding to none of them. He could work hard, but he found hard work was not selling at a premium. What the presidency demanded was the vision and grasp of a top-floor executive, not the diligence of a janitor. He had good will but not the perception to guide it. He wanted to be loyal, but he had nothing to be loyal to but a dead man's vague phrases and half-sketched plans. He who had always been a follower now had no one to follow.

But he had plenty of advisers. There was no need to ration the supply of opinions and ideas. The only thing that was lacking was the ability to decide.

In foreign affairs, he muddled along with inexperienced and over-confident Jimmy Byrnes, who learned the wisdom of a firm Russian policy but only after many painful missteps. Within a period of nine months, Truman oscillated violently between endorsing the "iron cur-tain" speech of Winston Churchill at Fulton, Missouri, and endorsing the "let's-mind-our-own-business" speech of Henry Wallace at Madison Square Garden in New York.

In domestic affairs, all was wild confusion. In January, 1946, during the General Motors strike, he let the remnants of the New Deal ele-ment talk him into backing public inspection of corporation books. By May, he was marching with Senator Byrd and calling for a draft of railroad strikers. He summoned Wilson Wyatt from Kentucky to be Housing Expeditor and gave him the stirring mandate, "Make no small plans." Within the year, Wyatt was dropped. Or, rather, he was allowed to get a divorce on grounds of nonsupport when court jester George Allen tied up the RFC's purse strings.

On the issue of a rise in the price of steel and on the general ques-tions of rationing, price control, and economic reconversion, Chester Bowles, John Snyder, Fred Vinson, Robert Nathan, John Steelman, Paul Porter, and others pushed and tugged Truman from all direc-tions, and he flipped, flopped, and wobbled like a rag doll. In the end, it all trailed off in a fog of confusion in the public mind: everyone in the administration working at cross-purposes, Congress passing a hopeless "compromise" bill, cattlemen staging a phony meat famine, and, through it all, like the sound of banshees wailing in the night, came the taunting Republican cry: "Had enough?"

Public confidence sagged still further as Truman made a rising number of shoddy appointments. Although he placed some strong figures in his cabinet, Truman still seemed to regard the presidency as a candy box with which he could get the thrill of giving choice pieces to his grubby friends. He took a positive delight in raising various obscure characters to important and high-sounding jobs, much as if he were playing "fairy queen" and had the power to make their fondest dreams come true.

Men like Harry Vaughan, John Snyder, "Jake" Vardaman, and

George Allen began popping up all over the Washington landscape. The climax came when Truman selected California oilman Edwin Pauley to become Undersecretary of the Navy and heir apparent to Secretary James Forrestal. Pauley, better known as a lobbyist against federal control of tidelands oil and as a prolific raiser of campaign funds than as an expert on naval affairs, had already served as Reparations Commissioner, where he established some sort of a record for always coming out as low man on the Russian totem pole.

What gave the Pauley selection the stature of a major crisis was the fact that Truman nominated him even though Interior Secretary Harold Ickes, a zealous defender of federal conservation policies, had given ample warning that he would not serve in an administration which included a man of Pauley's background. In effect, Ickes had said to Truman, choose him or me. The President chose Pauley. To the public it was not a palatable choice. A furor of protests arose; the Senate Naval Affairs Committee balked; and Pauley's nomination had to be withdrawn.

At this juncture, the big city bosses, led by Ed Kelly of Chicago and Ed Flynn of the Bronx, put pressure on Truman to fill the vacancy left by Ickes' departure with a man of real big-league size. They cared nothing whatever about tidelands oil or any other such issue. They did care about the next election, and they wanted in the cabinet a "strong man" who would serve as a kind of prime minister and give the domestic administration some of the leadership and coherence that Truman could not seem to give it.

Ironically, their choice for this role as receiver in political bankruptcy was Justice William O. Douglas, the man these same big-city bosses had euchred out of the vice-presidential nomination in 1944, in favor of Mr. Truman.

The President divined the real purpose in their move, and he had no stomach for such a vigorous, independent man as Douglas, anyway. But he wavered sufficiently to invite Douglas in for a talk, and made the offer to him. Douglas quickly turned it down. He was too shrewd to think that he could really pull the Truman regime out of the ruck, when he had no constitutional authority or traditional support for playing the strange role of prime minister. Truman was left to muddle through the chaos of confusion as best he could.

He was simply and hopelessly inadequate to the tasks that beset him.

At the very best, it would have taken a highly skilled and tough-willed chief executive to hold the reins during reconversion and drive the team in the direction he wanted to go. After four years of wearing war harness, the labor unions, the farm bloc, the big corporations, and assorted special interests were all bucking and plunging; they wanted to gallop into the green pastures and they weren't waiting for the Lord to lead them. Truman was not the man to be in the driver's seat at such a time. He did not have the requisite grasp of economic issues. But, worse than that, at this stage of his development in the presidency, he had not yet found his own operating level.

To the observer, at first glance, it seemed that Truman was just bewildered. He kept on reiterating the platitudes of the prewar New Deal with the same grim intentness and practical effect as a man selling sun-tan lotion in a snowstorm. It was this prevailing sense of incongruity that boss Ed Kelly summed up when he said, "These are chaotic times, and Mr. Truman makes a good chaotic President, in that he's matched to the times."

But what was even harder to explain was that, at the very core of this chaos, there was by no means an anxious or a gravely worried man. Truman actually seemed bored and indifferent to it all.

Visitors to his office reported that he heard them out with an air of polite civility. What manner of man was this who wore misfortune so lightly? Many looked at Truman's blithe self-control during the grave days of the railroad strike and echoed the query of the *New Republic*—is he "a man of iron . . . or one of stone?"

He was neither. The true answer contains several parts.

First of all, there was still a wide discrepancy between Truman's private opinions and his public utterances. He came to the presidency a moderate conservative, but he had inherited a liberal mandate and a set of liberal advisers. It was easy enough to fire most of the advisers, and that was quickly done. But it was not so easy to reset the intellectual orientation of the whole administration and to divert the currents of thought and practice which had been flowing strongly for a dozen years. Particularly difficult was it for a man who was laboring under a feeling of obligation to defer to his dead predecessor's wishes.

Inescapably, therefore, Truman found himself making statements and proclaiming policies in which he personally did not wholeheartedly believe.

It was this gap between compulsive public profession and genuine emotional commitment which caused much of his erratic performance. As long as the administration talked out of the left side of its mouth but turned its eyes wistfully to the right, it was bound to drag its feet and stumble quite frequently.

Secondly, this gap between practice and belief served, like dead air between outer and inner walls, to insulate Truman from any emotional grief over the failure of various policies and programs. It was not that he was deliberately and consciously pursuing a course of Machiavellian hypocrisy, but simply that he looked upon policies as expedients and palliatives to solve or ward off problems for which he had no personal solution.

Consequently, he suffered no agonies of indecision over any problem.

Some specific idea or solution would catch his fancy, and he would promptly adopt it. He did not spend a lot of time reshuffling and re-evaluating his reasons, because he scarcely had any reasons to start with. He could not worry about which card to play when they all looked the same to him.

This was true even when he decided, in the railroad strike of 1946, to take the extremely drastic step of asking for power to conscript labor. He casually decided to choose the card which read, "Use the Prestige of the President and Appeal to the National Interest Over All Narrow Selfish Interests." If that card won a trick, that was fine. If it did not, he would have to play another card. It was as elementary as that. When the pundits screamed "Fascist," he thought they were just acting silly.

Moreover, Truman was still not emotionally adjusted to the seven-league boots any successful occupant of the White House must wear. He was timid and eager to please.

He had been schooled for so long to be agreeable and to do what other people expected of him, whether it was dutifully learning to play the piano at his mother's behest or obeying political instructions from the Boss in Kansas City, that when, as President, he dealt with people toward whom he felt real hostility, his first instinct was not to express that feeling but to deny it. Moreover, not only did he mask his true aggressive sentiments but he felt compelled to deny even to himself that he had them—by expressing their exact opposite.

Thus it was that, several weeks after he became President, he summoned Treasury Secretary Henry Morgenthau to the White House. Truman had always been suspicious of Morgenthau and considered him cold and supercilious. The Treasury Secretary's voluntary resignation had lain on Truman's desk for over a month. It was natural, therefore, for Morgenthau to assume that this conference had been called for the purpose of giving him the ax. The President began, however, by discussing various routine tax matters, and then the conversation drifted aimlessly. Just as the Secretary's fifteen minutes were coming to an end, Truman, much to Morgenthau's surprise, rose, clasped his hand, and said earnestly:

"Henry, when I took this job, I didn't know you very well. But since I've worked with you, I've begun to feel like a brother toward you, and I want you to feel like a brother toward me."

The Secretary naturally left the conference much elated. A week later, Truman's true feelings having struggled to the surface in the meantime, he quite suddenly and unceremoniously fired Morgenthau. But, characteristically, even then he did not do this in person. He sent Judge Sam Rosenman to deliver the news.

Closely related to this habit was a second trait in Truman's personality. He seemed so eager to have people like him that, face to face with a man, he shrank from doing anything aggressive or unpleasant and often said things he didn't really mean.

This characteristic differed considerably from the same trait in Roosevelt. Roosevelt also did not like to be cruel, but when the issue was a major one, he could be as ruthless as was necessary. Roosevelt, moreover, was the master of the blurred ambiguity. He left visitors feeling that perhaps he was with them or at least he hadn't made up his mind. Truman was not so adept at spinning verbal fuzz and consequently found himself making sweeping and explicit statements which went far beyond the necessities of letting the other fellow down easily. Then, when he was alone again, Truman would think about it for a time and work up courage and will power enough to do what he had wanted to do in the first place.

These two facets of Truman's personality became painfully familiar to top-bracket officials.

Spruille Braden, the Assistant Secretary of State in charge of Latin American affairs and a staunch foe of dictator Perón, was discussing Argentine affairs at the White House one afternoon and reviewing the points of controversy between him and pro-Perón Ambassador George Messersmith. After a while the President said, "Spruille, I want you to know that I'm one hundred per cent behind you. I'll back you all the way."

Warmly pleased, Braden went back to the State Department. But when he related the incident to a friend, the latter cautioned, "Maybe he means it. But that is exactly what he told Henry Wallace the day before he fired him. He told Henry he would back him all the way, too. Next day Wallace was out."

Sure enough, shortly afterward Truman asked for Braden's resignation.

The same dreary process was followed with regard to Housing Expeditor Wilson Wyatt, James M. Landis of the Civil Aeronautics Board, Marriner Eccles of the Federal Reserve Board, and other ace officials whom Truman eventually fired or demoted. He did all this backing and filling, and mumbled all these professions that he didn't mean, at the very same time that, in his public addresses, he woefully mourned the lack of capable public servants.

Handicapped by this insecure and inept leader, the Democratic Party entered the 1946 elections in an atmosphere saturated with defeatism. The liberal cause in the country missed the guiding hand of the White House and had lost all sense of purpose and direction. Among liberals in Washington, bitterness was so intense that the White House came to be known as Heartbreak House. Truman, except for making a clumsy gesture toward the Jewish vote in New York by reversing his stand on Palestine, sat out the campaign. The Democratic Party everywhere manifested all the symptoms of a Freudian death wish.

The crushing Republican victory in the off-year elections brought more comfort than despair to Harry Truman. It lifted twin burdens from his shoulders.

The mandate Roosevelt had won in 1944 was canceled out, and Truman was free to go ahead in any direction he wished. Secondly, the defeat gave largely to the Republicans the responsibility for finding solutions for new problems and permitted Truman, for the first time, to shift from the defensive to the offensive.

Almost simultaneously, a new and refreshingly brainy figure moved into the intellectual void around the President. Clark Clifford, smart, able, diplomatic young lawyer from St. Louis, had entered the White House service earlier as Assistant Naval Aide and had been rapidly promoted under the aegis of Judge Sam Rosenman to the post of legal counsel to the President.

Clifford had had his baptism of fire, rather inauspiciously, in the assignment of drafting Truman's reactionary message to Congress recommending the draft of strikers into the Army. But Clifford, though he lacked the ebullience and crusading fire of his New Deal prototypes, was shrewd enough to see that the only hope for Truman's political success lay along liberal rather than conservative lines. In his suave, adroit way he began to guide the President in this direction. Simply because he did not talk or look like a doctrinaire liberal, Clifford gradually won the Chief Executive's full confidence and became his chief speech writer and administrative coordinator.

Though the pupil himself did not realize it, the education of Harry Truman had begun.

Clifford's first victory came shortly after the 1946 election, when he persuaded Truman to stand firm against John L. Lewis. This represented a triumph over the mealymouthed counsels of White House Assistant John Steelman, who urged a continuation of the policy of appeasement. Clifford's strategy was successful; the government broke the coal deadlock, and the Truman regime won the first real victory in the domestic field in its two-year history. The defeat of Lewis was not of itself an augury of a liberal future. Its main significance was that it restored a dash of vigor to the flabby spiritual tone of the executive office.

In the months that followed, the administration pursued a cautious policy. Truman enjoyed a synthetic rise in his popular prestige, especially in the conservative press, following his appointment of General George Marshall as Secretary of State and Lewis W. Douglas as Ambassador to England. Toward Congress, Truman played Fabius.

He issued mild, conciliatory statements at his press conferences, lowered the sights on his domestic program, proposed a watered-down revision of the Wagner Act, and tried to steal some Republican thunder by giving Attorney General Tom Clark the go-ahead signal for a loud, showy campaign to rid the federal government of "Reds."

For a time, this strategy became so pronounced that liberals grumbled that Truman kept his ear to the ground trying to find out what the Republicans were going to do so he could beat them to it. GOP Floor Leader Charles Halleck wisecracked, "Harry knows a trend when he sees one. Why, I expect any day now to see him register as a Republican."

Actually, however, this was only a few rounds of sparring while the contestants waited for the main event. The bell rang for action when the Republican Congress placed the Taft-Hartley bill on Truman's desk for his signature.

At this point, a savagely fought struggle began within Truman's circle of advisers. The majority of the cabinet, led by Navy Secretary Forrestal, Treasury Secretary Snyder, and Commerce Secretary Harriman, urged the President to sign the bill. Only Postmaster General Hannegan and Labor Secretary Schwellenbach, both ailing and fading from active participation, held out against signing.

Energetically backing them up, however, was Clark Clifford—also, it was political wisdom not to ignore the mingled threats and exhortations from the leaders of organized labor and their Northern political allies. Clifford prepared an incisive and comprehensive analysis of the bill, which succeeded in convincing the President he had a sound case for a veto. Though Truman postponed his public decision until almost the last minute and heard everyone's arguments patiently, he had in fact made his decision intuitively almost at the outset.

Faced with a choice in stark and unmistakable terms between holding to a moderately leftish course or turning sharply to the right, Truman sensed that this time there could be no easy, roundabout escape, no bland compromise. Any decision would be irrevocable. Whatever his reason, whether it was that the crisis of decision gave his pallid liberalism a shot of adrenalin, or whether his action was a piece of calculated political opportunism, Truman made his decision to veto the bill and side with organized labor. It was his own choice, consciously and deliberately made. And, since it was his own, he inevitably felt emotionally committed to it and would have to come to its defense when it was attacked.

This Taft-Hartley veto was the first step in closing the gap between the inner convictions and the public platitudes of Harry Truman, between the man and the President.

The bitter and protracted struggle with the Eightieth Congress over tax reduction further clarified the liberal-conservative issue in Truman's mind. He saw clearly that the "reasonable," "sensible" course of action long urged upon him by the conservative press and conservative interests generally was only a decoy move on their part. The right-wing spokesmen were themselves now in the saddle and evincing no interest in halfway measures.

The views of the Joe Martins, the Hallecks, and the Wherrys had not changed from the days of Coolidge and Hoover. They still put tax reduction and quick profits for a few fat-cats ahead of debt retirement and long-term financial stability. And where were the newspaper editors and the others who always clamored so loudly for caution and prudence in economic policy-making? Truman found them cheering on the GOP work. Thus, the tax vetoes of Truman represented more than the financial attitude of the administration. Each veto message underscored the political distinctions which for the first time were emerging clearly in the President's mind. Each veto was another act of faith, another tie binding Truman to the liberal cause.

The fulfillment of this educational process came for Truman in the fall of 1947 and the early winter of 1948.

That fall, the President called a special session of Congress to deal with the skyrocketing inflation. Shortly before the session, a reporter at the weekly White House press conference asked if plans were under consideration for a return to rationing and price controls. "No, sir," Truman said grimly, "those are police-state methods." At these words, Clark Clifford, standing at the President's right, winced visibly. Clifford realized the only way Truman could distinguish his position from that of the Republicans was to come out clearly for a program of strong government controls.

In the days that followed, he argued this question out with Truman. He showed him how futile and ineffective had been the washed-out substitutes advocated by Treasury Secretary Snyder and other administration conservatives. Truman's main opposition was not so much intellectual as emotional. Price controls and rationing were identified in his mind with the unpleasant experiences he had had in the losing OPA fight of 1946. But in the end he swallowed his distaste and made a fighting speech for all-out action.

Almost simultaneously, the President adopted the recommendations of the Committee on Civil Rights appointed a year earlier. Truman's private views on the race problem had always been those of a well-intentioned Southerner. He had no fighting convictions about Negro injustices, no personal eagerness for a full-fledged policy of social equality, but, on the other hand, neither did he have any violent prejudices. It was, therefore, not too difficult for him to go along with the civil rights report, especially since he privately viewed the recommendations as more in the nature of long-term goals rather than immediate objectives.

He felt Southerners would have the good grace to view it in this light also. When Southern reactionaries made this an excuse for bolting the party, he was shocked at their ruthlessness in driving him to the wall and calling his bluff. But he readily identified the program with himself and prepared to fight it out on this line in fullhearted fashion.

Ironically, at this very time, Truman's stock began to drop.

He was still surrounded by many mediocre associates and ill-chosen friends. General Wallace Graham, his personal physician, and the ineffable Ed Pauley were revealed as grain-market gamblers at the very time Truman was denouncing commodity speculation as a contributing cause of inflation.

A further source of grief was the snarled situation in Palestine. Stirred by personal sympathy and political instinct, Truman at first took a wobbly stand on behalf of the Israeli. Then, under pressure from Defense Secretary Forrestal, he reversed himself, in a misguided attempt to curry favor with the oil-rich Arab states. In each instance, his intentions were of the best, but chaos was his only achievement.

The Palestine dilemma merely highlighted the deteriorating conditions in the whole realm of foreign policy in the winter of 1947-48.

Domestic affairs were also in a drifting and embittered stalemate, but it was in the perplexing and delicate diplomatic field that that sad winter of the Truman administration really had its worst effects. Walter Lippmann summed up the situation cogently when he wrote, that spring:

"It is not, I think, an alarmist exaggeration to say that the condition of the Truman administration is a grave problem for the nation. The problem is . . . how in the perilous months immediately ahead the affairs of the country are to be conducted by a President who has not only lost the support of his party but is not in control of his own administration. The heart of the danger lies in the fact that Mr. Truman is not performing, and gives no evidence of his ability to perform, the functions of the Commander in Chief. . . . At the very center of the Truman administration, at the critical point where the fateful decisions of the highest diplomatic and military consequence are made, there is a vacuum of authority and responsibility. There is, that is to say, no one who guides, directs, coordinates, and disciplines the actions of the government."

It was against the background of this failure to coordinate the State and Defense Departments' views on foreign affairs and to give an integrated domestic policy strong backing, plus the general picture of administrative disorganization, political ineptitude, and intellectual sterility, that the frantic revolt broke out against Truman within the Democratic Party.

The blundering attempt to draft General Eisenhower was more than an awkward expression of the latent desire of the big-city bosses and inveterate New Dealers to lower the boom on Harry Truman. The "Good-by Harry" movement was a desperate attempt to find creative leadership for the solution of the nation's travails.

The movement became so strong that by the time the Democrats gathered at Philadelphia, it seemed that the only person who wanted Truman was Truman. He got the nomination, of course, but the delegates gave it to him with all the enthusiasm of a six-year-old giving his baby brother the candy.

The Democratic dissidents had wanted a new man. Before the campaign was over, they realized they had a new man.

It was a very different Truman who tore into the "gluttons of privilege" and the "greedy, selfish few" from the alternately harried and frozen man who complained to visitors because fate had made him President, and who sat throughout the 1946 campaign like a numbed spectator in the wrong cheering section. He was once again on the defensive. But this time he was defending not himself alone but his policies as well.

Every major issue of the 1948 campaign—Taft-Hartley, inflation, farm aid, and civil rights—was one on which Truman had taken a decisive personal stand. There would have been no labor issue if he had not decided to veto the Taft-Hartley bill. There would have been no civil rights issue if he had not decided to appoint a special commission and then had the courage to defend its recommendations. There would have been no inflation issue if he had not finally decided to come out for price controls. Unlike his 1944 tootling, he was not an amiable, easygoing fellow, loyally repeating New Deal platitudes. This time, he knew what the fight was all about and on what side he was scrapping.

To the impartial observer, the Fair Deal baby looked just like its New Deal big brother. But to Harry Truman there was one big difference. It was his baby.

The big brother had come from an intellectual foundling home. The baby was his own—and the President did not love it any the less when he woke up the day after election and found it had been weaned with the silver spoon of victory in its mouth.

Victory at the polls did not alter any fundamental features of the Truman administration—except one. It served to consolidate the psychological changes that had been at work within the President during his three years in office.

If it gave him only nominal control of Congress, it did tighten his grip on his own administration and did give a very real boost to his own morale. He emerged from the campaign the man he is today. Harry S. Truman is President of the United States in his own right and at the peak of his power.

Visitors to the President's office find an erect, compactly built man of medium height, with a lean, clean-cut face. There are no jowls, and no bags under his eyes. He is fifteen pounds heavier than when he entered the White House, but he does not look his sixty-six years.

Truman is very friendly and quite easy to talk to. During a conversation, his customary position is to cross one leg, clasp his hands across his knee, and lean forward slightly. Unlike Roosevelt, he does not monopolize the talking. In fact, he frequently says only enough to keep the discussion going smoothly.

He is quite regular in all his habits and is almost never late for an appointment. He keeps his schedule of interviews running smoothly and manages to bring each one to a close, unobtrusively, just as the fifteen minutes is ending. He keeps his desk clear and neat. He has a passion for orderliness and has everything in its regular place. Press Secretary Charles Ross relates how, one evening, he placed the President's engagement calendar casually on his desk. Truman kept right on talking, but reached over and very carefully lined it up in its proper place.

He carries this instinct for neatness over into his personal regimen. His daily routine is extremely regular, to the point of being meticulous.

He breakfasts at eight every morning, has lunch at one and dinner at seven. He has no favorite foods, eats fairly rapidly and sparingly, and never raids the icebox between meals. He rises each day at six-thirty A.M. He dresses and shaves himself. For shaving he uses a safety razor. There is a Negro servant assigned to the staff as barber, but his work is limited to giving the President a haircut approximately twice a month. Truman dresses very quickly, and usually tries to go out for a brisk walk. He used to walk in Washington itself, but even early in the morning his arrival in any neighborhood caused such commotion that now he generally rides to the outskirts of the city and walks in fairly secluded areas. Truman clips along at 120 strides a minute. Unlike Theodore Roosevelt, the last Chief Executive who loved to walk, Truman does not impose this early-morning constitutional on his staff or on visiting dignitaries.

At eight-thirty, he is at his desk. By nine he is seeing Ross, Matt Connelly, Charles Murphy, and other members of the staff who have anything to do with his morning schedule of fifteen-minute conferences with visiting delegations, personages, and cause-pleaders.

The President wears tailor-made, double-breasted suits. He rarely wears a boutonniere (his favorite campaign picture in 1944 showed him wearing a World War I discharge button in his lapel), and his cravat may be either a four-in-hand or a bow tie. His suits are made just a shade too tight, so that they draw attention to his somewhat bandbox appearance instead of featuring the "natural drape" which is now more in fashion, but Truman has excellent taste in accessories. As becomes an ex-haberdasher, he sports very natty bow ties. Once he startled a formal dinner by wearing a silver-streaked black bow tie. His suits emphasize his soldierly carriage, of which he is extremely proud.

Because of this pride, Metro-Goldwyn-Mayer had to make some costly changes in a film about the atomic bomb. They had a shot of an actor portraying the President. The actor had a good resemblance but seemed to be a bit round-shouldered, and at Truman's behest he was replaced by a player with better posture and the scene was refilmed.

Shirts are something the President has plenty of. He now has a bigger supply than when he was in the business of selling them. Also, he does not have to worry about buying them. Every year, well-wishers from all over the country send them to him by the dozen. He prefers whites or blues with collars attached and stiffly starched. His collar size is 15½.

The President's overcoats, like his suits, are tailor-made by a Washington tailor whose identity is a closely guarded secret. Truman buys his hats (size 7⅜) and his shoes (size 9-B) from regular specialty shops. His brands, like his tailor, are a secret, but it is fairly certain he does not buy the brand of hats which used to sponsor a certain columnist on the radio. Truman methodically wears black shoes with his gray and blue suits, and brown shoes with his brown suits. In the spring and summer, he sports two-toned shoes. He dresses in sports clothes only on board his yacht or during vacations. In the summer, he goes in for light worsted suits and Panama hats.

But, summer or winter, the handkerchief in his breast pocket always shows four points and resembles a miniature white picket fence.

Aside from walking, the only physical recreation the President enjoys is swimming. One story had him pitching horseshoes, but he almost never does. He is a tie with Calvin Coolidge for the title of least athletic President. Truman, however, stays awake at ball games and enjoys munching peanuts; Coolidge always wanted to go home after the second inning. Truman is a good swimmer but not a fast one. He swims twice a week in the White House pool, invariably accompanied by Military Aide Harry Vaughan. He swims with his head out of the water and his glasses on, using a side stroke.

After his late afternoon swim and dinner, Mr. Truman's evening schedule varies considerably. Often he has official parties or receptions to attend. Society columnists, who over the years have watched several Presidents attend these affairs, say that Mr. Truman, by all odds, enjoys parties more than any other Chief Executive in recent decades. Only Warren Harding was equally sociable.

Mr. Truman frequently goes not only to official functions but also to little private parties given by administration bigwigs. His favorite spot for these affairs is the 1925 F Street Club, a private house which has been converted into a small, swanky club. As often as once a week, he may go to stag poker games. Unlike Harding, Mr. Truman never plays poker in the White House or Blair House. Mr. Truman does his gaming in nonofficial places.

Other evenings he reads, his intellectual fare ranging from government reports and memoranda to history and biography. He has always been a great reader and has an unusual memory for places, dates, and details. As a boy, he read practically every book in the Independence, Missouri, library. His greatest interest is in military history and strategy. He is an authority on the Civil War, and the halls of the White House leading to his office are covered with prints of Civil War battles and pictures of both Union and Confederate generals.

Early in his term as President, he paid a brief visit to Gettysburg and surprised newspapermen by giving them a lengthy and detailed account of the whole battle. The President considers Hannibal's battle of Cannae, Napoleon's victory at Austerlitz, and the battle of Chancellorsville as the three most decisive battles in history.

Truman purchases large quantities of books and magazines. Every morning he reads the Washington papers and *The New York Times* and the *Herald Tribune*. He does not see as many newspapers as President Roosevelt did, but various members of his staff go over papers from all sections of the country.

Truman rarely listens to the radio and almost never uses his television set. Nor is he as avid a movie fan as Mr. Roosevelt was.

The White House books its movies from Washington film exchanges. When the President wants to see a currently popular film, the White House rents it. The standard fee for one picture for one evening is $300. Truman's favorite movies are newsreels, which are exhibited regularly every Thursday after lunch in the White House. He is also very fond of pictures with shots of the White House, like the cloak-and-dagger thriller, "13 Rue Madeleine." This picture also included a brief scene showing General Harry Vaughan, who was billed—at the White House, at least—as Jimmy Cagney's co-star. Truman likes good Westerns such as "My Darling Clementine" and "California." He does not care for musical pictures as a rule, but daughter Margaret does. The Walt Disney film, "Make Mine Music," in which Nelson Eddy's voice took over for a Metropolitan Opera whale, was a big favorite with her.

Washington movie critic Richard Coe tells one Truman movie anecdote which is in the ought-to-be-true-but-it-isn't category. The story is that the first picture Truman happened to see after the 1946 elections presented him with a Republican Congress was "Two Years Before the Mast."

The President is the country's most famous amateur piano player. This, of course, has been the basis of innumerable anecdotes and wisecracks. In the rough days of 1948, one California politician begged indulgence for the President's mistakes with the old barroom punch line, "Don't shoot the piano player, boys, he's doing the best he can."

Another gag along the same lines had a soldier returning from the war and saying to his grandfather, "How's this new fellow doing in Washington?"

Grandpappy: "Reminds me of your Uncle Jack; he played the piano in a place for five years and never knew what was going on upstairs."

The President takes this ribbing in good spirit. As an amateur pianist, he is fond of Chopin's works in particular, and of all serious music in general. He is constantly hearing the "Missouri Waltz" and has played it on many occasions, including the 1945 Potsdam Conference and affairs such as the Gridiron Club dinner. He thinks that of all modern pianists, Paderewski was the master. He takes special in-

terest in GI pianists of virtuoso stature. One of these, Sergeant Eugene
List, also played at the Potsdam Conference.

The President goes to concerts as often as he can. Back in January,
1947, he attended the musical, *Blossom Time,* at the National Theater.
The theater was at that time being picketed by liberal groups because
it denied admission to Negroes. The next day, at his press conference,
Truman explained that he had crossed the picket line unwittingly and
had not learned there was one until he read the morning papers. He
remarked that he had never seen the show and had wanted to for
twenty years.

A reporter in the back row, hearing this revelation, remarked (*sotto
voce*), "That's a real man-bites-dog story. At last we've found someone
who hadn't seen *Blossom Time.*"

Truman is an avid traveler. He takes a boyish delight in sitting up
front with the pilot or the locomotive engineer.

As is apparent, this sketch of Truman the man, as distinguished
from Truman the President, could not have been achieved without
cooperation from him and his staff. Mr. Truman is fairly cooperative
in giving out biographical and personal information. During his first
few months in the White House, he was often asked queries which
astounded him because of the type of intimate personal details requested. On one occasion, during a visit to Independence, he arose
early and, finding a flock of newsmen on hand to ascertain what he
was and wasn't doing, he assumed a tongue-in-cheek attitude.

He told his aide to tell the press the precise hour at which he moved
his bowels.

In the early months of his presidency, many people expressed the
hope that Truman would grow to presidential size. It is a fact that he
has matured emotionally. He now has a vigor and *esprit* he never had
before. The cocky inner man has broken through the outer shell of
submissiveness and timidity and taken full command.

The evolution shows up vividly in the changed mood and tempo of
his weekly press conference.

During the first year, he talked volubly and readily on almost every
subject. He was one of the boys, and the reporters were his pals. Then,
as the problems and the criticism grew, he became increasingly close-

mouthed. In 1947-48 he blurted "No comment" or offered brief explanations with all the *savoir-faire* of a YMCA secretary answering questions on sex.

But since his re-election he has become at once more relaxed and more defiant.

When reporters heckled him after he granted an exclusive interview to Arthur Krock of *The New York Times,* he told them, "I'll see whomever I damn please." The hostile "plants" and the purely speculative questions he bats right back at the questioner. More and more, he takes on the character of the dapper night-club emcee exchanging wisecracks with regular patrons. He's either heard that one before or is sure he can top it.

But, though Truman today uses his talents spontaneously and to their fullest extent, his are inherently limited talents.

Despite what the pundits say, he is neither a distinguished administrator nor an adroit politician. Really able administrators not only can chart a policy but also guide and stimulate its implementation if necessary. Many a top-ranking official, however, has gone to the White House sorely beset with critical problems, most anxious to hear the President's views and suggestions, but, after carefully outlining his difficulties, has received a reply along this line, "Well, I can see that you've got a big headache on your hands. You're up against a tough situation. I'm all for you and I am confident you can work it out."

No incisive observations, no clear directives. Nothing, just a cheery pat on the back.

Having had no practical experience of his own in organizing and handling large affairs, Truman does not have any specific ideas on how to proceed. Presumably, five years in the presidency would give him some definite ideas, but this is not the case because of the way in which Truman works.

When someone presents an idea or a new policy to him, he does not think along as his visitor explains, and cut in with questions now and then. He does not interrupt to say something like, "Well, now, to sum it up in my own words . . ." or "What you are really trying to get at, as I understand it, is . . ." Instead, Truman listens with a patient and somewhat resigned expression, almost never interrupts or summarizes the conversation, but at the end, if he is favorably impressed, says,

"Well, that sounds okay to me; let's go ahead on that"; or, if he is not impressed, he refers the matter to a subordinate.

Truman's advisers and lieutenants usually leave such an interview convinced that he does not really understand the reasons they have advanced. And they are right.

He has grasped only the broad outlines of the problem. The plausible presentation, rather than the intellectual content, has won him over. It is personal confidence and not intellectual coherence that is the key to Truman's operating procedure. He supports men, not policies.

Advisers like Agriculture Secretary Brannan and economic adviser Leon Keyserling, who have won his trust and confidence, sell him packaged programs, which is quite different from explaining ideas and convincing him of their merit. A Truman decision is a vote of confidence in a man, and not necessarily a sign of inner conviction. Truman does not administer. He presides. This central fact is at once the blessing and the curse of his administration.

It is a blessing because this approach precludes his meddling in foreign affairs. Had a man of Truman's ignorance of foreign affairs been as opinionated as he was ill-equipped, it would have been tragic. But, instead, Truman has allowed each of his Secretaries of State to carry the full, crushing burden alone, just as he allows the Attorney General or the housing administrator to work uninterrupted and unsupervised.

But the results have been less happy in domestic affairs. This laissez-faire approach accounts for the shapeless character of the executive department. Great chunks of power are dispersed in the hands of subordinates who exercise it in semiautonomous and often contradictory fashion. The administrative tone is flabby and listless.

Mr. Roosevelt had a much clearer idea of what was going on in each agency and department, worked hard to keep himself well informed, and sent a constant stream of memos prodding here and praising there. Mr. Truman doesn't do this follow-up job. He feels he has done his duty when he gives the green light. But the traffic flowing by the President's desk is too heavy and complex to be regulated with a semiautomatic traffic signal. There has to be a live cop on the job, blowing his whistle, waving his arms, and seeing that all the cars really keep moving. Things may look all right to Mr. Truman from his vantage point, but he rarely looks down the line or around the corner.

That is why his administration gets jammed up, or, more frequently, does not move at all.

A concrete example is the Housing and Home Finance Agency. Not even Roosevelt fought as hard or as consistently for housing legislation as has Harry Truman, but once the bills were finally passed and the programs authorized, he forgot about them. This is tragic because the Housing and Home Finance Agency, which coordinates the assorted housing programs, is one of the most bumbling and molasses-minded bureaucracies in Washington.

Its chief is Raymond Foley, who can never quite make up his mind whether his heart belongs to the public that pays him or to the real-estate industry he is supposed to deal with. He does not oppose government action in the housing field, but neither does he push it. One subordinate summed him up this way, "Ray will never die storming a barricade." Foley surrounds himself with yes men. The worst of these is Public Housing administrator John T. Egan, a government careerist and a notoriously weak executive who should never have been promoted to a responsible, policy-making level.

When Egan was head of the New York regional office, he was known for his inability to fire anyone. If an economist on his staff was inefficient, Egan would call the chief economist in Washington to come up and do the axing. If he had an incompetent staff attorney, he would pass the buck to the chief counsel in Washington.

It has been no surprise that the much-heralded low-cost housing program of 1949 has bogged down under this kind of jellyfish leadership, and that the housing agencies in general have done little to curb the vicious antisocial practices of the real-estate industry.

A President who was an alert and conscientious executive would have forced Foley to dump Egan, or would never have appointed Foley in the first place. But Mr. Truman feels that, having signed the housing bill and told Foley to go ahead with a public-housing program, he has done his duty and that is sufficient.

Another serious defect is the fact that the President still has the idea that an administrator is a sort of sexless technician. He fails to realize that it takes militant liberals to put across a liberal program.

In his first State of the Union message after his re-election, Truman again advocated price controls. Two weeks later, he sat silent when Commerce Secretary Charles Sawyer trotted up to Capitol Hill and pompously informed a committee that he personally was against controls. Similarly, Truman has consistently urged a federal health-insurance program. For a considerable time, one of the most active and well-paid lobbyists against such a program was a Californian named James J. Boyle. Yet, in 1949, Truman appointed this same Boyle to the attractive job of U.S. Marshal in Los Angeles. When someone gently suggested to the President the need for more inspired liberal leadership in government posts, Truman replied, "We have plenty of liberals around here—my kind of liberals."

The truth is, Mr. Truman likes liberals in the abstract, but he doesn't like them in the flesh.

Anyone with an Americans for Democratic Action tag starts off with two strikes against him on the Truman score card. This is because Truman recoils instinctively from people who have cold, sharp convictions and who refuse to temporize or evade a fight. He may pay his grudging respects to their glittering intellects—but he doesn't want them around him. He prefers the less dynamic and aggressive, the more amenable and conciliatory.

The result is that Truman moves into the shadowy future guided only by the flickering light of his poker-playing cronies. Like an executive operating a firm on its capital assets, Truman has financed his two administrations on the inherited intellectual capital of the New Deal. It is to be hoped that in the near future destiny does not stage a run on the bank. The firm of Truman & Co. will be caught fearfully short.

Similarly, Truman is far from the able and consummate politician he is often pictured. The only objective evidence ever offered for this claim is his uphill victory in 1948. What is consistently overlooked is that this is far more a case of Dewey's being defeated than Truman's being elected.

This is strikingly demonstrated by the fact that Truman almost everywhere ran far behind his ticket, the exact reverse of the normal trend in presidential elections.

In Illinois, his plurality was 549,000 below that of Governor Adlai

Stevenson and 374,000 behind Senator Paul Douglas. In Massachusetts, he ran 148,000 votes behind Governor Paul Dever. In Iowa, he trailed Senator Guy Gillette by 135,000. In Indiana, the local Democrats swept the State, but Truman lost it. And so it went.

These figures cannot be explained away by saying that Dewey was a much tougher candidate than most of the local Republicans. Dewey was actually a weak candidate: cold, colorless, and unpopular with his own party. He has been beaten every time he faced a capable opponent such as Herbert Lehman or Franklin Roosevelt. His two gubernatorial victories were both won over spectacularly weak opponents in years when the Democratic vote was abnormally low. Few people voted *for* Truman; they voted *against* the Republicans who seemed desirous of turning the clock back to the pre-Roosevelt era.

The vote in 1948 was a testament to a dead man's vision of the liberal future.

Despite all of Truman's bungling and reactionary mistakes from 1945 to 1947, once he rededicated himself to the Roosevelt program, the political coalition Roosevelt had formed proved inherently strong enough to stagger in again. This alone pulled Truman through. In his hour of victory, Truman was humble; he had much to be humble about.

His reputation for political acumen also stems from the fact that Truman is for everything Roosevelt was for, and in some cases more so, and yet he does not arouse the same antagonism. But this is obviously due to the President's unspectacular personality, the flabby tone and ineffectual character of his administration, and the badly written, unprovocative scripts his speech writers turn out, rather than to any skill or deliberate planning on the President's part.

Truman loves politics, but it is politics of the pre-1933 variety. He knows, understands, and is reasonably skillful at the old-fashioned post-office and courthouse kind of politics. But this style is passé. He is out of his depth in maneuvering in the politics of issues.

Effective modern politics requires keen judgment of the public temper, and astute, high-level salesmanship. At this level, Truman simply hasn't got it. The subtleties of the trial balloon, the shrewd hint, the well-timed gesture, the psychologically "right" appointment are all beyond his repertoire.

Further, he has wantonly abandoned or debased the two public-relations media which Roosevelt so adroitly built up and used with such great skill and potency—the press conference and the radio fireside chat. Truman practically has dropped radio talks and cut his press conferences from two to one a week, and the one he does hold, he fails to use as an effective sounding board.

A President must articulate the needs and problems and anxieties of the nation. But at this still higher level, Truman is sterile. When he tries to rise above the slashing, off-the-cuff, "give-'em-hell" level—which is exactly the same kind of speech he made running for county judge thirty years ago—he comes forth with nothing but dry platitudes and wet sentimentalities.

Everyone believes in God, motherhood, and the dignity of man. The question is, how do we apply our basic beliefs to the control of atomic energy or to any of the other grim perplexities which confront us?

Illustrations of Truman's ineptness as a national leader occur almost daily and are now numerous enough to fill a mail-order catalogue. One or two will suffice.

In January of 1950, Myron Taylor, the President's special envoy to the Vatican, after giving Truman weeks of advance notice, finally submitted his resignation. Truman accepted it. He then hopped from one foot to the other for months, trying to make up his mind whether to appoint another personal representative, to raise the mission to a regular embassy, or to abolish the mission altogether. In the meantime, he had given both Catholic and Protestant adversaries time to kindle backfires of public sentiment, write editorials, make speeches, send delegations, and attempt to embroil Congress.

A smart executive would have avoided all that. He would have made up his mind on a course of action before Taylor quit, and announced it simultaneously with the publication of Taylor's resignation. Thus, any controversy would have been over before the partisans realized it had begun. A wrangle harmful to national unity would have been averted. From the strictly political angle, Truman made a further error, for by procrastinating he pushed the time of decision dangerously close to the fall elections.

Another illustration is his handling of atomic energy developments and the H-bomb.

With little advance warning and with no effort whatsoever to offer guidance or inspiration to the public, he divulged the agonizingly important news of the decision to manufacture the H-bomb. Yet anyone with a sophisticated political intelligence would have realized that, at the very least, a public statement or a full-dress radio address was called for. Popular psychology simply demanded it. But a feeling for the public temper requires imagination, and Truman has no more imagination than a horse with blinders.

Moreover, as the clamor rose, keynoted by a speech by Senator Tydings and two speeches by Senator McMahon, the President not only did not meet it but he encouraged it to grow by allowing two places on the Atomic Energy Commission, including the chairmanship, to remain vacant for many months. When the people are concerned, they have a right to expect their President to be similarly concerned.

Nor is Truman an effective political leader in the sphere of legislative tactics. Now, at least, he occasionally tries a little bluffing and whipcracking. But he is not very good at either. There are only two cards in his deck: loyalty and horse trading. When an obstreperous congressman will not respond to the first, he tries the second. But when it comes to backstairs bargaining, Truman is no David Harum.

Both Mr. Truman and the nation have learned to live with his inadequacies.

He is a strong and likely candidate to succeed himself in 1952. The country likes him because he is a decent, likable person and because the opposition is bankrupt. Mr. Truman likes the presidency because it gives him a warming sense of personal importance. Without it, he might dwindle to his old size.

It is a tough job, but he has not aged under the strain because his noninterference method of governing does not involve him emotionally in the success or failure of day-to-day policies. He has made up his mind, after three years of fumbling, as to where he stands on the big issues. He sticks to the steel framework of his platform and is not overly concerned at the slowness with which Congress covers it with mortar and stone.

Mr. Truman has partially filled the vacuum which Lippmann described in 1947-48. But he remains a calm center—if not exactly a dead spot—in the tense and momentous Washington whirl.

In March and April, 1950, in the middle of the congressional session, he took a four-week vacation in Key West. He kept in daily communication with Washington. The weekly chat with the "Big Four" congressional leaders was held over a three-way telephone hookup. In one of these conferences, he talked to his congressional lieutenants for twenty-five minutes. In the House, at that time, Republican Leader Joe Martin had just announced he would seek a deep cut in the ECA appropriation bill. In the Senate, the bitterly controversial Kerr natural-gas "ripper" bill was up for debate. There was much speculation as to what Truman and his top lieutenants had discussed and what strategy they had devised.

But here is a characteristic portion of what the President and his leaders actually talked about:

HOUSE FLOOR LEADER JOHN MC CORMACK: How're you doing, Mr. President?

TRUMAN: Not so well, John. The boys are cleaning me out. My poker isn't so good.

SPEAKER RAYBURN: Who took you?

TRUMAN: Well, Fred Vinson for one. Fred left here in good shape. He really took me for plenty. But so did the others.

MC CORMACK: I've told you, Mr. President, you've got a bad weakness, you can't resist keeping in the pot. You keep on sticking it out no matter how bad the cards.

TRUMAN: Guess you're right, John.

VICE-PRESIDENT BARKLEY: How are you feeling?

TRUMAN: Fine. I've got a swell sun tan. My only complaint is the way the boys are cleaning me out.

SENATE FLOOR LEADER LUCAS: Remember, Mr. President, play them close to your chest.

Mr. Truman's cautious days are over, however. They have a saying down in Kentucky that it takes a lot of luck "to catch lightning in a whisky glass." That's what Mr. Truman did when he won in 1948. After doing that once, it is likely that, no matter how inadequate his skill or what his cards, he will keep trying to fill an inside straight.

THE WHITE HOUSE GANG

EIGHTY years ago, Henry Adams, then a young man of thirty, was heartsick at the mediocrity and incompetence of the men around President Grant. Looking back on that period years later, he wrote in his autobiography: "One dull administration can rapidly drive out every active subordinate. At Washington in 1869-70, every intelligent man about the Government prepared to go."

"Grant," he observed, "avowed from the start a policy of drift; and a policy of drift attaches only barnacles."

What the Boston Brahmin wrote in 1870 applies equally well today.

Harry Truman's White House staff has a double distinction: in size it is the largest in history, and in ability it is the weakest in decades. Nowhere do the barnacles cluster so thickly and so tenaciously as at 1600 Pennsylvania Avenue.

Twenty years ago, it was a national sensation when President Hoover expanded his secretarial staff to four people; his predecessors had gotten along with two. Today, Truman has three secretaries, six administrative assistants, a legal counsel, two legislative representatives, three economic advisers, a Security Council secretary, and three military aides. There are also a score of young military officers assigned to White House duty as props for big dinners and diplomatic receptions.

Further, each of these assistants has at least one assistant of his own; some, like Dr. John Steelman and legal counsel Charles Murphy, have four apiece. This massive entourage takes up both the east and west wings of the White House proper and part of the building across the street, which in Hoover's day housed the State, War, and Navy Departments.

45

Even as compared to the Roosevelt staff, there has been a phenomenal growth. In 1939, the White House payroll listed 109; in 1950, it is 232.

For years, American Anglophiles and theorists have longed very audibly for a cabinet-style government on the British model. What has happened, in fact, is exactly the reverse.

What has grown up in America is Staff Government.

Anonymities such as the omnipresent administrative assistant and the budget official, who do not require Senate confirmation and who serve wholly at the pleasure of the President, frequently have more influence over the course of government than the average cabinet member does.

The Attorney General is the titular director of the politico-judicial machinery of the government, but the President now gets most of his legal advice from his own special counsel. Dr. Steelman has made more labor policy than the Secretary of Labor. Economic adviser Leon Keyserling and Budget Director Frederick Lawton influence economic policies far more than the Secretary of the Treasury. And almost any administrative assistant is of more real consequence than the Secretary of Commerce and the Postmaster General.

Because this silent transformation has taken place, the quality and character of these men in the White House become of greatest importance. They do more than write speeches or serve as boon companions. They determine in a very large degree the tone and temper of the administration.

As a group, the present "White House gang" has certain characteristics in common.

By birth and long association, they are largely border-state men. In fact, to an extraordinary degree, they are drawn from three states on the fringes of the Southern black belt— Missouri (Vaughan, Ross, Dawson, Clifford, Vardaman, Dr. Graham, and Admiral Souers), North Carolina (Stowe and Murphy), and Arkansas (Steelman, plus an unofficial intimate, Senate Secretary Leslie Biffle).

Secondly, with the partial exception of Ross, they were all totally undistinguished in private life. There is no Robert E. Sherwood or Archibald MacLeish in this circle.

Finally, with few exceptions, they are opportunists or career men by temperament. They are wedded to no concept of social policy, have no large or controversial ideas, have never fought for any liberal or unpopular cause. As far as their private opinions are concerned, if they have any, they could just as easily work for Senator Taft.

If the almost India-rubber elasticity of John Steelman is characteristic of their ideological indifference, so also is his stodgy mediocrity typical of their intellectual level. To attempt to contrast any or all of them with their opposite numbers during the New Deal is almost too painful to consider. There is no one in the Truman "gang" who has the ingenuity and political savvy of Tom Corcoran, the brilliant legal mind of Ben Cohen, the literary flair of Adolf Berle, the public relations sagacity of Steve Early, the shrewd economic mind of Isador Lubin, or the charm of Harry Hopkins.

A concrete example of the intellectual poverty of the incumbent welter of advisers is in the field of speech writing.

To prepare the best and most significant Truman declamations, it has been necessary to import an alumnus of the New Deal. Judge Sam Rosenman, former counsel to Roosevelt, has been repeatedly summoned to Washington for this purpose. It was Rosenman who wrote Truman's acceptance speech at the Philadelphia convention, a gem of political oratory and the best speech he has ever made. Rosenman also wrote the 1949 State of the Union message and the last half of the inaugural message in which Truman broached the "Point Four" proposal.

Truman drove able and competent men away from him because in his early years in office he sought no counsel, encouraged no new ideas, rewarded no show of originality, gave no opportunity to serve and no encouragement to do so. The few, like OPA Administrator Paul Porter and Housing Expediter Wilson Wyatt, who struggled on persistently, received only indifference, mounting hostility, and ultimate dismissal.

As a result, at every level of government, "every active subordinate . . . prepared to go." All the abler young and middle-aged men who had come to Washington before the war and during it now left government service and returned to their law offices, to their editorial desks, to economic consulting work, and to a hundred college campuses throughout the country.

In the history of Washington, the period 1945-47 will be known as the years of the flight of the intellectual.

In a few corners of the State Department and the Pentagon, new men appeared, most of them conservative but at least possessed of bright and live intellects. But no such newcomers arrived in the precincts of the White House. The gang there grew and grew and grew. But the recruits were all alike, political stumblebums and weary, faceless hacks.

Of these there has been no shortage. The mere announcement in April, 1945, that Harry Truman was President flushed them out of every dark cove and secluded thicket.

They came in droves. High-school classmates and wartime buddies, provincial editors and obscure politicians, business failures and lame ducks, the alumni of Pendergast politics and the bootblacking profession, country bankers and county judges, broken-down bureaucrats and professional glad-handers—all who had "known Harry when" or who had ever given him a kind word or done him a good turn came rushing to Washington or clamored for a more comfortable berth if they were already here. Smug, smiling, hopeful, pompous, eager, wary, they entered the never-never land of presidential patronage.

If the sounds at first were a little incoherent, this was only to be expected when each one was asking two questions simultaneously, "How the hell did we get here?" and "What'll we do first?"

Colonel Harry Vaughan, veteran of six months in France and ten years in the tea business, overnight became a brigadier general and Military Aide to the President. Sleepy-eyed, social-climbing Jake Vardaman, head of a bankrupt shoe company in St. Louis, was transformed into land-based commodore and Naval Aide to the President. Vardaman's personal attorney, able, alert Clark Clifford, became Assistant Naval Aide and went on to fame and fortune. The vast and complex duties of Director of Economic Stabilization were assigned to Caskie Collet, a diminutive, unknown judge from Missouri. Amiable Charley Ross, faded veteran of forty years of newspapering, was installed as Press Secretary. John Snyder, the Arkansas bank teller, was installed as War Mobilization and Reconversion Director, but his face remained screwed into the expression of a man who has a stench in his nose and a cold in the head. George Allen, the professional gaiety boy, moved in as an unofficial master of ceremonies. Hugh Fulton, the big apple-cheeked lawyer who had written the Senate committee reports which made Truman famous, became Special Counsel. Edward McKim, Nebraska insurance man and World War I buddy, caught a fast train and took over as "the assistant to the President."

With all the pap to be distributed, it might have been expected that there would have been enough for all. But that was not the case. There was, in fact, some unseemly pushing and shoving.

Messrs. Snyder and Vaughan soon convinced their chief that Special Counsel Fulton was too ambitious. He was talking so much and making so many decisions . . . why, folks would think he was the President. So Mr. Fulton was soon asked to retire to the practice of private law. A few weeks later, after making all the blunders he could think of, well-meaning Ed McKim was also asked to catch a fast train back to the prairies.

But still those were halcyon days. America had won the war. Truman's popularity was sky-high. It seemed as if General Vaughan were right when he told the ladies of the Presbyterian Church at Alexandria, Virginia, that "after a diet of caviar, you like to get back to ham and eggs."

After glory with Roosevelt, why not relax with Truman?

The crowd around Truman, the public felt, was funnier than it was dangerous. They were not putting their hands in the till; they were too busy putting their feet in their mouths.

Characteristic of this was the same speech by Vaughan, in which he not only settled the respective merits of Roosevelt and Truman by a gastronomical metaphor but also disposed of Churchill ("a garrulous old man"); Stalin ("he was a day late at Potsdam to get even with Churchill who was a day late at Yalta"); and Protestant chaplains ("appointed because they wanted a three-year vacation").

But in January, 1946, the President's addiction for amateur comedians and poker-table pundits took a somber turn.

Previously, he had mostly restricted these intimates to the exalted but confined quarters of the White House itself. Now, in one fell swoop, he proposed installing three of them in some of the most potent and far-reaching policy-making jobs in the government. In one day,

he nominated George Allen to be a director of the Reconstruction
Finance Corporation, Naval Aide Jake Vardaman to sit on the Federal
Reserve Board, and power-hungry Edwin Pauley, of tidelands oil
fame, to be Undersecretary of the Navy. Not one of them was qualified
by experience, training, or social outlook for the job he sought to fill.

Mr. Truman's "being a good fellow" was casting the dark shadows
of government-by-crony.

The Senate swallowed Allen and Vardaman, but gagged on Pauley
and ultimately forced the withdrawal of his nomination. At the same
time, the stormy resignation of Interior Secretary Harold Ickes and
the nationwide uproar momentarily put a halt to the attempt to give
fat jobs to fatheads, no matter how affable.

But Truman has repeatedly reverted to this practice, since it is his
natural instinct to get along with people and do nice things for his
friends. It is a course which has caused him all sorts of grief. The
President, apparently, is wholly impervious to the realization that
every time he makes a worthless and indefensible appointment, he not
only weakens his administration but he also gives a powerful hostage
to his enemies.

By the arduous summer of 1946, the permanent pattern of relationships among the White House insiders had emerged.

Fulton and McKim had long since gone. Pauley had disappeared,
to lick his wounds and concentrate on the commodity markets. Allen
and Vardaman were snug in their respective sinecures. Judge Caskie
Collet had taken his still-undisplayed administrative genius back to
Missouri. John Snyder had been promoted from War Mobilization to
the Treasury, where he had a larger field to exercise his bad prognosti-
cations and reactionary views, but where their consequences at least
would not show up in daily headlines. Clark Clifford, having worked
his way up to Special Counsel, and Dr. John R. Steelman to that of
top White House economic adviser, were about to begin their long
and bitter duel for supremacy. David K. Niles and one or two other
battle-scarred, elephant-hided members of the Roosevelt staff had survived the first big rush to the Truman banquet table and seemed
likely to hang around a while longer.

And, of course, General Harry ("I'm still with ya, Chief") Vaughan
was, to put it mildly, still with us.

The three men who see Harry Truman most regularly are secretaries Matthew Connelly, Charles Ross, and William Hassett.

Connelly, who handles appointments and supervises the office routine; Ross, who handles press and radio; and Hassett, who copes with the heavy volume of correspondence, see the President every morning, precisely at nine o'clock. Together, they set up the day's schedule, discuss with the Chief Executive the announcements, press releases, and important letters that will go out. After this conference, which runs from one-half to three-quarters of an hour, the three scatter to their respective offices in the east wing of the White House. Each, of course, can see the "Chief" at any time during the day.

In making up Mr. Truman's schedule, Matt Connelly has certain fixed constants. Every day, following the staff conference, which may be attended by one or more of the President's administrative assistants, the Chief Executive hears a top-secret briefing on the general strategic situation in the world from both military and Intelligence standpoints. During the first Truman administration, aged Admiral Leahy, personal Chief of Staff to the President, made this oral report. After the "Gray Eminence" went into retirement, Admiral Sidney Souers and, more latterly, his successor as executive secretary of the National Security Council, civilian James Lay, have given this strategic roundup. Following this is a brief interim during which Truman signs various orders and other documents which require his signature.

Then, at ten-thirty or eleven, a round of fifteen-minute interviews with visitors begins. These callers range from foreign dignitaries to Elks from Walla Walla. Each day, the President usually sees at least one or two of these delegations of visiting firemen. Truman has almost a compulsive fixation about keeping up to schedule, and rarely does he allow a visitor to overstay his allotted fifteen minutes.

At one o'clock, Truman walks to the White House proper or, during repairs to the old mansion, across the street to Blair House. Unlike Roosevelt, who lunched from a tray on his desk, Truman likes to break up the day by leaving the office for a full-course meal. Also unlike Roosevelt, Truman frequently lunches alone or accompanied only by Vaughan or some other staff member. He rarely schedules a big shot for lunch.

The round of visitors is occasionally resumed from two o'clock to about three-thirty. From then until six, Truman devotes himself to paper work and to unscheduled visits from various staff members.

Appointment secretary Connelly can count on certain other constants. Thus, every Monday noon Secretary of State Dean Acheson arrives for a half-hour review of foreign policy. Every Thursday the President holds his press conference, one week in the morning, the next in the afternoon. Every Friday there is a cabinet meeting, lasting anywhere from twenty minutes to two hours.

It is obvious that, within this general framework, Matt Connelly has a great deal to say as to who sees the President. Only the topmost civilian and military brass can get in without Matt's approval. And once the daily calendar of visitors is announced, he can slip unscheduled callers in on his own initiative. Even routine office work can be an avenue to power when the office is that of the President of the United States.

No one knows this better than Matt Connelly, and no one enjoys that fact more.

Not that Connelly is pompous or arrogant. Rather, he takes a restrained but exhilarating and almost childish glee in the trappings, aura, and glitter of his position and his proximity to the President. Never before, and probably never again, has he had a job that paid him $18,000 a year, plus a limousine, week ends on a yacht, and regular trips to Florida. Matt is enjoying life on the Gravy Train Express.

He was born in the small town of Clinton, Massachusetts, in 1907. His father was janitor of the neighborhood school. On his modest civil service salary, he managed to send Matt to Fordham College in New York. Matt graduated in 1930, the first class to buck the depression. He held low-paid jobs as a runner in the New York Stock Exchange and with Western Union. In 1935, he arrived in Washington with a wife and child and no job.

After a considerable period of scratching about unsuccessfully, and first being refused a position by David Niles, then Harry Hopkins' right-hand man, Connelly finally landed a job as an investigator for the WPA. Later, he caught on with a short-lived investigating committee headed by Senator Lister Hill of Alabama. Through the latter, Connelly met the freshman Senator from Missouri, Harry Truman. They hit it off immediately.

They had much in common: modest abilities, limited intellectual interests, limited ambition, little imagination, and a good-natured interest in stag parties and in "relaxing." The Senator was not too demanding; the young man was not too aspiring. They relaxed perfectly together. Connelly went to work as Truman's personal assistant on the War Investigating Committee. He has been with him ever since.

Some "dope" stories have pictured Connelly as giving Truman "smart political advice" and in other ways playing a decisive policy-making role. Such stories are pure hokum. The only policy Matt Connelly is interested in is staying on good terms with Harry Truman. The only issue on which it is possible to determine what side Matt is on is the tradition against a President's seeking a third term.

Matt is strongly agin that one.

At the end of his life, a French bishop was asked what he had done during the French Revolution. He answered, "I survived." Kindly, soft-spoken Bill Hassett might make that same pertinent reply if queried in the future about his activities on the Truman merry-go-round.

During the last several years of the Roosevelt administration, Hassett served as correspondence secretary to the President. When Truman took over, Hassett was the only one of the incumbent secretaries kept on, largely because someone was needed who knew how the wheels went round. In the hectic years that have followed, palace favorites have come and gone, but tall, gray-haired, bespectacled Bill has survived.

His main assets are his nonabrasive personality and quiet efficiency. It has long been said around the White House that Bill Hassett can say "no" so gently it almost sounds like "yes."

A onetime newspaperman, he spends most of his time drafting answers to important letters for the President and, in a pinch, ghosting a speech. Bill also writes the innumerable proclamations which stream from the presidential office announcing "American Cookie Week" and "Be-Kind-to-Animals Week." As a letter writer, Hassett will be best remembered as the master of magnificently mixed metaphors.

Perhaps his most popular was the presidential letter he wrote to one housing official directing him "to sift out the bottlenecks in this area at every level."

Press Secretary Charley Ross is the only White House attaché who had a career of some note before he entered Mr. Truman's service. In fact, because he was once a first-rate reporter and is now a second-rate press secretary, Ross has capped his career with an anticlimax.

In Washington, Charley Ross and the *St. Louis Post-Dispatch* had for decades been almost synonymous. Actually, before joining the *P-D* as its Washington bureau chief in 1918, Ross had had a lengthy career in education. He went to Independence High School with Harry Truman and graduated at the head of his class. Graduating from the University of Missouri in 1905, he knocked about for three years with various small papers in Colorado and Missouri. Then he joined the faculty of the School of Journalism at his alma mater and taught there for ten years, with the exception of one year spent in Melbourne, Australia, as visiting editor of the *Melbourne Herald*.

As Washington chief of the *St. Louis Post-Dispatch,* Ross ran one of the best bureaus in town. One ace staff man, the late dynamic Paul Y. Anderson, won a Pulitzer prize for his outstanding coverage of the Teapot Dome scandal. Ross himself won the Pulitzer prize some years later, during the depression, for a series entitled "The Country's Plight—What Can Be Done About It?" He became a member of the Gridiron Club and its president in 1933. The following year he was called back to St. Louis to take charge of the editorial page.

Although well read, scholarly, and liberal, Ross failed to turn out a very distinguished editorial section. Essentially, he is a reporter with an innately dull but meticulously detailed and exhaustive approach.

Finally, in 1939, he was sent back to Washington as a "contributing editor." In this capacity he turned out special articles for the "prestige page"—the split page in the editorials-and-special-features section of the paper. Ross was still in this job when Harry Truman, his old high-school classmate, asked him to become White House press secretary.

In this role, Ross has been a distinct disappointment.

A press secretary's job is twofold in its nature. He must prep the President so that he will handle himself effectively during his weekly press conference, and he must also dispense important news in such a way as to give it maximum "play."

On the first score, Ross has done very little. Truman's helplessness in press conferences during most of his first administration was sometimes pathetic, sometimes amusing. For example: When he announced the appointment of Gordon Clapp as director of the Tennessee Valley Authority, Truman continually referred to the Authority as the TWA, an airline whose employees were then on strike. A titter ran through the room. The President frowned but kept right on. Finally, a reporter said, "Don't you mean TVA, Mr. President? The TWA is an airline." Truman nodded grimly, went on reading, and carefully enunciated the "V" in TVA.

On such occasions, Ross stands by silently, a stooped, lean, tired figure, with sad spaniel eyes and enormous pouches under them. Steve Early, his predecessor, would interrupt Roosevelt to correct such slips of the tongue and errors of fact. Early would say, "I think you mean something else, Chief; don't you mean so-and-so?" and the inadvertence would be cleared up. Ross doesn't do things like that.

Nor has he been responsible for the improvement in Truman's press conference technique.

It was largely Clark Clifford who persuaded Truman to switch from his disastrous impromptus to the bland diet of "No comment" which now enables him to hold his own in the conferences with something approaching jauntiness and *esprit*.

Essentially, the difficulty with Ross is that he is too fond of Truman as a lifelong personal friend to be an imaginative and helpful assistant. In fact, "fond" is not strong enough to describe his feeling. Ross idolizes Truman. His attitude is not only open-eyed, but open-mouthed. He speaks of "the *President*" in hushed tones of reverent awe.

It seems incredible that a veteran newspaperman like Ross, who was a significant Washington figure long before anyone ever heard of Harry Truman, and who knew him for years as the run-of-the-mill machine politician he was, should so completely mesmerize himself. Personal affection and esteem for an old friend would be understandable, but this kind of adulation surpasses belief.

Thus Ross, like so many others around Truman—but for a different reason—is a yes man. It is ironic that Roosevelt, who was so often criticized on this score, actually received considerable face-to-face criticism from his staff. Truman, himself, would probably not be averse to more independence from his associates, but for a variety of reasons he is not likely to get it.

In Ross's own news conferences every morning, he speaks his piece in a droning monotone which can scarcely be heard beyond the first row. Worse than that, he budgets the distribution of the news in a most inept manner. On one day, two or three big stories may be given out and then nothing at all the next day. Inevitably, only one of the stories receives a proper play, and the others get abbreviated treatment. A striking example of this was the handling of the launching of the Marshall Plan.

On the day in June, 1947, when Secretary of State George Marshall announced his epoch-making project at the Harvard commencement, Truman practically swamped his own press conference with news, including a fiery denunciation of the Hungarian Communists and an attack on Senator Taft's economic views. Thus, without Ross's lifting a finger to prevent this blunder, Truman inadvertently "scooped" his own Secretary of State right off the front pages.

Again, the following December, the White House, in conjunction with the State Department, released in one afternoon the following: the President's message to Congress on the proposed ECA program, the full text of Secretary Marshall's report on the London Conference of Foreign Ministers, the text of the administration's European Recovery Plan bill, and a 227-page memorandum explaining the European aid policy. As a result, only a few major papers carried the text of the Truman and Marshall messages, and the other two important documents, each representing months of expert work, were elbowed out of the papers altogether.

A simple phone call from Ross to Michael McDermott, press chief of the State Department, could have prevented this senseless jamming-up.

Quite characteristically, on the following day the White House had no news at all to give out, and the State Department had only one piece of information. It announced that wrestler Primo Carnera would be allowed to stay in this country.

Experience and the passage of time have made Ross look worse rather than better.

In April, 1950, he put on an amazing, bungling performance. On April 5, reporters at the Little White House in Key West, Florida, asked Ross about reports that John Foster Dulles would be appointed a bipartisan State Department adviser.

"It is not so," Ross replied, and the newsmen sent out flat denials.

Yet at that very time newspapers were already on the street with the story of Dulles' appointment, and the next day the State Department officially confirmed it. Ross lamely explained that he was only denying that Dulles was to be appointed roving ambassador. The ambassadorship, Ross continued, was still "vacant," and the President was still trying to find a "successor" to Philip Jessup.

The excuse was as sad as it was inaccurate.

Jessup was still very much in office, and there was no "vacancy" to be filled. Moreover, this stupid statement at that precise moment played into the hands of Senator Joe McCarthy, who was putting on one of his berserk acts and demanding that Jessup be ousted. Ross's remark seemed to indicate that the President was wavering in his support of Jessup.

After hurried calls to Washington from Key West by several reporters, the State Department issued an official declaration, with the concurrence of the President, that Jessup was "Ambassador-at-Large for the time being" but that the problem of his successor was "under consideration." This did not satisfactorily explain whether Jessup was returning to private life or whether he was to be shifted to another post.

The *Washington Post* commented wryly: "Reporters trying to keep their box score, chalked it up as no hits, no runs, and at least three errors."

Like almost all the other White House aides, Ross has an assistant. In his case, it is red-haired Eben Ayers, who has the unenviable job of holding the White House fort when Ross and the rest are away with Truman on vacation.

Ayers dutifully holds the daily press conference, though usually it is absolutely newsless. One day, as a gag, a newsman asked if it were true that atomic bombs were stored in a tunnel between the White

House and the State Department. "The only tunnel I know of," Ayers replied, "is a heating conduit." He reflected earnestly a moment and then reiterated firmly, "Yes, sir, the only tunnel between the White House and the State Department is a hot-air tunnel."

Truer words were never spoken.

Glamorous Clark Clifford is one of those people who is too good to be true.

His face is too handsome, his blond hair too evenly waved, his smile too dazzling, his voice too resonant, his manner too patently sincere, his family background, childhood, college record, romantic courtship, and legal career are all too storybookish to be real. Somewhere there must be a flaw, a glaring weakness, an idiosyncracy. But so far Washington hasn't discovered it.

Clifford, of course, is no longer a regular member of the White House gang. But he still holds the President's warm esteem and confidence and occasionally plays a significant role in behind-the-scenes deliberations. But, even as an ex, no study of the Truman era would be complete without an account of Clifford.

From 1946 through early 1950, no staff member besides the three secretaries saw the President more frequently, and no one, without exception, was more influential in his councils. Clifford's departure left a gaping hole which has not been filled and which is not likely ever to be completely filled.

When the young Naval Aide took over as special counsel to the President in mid-1946, it seemed as if he were ascending to the bridge of a sinking ship. The Truman administration was foundering. Clifford's first important action was carried out, according to him, only because his boss ordered it. With some misgivings, he wrote Truman's address to Congress asking for a draft of railroad strikers into the Army. But from then on, Clifford took a stronger and stronger part in shaping decisions.

He strengthened the President's determination to stand firm against John L. Lewis in late 1946, wrote the reverberating vetoes against the Taft-Hartley and Republican tax bills, and did much to encourage Truman vigorously to endorse the civil rights report. The happy re-

sults of the 1948 election gave the benediction of success to these policies and entrenched Clifford's position.

He had many initial advantages in building a successful relationship
with the Chief Executive. To begin with, Clifford is a Missourian,
and his speech, though not the flat border-state twang which rever-
berates through most White House offices, is sprinkled with regional
colloquialisms such as "right happy" and "mighty pleased." Unconsciously, therefore, Truman is conditioned to be more receptive than if
Clifford had a disconcerting Harvard "a."

Secondly, Clifford is not just an eager beaver with a shiny academic
record. For several years before the war, he averaged $30,000 a year
as a lawyer in St. Louis. Roosevelt respected brains. Truman respects
financial success.

But perhaps weighing most important of all in Clifford's favor was
the fact that he had no Washington background before he joined
Truman. His name had never been damned in senatorial cloakrooms,
and he had never been dangled before a congressional committee. Not
only did Clifford appear to Truman completely free of the odor of
bitterness and controversy but he also did not suffer from the "Roosevelt complex." Truman never has the uneasy feeling that Clifford is
comparing him with his predecessor and making mental notes of dis-
crepancies.

Clifford capitalized these potential advantages because of his personality. He is an outwardly calm, even-tempered, hard-working, dependable young man who can get others out of trouble and who
never gets into it himself. He used to arrive at his White House office
before nine in the morning (a habit Truman much admires) and work
till early evening. In conference, his advice inevitably carries extra
weight because his warm smile and rich voice simply radiate firmness
and confidence.

Many observers have tried to define Clifford's relation to Truman
as that of a lawyer to his client. This does Clifford an injustice. It
implies that if he thought reactionary policies would serve Mr. Truman better, Clifford would counsel reaction. Clifford's liberalism is not
messianic, but it is genuine.

The misconception arises because it is impossible to apply any neat
class analysis to his development. Everything in his background would

seemingly ally him with the country-club crowd rather than with the people from the other side of the railroad tracks.

His father was an auditor for the Missouri Pacific Railroad. His mother in her younger days was a well-known lecturer and professional teller of fairy tales ("Good background for a Fair Dealer," snorted one Republican). As a youngster, Clifford sold magazines and sang in the Episcopal Church choir. In college, he acted in shows, played tennis, got fairly good grades, and was a Big Man on Campus. He attended law school, traveled in Europe, married the graduate of an Eastern finishing school, and settled down as a lawyer in his home city. He and his wife were patrons of the St. Louis Opera and furnished frequent items for the society page.

Clifford's law partner was Jacob Lashly, a shrewd, successful leading citizen noted for his religious orthodoxy and his sponsorship of the local "Youth for Christ" program. Lashly has long been a loyal Democrat, but of the old-school, Southern conservative type. As a member of the Mayor's Race Relations Committee, Lashly had one standard comment, "It is not the business of this committee to be pro-Negro but only to see that there are no disturbances in the city."

The firm of Lashly, Lashly, Miller and Clifford had a lucrative corporate practice, with junior partner Clifford specializing in automobile accident cases and labor law. He was highly effective as a courtroom pleader, but he was also noted for his thoroughly prepared briefs. In his labor work, Clifford was fortunate in never having to deal with a genuinely militant union. Most of his clients bargained with cautious, old-line craft unions or with company-dominated outfits.

Since neither academic insemination nor economic background explain Clark Clifford as a Fair Dealer, other factors must be sought. One obvious explanation is that Clifford's family and that of Lashly were Democrats, if only by inheritance. (On one occasion, Clifford helped manage the unsuccessful campaign of ex-Congressman Charles Hays, a genial Democratic politico and a Lashly intimate.) Secondly, he was influenced indirectly by the ideas of his uncle, Clark McAdams, who in his day was a crusading liberal editor of the *St. Louis Post-Dispatch*. Moreover, even a young man moving in country-club and chamber-of-commerce circles could not help but be influenced by ten years of depression and New Deal thinking, especially if he was oriented by background toward the Democratic Party.

Lastly, any man with intuitive political sense and without cast-iron preconceptions could perceive in 1947-48 that, while Truman had some chance to outbid Henry Wallace for liberal support, he could not possibly outconservative the Republicans. Clifford himself underlines these last two points with the cryptic remark, "I studied American history in college."

Clifford's great contribution was to reorganize the shambles and produce some semblance of an intellectually coherent program. He likes to think that it is more than a reinvigoration of the prewar New Deal.

In his opinion, old ideas that did not work were discarded in a process of critical selection, and new ideas added. Actually, of course, and in no way to Clifford's discredit, it is still the same old "streetcar named desire." Almost nothing has been thrown away. The only extra attachment that has been added is the Brannan farm plan.

Clifford himself added nothing new. And, in the end, that is perhaps precisely the secret of his success with Truman. Clifford does not have in him a trace of the doctrinaire. He has no "line" to sell, no new programs or proposals. He is not a creator of ideas but a highly skilled administrative diplomat and an astute political strategist.

He also has one other outstanding distinction.

Alone of all the Truman entourage, Clifford has the brains, the personal *élan,* and the *savoir faire* requisite for a big-leaguer. He is really of White House class. None of the others are, or ever can be.

With his departure, the administration to which he gave at least superficial coherence is again left in a vulnerable position.

No man was happier to see the dapper figure of Clark Clifford leave the White House than his archrival, red-faced, pushing, opportunistic Dr. John Roy Steelman.

The "Doctor" is now free to resume mining and sapping the liberal program he never thought much of anyway. As "*the* assistant to the President" (and the article "the" is very, very important to Steelman), he fought Clifford every step of the way.

Always a jovial, booming sort of fellow, Steelman in recent years has exhibited all the panting optimism and perspiring heartiness of a man who has returned from the dead. As far as Washington is concerned, Steelman did just that.

After hanging on to his job as head of the Federal Conciliation Service long after his immediate boss, Frances Perkins, and Roosevelt had both grown cold to him, Steelman finally gave up in the fall of 1944 and went to New York to open a public-relations office. By thus getting out in time, some cynics suggested, he at least preserved the long-shot possibility that Dewey might call him back as a nonpartisan authority on labor problems. But Dewey's defeat blasted that possibility. It was from this limbo that the advent of the Truman administration rescued Steelman.

Truman's first Secretary of Labor was the late Lewis Schwellenbach, a well-intentioned liberal with a good record as a one-term senator and a federal judge, but utterly without experience in the labor field. At Schwellenbach's suggestion, Truman asked Steelman to come to Washington temporarily as a special White House consultant on mediation problems. Steelman answered the call with bug-eyed alacrity. He has never left.

Almost from the outset, he appropriated the handling of all major labor disputes. Schwellenbach at first was too innocent and then too ill to offer the tenacious opposition Miss Perkins had put up against Steelman's machinations. As a result, Steelman was soon Secretary of Labor in all but name. For a time, he was even more.

As one of the greatest apple-polishers (GI's had a more pungent and fitting expression for it) in a town which is not exactly short of them, Steelman quickly worked his way into the President's confidence. Strongly backed by Treasury Secretary John Snyder, he became the No. 1 economic adviser at the White House. Much of the blame for Truman's jellyfish stand on reconversion, price controls, veterans' housing, and taxes during 1945-46 can be attributed to Steelman.

Sycophantic, Old Guardish, and a jealous self-seeker, Steelman played a strongly antiliberal role during this bedraggled period. If the White House overlooked any mistakes, the fault was not Steelman's. A bombastic hack if there ever was one, he and Snyder came within an ace of wrecking the administration.

Curiously, though much touted as a labor expert (especially by himself), Steelman has virtually no standing with labor leaders. Nor is he sympathetic to union labor. Indeed, he inspired most of Truman's antipathy to CIO and AFL chiefs during his difficult early years.

Truman at one point during the 1946 railroad strike told an intimate that all labor leaders were s.o.b.'s, and the only one who could be trusted to keep his word was John L. Lewis. That was pure Steelman doctrine. He is renowned in Washington as the one man who gets along well with Lewis and apparently enjoys it.

But Truman's patience with Steelman's pal finally wore thin, and, with Clifford's assistance, the President cracked down on the defiant miner czar. This deeply pained Steelman, but he went along. It always pains him much more not to go along.

He has the unique and serviceable ability to be firm—on every side of every issue.

A congenital glad-hander, Steelman can, by natural instinct, be all things to all men, with great sincerity and ardor. His greatest dislike is to disagree. He just loves to love, and be on warm and ingratiating terms with everybody—especially those with money and in high places.

Newsmen who deal with Steelman have had the experience of calling on him one day to ask him what he thinks about Plan A. He's all for it. Then, when they call on him several days later and ask him what he thinks about Plan B, he is just as enthusiastically for it as he ever was for Plan A. Never was this mealymouthing clearer than during the inner White House debate over the President's stand on the Taft-Hartley bill. To this day, no one really knows where Steelman stood on the issue. He was on all sides at the same time.

Steelman's basic Old Guard viewpoint was again strikingly displayed during the 1948 campaign.

He consistently counseled Truman to tone down his attacks on "selfish interests" and to appeal to the folks "right down the middle of the road." He also fought hard against the President's endorsement of the civil rights report. An Arkansan by birth and an Alabamian by adoption, Steelman tooted the theme that a civil liberties pronouncement would only make people "mad," and "even if we did get an FEPC, it would only be ignored and wouldn't work."

Fortunately for the President, he disregarded Steelman. By that time, the President had reached the point where he paid very little attention to Steelman's blundering advice.

Steelman's main stock in trade is his enormous capacity for hard work. A big, strapping, 215-pound six-footer, he is still the overeager, slightly clumsy country bumpkin come to the big city.

Born on a farm in Thornton, Arkansas, in 1900, he attended Henderson Brown College at Arkadelphia and then spent half a dozen years taking graduate work in sociology and economics at Vanderbilt, Harvard, and the University of North Carolina. Summers he worked in the Arkansas cypress swamps and logging mills, in the wheat fields of the Pacific Northwest, and as a map salesman. Finally, he received a Ph.D. degree from Chapel Hill in 1928 and, as a "Doctor," went to teach at Alabama College for Women. He was still there in Montevallo, Alabama, in 1934, when he met Labor Secretary Frances Perkins at an economic conference. She was favorably impressed by his energy and affable manner and hired him as an agent for the Conciliation Service. He quickly worked his way to the head of the organization.

Steelman had considerable success as a conciliator, especially at first, largely because he exuded good will and could with equal ease exhibit sympathy for all parties in a dispute. A useful trait at a lower level, it is scarcely a valuable quality for a man who must implement his chief's decisions in the face of tough opposition.

As *the* assistant to the President, Steelman passes on almost every kind of White House business. Affairs of most of the independent agencies, from the Federal Trade Commission to the Housing and Home Finance Agency, come under his eye. For a time, he also served as acting chairman of the National Security Resources Board, the supercoordinating unit for the various boards and commissions engaged in defense and emergency planning.

Steelman starts his day around eight in the morning and often works until midnight. At the end of a day, even if it be late at night, he frequently calls up select newspaper friends and "plants" stories with them. These calls are from the privacy of his home. Other insiders in this and previous administrations have "leaked" news which was to their own advantage if a newspaperman called and asked them. But few men have ever attempted to manipulate the press so consistently, in an underhanded effort to advance their own ends, as has Steelman.

Throughout his long feud with Clark Clifford, Steelman regularly gave out disparaging reports and gossip about his younger and abler adversary. Whenever Steelman lost an inner administration battle or seemed in danger of doing so, he would call up his press pals and spill the beans on the whole affair, even though he was violating every personal confidence in doing so.

Steelman's loquacity is particularly pronounced when he has anything to do with a major labor controversy. On such occasions he becomes a veritable sieve of information.

He is usually serving several purposes at once. He is trying to grab the headlines and glory, if any, for himself; he is trying to smoke out colleagues on the inside who may be urging a course different from his; and he is jockeying among the various participants of the dispute, in an effort to wheedle them into a settlement.

A graphic example of Steelman's technique was his "double leak" in the coal strike of the winter of 1949-50.

The three impartial arbitrators appointed by the President to settle the protracted deadlock reported to the White House that it was the coal operators who, by their obstinacy, were delaying a settlement. Steelman promptly leaked this information to the operators, in an effort to disconcert them. Then Steelman leaked the story to some of his newspaper friends, so he would get the credit for engineering an agreement.

An ambitious mediocrity, Steelman courts his enemies, is a sycophant to his superiors, and betrays the confidences of both.

Although he is a teetotaler, Steelman and his pretty wife, a former stenographer in the Washington office of the AFL, greatly enjoy Washington social life. Whenever the pressure of work lets up slightly, he hits a three-cocktail-parties-an-evening pace.

Some of his closest friends, both personal and political, are Republicans such as House Floor Leader Joe Martin and that other well-paid John L. Lewis intimate, Senator Styles Bridges of New Hampshire.

Steelman has neither time nor inclination for sports, nor is he well read. He has only one diversion, but he sticks to it with heart-warming constancy. No matter what business may be at hand or how great the pressure of work, the Doctor never misses a broadcast of Amos 'n Andy.

The tall, gaunt, stooped figure of Averell Harriman seems strangely out of place as he moves through the corridors of the White House. It is not that he doesn't fit there. He does. He goes very well with the mansion. Where he doesn't fit is with the crowd now occupying it. Harriman is a man apart from the entourage around Harry Truman.

Possessed of great inherited wealth, wide executive experience, personal charm, intellectual acumen, and a well-merited international reputation, Harriman has nothing in common with the White House gang. Further, the wide gap between them is due to more than differences in capacity and experience.

The figure of Harriman recalls memories of another era of historic crisis: the hectic, fervent, high-spirited, crusading days of Franklin Roosevelt and World War II; days that were only yesterday but now seem another world from the flaccid tone and spiritual emptiness of the past five years of Truman. Harriman is not himself alone; in his footsteps the ghost of Harry Hopkins walks the White House once again.

When the President summoned Harriman home from Paris in the spring of 1950, on the eve of the unexpected Korean war, he acknowledged, in effect, that his large and unwieldy staff contained no one of the stature he urgently needed.

Among that small army there was no one of sufficient capacity to pull together the myriad loose ends of foreign policy, military strategy, and economic aid. To fill this serious gap, Truman belatedly brought a first-class man into the White House staff. Harriman was made "special executive assistant" in charge of all the vast untouched domain, a post and a responsibility which have no precedent in our history save that of Harry Hopkins' peculiar relationship to Roosevelt in time of war.

Harriman, like Hopkins, has free access to his chief. He has an office only a few doors away and sees Mr. Truman several times a day. He also has access to all secret information. He is the eyes and ears of the President on a wide range of subjects and in dealings with the highest level of officialdom.

All this is nothing new to Harriman. He is no stranger to high places, special tasks, and great authority. He began to move into the inner sphere of power in 1939 when Hopkins, then Secretary of Commerce and Roosevelt's intimate, drafted him to be chairman of the Business Advisory Council, an important political sounding board. Earlier, Harriman had served under General Hugh "Ironpants" Johnson in NRA days. Harriman soon became as close to Hopkins as the latter was to Roosevelt.

In 1940-41, as the country's furious drive to arm itself and save Britain gathered increasing momentum, Hopkins and Harriman moved from the field of domestic affairs and politics to the far more challenging and exhilarating arena of war and foreign policy. Harriman, as deputy Lend-Lease administrator and roving envoy, became Roosevelt's topmost "leg man" on the international stage. Later in the war, Harriman became Ambassador to Russia.

In this role, he attended the Potsdam Conference in July, 1945, and met for the first time the new President, Harry Truman. Harriman came away from Potsdam elated. He told intimates he was "very optimistic about my future in this administration." By chance, the two men had hit it off at once.

Next spring, Truman shifted Harriman to London as Ambassador and, that fall, called him home to become Secretary of Commerce, Hopkins' old job and the one recently vacated by Henry Wallace.

In the cabinet, Harriman generally followed the right-of-center viewpoint which might be expected from an alumnus of the Wall Street banking fraternity and a former board chairman of the Union Pacific Railroad. He was one of those, for example, who counseled signing the Taft-Hartley Act. But essentially Harriman did not play an important role in domestic affairs. Being Secretary of Commerce was in the nature of a hiatus from his true interests and vocation.

His mind and dominant instincts turned strongly toward Europe, where Russia and the United States were drifting farther and farther apart. In foreign policy, Harriman leaves his instinctive economic conservatism at home. Unlike most rich bankers, such as former Undersecretary of State Robert Lovett and the late Defense Secretary

James Forrestal, Harriman unerringly recognizes that trade unions, the Socialists, and other left-of-center non-Communist elements are our sole hope in Europe.

The political henchmen of big business and the cartels have no popular support in the European democracies. They have nothing to offer but empty claptrap. Harriman realizes that we are engaged in a struggle not only of competing material forces but also for the minds and loyalties of men. He sees the broad sweep and has a realistic perspective of the whole field. It is his tragedy that he usually fails to communicate that vision and insight in public appearances. In personal conversation and in small groups, he is given to bursts of eloquence that kindle the ardor of his hearers with the fire of his conviction.

As a result, there is a small but active Harriman cult in Washington. Like his good friend Dean Acheson, who has much more of a platform personality, Harriman is a man who attracts personal zealots.

Harriman has few relations with the White House gang. He towers above them in a position of his own. All his nominal colleagues in the executive offices stand aside for him. Even Steelman does not dare intrigue and backbite against Harriman—at least not as baldly as against Clifford. After all, think how rich and influential Harriman is!

Harriman's future holds many possibilities. There is the post of Secretary of State; yet he and Acheson are close friends. It can be stated flatly that if Harriman does succeed Acheson, it will be only after the latter has left of his own accord and in circumstances as yet unseen. It will not be part of a preconceived plan.

Harriman is reminiscent of Hopkins because he brings with him some of the aura of wartime glamour (the only present White House figure who played an important role in the last conflict) and some of the sense of contact with the drama of great world events. Of all the mediocre array, he is the only man of full-sized proportions. But how long he will stay and how well he will make out is uncertain. These reasons make the analogy with Hopkins dangerous.

For Harriman has no such personal intimacy with Truman as existed between Hopkins and Roosevelt. And Harriman, who has held big assignments overseas before, may at any time be drafted again. But for an uncertain interim, at least, he helps to fill a yawning void.

Steelman stands at the dividing line which runs through the White House staff.

On one side is the group of intimates who not only make policy but also are presidential pals and confidants. Steelman is clearly in this element. But, on the other side, he has also served tours of duty as director of the Office of War Mobilization and Reconversion, and acting chairman of the National Security Resources Board. Thus, he has something in common with those members of the entourage whose work brings them into close personal contact with the President but who are not cronies of his.

These members of the staff include the other five administrative assistants, the legal counsel, the Council of Economic Advisers, and the Budget Director. Any one of these positions is of sufficient importance to entitle its holder to play a strong role in White House councils. But none of the present occupants has the needed combination of brains and personality to do so. As a group, the atmosphere they create is one of intellectual aridity.

Most of them are quite self-effacing, something they do not find it difficult to be.

Tall, lanky David Stowe is a onetime North Carolina schoolteacher and a Steelman protégé. After, as Stowe puts it, "backing into the teaching profession" because he could find nothing else to do during the depression, he joined the North Carolina State Employment Service in 1937 and soon rose to be assistant director. Four years later, he came to Washington as an examiner for the Budget Bureau, where he worked closely with Sidney Hillman and Paul McNutt on man power mobilization problems. It was he who drafted the special committee report which was the basis for the setting up of the War Manpower Commission.

Although Stowe worked four years in an employment service, he makes the curious admission that it was not till he got to know Secretary Frances Perkins during the war years that he "came to see labor as a human problem."

Because he handled the budgetary requests of the Conciliation Service, among those of other agencies, Stowe became acquainted with Steelman, who, on his return to office under Truman, made Stowe his deputy. In 1949, he was elevated to the status of administrative assistant to the President. But he still works more for Steelman than he does for the President. During most of 1949, he was the former's eyes and ears on the National Security Resources Board. More recently, Stowe has been a trouble shooter on everything from interdepartmental wrangles over ECA to congressional strategy on repeal of the Taft-Hartley law.

Physically nondescript and personally colorless, Stowe is the epitome of the politically sexless technician.

Handsome George Elsey is a product of his time.

From a middle-class Pittsburgh background and four years at Princeton, class of '39, Elsey, a generation ago, would have become a bond salesman or a Cadillac dealer. But, unlike his fictional prototypes —the nice young men in John O'Hara's novels—Elsey, upon graduation, had nothing to look at but the bleak tail end of the depression. So he decided to become a scholar.

He spent the next two years at Harvard in quest of a Ph.D. in history. But by an alert pursuit of his own opportunities, he has thus far eluded the necessity of teaching.

Joining the Navy as an ensign in early 1942, he wangled an assignment to the secret White House "war room," where maps showed the situation on every front down to regimental level. President Roosevelt visited this center almost daily, and, on the days he did not, Elsey brought him portable desk maps. Early in 1944, Elsey went to England, where he served on the staff planning the Normandy invasion. When those preparations were completed, he returned to the White House. By the time the war ended, Elsey had soared to the rank of commander. He lingered on, and finally, on April Fool's Day, 1947, he was demobilized and joined the staff of his old boss, Clark Clifford, now promoted from Naval Aide to Special Counsel.

It was commonly said around the White House that the better a man dressed, the more Clifford—a natty figure—liked him. Elsey, a tall, slender, good-looking blond, is a very sharp dresser. His rise was rapid. In 1949, Clifford secured him the appointment as administrative assistant.

Elsey devotes half his time to collating documentary material on the foreign policies of the Truman administration and writing explanatory memoranda for the benefit of future historians. The other half is spent as liaison man for the National Security Council and on minor assignments in the field of foreign relations and national defense.

During the 1948 presidential campaign, Elsey wrote rough drafts for Truman's whistle-stop speeches. His only previous political experience had been in 1940, when he struck up a friendship with Philip Willkie, then at Harvard, and became one of Cambridge's most ardent Willkie Republicans. Some of the speeches Elsey wrote for Truman, however, were pretty radical stuff. To turn them out must have required considerable mental readjustment.

It just goes to show what a Princeton man can do when he puts his mind to it.

Administrative assistant Stephen Spingarn comes closer than any of his associates to having an authentic liberal background.

Spingarn's father was a distinguished professor of American literature who resigned from Columbia University in 1911 in the course of a spirited battle with President Nicholas Murray Butler over a question of intellectual freedom. Butler fired Professor Harry Thurston Peck, not because of anything he had done or not done as a professor but because he became involved in a love affair which got into the papers. Spingarn offered a resolution at the next faculty meeting praising Peck for his distinguished services. Butler promptly threw Spingarn out, too.

None of Spingarn's colleagues supported him, which prompted him to write a bitterly satiric poem called "Héloïse Sans Abélard" which closes with the stanza:

> O passionate Héloïse
> I, too, have lived under the ban,
> With seven hundred professors,
> And not a single man.

The closing years of the elder Spingarn were devoted to work on behalf of the National Association for the Advancement of Colored People, of which he was one of the founders.

Steve Spingarn, native of Franklin Roosevelt's Dutchess County, moved to Arizona as a young man to seek treatment for a sinus condition. He graduated from the University of Arizona and also from its law school. He entered the government in 1934 as a lawyer in the Treasury Department. He worked there for eight years, until he entered the Army in 1942. In the service, Spingarn was chief of Combat Intelligence for General Mark Clark's Fifth Army in Italy. The unit he commanded captured more than five hundred enemy spies.

When Spingarn returned home, he went back to the Treasury as Assistant General Counsel. Later, he shifted to the White House staff through the influence of Charles Murphy, the present Special Counsel and an old personal friend.

Spingarn, a capable and experienced lawyer, handles the drafting of administration bills, particularly those of an economic nature. He is also given assignments on Loyalty Board matters, because he was secretary of the "working committee" which set up the original Loyalty Board system. Spingarn feels he is especially qualified for this kind of work, because his wartime experiences taught him the importance of security, while his family tradition taught him a regard for the equally important rights of the individual.

A big, jovial six-footer who weighs around 250 pounds, Spingarn has a ready smile and a hearty laugh to match. He dresses carelessly and usually doffs his baggy coat in his office and works in shirt sleeves. (Mr. Murphy, unlike Mr. Clifford, is unconcerned about the sartorial elegance of his protégés).

As regards ability, Spingarn is safely in the upper half of the White House staff—questionable as that compliment may be. One of his pet enthusiasms is to try to persuade newspapermen that the White House gang is better than it is usually pictured.

"Now, I know I am just a mediocrity," he will say with a booming laugh, "but all of these fellows here are not. Now, you take . . ."

But so far Spingarn has found no takers among the reporters.

Big, smiling, capable-looking Donald Dawson is the President's personnel expert and political liaison man. Dawson bears a striking facial resemblance to Senate Republican Floor Leader Kenneth Wherry of Nebraska. But once Dawson opens his mouth, this taint vanishes. He's from Missouri.

Dawson has been in Washington since 1933. He arrived during the "hundred days," in the wake of the wave of bank failures, to join the RFC as a bank examiner. He stayed six years, caught the eye of RFC boss Jesse Jones, who took him along as a right-hand man when he became Federal Loan Administrator. When war broke, Dawson joined the Army as a private, against his wishes became a personnel officer in the Air Transport Command, and came out a major. He returned to the loan agency and by mere chance was "loaned" to the White House for "a few weeks'" special work. One assignment led to another, and the temporary arrangement eventually became permanent.

From obscure beginnings and chance developments such as these are White House careers molded.

During the 1948 election, Dawson did advance work for the Truman train. Since then, he has served as the clearinghouse for all presidential appointees. For this reason, Dawson, unlike his fellow administrative assistants, sees a long list of callers every day. He screens with the FBI and other sources the background of all proposed nominees.

On patronage matters, Dawson works closely with National Democratic Chairman William Boyle. Anyone seeing hefty, ruddy-cheeked Bill Boyle in, say, the lobby of the Mayflower Hotel (or anywhere else, for that matter) would have no doubt as to his profession. Bill looks like a machine politician.

A well-to-do Kansas City lawyer, he is an old Pendergast ally and a personal friend of Truman's. When Harry Vaughan went into the Army in 1941, Boyle came to Washington to replace him as Truman's secretary. Three years later, and months before the Chicago convention, Boyle joined the National Committee for the express purpose of promoting Truman for Vice-President. The election over, Boyle opened law offices in Washington. During the 1948 campaign, he acted as contact man with state leaders and was on the phone almost continuously from his office in the Capital. Each evening he telephoned to Matt Connelly, on the campaign train, the results and conclusions of his day's work.

One of the principal reasons for Truman's eagerness to promote Senator and National Chairman McGrath to the cabinet was the ardent desire to have his old side-kick Boyle in the chairmanship. Whether the President will do any better playing politics by crony than he has running the government by crony remains to be seen.

On the basis of Boyle's record so far, he has shown up pretty well. He may not be a Fair Dealer by conviction, but he seems to realize clearly on which side the administration's political bread is buttered. Since he has headed the National Committee, liberal and labor leaders have been accorded a far more cordial response than they ever got from McGrath.

Repeatedly, in the 1950 session of Congress, Boyle worked hand in glove with militant Democrats, such as Senators Paul Douglas and Hubert Humphrey and Representatives John Carroll and Mike Kirwan, to obtain a presidential veto on boodle bills that they couldn't defeat in Congress. Boyle did not get the public credit for it, but he had a lot to do with the vetoes of the grab-bag natural-gas "ripper" bill and the price-fixing basing-point measure—both products of Democrat-Republican deals in behalf of special interests.

However, the team of Dawson, Jesse Jones's personnel expert, and Boyle, Harry Truman's Man Friday, has had its crude moments, particularly on delicate patronage problems. They have been fewer and less crude than any previous combination in the White House gang, but they have occurred and may occur again at any moment.

That there has been this improvement is welcome news, but it is still only relative and of uncertain duration.

Special Counsel Charles Murphy, as his predecessor Clark Clifford demonstrated, has the job with the biggest opportunities of anyone around the President. However, shy, baldish, bespectacled Murphy is a man who believes in consistently underplaying his hand.

Where Clifford was persuasively fluent, Murphy is inarticulate. Where Clifford had the courtroom lawyer's sense of the dramatic and ready grasp of the essentials of an argument, Murphy has the desk lawyer's feeling for precision and detail. Clifford consistently outmaneuvered and outthought John Steelman; Murphy, cautious and slow-moving, is no match for Steelman's wheedling and intriguing.

Above all, Murphy has no incentive to fight back, because he is intrinsically as conservative as Steelman himself.

Murphy, another North Carolinian in Truman's councils, has spent almost his whole adult life in Washington. He came to the Senate as a legislative assistant after leaving law school almost two decades ago.

In the years since, he has become an expert in drafting legislation. Before his appointment as Special Counsel, Murphy worked on the Hill as the President's liaison man, supervising and checking measures in which the administration was interested.

In this role, he did not follow the Tommy Corcoran technique of administering a sophisticated blend of intimidation and cajolery. Murphy merely made himself available to advise and assist the reliable congressmen and confer with the doubtful. He pressured no one.

As his legal counsel, Truman need never doubt Charley Murphy's loyalty and dependability. Charley will always stand behind him; but as the vaudeville gag went: Will he also push?

David Niles is the Berlitz School edition of Dorothy Dix.

Not that Niles is an expert on linguistics. But he does know the leaders of the innumerable racial and religious minorities, and, wherever he may be in his travels, and no matter how tight his schedule, they can always get in to see him and pour out their woes.

For Niles is the administration's portable wailing wall.

He is also the only member of the Roosevelt staff held over by Truman, with the exception of correspondence secretary Bill Hassett. Niles knows intimately the world of the urban immigrant community and the assorted minorities. In their effort to play the full role in American life for which their talents fit them, these minorities have thrown up a whole set of congresses, conferences, committees, alliances, unions, fronts, clubs, special newspapers, societies, and countless other organizations which make up an exciting but complex world which no Missouri farm boy would want to enter unguided. For this reason, and this reason alone, Niles has a high survival value.

Truman keeps him on and allows him to perform his work uninterrupted and unsupervised. Roosevelt himself was no mean operator in this field. The intricacies of Jacob Potofsky vs. David Dubinsky vs. Vito Marcantonio, or the difference between the Civil Rights Congress and the Civil Liberties Union were quite clear in his mind. But in this kind of game, Truman is just a rookie from the Three-Eye League. Niles has to do a lot of coaching and steering.

Naturally, he concentrates on the Jewish and Negro groups. In 1947-49, he was very active in the Palestine problem. How much weight Niles actually exercised is debatable, but he was busy. In the field of civil rights, much of the masterminding and the lobbying by interested groups is coordinated in his office. With Catholic elements, Niles's influence is considerably less, but even here he is an astute listening post for the administration.

Niles personally is most likable. A short, dark-haired, barrel-shaped man with horn-rimmed glasses, he speaks in soft, velvety tones and has an ingratiating manner. He frequently tells his visitor a titbit or two of backstage gossip and thus creates the warming illusion he is taking him into his confidence. Niles's favorite technique for winding up a conversation is, "Come in to see me again, and we'll talk about this some more." In this way he sends callers away with the feeling that, if he said next to nothing this time, there was a good chance he would do better later.

Niles has helped to swing some valuable appointments to minority groups. But patronage is not Niles's main concern.

His chief function is to serve as a portable wailing wall. Delegations from various minorities come to the executive offices with problems and complaints. Often they endeavor to see the President and some-times succeed, but in any case they are inevitably shunted off to Niles. He hears them out with great patience and sympathy, lends them his shoulder to cry on, and assures them he is heartily on their side.

"Of course," he will explain, "there are great difficulties, and some things are just impossible. But the President is a very good man, and something will surely be done for you if it is humanly possible."

More often than not, nothing more ever happens. But Niles has served the administration by turning aside dangerous wrath, and the callers have relieved their feelings by this confessional procedure.

Since anti-Semitism is never eliminated and the majority of Negroes continue to live in squalor, no matter how much Niles does or does not do, business is always brisk at his stand.

Niles has a good background for this work. Born in Boston's North End slums in 1891, he is the son of immigrants. (The family name was Neyhus, as Westbrook Pegler is so fond of pointing out.) As a young man just out of high school, he became an assistant to George Cole-man, the colorful, goateed manager of Boston's famed Ford Hall

Forum. Eventually, Niles succeeded his mentor and also established himself in the lecture-bureau business.

His first fling in politics came in 1924, when he managed the speakers' bureau for Robert M. La Follette's campaign for President. One of Niles's co-workers in this crusade was a young man from Wisconsin named David Lilienthal. Niles also made the acquaintance of Senator George Norris of Nebraska. Today, a small autographed picture of Norris is the only photograph on his desk. In 1928, Niles helped run the Committee of Independents for Al Smith, and in between he was tirelessly active in the futile liberal struggle to save Sacco and Vanzetti. Naturally, Niles was with Franklin Roosevelt from the very start. He became Federal Emergency Relief Administrator for Massachusetts and later came to Washington as one of Harry Hopkins' top aides in the WPA. In 1940, he shifted to a desk in the White House.

Over the years, Niles has developed a three-way division of his life.

From Monday through Wednesday, he works at political wirepulling for the President. Wednesday evening he goes to New York, where he is an inveterate theatergoer. (He is one of the minor "angels" of *South Pacific*.) Late Friday, he arrives in Boston. All the next day, he holds open house in his suite of offices in a downtown building. His schedule of visitors on these Saturdays in Boston is very long, and very little goes on in Boston and Massachusetts politics about which he does not know and in which he does not frequently dabble. On Sunday evening, he shepherds the visiting lecturer to the Ford Hall Forum, which he still runs, and after the lecture takes the train back to Washington.

Probably no other man gives the Pennsylvania Railroad's midnight runs so much business.

But, whatever city Niles is in or whatever project he is at work on, he has little to say for publication and prefers to operate under cover of anonymity. This has given him a considerable reputation as a "mystery man." A legend has developed concerning his Machiavellian machinations and his supposedly far-reaching power.

One writer recently went so far as to state, "Many a cabinet member or other top official today has an uneasy feeling that he might rise or fall on a casual word from Niles."

That is silly. Under Roosevelt, Niles had no more influence than a hundred other persons. Under Truman, he has even less, except that in his own bailiwick—minority relationships—he now has unchallenged sway, since Truman has no one else around who knows anything about such matters.

Indeed, this is the essential fact underlying Niles's position in the White House gang. He has almost nothing in common with his associates except a taste for power. What he privately thinks of them, no one knows. It is doubtful if Niles even lets his mind dwell for long on such dangerous notions.

Except where his own specialty is involved, he is largely a background figure. If he is for someone or some program, he can help a little. If he is opposed, it counts for nothing.

David Niles still turns shrewd eyes and an urbane, smiling countenance toward the world. But he is today more often a spectator than a manipulator of great events.

The legal counsel and the six "anonymous" assistants all have aides and assistants of their own.

Niles, for example, has as his deputy Philleo Nash, a Ph.D. in anthropology who is an expert on Indians. Nash, when he isn't occupied backstopping Truman and Niles, runs a country day school in Washington and a big cranberry farm in Wisconsin.

Murphy has several people on his staff. One of them leaped briefly to the front pages of the nation's press when he was plastered by Senator Joe McCarthy as one of the State Department's "pro-Communists."

David Lloyd, the man "Jumpin' Joe" accused, is a lawyer and speech writer from New York. Lloyd graduated from the Harvard Law School in 1935 and has been working in Washington ever since in various positions on the Hill and in downtown agencies. He arrived at the White House by a somewhat circuitous route.

In 1947-48, he was a lobbyist for the Americans for Democratic Action, the liberal, anti-Communist political organization. When the presidential campaign got under way, ADA "loaned" him to the research division of the Democratic National Committee to prepare speeches for party bigwigs. During the course of the campaign, the National Committee "loaned" him to the White House to prepare talks for Truman's whistle stops. Lloyd's work stood out so distinctly above the average of his associates that he was invited to stay on after the election.

Lloyd, like a number of others whom McCarthy smeared, actually never worked for the State Department.

During the war, he was in the European branch of the Foreign Economic Administration. After V-J Day, this organization's duties were taken over by the State Department, and the agency was "liquidated." Lloyd was still overseas at the time, and, for purposes of payroll accounting, he was carried briefly on the State Department lists, though he never performed any regular Department duties and soon left the government altogether, to work for ADA.

Lloyd is a tall, thin, sandy-haired man of thirty-nine, with a high forehead, spectacles, and a ready smile. He has a mild, easygoing manner and a reflective mind. In his whole make-up, there is not a trace of the doctrinaire or the conspirator.

Leon Keyserling, chairman of the Council of Economic Advisers, is proud of one thing. The President called his predecessor, Dr. Edwin Nourse, by his academic title, but he calls him "Leon."

For a man who suffers from as massive an inferiority complex as Keyserling does, this simple matter of nomenclature means a great deal.

Keyserling's profound personal insecurities have caused him to erect a protective shell of arrogance between himself and the outside world. When he worked as secretary to New York's former Senator Robert Wagner (though he was really his legislative counsel and did not do secretarial work, as Keyserling is always careful to explain), he had few friends on the Hill and was cordially disliked by the girls in the office. His first big job "downtown" was as head of the old U.S. Housing Authority, where he had a reputation as a martinet. Now, as chairman of the Council of Economic Advisers, he suffers anxieties because he knows that professional economists look down on him as a mere lawyer who does not have the proper string of academic degrees in economic theory.

But still, there he is, and the President calls him "Leon."

The three-man Economic Council was set up in 1946 under the Full

Employment Act. It is one of the three agencies which operate direct from the President's office. It recommends economic policy, just as the National Security Resources Board recommends policy on civilian defense and war mobilization, and the Budget Bureau handles the administrative management problems of the President.

For a long time, the Council's exact function was obscured by a smoldering controversy between Dr. Nourse and his two associates as to whether they should testify before congressional committees in behalf of the President's program or whether they should remain in the background and devote themselves solely to preparing "impartial and objective" reports for the President's guidance. Nourse insisted Council members should not testify; his colleagues contended they should. At first, a makeshift compromise was arranged, whereby Keyserling and Clark would testify but Nourse would not. But finally, in early 1950, the friction broke into flame and Nourse resigned—without regret or loss to anyone.

The controversy was asinine from the outset.

An agency like the President's Council of Economic Advisers has as much chance of keeping pure of politics as a sixteen-year-old virgin has of preserving her chastity in an Arab harem.

There is no such thing as "objective" and "impartial" economics. There are as many economic theories as there are economists.

Moreover, as Nourse's critics pointed out, he was saying one thing and doing exactly the opposite. While making a great ado about his lofty squeamishness regarding testifying before Congress, he was at the same time busier than a queen bee, buzzing about the country expounding his views to almost every conceivable group that would listen to him.

Of course, what Nourse was really yelling about was not this question at all. The real core of his complaint was the nature of the economic advice his two colleagues were giving the President.

They are liberals and Nourse is a conservative. They differed continually with Nourse's orthodox and unimaginative concepts. That's what the protracted wrangling was actually all about.

Characteristically, Nourse refused to state the dispute in its proper terms.

The President, in his usual offhand manner, summed up the situation patly when he remarked, at the first meeting of the Council after Nourse resigned, "Well, the Doctor was a very nice old gentleman, but he wasn't very practical."

Keyserling and his two colleagues, John D. Clark and Roy Blough, see Truman far less frequently than do the "anonymous assistants." They have a standing date with him once each month, when they give him their monthly survey and have a conference that lasts usually about a half hour. They also see the President once or twice a week for the four or five weeks preceding their semiannual reports. Keyserling, however, as chairman, sees Truman informally on other occasions and does various odd assignments, including assisting in the preparation of important speeches.

Keyserling is the closest thing to a brain-truster on the President's staff. But his position is difficult, for he has always been insecure about himself, and now he is insecure about his job.

Keyserling has Truman's confidence for the moment, but he has to contend constantly with the suspicions of him in many congressional quarters as a "dangerous radical" and with the ambitious machinations of John Steelman. Steelman has long distrusted Keyserling as being "too liberal," and he frequently duplicates the Council's work by secretly preparing for the President lengthy reports on economic affairs.

Nor does Keyserling have any of the solid psychological advantages of Clark Clifford. Though born in South Carolina, Keyserling is really a New Yorker with a Harvard and New Dealish background, and he looks very much the intellectual.

Pudgy and fortyish, he has a receding pompadour hairline and pale, bulging eyes which peer nearsightedly from behind thick glasses. His defensive manner betrays the pressure he is under. Personally cold and unable to make friends easily, he has developed a somewhat stuffy, pompous manner and tends to talk in blurry circumlocutions which obscure rather than illustrate the fact that he really has a first-rate mind.

If Keyserling survives, it will be one of the few times Truman has let brains triumph over conviviality.

Frederick Lawton is one of the most powerful and least-known men around the President. It is his office and not his personality which gives him this power. Lawton is Director of the Bureau of the Budget.

In discussing the Budget Bureau, it is necessary first to clear up some widely held misconceptions. The popular belief is that the agency consists of a bunch of bookkeepers who tote up the budget estimates prepared by the various department heads, compare this figure with the total anticipated revenue, and then suggest ways of making the two meet as closely as possible. This, however, is only a small part of the Bureau's work.

There is also what is called the Division of Legislative Reference, which must clear every recommendation for legislation proposed by any agency. Bills on everything from reclamation to bombs pass through the Division on the way to the Congress. This is supposedly for purposes of "coordination."

The Bureau also has a Field Service, with offices in Chicago, Dallas, Denver, and San Francisco, and a Division of Administrative Management, which keeps a continual check on the operations of every government agency. There is, further, a Division of Statistical Standards, which analyzes and coordinates everything down to and including the style and format of government questionnaires.

Thus, begun as a small unit of the Treasury in 1921, and switched in 1939 to the President's office, the Budget Bureau has mushroomed to major bureaucratic importance. In the name of coordination and managerial efficiency, it has grabbed for power in all directions and has become a kind of super-holding company of bureaucracy, a government within a government. It is the most feared and damned agency in Washington.

Frederick Lawton, as Director of the Budget, is therefore a man of great power. For long stretches of the year, he sees the President every day; at any time he has ready access to him. Lawton likes to emphasize that he does not make policy; he only points out to the President what the "consequences" of any given policy will be, not only in terms of cost but whether it will work "in administrative terms."

The incumbent of this key job has traditionally gone on to bigger and more glamorous, if not more influential, positions. The first director was Charles G. Dawes, who later became Coolidge's Vice-President and Hoover's Ambassador to England. Lewis Douglas, the current

American envoy in London, was Roosevelt's first chief of the budget. Truman has upped two of his selections to high place: James Webb to Undersecretary of State, and Frank Pace to Secretary of the Army.

It is uncertain how much farther Lawton will climb. He has already gone a lot farther than he expected.

He started as a career employee thirty years ago, at the very bottom of the civil service ladder. He studied nights and eventually attained a law degree at George Washington University. For the last several years, he had been the Bureau's assistant director.

Frank Pace, Lawton's predecessor, was bitterly resented in various departments for his insistence on trimming expenses for social-welfare and natural-resources-development programs. Reclamation projects and public power lines suffered particularly under Pace's brand of economy. A wealthy young Arkansas lawyer, he has a thoroughgoing conservative background and outlook. He economized at the expense of such projects with no personal qualms whatsoever.

Lawton is a very different type: a cautious, self-contained, middle-aged bureaucrat. He is unlikely to stick his neck out and get into any bitter intra-administration rows. For this reason, the Budget Bureau may, perhaps, for the next few years at least, recede somewhat into the more modest, nonpolicy-making role originally envisaged for it.

That would be a wholesome and long-needed development.

The National Security Resources Board is a striking contrast to the Budget Bureau.

Budget is an agency which was modestly conceived but which expanded to fabulous size. NSRB is an agency born with a grandiose conception of its huge power, but which did little until forced to bestir itself by the Korean eruption. The agency has still to demonstrate what it can do, if anything.

It was originally set up as the superagency to do all the planning for war mobilization and civilian defense. The next war, if there was to be one, would be a conflict we were prepared to meet, unlike our stumbling approach to the last two global melees. But with all its much-vaunted authority and high purpose, the agency did virtually nothing.

Chief reason for this was Mr. Truman.

Instead of naming an outstanding man to the chairmanship, he

piddled around and finally sent up the name of Mon Wallgren, whom
the Senate refused to confirm. For more than a year, Truman left the
post in the hands of John Steelman. The Doctor, ever willing to en-
hance his importance, took the job but threw much of the work of the
chairmanship on an assistant, David Stowe. Between them, Stowe and
Steelman managed to smother the agency in red tape.

Endless plans, memoranda, and paper programs were concocted.
Their purpose wasn't to do anything, but to "clarify" the previous
clarification of what the agency was *supposed* to do.

A typical product of this process is the following sentence from a
memo drafted by Stowe: "The Resources and Requirements Office,
in addition to rendering central staff guidance on the peacetime inter-
relation of anticipated wartime requirements data, is responsible for
the development of techniques required to balance and program resources and requirements in wartime."

Needless to add, after this saturation of bureaucratic hogwash, the
situation at NSRB was denser than ever.

Stuart Symington, the chairman finally appointed in the spring of
1950, has earnestly endeavored to change all that. He has a reputation,
at least in some quarters, as a hot-shot administrator, but he came to
NSRB in a very inauspicious way. The appointment was definitely
warmed-over biscuits for Mr. Symington.

He was angling for David Lilienthal's old job as chairman of the
Atomic Energy Commission. Truman did not wish to give him that,
and used Symington's poor health as an excuse. (Symington suffers
from severe and chronic high blood pressure.) Truman gave him
NSRB as a consolation prize.

Symington is a tall, handsome, dapper, forty-nine-year-old millionaire who makes an elegant addition to any hostess's dining table, and
he and his pretty wife are not at all averse to the lure of the social
whirl. Symington was born in Massachusetts and educated at Yale,
but spent most of his business career in Rochester and St. Louis.
From 1938 to 1945, he was president of the Emerson Electric Manufacturing Company in St. Louis and supervised its wartime expansion
when it became the world's greatest airplane armament manufacturing
plant.

Shortly after Truman took office, he brought Symington to Washington to head the Surplus Property Board. But the latter quickly dropped this hot potato, and early in 1946 adroitly shifted to the War Department as Assistant Secretary for Air. The next year, under unification, he became the first Secretary of the Air Force. In this role, Symington was the glamour boy of the administration. He was very popular on Capitol Hill and could sell congressmen on any Air Force program. In fact, his main achievement was to get money for more airplanes than his nominal chief, the Secretary of Defense, and the President wanted to build.

Symington was a wonderful salesman, but he was operating in a seller's market.

Most people, and that especially includes the President, consider Symington suave and ingratiating. But newsmen trying to track down information, and Pentagon officials at variance with Symington's views, often found him more slick than suave. He is very good at "inside politics," and he is also skillful at ducking, evading, and jabbing. When in a tight spot, he does not hesitate to brazen his way through.

Putting the National Security Resources Board into shape is a long and difficult job, and Symington has only begun. Whether he will prove himself the deft administrator the President thinks he is, remains to be seen.

The size and scope of the task became compellingly clear after the Communist aggression in Korea. NSRB, the great planning agency, had no plans. Everything in the economic mobilization program had to be hurriedly whipped up on the spur of the moment. The long-moribund NSRB staff was very creaky and rusty when it tried to function under pressure. Some suggested the difficulty was that the staff had spent three and a half years preparing for a total war requiring full mobilization, and the damned Russians crossed them up by starting a small war requiring only piecemeal mobilization. This was a good wisecrack but a lame excuse. The truth is, NSRB was unprepared to meet any kind of emergency, big or little. Little had been done before Steelman took over, and after that, even less was accomplished, if such was possible. If Steelman had any concept of the function of NSRB, he displayed little sign of it. The country can thank

God that bitter events gave the whole time-squandering gang a swift kick in the pants.

One thing is certain. Whether Symington regrets it or not, he is now the head of NSRB and very much on the spot. He must deliver. The job is the biggest and toughest he has tackled in his five years in Washington, and it will take a lot more than sweet talk and photogenic glamour to put it over.

The Army, Air, and Naval Aides to the President form a special segment of the White House staff. In other administrations, they were completely unimportant. Who remembers Hoover's military aides? Who but the historians of the Roosevelt era remember FDR's kindly, unobtrusive General "Pa" Watson?

But who can possibly forget Harry Vaughan?

That anyone as gross and blatant as Vaughan should be an inner member of the President's staff is a devastating commentary on the intellectual level of this administration.

The National Guard must take the blame for putting Harry Vaughan where he is today. Vaughan and Truman served in the Missouri National Guard together and became fast friends. Vaughan, like Truman, saw duty in World War I. In the intervening years, he wandered about from job to job, a very round peg never finding a niche small enough to drop into permanently. He held an assortment of jobs—one with a chemical company, the longest as a tea salesman.

Vaughan was just a jolly, foot-in-the-mouth kind of guy whom nobody disliked or gave a second thought to. In 1940, Truman brought him to Washington as an office assistant. When Truman became Vice-President, he made Vaughan his Military Aide. No Vice-President had ever had a Military Aide, but that did not stop Truman. Once the Missouri gang moved into the White House, Vaughan was quickly upped to brigadier general, and then to major general.

Practically overnight, he skyrocketed from obscurity to notoriety.

He began to make speeches and expound his views on public questions. This rapidly grew embarrassing, and Vaughan was curtly silenced. But he remained active in White House affairs.

In addition to being boon companion and Military Aide, Vaughan acquired another function. The President made him Coordinator of Veterans' Affairs. His task was to cut red tape and to help servicemen who needed immediate government assistance. Considering the inefficiency of the VA, there was no doubt of the need for such a position, and Vaughan in his blunt, stable-sergeant manner actually did some good.

On one notable occasion, he solved a problem which had been stumping the great minds for months—the shortage of medical personnel in one service and a surplus in others. In a sensible three-cornered swap involving the Army, Navy, and the VA, Vaughan arranged to transfer doctors and dentists from one to the other and thus satisfy all their needs.

But while doing some good work, Vaughan also gravely abused and exceeded his authority.

He intervened to get a race-track promoter scarce building materials at the height of the housing shortage. He allowed Johnny Maragon, the ex-bootblack turned five-percenter, turned convict, to use his office and telephone to carry on business which was not only strictly personal but strictly shady. And he capped it all by stupidly accepting a gaudy gewgaw from Argentina's tinhorn Dictator Perón.

For ends that were vain, cheap, and degrading, Vaughan embarrassed himself and compromised the President.

But Truman, characteristically, has defended him throughout his scrapes and continues to keep him on. He did give him strict orders to keep out of sight and sound during the 1948 campaign, but that is the only known hobble put on him.

Truman likes Vaughan because he is a jovial drinking and card-playing companion. He also relishes his raucous barnyard humor. Most of Vaughan's stories are too crude to print, but a few of his cracks can be published without being sent to the laundry first. For example, when Truman was making one of his periodic trips to Key West, Vaughan was afflicted with seasickness. "But what the hell," whooped the General, "it tastes just as good coming up as it did going down."

It is the carefully cultivated practice around the White House to picture Vaughan as nothing more than a playtime companion, with no influence with the President on big issues. To a large extent that is true. But it overlooks one psychological fact that is of prime significance in analyzing the importance of the White House staff.

The President trusts Vaughan as a very close and intimate friend who will not fail him in a showdown. Further, he not only sees Vaughan every day, but he sees him late in the afternoon and in the evening, when he is tired and in a reflective mood. Vaughan's comments at such moments, even in ostensible jest, carry special weight.

Harry Hopkins, who was a far different man from Vaughan but who occupied a position of comparable intimacy, once remarked to another White House intimate in a burst of unaccustomed candor, "I don't give a damn who sees Roosevelt during the day. I see him at night, the last half hour before he goes to bed. People forget how lonely a President is, how often he sits alone, eats alone, thinks alone. I see the Chief when he is alone and tired, and a half hour then is worth two hours any other time."

Truman, because he has normal use of his limbs, moves around more and meets more people socially than Roosevelt could. But he, too, has his tired and lonely moments. And Vaughan is usually there.

He is no Harry Hopkins. But he does have strong opinions on many subjects and many people. Truman hears these opinions when he is peculiarly receptive to influence.

Vaughan thus plays a subtle, and occasionally an important, role in presidential decisions, particularly with regard to appointments.

Vaughan is a benighted reactionary on all economic matters, and his words always serve the Snyder-Sawyer-Steelman legion of death. He has violent likes and dislikes of various people. Two persons he was particularly "down on" were Henry Wallace and James Byrnes. When Wallace was finally forced out, Vaughan remarked, "We haven't had a decent Secretary of Commerce since Herbert Hoover." Byrnes's fall as Secretary of State was partially due to Vaughan's constant needling of Truman with the charge that Byrnes was too independent and was playing to the grandstand too much.

Despite the carefully planted stories to the contrary, Harry Vaughan still has influence in the White House, and there can be little doubt that any influence this character wields is not desirable.

The Truman gang is an extraordinary group, unparalleled in the history of the White House. Never was there such a large, weirdly assorted, and variegated crew, and never one which ran so instinctively and unerringly to the banal and the second-rate.

Members of the gang are not unaware of the general low repute they have with the public. But this has not given them an inferiority complex. Quite the contrary. They have developed an elaborate defensive rationale.

Taking their cue from one of the Boss's favorite themes, the Truman coterie constantly refer to themselves as a "team." "We may not have any stars," their argument runs, "but in the long run we make up for it in balance and coordination. Everything works smoothly and harmoniously, whereas with a 'star' trying to do everything, nobody knows where he's at."

Like the old European saw that the only thing the Balkans needed was unity, this sounds pretty good until it's examined. Then it becomes clear that nothing particular is gained by uniting weakness. Mediocrity, even in massed and well-balanced formation, does not equal distinction or effectiveness.

But the worst thing about the Truman gang is their complaisance, their lush sense of self-satisfaction, and their utter lack of any sense of moral commitment, personal urgency, or intellectual fervor.

When Roosevelt signed the law in 1939 creating the six administrative assistantships, he declared that he would fill them with men who had a "passion for anonymity." Some of the men he appointed had a passion for authority, others a passion for ideas.

Truman's staff needs some passion, period.

MEN OF DISTINCTION

THE nine members of Harry Truman's cabinet are like nine men in a stranded bus.

Some came complete strangers, and others knew one another only casually. Unlike the vaunted British cabinet, they do not represent either a common social background or a common ideological viewpoint.

The group includes a socially aristocratic Brahmin lawyer, a career civil servant who has always lived on his modest salary, a rich upper-middle-class corporation lawyer, a couple of big-city politicians from the low-income brackets, a self-made Midwestern businessman with arch-Tory ideas, two liberal lawyers from the West, and a small-time conservative banker from Arkansas. Nor have the members served together in any body like the British Parliament, where long association rubs off social distinctions and creates a commonly shared outlook. Individually and as a group, the cabinet constitutes one of the most diverse and variegated assortments of its kind in more than fifty years.

Under the sheer necessity of living together, the members strike up a lighthearted friendship, call one another by first names with an unduly hearty emphasis, and generally act as if this is just what they would be doing if they had any choice in the matter, which they don't have.

No one fully trusts any of the others ("I bet that bastard will leak my stuff the first minute he gets out of here"). Each may think that one or more of the others is a fool or an incompetent or politically unreliable, and not be far wrong. But these suspicions generate no hostility, because each knows he is completely autonomous and will stand or fall on his own merits or lack of them. Only on paper are the Commerce and State Departments, say, in the same administration.

As in a smoking car or a bus, the discussions at the weekly cabinet meetings proceed at a very low intellectual tension. They consist mostly of amiable pleasantries, anecdotal reminiscences, and mildly ribald stories. No policies are threshed out, no decisions made. How can the Secretary of National Defense explain the "strategic bombing" controversy to eight amateurs and expect them to arrive at any intelligible common decision in thirty-five minutes?

The cabinet has no intellectual unity; it ranges from extreme conservatives to extreme liberals and includes two or three members who are, or pretend to be, neutral on the great domestic issues. Most important of all, the cabinet has no common destination; this is not an express bus. Each man will probably get off at a different stop, and each keeps his own career and his own destination uppermost in his mind.

When Mr. Truman took over the driver's seat in 1945, he made a great point about revitalizing the cabinet as a policy-making instrument. It was to be the top council of strong men to whom great responsibility would be delegated and with whom all great issues would be discussed and decided.

For a few months, this approach was actually carried out. Weighty problems, such as the Japanese surrender, were argued out at the cabinet table. But soon all that passed, and the old "inefficient" order that had existed under Roosevelt prevailed once more. It was the inevitable nature of things. Truman, like most of his modern predecessors, discovered that he was not a prime minister or the chairman of a board of directors. His job was comparable to that of military commander.

In the formal sense, a President, like a commander, has no cabinet; he has a staff. Under the British cabinet system, the responsibility for carrying on the government is a collective one; the premier is just that—first among his equals. In the American system, the responsibility for the administration is centered solely on the President. No one is even close to him, and no one can share his power.

Only one aspect of Truman's original conception remains unchanged. He still delegates great chunks of authority, much vaster grants than Roosevelt or any other strong President ever made.

But, for the very reason that he is not on top of every cabinet member's job, knowing it almost as well or better than the officer knows it himself, Truman cannot readily guide a cabinet discussion which ranges over every field. Roosevelt, for example, was his own Secretary of State and his own Secretary of Labor, and, in a sense, he served as a bond uniting the two Departments and could profitably conduct a multicornered discussion in which these two Secretaries took part. Truman does not have such a grasp of working policy and practical detail.

On any single subject, his knowledge is inferior to that of the secretary concerned. He is thus heavily dependent on private briefing sessions with that official alone. He cannot in any real or practical sense unite and coordinate policies in his own person. Truman, seen in this perspective, is thus the missing link without which the nine members cannot be bound into a coherent cabinet.

This overriding fact is so important that the Secretary of State and the Secretary of Defense are more than members of the cabinet. They form with the President a kind of superdirectorate for the conduct of the interrelated fields of foreign and military affairs. Because of this, these two Departments are considered in separate chapters in this book.

The cabinet meets with the President once a week, usually on Friday mornings, and then again for lunch on Monday, when the President ordinarily does not attend. But the degree of personal intimacy which exists may be judged by the fact that though Secretary of Commerce Charles Sawyer and Secretary of State Dean Acheson have houses in fashionable Georgetown only a stone's throw apart, they have never visited one another.

Interior Secretary Oscar Chapman is the newest member of the Truman cabinet, but he has a long background of continuous public service in Washington. He came in 1933 as Assistant Secretary of the Interior.

Chapman has a fabulous grasp of all the complex details of his far-flung jurisdiction. He has lived with it, run its machinery, fought its

battles, and dreamed its dreams for over seventeen years. Few cabinet
officers, and certainly no Interior Secretary, have ever brought to their
task a wider experience, more profound grasp, and loftier concept of
their duties.

But Chapman has other attributes in addition to exceptional administrative capacity and a wealth of experience. He is the suavest, most
adroit, and most effective politician in the Truman administration. It
was Chapman who managed the President's unprecedentedly successful "nonpolitical" tour in the spring of 1948. He did much of the
masterminding in the election that fall and again in 1950.

Chapman did not acquire his political savvy in the smoke-filled
rooms. He learned it battling for liberal causes under three of the
doughtiest warriors old-time American progressivism ever had—Judge
Ben Lindsey, Senator Edward Costigan, and "Honest Harold" Ickes.

Chapman met Lindsey and Costigan when he moved to Colorado
as a young man. He had been born on a tobacco farm in Virginia,
and his quiet, mellow voice still carries a hint of Southern drawl.
Chapman enlisted in the Navy in World War I. In the course of that
service, he crossed the Atlantic thirty-six times. On one voyage he
contracted tuberculosis, which later caused him to move to Colorado
in search of a cure. In 1922, attracted by Lindsey's great liberal reputation, he persisted until the Judge granted him an interview and soon
after a job as assistant probation officer in juvenile court. Later, Chapman went into private law practice as partner of Edward Costigan.

Costigan was the grand old man of Colorado liberalism. He had
been a Republican in his younger days, but in 1912 he followed Theodore Roosevelt down the trail of the Bull Moose and never went back.
Over the next decade and a half he struggled to make the Democratic
Party in Colorado a vehicle for liberal policies. Every prominent Colorado New Dealer—Oscar Chapman, Agriculture Secretary Charles
Brannan, Representative John Carroll, and Josephine Roche, onetime
candidate for governor and now secretary of the United Mine Workers Pension Fund—felt the mark of his leadership and inspiration.
Costigan, a small, dark-complexioned man, the son of an Irish father
and a Spanish mother, worked tirelessly to gain social justice for the
coal miner, the migrant worker, the debt-squeezed dry-land farmer,
and all the other struggling poor of the West. Of all his disciples,

Chapman, the modest, soft-spoken, hard-working young Southerner, was personally the closest. It was Chapman who, in 1930, managed the campaign that put Costigan into the Senate.

Two years later, Costigan took Chapman along with him when he went to Albany to talk with President-elect Franklin Roosevelt. It was the first time Chapman had ever met him. "Ed," said Roosevelt to Costigan when the conference ended, "I want to keep this young man in Washington. He is the kind of man we want in the government."

The next spring, Chapman got the offer to become Assistant Secretary of the Interior under Harold Ickes. In their introductory meeting, the Old Curmudgeon asked only one principal question, "What is your philosophy of conservation?"

Chapman replied, "I am in complete accord with what Gifford Pinchot and Theodore Roosevelt did."

"That's good enough for any man," said Ickes.

At this hour of their mutual triumph, Chapman had to stand by helplessly and watch the aged Costigan, his health broken by his long struggles, die a slow, lingering death in circumstances of near poverty.

Costigan's vision has remained Chapman's indelible inspiration. The decade of struggle they shared in the futile 1920's and the at once challenging and heartbreaking early 1930's gave him a sense of long-range perspective and a feeling of sureness in liberal purposes and objectives which many noisy Fair Dealers sorely lack. Bitter experiences and vivid memories make Chapman the soundest liberal in top-bracket Washington.

As Assistant Secretary, Chapman put in years of useful work. He fought the scourge of child labor in the Western sugar-beet fields. When the Taylor Grazing Act of 1934 put thousands of acres of public domain, previously overgrazed by big sheep and cattle ranchers, under strict conservation controls, it was Chapman who toured the Far West explaining the law and appeasing the wrath of the private owners. He took a leading part in the program to improve conditions in Puerto Rico and Alaska and to bring statehood to the latter and Hawaii. With high integrity, perseverance, and courage he handled the politically dangerous and sensitive assignment of the oil leases and public-power contracts. He pioneered the development of the synthetic-fuels program, including the extraction of oil from shale.

Chapman is more than a courageous and constructive champion of the West. He is a liberal on all fronts and a man of national stature.

Chapman has made the welfare of minority groups a kind of personal avocation. He worked effectively to assist persecuted Jews and was influential behind the scenes in aiding the establishment and diplomatic recognition of the Republic of Israel. It was his idea to have Marian Anderson give a concert on the steps of the Lincoln Memorial after the famed Negro singer had been denied permission by the D.A.R. to use Constitution Hall.

Meanwhile, as he toiled and battled year after year, he saw a succession of less worthy and less able men promoted over his head. The climax came in 1946, when Truman imported Julius Krug from outside the administration to replace Ickes.

"Cap" Krug, a huge 6′ 3″, 260-pounder with a colossal egotism to match, was the protégé of Bernard Baruch. The "park-bench statesman" was then influential at the White House. Wisconsin-born, Krug had worked his way through college and established a good record with the Tennessee Valley Authority. In 1944, Roosevelt promoted him to the chairmanship of the War Production Board, where he began the premature scrapping of production and allocation controls. Krug is a capable engineer but is hopelessly naive in political matters and sadly defective in administrative judgment, as he proved more clearly the higher he went in government echelons.

Less important but more readily noticeable was that he lived on a rather grand social scale and was eternally preoccupied in straightening out his tangled private affairs. As a department head, he mush-mouthed along from one minor crisis to another, never quite reversing the liberal precedents laid down by Ickes but frequently vitiating them by indirection or neglect.

His undoing came in 1948.

Baruch, Krug's mentor, and by that time at odds with the White House, told him to lay low in the presidential campaign, with the implication that after Dewey was elected Krug would be available as a kind of Democratic Dulles in any bipartisan administering that needed to be done. Krug obediently hotfooted out West, not to campaign for Mr. Truman but to make "inspection tours." When the big show was over, Krug returned to Washington as sunny and cocky as ever. He answered all queries by explaining that he had been visiting Indian reservations and wildlife refuges.

For Harold Ickes, his old enemy, this was too good to pass up.

Ickes would have been at least a little jealous of almost any successor, on the age-old human principle of what always happens when the new queen lies in the old queen's bed. But the spectacle of this bumbling conservative particularly excited the ire of the Old Curmudgeon. At every turn, he harped acidulously on the theme, "Where was Krug during the campaign? Oh, he was visiting wildlife reservations, was he? Well, now, isn't that interesting! And did he get a lot of votes from the ducks?"

Truman also had it in for "Cap," but he dallied about doing the nasty job of firing him, in the hope that Krug would do it himself by resigning. But Krug showed no disposition to leave.

Finally, Truman wrote him a caustic letter concerning a relatively minor matter, and the big, burbling engineer had no choice but to get out. As usual, Senator Clinton Anderson of New Mexico, still grunting and groaning about jumping out of his berth as Secretary of Agriculture when it turned out the ship wasn't going to sink after all, issued a mumbly statement to the effect that his good friend Krug had been "let out because he kept pressing for reclamation projects." Krug, of course, had never offended anyone by his zeal for reclamation projects or anything else. But it was one way of putting a halo around his head, even if it did hang lopsided.

When Chapman became Secretary in the fall of 1949, he was fifty-two. He had been Assistant Secretary for thirteen years and Undersecretary for three and a half. He fitted into his new job as smoothly as a key clicking in a lock. As Secretary, Chapman has fulfilled all the expectations of his friends, and then some.

But he has received very little public acclaim for his magnificent work.

One reason for this is his own persistent refusal to play to the grandstand. Quiet, charming, affable, he lets his deeds speak for him. A more fundamental reason is that the policies he administers are not the kind that make headlines. They are of crucial importance to the development and welfare of virtually every section of the country and its possessions, but they are not spectacular. This is not to say that the Interior job is not an exacting one. It is.

Interior, essentially, is the guardian of the nation's natural resources —land, water, coal, oil and other minerals, as well as wildlife and scenic beauty. At every turn, there is some private group or special interest striving openly or covertly to get a little extra or to grab off some resource which properly belongs to all the people. The main job of the Secretary of the Interior is to wield a big club and periodically crack the assorted hogs across the snout when they venture too far. Harold Ickes was expert at this. But Chapman goes him one better.

He not only wields a mean cudgel but, after dealing a lusty blow, he supplies free bandages and arnica. No one in Washington can say "no" in such a friendly, kindly way as Oscar Chapman.

His deft operations pay off again and again. When his name came up for Senate confirmation, Senator Pat McCarran of Nevada, a hungry hog if ever there was one, sent word that he expected to have the right to name the new undersecretary or else he would block Chapman's confirmation. Chapman sent back word that McCarran could go chase himself—there would be no deal. The sequel was very funny. Who should show up at the committee hearing to testify in Chapman's behalf but Senator George Malone, McCarran's Republican colleague from Nevada, and Senator Eugene Millikin of Colorado, one of the GOP's grand sachems. McCarran never raised a squeak.

In 1950, when his first budget went up to Congress, Chapman called up Representative Michael Kirwan (Dem, Ohio), chairman of the Interior appropriations subcommittee, and said, "Mike, this new budget is pretty complicated, and it's been figured on a new and somewhat different basis. If you want, I will be glad to come up to the Hill this afternoon and go over it with you." Kirwan accepted. Then, recovering from his surprise, he told a colleague, "I'm flabbergasted. I've been in Congress a long time, but this is the first time a cabinet member ever volunteered to come up here and explain his budget."

Chapman's most masterful performance of backstage diplomacy thus far was his successful engineering of the presidential veto of the boodle-loaded Kerr natural-gas "ripper" bill.

Truman had promised Speaker Sam Rayburn to sign the bill, and the promise was still very much in force three days after the measure reached the White House. Then Chapman swung into action. He drafted a lengthy memorandum showing the President in detail that he need not feel bound to his promise to the oil and gas crowd, for they had deceived him in declaring the bill would not raise consumers' gas rates "one red cent." Next, he persuaded Commerce Secretary Charlie Sawyer to write a memorandum counseling a veto because many industries would be adversely affected by an increase in gas rates. Then he collared pussyfooting Mon Wallgren, the oddman on the five-man Power Commission, who had made a hurry-up trip to California in order to escape the backstairs pulling and hauling on the bill. Chapman convinced Wallgren that he should vote for a veto. Wallgren capitulated, and thus the Federal Power Commission went officially on record against the bill by a 3 to 2 count. It was this lightning-fast triple play, with Chapman the man in the middle, that shut out the Kerr bill.

It was a brilliant feat, for which Chapman neither sought nor got any credit. The satisfaction of undoing an unconscionable gouge was sufficient for him. Further, he was already busy battling a number of other grab deals.

Chapman figures that a man who waited so long for the big opportunity to fight the good fight can't act too fast when the chance comes his way.

The story of Attorney General J. Howard McGrath is the story of the triumph of the deadly perseverance of mediocrity in motion.

McGrath was vice-chairman of the Democratic State Committee of Rhode Island when he was still in law school. In rapid succession, he has been State Chairman, U.S. district attorney, three times governor, Solicitor General, United States Senator, Democratic National Chairman, and Attorney General. As soon as the next member of the Supreme Court dies or retires, he will probably become a Justice. And all this by the age of forty-six.

To explain McGrath's "strange affinity" for political power and high offices is a bit difficult.

He has all the charm and personal warmth of cold tea, the magnetism of a lead dime, and the intellectual interests and outlook of a deputy sheriff. In themselves, of course, these qualities illustrate why he fits perfectly into Mr. Truman's official family, but they do not explain how he got to Washington in the first place.

As in most nice success stories, the rise and heroic struggles of Howard McGrath can be illumined by reference to a few copybook maxims.

There is the one, for example, which says: "The world turns aside to let a man pass who knows where he is going." McGrath always knows where he is going. After all, you know, "a man without a purpose is like a ship without a rudder." Or the line from Ovid: "That load becomes light which is cheerfully borne." McGrath, come hell or high water, always keeps his mouth shut. Then, of course, there was Robert Browning who said: "Let us be content in work, to do the thing we can do, and not presume to fret because it's little." McGrath has come up step by step and has done every tough, dirty job from ringing doorbells and watching the polls to presiding at smoke-filled caucuses and begging fat-cats for campaign contributions. Finally, André Maurois advises, "Almost all men improve on acquaintance." McGrath is sure of it. So great is his confidence that he simply refuses to let any man be his enemy—besides, it doesn't pay.

In addition to the push, pluck, perseverance routine, there is another conventional element in the McGrath story—a fairy godfather. The man who has opened many doors for McGrath and in some cases booted him through them is Rhode Island's aged patrician politician, Senator Theodore Green.

This amazing eighty-three-year-old gentleman possesses one of the wisest and most acute political intellects in the country. For forty years, he has been the strategist, financial angel, and intellectual backbone of the Democratic Party in Rhode Island. It is accurate testimony to his ability that in those four decades Rhode Island has been transformed from one of the most moss-bound Republican states into the most tightly organized, rigidly controlled, one-party Democratic stronghold outside the Solid South. Pretty soon, when everyone over sixty dies off, there just won't be any Republicans left in Rhode Island.

Green comes from a very old and highly distinguished New England family. He was born in Providence in 1867, graduated from Brown University and Harvard Law School, studied in Europe at the universities of Bonn and Berlin, and returned to teach Roman law for three years at Brown. He then entered full time into the practice of law and built up a wide corporate practice which further added to his inherited wealth. He became an absolute rock-based pillar of society. He was an officer or director (or receiver) of the leading banks, railroads, insurance firms, and manufacturing companies; for three years in the 1920's he was also national president of the Morris Plan Bankers Association, the giant small-loan syndicate. A ruling Brahmin and the apotheosis of respectability, he was for twenty years a trustee of the leading hospital, for several years secretary of the State Red Cross; for fifty years he has been a trustee of the Rhode Island School of Design, since 1903 a trustee of the Providence Public Library, and he is a hereditary member and now president of the colonial Society of the Cincinnati. To Brown University, he has been practically an uncrowned king. For twenty-nine years he was a trustee; he is now a life fellow. Of Brown, it may roughly be said that it is to Rhode Island what Harvard is to Boston. And that is saying a lot.

Yet, along with all this, Green was also a Democrat. Yankee Democrats are a thin but hardy breed in New England.

In the old days before Franklin Roosevelt made them a social menace, they were regarded by their dominantly Republican friends as mild eccentrics, like Mormons. They were still admitted to the best clubs. But Theodore Green, unknown to his neighbors, was something more than just a Democrat.

He has a brilliant radical mind.

He foresaw the coming shape of things and long ago advocated ideas like minimum wages and slum clearance and other social-welfare measures. Neglected by his contemporaries, Green was a New Dealer twenty years before there was a New Deal.

For decades Green led the Democrats through the wilderness of defeat and futility. He ran for governor again and again before he finally made it in 1932. "I was elected twice before," he says with a quiet, knowing smile, "but both times I was 'counted out,' until the third time I got so many votes they had to count me in." During these trying years, Green kept his eye out for promising young men, particularly those from the "newer races"—the Irish, the French, and the Italians. Nineteen twenty-eight marked the turning of the tide.

Al Smith, running that year, snapped the immigrant community out of its lethargy and aroused a vote big enough to carry the State. Also, in that campaign, a pale, earnest young Irish law student attracted Green's attention by his hard and faithful work at campaign headquarters. Green, insisting that the youngster had the "makings," forced his election as Chairman of the State Committee over the grudging opposition of the hack old-timers. The young man was J. Howard McGrath.

McGrath's father had been interested in politics in a small way. By profession, the father was an organizer for the Catholic Order of Foresters, a once flourishing fraternal society. As a boy, Howard went with his father on speaking trips and to conventions. He was seeing back-room lodge politics at work when other kids were out playing marbles. It was an experience that made a profound impression, and one he never forgot. In a way, McGrath was never young—at least, not young in the carefree, irresponsible sense. Almost since anyone can remember him, he has been the intense, tight-lipped, cigar-chewing, professionally affable, and slightly grim ward and lodge politician.

Green took his protégé under his guidance, and McGrath was a willing pupil.

Yankee Democrats have been in the minority for so long that there are a good many tricks they have learned to get the maximum advantages out of very little strength. These tactics and maneuvers Green explained to McGrath. He also did something else for the young politician. He gave him a ready-made philosophy.

McGrath did not have then, and has not now, any rational grasp of social issues or the trend of social forces. He was an operator, a vote-getting machine humming and clicking in an ideological void. On the blank sheet of paper that was his mind, Green stamped like an indelible stencil a complex of liberal social attitudes and simplified beliefs. Fortunately for McGrath, this ideological design was an advanced one for its time but admirably fitted for the depression era that was about to open in 1930. When the New Deal interlocutor began to ask the questions, Howard "Mr. Bones" McGrath knew all the stock responses.

Queried closely on this tutoring process, Green, now a slightly grizzled old man with a faded gray mustache, a limp handshake, a skepti-

cal smile, and very shrewd eyes behind thin spectacles, comments
suavely, "I have always thought that one of the great pleasures and
rewards of public life was picking out young people and giving them
the chance they deserve but might not otherwise get. Don't you
agree?"

Sheer accident also intervened, the better to equip McGrath for the
political role he was to play.

He fell in love and married a beautiful French-Canadian girl whose
father was mayor of the small city of Central Falls. Assuming that
Cupid played the dominant role, this was still a master political stroke.
The missing link in forging a strong immigrant-Democratic alliance
had always been the French-Canadians—culturally isolated, politically
mercurial, and traditionally hostile to both the "uppity" Irish and the
"inferior" Italians. It would do no Irish candidate any harm whatever
to have a charming French wife to accompany him on campaign tours.

Under Green's guidance, McGrath moved up the ladder rapidly. In
1940, at the age of thirty-seven, after several years as U. S. District
Attorney, he won the governorship. He successfully survived a Republican trend in 1942 and was re-elected to a third term in 1944. His chief
claim to fame as State executive was economy (which was automatic
and painless during a war when both public works and relief rolls
almost disappeared), and the creation of a state-wide system of juvenile courts (about the only social-welfare legislation Green had left
undone during his own two terms as governor).

Where McGrath really shone was as a political operator.

He healed a breach which had appeared in the Democratic ranks,
distributed patronage judiciously to the French and the Italians to
bind them to the Irish core, enticed away the more ambitious and
opportunistic young Republicans, making them Democrats at least in
name, and greased the whole State machine from precinct to State-
house so that with noiseless efficiency it rolled out safe majorities for
any and every candidate.

This is work he loves to do and does well, for he is his father's son.

In 1945, President Truman, looking for a New England Irishman in
order to widen the political base of his administration, appointed
McGrath as Solicitor General. In this job he was, to put it judiciously,
anything but a howling success.

Not only had he never handled an important case up to that time, but he is a flat, banal speaker, and his mind is not quick enough or sharp enough to combat the tricky questions which often rain down from the Supreme bench with machine-gun rapidity. The Court several times complained to the Attorney General that McGrath's presentations were not up to the quality expected of the government's chief advocate. But since McGrath's boss, the Attorney General, was that well-known legal giant, Tom Clark, there was obviously no one to censure him or improve his work.

All in all, everyone was happy and relieved when, after one year, McGrath decided to give up the whole business and go back to politics.

In 1946, he ran for the United States Senate. In the course of the campaign, he felt the hot breath of the opposition blowing down his neck for the first time in his career. He reacted in a most interesting way.

Whereas Secretary of Labor Maurice Tobin, then facing an equally tough fight for re-election as governor of neighboring Massachusetts, went down the line for the national administration, Howard McGrath acted as if he didn't know Harry Truman from a hole in the ground.

As for OPA, those letters were banished from his alphabet. The initials, for all McGrath indicated, might have stood for Old Peanut-Vendors Association or something equally esoteric. Most significant of all, McGrath, in the last week of the campaign and against the frenzied advice of many of his associates, made a savage attack on the "excesses" of organized labor and implied that he would vote for restrictive labor legislation in the next Congress if he were elected. Whether this saved him or not, McGrath squeaked in.

The next spring, when the Taft-Hartley bill came up for final passage, he was subjected to the most intense kind of pressure to come through on his promise. Several leading businessmen called him long-distance from Rhode Island on the final day to remind him of his campaign pledge. But McGrath, also strongly under heat from labor, decided to follow Senator Green's lead and voted against the bill. One of his close associates remarked recently, "Boy, that was a close one. You know, if Howard hadn't backtracked on that one, he would never have been acceptable to the labor crowd as National Chairman, and he certainly would not be Attorney General today, pining for the Supreme Court."

Many ask if Howard McGrath is a liberal. If by that is meant his voting record, the answer is easy: it is one hundred per cent liberal. But in a strict sense the question is irrelevant.

McGrath warbles a liberal tune because it was the one his teacher taught him and it is the only one he knows. Further, in the whole twenty years he has been in public life, it has always paid off in votes. But if two or three defeats (or maybe only one) showed that liberalism had dropped from the head of the hit parade, McGrath could be depended upon to learn new melodies quickly.

In October, 1947, Truman selected McGrath to be Democratic National Chairman. McGrath helped as well as he could to bludgeon the party into renominating the President. He bungled the convention arrangements badly and put Mr. Truman on the air to give his really excellent acceptance speech at two o'clock in the morning, after everyone had gone to bed.

During the ensuing campaign he was like a master of ceremonies full of ideas and suggestions, only the show he's supposed to introduce has left town.

Mr. Truman ran his own campaign, closely advised by Clark Clifford and a temporary crew of speech writers. Bill Boyle, Truman's former Kansas City side-kick, kept in touch with the local leaders by phone from Washington, and he kept Truman advised on shifting trends. Oscar Chapman did the important work on advance arrangements, and Louis Johnson was the chief money raiser. Throughout all this bedlam and intrigue, McGrath issued a few press releases, an occasional weary exhortation, and looked most of the time as if he wished he knew what was going on.

After another ineffectual year at National Headquarters, McGrath got Truman's offer to go upstairs and become Attorney General. Ostensibly a promotion, the appointment, as McGrath well knew, was actually only part of a squeeze play.

On the one hand, the President wanted to give Tom Clark the appointment to the Supreme Court which had long gone to a Catholic. He therefore needed a Catholic to step into Clark's shoes. Further, the President wanted to "kick McGrath upstairs" so he would have a plausible excuse for removing him as National Chairman to make way for Bill Boyle. This was doubly galling to McGrath because he looked down on Boyle as incompetent and because he wanted the "Catholic appointment" to the Supreme Court for himself.

Why a youthful, vigorous machine politician would want to go into the dim-lit obscurity of the mothproof bag which is the Supreme Court is an almost inexplicable mystery. Of course, McGrath is totally unqualified to be a Justice, but that is doubtless an irrelevant observation. The soundest hypothesis is that he subconsciously wants to soothe and compensate his battered ego for the slights it received in his dreary year as Solicitor General. It is almost axiomatic that any lawyer who has ever taken the grilling from the bench that a Solicitor General is subjected to longs to get up there on the dais and ask the questions himself.

In any event, after some hemming and hawing, McGrath took the Attorney Generalship. It was about the last job in the world he wanted. Or that any sane man would want. No lawyer who knew the absolute collapse that had taken place in the Justice Department during the four years of Clark's tenure would welcome the invitation to go in and clean up the Augean stable.

Morale had sunk to all-time lows. Favoritism and inefficiency were everywhere. The Criminal Division was the broken tool of a politically minded hack. The Antitrust Division had been frustrated by Clark's clownish headline-grabbing on monopoly suits, followed by cozy little conferences in which everything was fixed up with a "consent decree." The civil rights section was starved and neglected. The Tax Division was woefully understaffed, for a long time had no chief, and was, as a result, far behind in its work. In a word, the whole Justice Department had gone to pieces while Tom Clark, with his oozing smile and big sombrero, went off chasing the vice-presidential nomination he never got.

McGrath will never win a master builders' citation for the job he has done in putting those pieces together. There has been a little improvement and a lot of fumbling and procrastination.

On the trust-busting front, McGrath has talked well in public and has acted effectively in a cautious, crabwise fashion. But trust cases are notoriously long drawn out. It remains to be seen whether he follows

'Clark's shoddy record of yielding in consent-decree negotiations what he so thunderously demanded in public. The civil rights section is still starved for money and staff. After months of delay, McGrath finally brought in a new chief. But instead of hiring a liberal Southerner who would bring both tact and prestige to the office, McGrath got an old political friend from Rhode Island who is a competent lawyer but without experience in the civil rights field. McGrath's other appointments have usually gone to men who are knowledgeable bureaucrats but uninspired. The general administrative tone is flabby.

It is in the Criminal Division that the greatest sins of omission have occurred. McGrath has done absolutely nothing to break the grip of the nationwide gambling syndicates which infest every city of any size from coast to coast.

In fact, at the very time when newspaper stories were popping in many places, when Senator Estes Kefauver was demanding a bare-knuckled probe of vice lords and their rings, and when Charles Binaggio, the gambler-politico, was slain in Kansas City, two of McGrath's top men in the Criminal Division were preparing a report attempting to prove that interlocking crime directorates were a myth and that it was all a matter for local authorities to handle.

Such a claim is ridiculous and outrageous. It goes counter to an incontestable mass of evidence accumulated by many sources, both private and official. It is true the federal government has no power to prosecute gamblers as such. Gambling is a local offense. But the government does have the power to send men to prison who violate the narcotics, white-slavery, immigration, and income-tax laws. And every big-time gambler, no matter how respectable his "fronts" and associations, has slimy tie-ups in these related fields. Many of the biggest crooks of the past, such as Al Capone, were sent to the penitentiary on less serious violations, like income-tax frauds.

Frank Costello, the most touted of the big-shot gamblers, is the known chieftain of a slot-machine syndicate which, according to the report of the California Crime Commission, takes in $2,000,000,000 a year and spends $400,000,000 bribing public officials throughout the country. Back in 1935, after the syndicate had been driven from New York by the late Fiorello La Guardia, Costello arranged to pay the Huey Long gang $100,000 to open up in Louisiana. The mob still operates there under the leadership of Costello's henchman, "Dandy Phil" Kastel. Not until 1946 did Reform Mayor "Chep" Morrison smash them in New Orleans, but they are still powerful elsewhere in the State. Miami Beach is another large city which has long been a haven for the big-time gamblers. But it is impossible to detail the operations of an empire which extends from Costello's swank apartment in New York to Kansas City to the Flamingo in Las Vegas to the Plantation Club in Fresno and to a hundred other "hot spots" in between.

What is significant is that, as Attorney General, McGrath has done nothing whatsoever to break crime syndicates. His only move was to hold a one-day conference of municipal and state officials on February 15, 1950, to discuss the problem. This was an utterly phony, meaningless gesture, and the meeting accomplished—zero.

Then, while the ambitious Kefauver probe was pending before the Senate Rules Committee, McGrath suddenly trotted out a bill to ban interstate shipment of slot machines and arranged for another committee to "investigate" and report out the specious measure.

When this diversionary maneuver failed to head off the full-scale crime probe, McGrath quietly backed an amendment to the pending tax bill which would have had the effect of blocking the Bureau of Internal Revenue from prosecuting any tax dodgers who offered to pay their defaults after learning the government was on their trail. The Bureau has long had discretionary power to waive criminal action, depending on the nature of the case. But it fought hard against being stripped of the power to enforce the tax laws. One immediate effect of the amendment would have been to deprive Senator Kefauver of a potent weapon in getting at powerful "tygoons" through their failure to pay taxes on all their illicit income.

The author of this extraordinary amendment was none other than Representative Aime Forand, Rhode Island Democrat and staunch member of the McGrath organization.

The reasons behind these devious and obstructionist tactics are not difficult to find.

No one would be surprised at McGrath's let's-sit-on-our-haunches-and-do-nothing policy who was familiar with his record in the matter of crime and law enforcement in his own home territory. No state in the Union is more "wide open" to every kind of gambling than the Attorney General's own State of Rhode Island.

Nor is it anything new. "Little Rhody" was wide open throughout the period when McGrath was U.S. Attorney for Rhode Island and governor. Not once did he attack underworld activities.

The police departments both of Providence and Woonsocket were, and still are, a reeking shambles of graft, protection, and pay-offs. Gamblers have been slain on the streets. Rookie cops who busted up gambling and slot-machine joints were themselves "busted." Never once did Howard McGrath lift a finger to interrupt these underworld operations.

Not only did he do nothing to check the mastery of the undesirable elements but he himself was personally friendly to many of their leaders. That fact leads to the complex and interesting question of how McGrath became a rich man.

The story begins in 1940. He was then U.S. Attorney, running for governor. It was fairly well known that he was worth in the neighborhood of $25,000. Nine years later, when he became attorney general after five years as governor, one as solicitor general, and three as senator, McGrath was a millionaire with a fortune of at least $4,000,-000. How had he accumulated these millions?

New Hampshire's Senator Charles Tobey supplied at least part of the answer.

Tobey in 1948 investigated the network of charitable trusts set up by Royal Little of the Textron Textile Company. The probe revealed that McGrath was a trustee of one foundation called the Rhode Island Charities Trust. This and other Textron "charity trusts" were exposed as tax-evasion devices by which Royal Little put aside large amounts of money ostensibly for charity, and therefore not subject to income tax, but actually for future business purposes. With the exception of McGrath, almost all the trustees were officers or directors of Textron or one of its subsidiaries, and they supplied the money from the foundation for Little to lease machinery and for other business purposes.

Over a period of several years, the Rhode Island Charities Trust took in over $4,500,000, and the only disbursement it made to charity was $85,000 to the Providence Community Chest.

When McGrath was asked why he and his two fellow trustees did not give away the rest of the money, he replied blandly that the funds "were being kept in reserve." McGrath, most observers are agreed, is kind of dumb in some ways, but he's been around too long to be that dumb.

Tobey's report, which politely did not mention McGrath by name, declared: "Over and over again the trustees have demonstrated that they have been at the beck and call of the president of Textron to make available the Trust funds for the benefit of this company. These trusts have never paid a cent of income tax. Thus, by this system of using charitable trusts, Textron has gained an unfair competitive advantage over the orthodox textile manufacturers, and the burden of taxation has been thrown more heavily upon the shoulders of all other taxpayers."

But Howard McGrath didn't worry; he got his $15,000 salary regularly from the "charity."

McGrath did more for the foundation than lend his name. He personally intervened in the fall of 1947, when the Bureau of Internal Revenue warned the trust that its business activities did not entitle it to tax exemption. McGrath was then Democratic National Chairman, and the Bureau discreetly called off its tax dogs.

But, revealing as the Textron episode is of McGrath's acquiescence in a tax dodge, a $15,000 gratuity does not explain how he became a millionaire in nine years. McGrath's friendship for the horse-racing crowd does.

The only split that has marred the last eighteen years of Democratic control of Rhode Island came in 1937-38 as a result of a long and politics-riddled struggle for control of the huge Narragansett race track. The loser in the struggle, a now deceased textile-machinery manufacturer named Walter O'Hara, ran for governor in 1938 as an independent candidate on a "square deal" platform. He polled just enough Democratic votes to put the Republicans in. McGrath took over in 1940 and smoothed out the racing tangle.

He made many friends in the race-track crowd, and he has retained them.

As soon as the war was over, McGrath and his friends built another track, Lincoln Downs, of which he is a stockholder. Further, the State, by some strange coincidence. immediately constructed a beautiful superhighway that passed the new track. Also, State authorities granted the new track one hundred days of racing, which is considerable even by Florida standards.

When it is realized that one of the underworld's most profitable activities is supplying racing wire service to bookies who do off-track betting, it can be seen why McGrath in April, 1950, did not throw his hat into the air with joy when Federal Communications Commission Chairman Wayne Coy recommended that such wire services be banned even to legitimate newspapers.

McGrath is also heavily involved in various business enterprises such as the sale of automobiles, the wholesaling of fruit and produce, and the always politically sensitive insurance business. He owns openly, and as a silent partner, large tracts of real estate and an interest in the great Walsh-Kaiser shipyards in Providence.

Howard McGrath's known record of complaisance with regard to gambling and police corruption in his own State during his service as federal attorney and governor, his personal holdings in the Lincoln Downs race track, his public association with race-track elements, his quick acquisition of great wealth during a period spent wholly in public office, his open connivance in the Textron tax dodge, and his year-old record of indifference and obstructionism in gambling matters as Attorney General, brand him unmistakably as unfit to hold the post of highest law-enforcement officer in the land. His record, while always on the safe side of legality, has not been one to inspire confidence and respect.

He would serve his government best by returning to private life.

Jesse Donaldson is an extraordinary person to be head of the Post Office Department. Donaldson actually knows something about the Department.

He is the first Postmaster General since Benjamin Franklin against whom this charge can be made.

Not that there haven't been men of distinction in the job. There was John Wanamaker, the Philadelphia merchant prince, who, as Benjamin Harrison's Postmaster General, became famous for "firing a Democrat a minute." Theodore Roosevelt had George Cortelyou, who collected campaign funds with a ruthless efficiency which was

sometimes embarrassing. Harding appointed Will Hays, whose ex-
pansive political morals qualified him perfectly for his later job as
censor of Hollywood's morals. Hoover's Postmaster General was Walter Brown, the long-time political boss of Toledo, who had "an iron
stomach, a nimble conscience, and the silken manners and irreproachable appearance of an Episcopal rector."

Then, of course, there was the irrepressible Jim Farley, who loved
his job because the frequent "inspection" trips gave him plenty of
opportunity to do what Roosevelt called "a little proselyting." But in
each case, the distinction of these undeniably eminent gentry had
nothing to do with running the Post Office. That honorable institution
ran itself.

All this has changed. Jesse Donaldson knows what the score is on
every little detailed operation of his Department, because he has lived
and breathed its minutiae for forty-six years.

Donaldson's father was postmaster of the fourth-class post office at
Hanson, Illinois. Young Jesse went to the Shelbyville Normal School
and during summers helped his father. In May, 1908, when he was not
quite twenty-three, he decided to quit teaching and seek fame and
fortune elsewhere. He became a letter carrier.

Slowly he rose through the ranks of the civil service. In 1911, he
went to Oklahoma as a postal clerk and supervisor. Four years later, he
became "a gun-toting member" of the famed Postal Inspection Service. Operating out of Kansas City, Missouri, he spent the next eighteen
years traveling through the Midwest and the upper South checking
service and investigating postal frauds. In 1933, he came to Washington as a Deputy Assistant Postmaster General. Here he served in a
succession of administrative posts. When the late Bob Hannegan became Postmaster General in 1945, he selected Donaldson as his right-
hand man.

In the two years that followed, Donaldson, for all practical purposes,
ran the Department, since Hannegan was always preoccupied with
political chores and later was sidelined with a chronic heart ailment.
The smiling Irishman finally stepped down in the fall of 1947. Donaldson then became acting head of the Department.

One day, Truman called Donaldson on the phone and said, "Jesse,
how would you like to be Postmaster General?"

Donaldson, thinking the President was joking, played it straight and replied, "Mr. President, being appointed Postmaster General is the finest thing that could happen to a man." Truman wasn't joking. He said simply, "Well, you're it, then."

Donaldson has been a capable and conscientious Department chief. He has wrestled persistently with problems that are almost insoluble. The Post Office runs up an annual deficit of over half a billion dollars. But the basic decisions causing this deficit are beyond Donaldson's power to control.

Congress sets the rates for postal services and sets the salaries postal employees are to receive. The Civil Aeronautics Board determines the amount the Department must pay the airlines for carrying air mail. The Interstate Commerce Commission fixes the rate the Department must pay the railroads for hauling regular mail. Donaldson has the power—to stand in the middle and catch the bricks with his head.

There is nothing new in that. But the recent Hoover Commission report has spotlighted public attention on the Department and renewed the periodic cry for "more efficiency." The critics cry, "Why can't the Post Office be run like a private business?" The answer is twofold.

First, it has never been run that way. In the last year of President Hoover's own administration, the deficit was $205,000,000. That was approximately thirty-two per cent of the total Department revenue. The volume of mail has increased three and one-half times compared to ten years ago, but in 1949 the deficit was $550,000,000, which once again was approximately thirty-two per cent of total revenues. In only seventeen years of the past one hundred has the Department made money, and those were almost all boom war years.

Secondly, the Post Office cannot be run as a business because by its very nature it is a government subsidy. For example, the government is in the parcel-post business, to the tune of an $85,000,000 deficit, because the private express companies could not serve the isolated rural areas at a profit and therefore refused to serve them at all. Once in the business, it was impossible to limit the government delivery service to only the farm sections.

The Post Office also pays the airlines $50,000,000 a year to transport air mail, which is excessive, but Congress, despite repeated exposés in the 1930's and one short-lived attempt to fly the mail with Army planes, long ago surrendered to the aviation lobby on this question. Railroads get $225,000,000 a year and seek much higher compensation for mail transportation—this despite the fact that an investigation, which Donaldson ordered, revealed clearly that the railroads were using obsolete equipment, even more antiquated practices, and were grossly inefficient.

Further, second-class mailing privileges are extended to almost all magazines, including giants which, as Donaldson remarked, "contain fifteen minutes of reading material and seventy-five minutes of advertising material. I just haven't any patience with the Post Office Department subsidizing such a practice." But subsidize it does. Second-class mail costs $250,000,000 to deliver and brings in only $40,000,000 in revenue.

So it goes. Special-delivery letters that cost the sender fifteen cents cost the Department thirty cents to deliver. Only first-class mail pays for itself and sometimes makes a modest surplus.

In one sense, it is probably no worse for the taxpayer to subsidize mail service and magazines (and railroads and airlines) than it is to subsidize the growers of cotton and potatoes and tung nuts. But it is a key factor to keep in mind whenever the rhetoric spouts start gushing about the deficit in the Post Office.

What role does Donaldson play in the administration and in the Washington political scene?

Although his promotion to the top has undoubtedly been an inspiration to the rank and file of civil service employees, it should not be forgotten that Donaldson has always been in a quiet, discreet way a thoroughgoing organization Democrat. He is profoundly loyal and grateful to the President who gave him his great opportunity. Unlike some of Mr. Truman's 1948 cabinet, Donaldson worked mightily for his boss's re-election. Naturally, he knew every postmaster from Passamaquoddy to Santa Barbara, and he did his best to stimulate Democratic organizational work.

But, as a cabinet officer, Donaldson is a background figure. A stocky, thickset man of sixty-five, whose full, serious face looks younger than his age, he keeps clear of ideological conflicts and power grabs, sticks to his knitting, and keeps his mouth shut.

That such a quiet, able, self-effacing career man should become the occupant of what has traditionally been a politically hot, power-laden job is the outward mark of a silent revolution. It fits into a pattern with the President's recommendation that first-, second-, and third-class postmasters be taken out of the patronage system and put under civil service. Both these moves are unconscious recognition by Truman that, in this postwar era, social issues have far more to do with deciding elections than the old-style dispensing of patronage.

Great masses of people have become politically alert and have been organized into great pressure groups like the farm organizations and the labor unions. All the postmasters of Iowa laid end to end did not have one-tenth the political importance that Truman's own speeches on farm policy had there in 1948. No number of political appointees have the weight in Pennsylvania and West Virginia today that the United Mine Workers possess. Donaldson's work in 1948 was thus useful but of marginal importance.

An active politician may some day head the Post Office again, but that probable event does not gainsay the fact that the age of social politics is here. The shy, conscientious figure of Jesse Donaldson is a perfect symbol for the twilight age of patronage politics.

Harry Truman probably finds his Postmaster General restful. He is one cabinet member who is not constantly angling to ensconce himself in the White House.

The same cannot be said of bald, bustling Charles Brannan, the forty-seven-year-old head of the Agriculture Department. Brannan is completely loyal to the President, but if "the chief" decides not to run again in 1952, Brannan knows a very good man who is just itching to take over.

When Truman appointed Charley Brannan Secretary of Agriculture in June, 1948, the general opinion was that he was merely another of the likable, reasonably competent, and thoroughly undistinguished guys that Truman likes to have around and seems to have a positive genius for discovering. Brannan's work during the 1948 campaign began to modify that notion. His work since then has changed it completely.

Brannan has put on a powerhouse performance that has electrified

Washington. He is the most bitterly controversial man in the cabinet. Many Republicans and quite a few Democrats cannot pronounce his name without mussing up their hair and gnashing their teeth.

The atmosphere of the Agriculture Department now more closely resembles the purposeful tone and stimulating enthusiasm of government agencies during stirring and hectic New Deal days than does any other. Activity pulses, and a quickening undertone of intellectual excitement—which is sadly lacking in empty hulks like Labor and Commerce and the Treasury—runs through the whole organization. There is more afoot down in "Aggy" than just the mailing of seeds to Uncle Herbert.

That something is the struggle to put across the Fair Deal agricultural program commonly capsuled as the "Brannan Plan." The plan is not a personal invention of Brannan; it is a staff-created program in which he took an active but not an encompassing role. Yet, to understand the guiding philosophy of the Brannan Plan, it is necessary first to know Charley Brannan.

Such an understanding is easily gained, for he is essentially an uncomplicated man. He has his opportunistic side, but basically he is honest and straightforward.

Born in Denver, Colorado, in 1903 and educated at the Denver University Law School, Brannan has been a lawyer, not a farmer, all his life. As a young man, he was a liberal Democrat and thus came inevitably under the sway of Senator Edward Costigan, the grand old man of the Colorado Democratic Party. He imbibed Costigan's humane philosophy and worked closely with Oscar Chapman, the future Secretary of the Interior, in the local Young Democrats group.

When the New Deal came, Brannan did not rush to Washington. He stayed in Colorado. In 1935, he went into government service as regional attorney for the Resettlement Administration, with home offices in Denver. The Resettlement Administration was created by brain-truster Rexford Tugwell to lift marginal and submarginal farmers off their worn-out or arid land and help them build new lives on new land or in planned projects.

Resettlement was a particularly urgent and appealing problem in Colorado, for the whole western half of the State is a part of the historic cradle of the recurrent dust bowl. Thousands of dry-land farms were abandoned during the tragic mid-1930's. The plight and suffering of these desperate farmers and their families made a profound impression on Brannan. When he thinks of farmers, it is of men like them he thinks and their cause he champions. In 1941, Brannan became regional director of the larger Farm Security Administration which had absorbed the old Resettlement agency. His territory embraced Colorado, Wyoming, and Montana, but his home base was still Denver.

In 1944, Brannan was promoted to Assistant Secretary of Agriculture and moved into the Washington picture. Most of his work centered about world food problems and international agricultural conferences and negotiations. This job gave him an added dimension of experience and a new perspective that is important to understanding his work as Secretary. Four years after he came to Washington, and three months before his forty-fifth birthday, Brannan, in June, 1948, became Secretary of Agriculture.

He was one of the heroic handful who sincerely believed that the people were capable of re-electing Truman. Whether this proves he has the perspicacity of a brilliant politician or merely a useful capacity for self-intoxication is now an academic point. But, whatever his reasoning, Brannan strove mightily and potently for his patron.

In September of that year, he seized upon Harold Stassen's incredibly gauche attack on the farm price-support program, made after an Albany conference with Dewey, and immediately began shouting from the silo tops that the Republicans were out to cut the farmer's throat. Stassen's statement was actually somewhat ambiguous and never properly clarified, but Brannan was scarcely going to wait for the Republicans to figure out just what it was they did mean. He stridently stumped the Midwest and kept assuring the President that he could carry the region.

Naturally, the election returns zoomed him to an impeccable place of honor at the Truman council table.

After the inauguration was safely out of the way in early 1949, Brannan got to work. He held a series of intensive secret seminars with his staff to devise an alternative to the GOP Hope-Aiken Act which was scheduled to become effective in 1950. He gathered together a large number of Department people for a wide-open discussion every Monday evening from seven to nine o'clock.

These meetings discussed basic questions such as "What is parity?" (note to nonfarmers: parity, in nontechnical terms, is a government payment system designed to assure the farmer he will get the same share of the national income as he did in 1909-14, the last period before the artificial war boom and the long postwar slump); "Do we still need parity?"; "Should it be modernized?"

The subjects were kept secret for fear that if farmers knew that abandonment of parity was even discussed, they would be appalled. Brannan, nonetheless, wanted to start with fundamentals, in order that the new policy would be the result of a complete rethinking of basic issues—a process that had not taken place since 1933-34. After some two months of weekly conferences, and after the broad outlines of a program had been formulated, Brannan cut the number of people engaged to a small core of advisers, who then worked every evening far into the night to blueprint the details.

Out of this exhaustive, three-month cooperative effort emerged the Brannan Plan. Mr. Truman gave his assent, and Brannan presented the program to Congress.

A storm of controversy immediately broke over his head. The plan was assailed as a political concoction cleverly designed to snare the largest number of votes and to buy both farmers and consumers.

There is no doubt that the Brannan Plan has now acquired heavy political overtones and that the enthusiasm of Mr. Truman and some of his political associates stems largely from the pleasing possibility that it will consolidate Democratic control of the farm belt. But there is also no doubt that Brannan was a little surprised at the vehemence of the reaction and that the plan was not politically inspired but rather was immaculately conceived in an expert scientific womb.

The core of the Brannan Plan is his militant faith in the small family farmer and his equally militant distrust of the huge, corporation-owned "factories in the field." Brannan wants to take the family-sized farm out of the preamble and put it into the law.

To do this, Brannan begins by modernizing the parity concept.

He shifts the base for parity payments from the 1909-14 period to the ten years preceding the present. Parity is further redefined in terms of total farm income rather than by the price received for individual big crops like cotton and wheat. The price floor is extended under every major farm crop, including perishables like meat and milk. This is designed to increase the production of these basic items in the human diet, thus giving the consumer a break and achieving a balanced farm output. This would tend to discourage such ridiculous situations as in the Central Valley of California, where big farmers are shifting from the raising of fruits and vegetables, which the people need, to the growing of government-supported cotton because it's more profitable, even though government warehouses are already glutted with surplus cotton.

To establish a coherent relationship between the perishable and the nonperishable crops, Brannan proposes a system of units of farm production. One unit, for example, is ten bushels of corn. This unit would be equivalent to twenty-two pounds of butterfat, seventy-nine pounds of lamb, twenty-nine pounds of wool, thirty-two dozen eggs, seven boxes of oranges, and six bushels of rice. Brannan uses this unit system to take a whack at the big growers.

Government supports would be limited to eighteen hundred units of produce for each farm. Thus, if a farmer produced more than eighteen hundred units of all his produce combined, he would have to choose which items he would get support on. He could continue to raise and sell all the excess he wanted to. There would be no limit on that. But the government would not guarantee the price he would receive, as it does under the existing support program.

This eighteen-hundred-unit limitation would hit only two per cent of all U.S. farmers. But this two per cent is made up of the largest producers of wheat, cotton, cattle, and fruit, who grow about one-fourth of all farm output.

The present price-support law aids and encourages the growth of these agricultural giants (and would-be monopolists). The Brannan Plan is designed to curb their growth and create elbowroom for thousands of small farmers who are being driven to the wall.

It is this issue, densely concealed behind many swaths of shoddy arguments about "socialism" and "regimentation," which explains why the Farm Bureau Federation, spokesman of the big farmers and headed by Allan B. Kline, who hoped to be Dewey's Secretary of Agriculture, is against the plan. Also, why the National Farmers Union, champion of the small farmer and headed by James Patton, an old friend of Brannan's, is so militantly for the plan.

The feature of the Brannan Plan which has drawn the bitterest fire of its opponents and won the fervent backing of labor and consumer groups is the proposal to make direct payments to farmers producing such perishable commodities as milk and eggs. (Farmers raising non-perishable crops like cotton and wheat would still be paid under the complex system of government loans and purchase agreements, as at present.) But the perishable products would be sold on the open market at prices which would be allowed to find their natural levels. The difference between these prices and the parity quotient would be made up by the government to the farmer with a direct cash payment.

This is the much-wrangled-over "production payment."

It is called that because of the concept that the device would stimulate greater production of meats, milk, and other produce which must be consumed in larger quantities if the average diet is to be improved.

The advantages of this system to the consumer are obvious. He would be able to buy food at a reasonable price, while at the same time his cost in tax money would be no greater, since he is already paying a whopping tax bill to finance the present price-support system from which he gets no direct benefit at all.

For the government, there would be a clear advantage because lower prices would increase consumption and thus prevent the accumulation of huge surpluses in government warehouses. Brannan points out that if his plan had been in effect with regard to the 1949 potato crop, the cost to the government would have been only $25-$30,000,000 in cash payments to farmers, and the potatoes would have been eaten. Instead, it cost the government $100,000,000, and the potatoes, rotting in storehouses, had to be destroyed.

Critics of the plan say the idea of direct payments is a subsidy, a degrading handout. If that is so, then there are a powerful lot of degraded folks in the U.S.—many of them in the most respectable business circles. High among the list of these far-from-degraded recipients of huge government subsidies, or handouts, are the railroads, airlines, and shiplines. For many years they found nothing repugnant about taking hundreds of millions of dollars from the government.

And neither have farmers. The simple fact is that we have had a managed, government-financed farm economy since 1933, and, as the staunchly Republican *Des Moines Register* declared in an editorial, December 14, 1949: "Despite Republican criticism of Brannan, the general public and agriculture are well aware that the GOP stands for essentially the same thing. To the extent that there are differences, the Democrats have the 'advantage.' . . . These innovations (that Brannan suggests) will hardly sound 'bad' to people who are accustomed to price pegging. In short, once you accept price supports as the basic method of protecting farm income, the Brannan Plan is hard to resist. The Republicans have fallen into this trap."

The basic difference between the Brannan program and the scheme envisaged under the Hope-Aiken Act is that the Republican idea is based on the belief that the best way to reduce overproduction is to let prices fall. Brannan's plan is predicated on the incontrovertible historical fact that crashing prices always result in greater overproduction as the farmer tries desperately to maintain his total income.

In essence, the Brannan Plan is nothing new. It is based on thirty years of experimentation in farm policy. As Angus McDonald summed up in a luminous article in the *New Republic,* "Brannan's program is a masterpiece of timing. Everything in it has been used in some form in the past. Every authority he seeks is already given to him in present legislation."

Under the white heat of furious controversy that has beat down on his head in the past eighteen months, Charley Brannan has blossomed rather than shriveled. He has displayed firmness and audacity, exhibited marked abilities as a public controversialist, and built a wide circle of supporters and admirers throughout the country. Whether he can capitalize on these assets politically is very uncertain. There is no doubt that he has political ambitions. But they may be his downfall.

Brannan has been plying his oar in certain local situations that may cause him trouble—if for no other reason than that they are laying him open to a growing suspicion that he is opportunistic and willing to play the game of expedients. So far, friends have covered up for him and protected him from press blasts. But if he doesn't restrain himself, he is headed for jolts that will do his yearning ambitions no good.

Meanwhile, he continues to enjoy the President's personal confidence and occasionally sits in on evening poker games with Stuart Symington, Fred Vinson, and other members of the White House gang. Whether Brannan does that because this otherwise sober, hard-working, serious-minded man likes poker, likes Mr. Truman's company, or has other things in mind is difficult to say.

Whatever the reason, Brannan has to play a wary, cautious game. He has force and brilliance, but in present-day Washington these qualities are not always the surest passport to power.

In that regard, Secretary of the Treasury John Snyder is absolutely safe. No one has ever accused him of brilliance.

Snyder, who took office in June, 1946, is the ranking member of the Truman cabinet in point of seniority. During his first eighteen months, Snyder was personally the closest man in the cabinet to the President and the most influential in shaping government policy. The first is still true; the second is not. Snyder, who never had any weight or influence with anyone else, now has little with the President.

What has happened is that Truman finally realized what everyone else spotted immediately. Snyder is a size 5-B man trying to fill size 12-AAA shoes. No wonder his face has a pinched, unhappy look. The man has an aggravated case of intellectual bunions.

He was born in Jonesboro, Arkansas, in 1895. He went to Vanderbilt University for a year, served in the Field Artillery during World War I, and afterward became a bank clerk. He spent the decade of the 1920's as a teller and minor executive in various small banks in Arkansas and Missouri. In the 1930's, he was a bank receiver for the Comptroller of the Currency and for a time manager of the St. Louis office of the Reconstruction Finance Corporation. An old personal friend and National Guard buddy, Snyder zoomed like a comet when Truman became President. In April, 1945, he became Federal Loan administrator; in July, director of the Office of War Mobilization and Reconversion, and the following June, Secretary of the Treasury.

The dismal story of Snyder's sorry bungling in the first year of reconversion has been told many times. But his basic attitude during this period is important for an understanding of the man. His stock response to every problem was, "All right, let's get it over with." Regardless of whether a proposed solution was sound or unsound, his primary impulse was a psychologically frantic desire to put the difficulty behind him. All that seemed to matter to Snyder was getting shed of problems.

Since his expulsion as the President's one-man brain trust, Snyder has slowed down considerably. But his resounding mental limitations are unchanged.

He is still bewildered by complex problems. When aides attempt to explain them to him, he cuts them short with irritable impatience. He wants a clear-cut policy, preferably a simple one leading to a quick decision. His sabotaging of price controls and a program of orderly and gradual decontrol of the war economy was the product not only of an inherently conservative and naive "back-to-normalcy" viewpoint, but also of an almost involuntary recoil from anything so subtle and complex.

Snyder is really not the rock-ribbed, flint-hearted reactionary he is often pictured. He has neither the sublimated selfishness of a modern Hamiltonian nor the craftiness and shrewd insight into human nature possessed by many small-town bankers. He is merely ignorant, shallow, and incompetent.

He is personally a cold and repressed man who occasionally tries to loosen up with a hefty intake of bourbon or by telling a dirty story. But beyond that he is not a bad sort. He harbors no bitter grudges or twisted prejudices and is generally even-tempered.

It is true he has driven all the good men out of the Treasury Department, but that was not by calculated design. It is simply that it is no fun to work there under such a frigid, do-nothing boss. He is not interested in new ideas, rejects most suggested changes, and inspires nothing and no one. Nothing ever happens in the Department, so, inevitably, the best men depart.

Since early 1947, Snyder has sat tight while the Treasury has steadily run downhill. Both under the Roosevelt regime and the Republican administrations that preceded it, the Department was a key coordinating center of national economic policy. Morale under Ogden Mills was high, and Henry Morgenthau raised it to the highest peak in its history. Some of the keenest and most original minds of the New Deal worked there. Under Snyder, all this has changed.

The Treasury has slowly sunk into a sleepy, stodgy, routinized bureaucracy.

From the role of economic high command, it has dwindled to a hack financial clearinghouse and bookkeeper. Initiative on taxation has been lost to the congressional committees. High-level thinking on broad economy policy has been captured by the President's Council of Economic Advisers. Leadership in budgetary and related government policies has been yielded to the Budget Bureau.

The office charged with planning international financial policy, which had been raised to a high state of creative leadership during the war, has been placed in the hands of William McChesney Martin, the former "boy president" of the New York Stock Exchange. Between them, Martin and Snyder brilliantly bungled the only important operation that has taken place in this field during their tenure. This was the devaluation of the British pound. Many authorities believe they heavy-handedly forced a sharper and earlier devaluation than was necessary or wise.

In effect, Snyder, by his own sterility and ineptitude, has by 1950 shattered most of the prestige and influence traditional to the office of Secretary of the Treasury.

He is little more than the nominal superior of such self-operating agencies as the Bureau of Engraving and Printing, the Customs Bureau, and Mrs. Nellie Tayloe Ross's Bureau of the Mint. But even these career service outfits have been allowed to run downhill under Snyder's "blind-monkey" rule.

The great and tradition-rich Coast Guard is at a low state of morale and efficiency. In the summer of 1949, the Coast Guard failed to make two important rescues off the coast of New England. Officers sheepishly explained that the failures, which resulted in loss of life, were due to the fact that the station in the vicinity was inadequately manned, that disaster signals had not been heeded because the men were not sufficiently trained, and that, finally, the Guard did not have the right kind of ships to navigate the treacherous waters where the accidents occurred.

President Truman reportedly plans to transfer the Coast Guard to the Commerce Department, along with part of the Customs Bureau. While no agency can view with relish the prospect of falling into

Commerce Secretary Charles Sawyer's clammy clutches, the Coast Guard could scarcely do worse than it has under Snyder.

Even more serious and tragic than the Coast Guard situation is the woeful low to which the Bureau of Internal Revenue has fallen.

The Bureau still does its routine job of collecting taxes in adequate fashion. But it is in the income-tax-enforcement field that affairs have deteriorated. Many big underworld figures, crooked politicians, and wartime black marketeers cannot be caught in any other way than by their failure to report for tax purposes the full amount of their illicit gains. But the tax investigation unit of the Treasury has not been utilized to anywhere near its fullest extent in this regard.

Experts estimate that the government could collect around a billion dollars a year in added revenue if the tax laws were enforced more effectively.

Most of the responsibility for this sordid situation rests on Congress —particularly the Republican Eightieth Congress. It slashed a large number of tax examiners from the Treasury payroll. The alleged reason for this was "economy"—almost always a spurious and hypocritical cry. In this instance it was viciously fraudulent. The sole purpose was to protect big tax cheats and dodgers by deliberately sabotaging the government's enforcement machinery.

Further illustration of the falsity of the economy claim is the simple fact that the staff of tax examiners consistently recovers in unpaid taxes many times the cost of its salary. The Eighty-first Congress partially remedied this outrage, but the staff is still far short of what it was under Morgenthau.

All this is bad enough, but Snyder has also played a part that is no better. Under him, even after tax crimes have been uncovered, very little has been done about aggressively bringing these cases to trial. Many big cases of tax evasion have been delayed for years or dropped altogether, with no satisfactory public explanation.

Actual prosecution of tax frauds is the responsibility of the Justice Department, and under Tom Clark few prosecutions were recorded. The situation has not substantially improved under McGrath. Between Alphonse Snyder and Gaston McGrath, morale in the Treasury Intelligence Unit, until 1946 very high, has steadily slumped.

In the summer of 1949, one revenue agent in the New York office was indicted and four others were suspended for "shaking down" tax violators and yielding to pressure from Tammany politicians. In the old days, such a betrayal of confidence would have been unthinkable. But a spirit of moral laxity and indifference now prevails throughout the Internal Revenue service. When no one goes after the big crooks, why should not the little fellows also enjoy the buggy ride?

Snyder is not dishonest. He is merely listless and obtuse.

He clings to his job with a pathetic intensity because it is the best one he ever had. It pays him $22,500 a year, plus a government limousine and chauffeur. In private life, Snyder never earned over $7,000. He gets a good press from leaders of the business community because he serves their purposes, but they are under no illusion as to his real capacity.

Unlike some men in government, Snyder is not serving at any sacrifice—unless it be the public's.

Secretary of Labor Maurice Tobin is a man who likes to belong.

From boyhood, he has sought a hero to worship and a gang to cheer for.

In pursuit of these, he has progressed from the fraternity of corner newsboys to the city-wide Curley gang, and from there to the leadership of Massachusetts' liberal-labor alliance. Today he champions one of the biggest "gangs" in the country—organized labor. In Harry Truman he has a leader, if not a hero, and in the Fair Deal creed he has a full and comprehensive text to quote from. Is it any wonder that Maurice Tobin is a happy man?

Tobin at forty-nine is a tall (6′ 3″), handsome, elegantly dressed politician who manages to look as unrumpled and Beau Brummelish at five in the afternoon as he does at ten in the morning. His beautifully tailored clothes, smooth, full face, pale-blue eyes, wide mouth, long piano-player's fingers, velvety voice, and graceful carriage all convey the impression that he is an aristocrat sired by Harvard out of a Brooks Brothers catalogue.

But that is not the case. Tobin was born in the slums of Boston. His father and mother had immigrated from Ireland. (His father came from the village of Clougheenfishogue.) Tobin quit the High School of Commerce at the age of sixteen to go to work. He had a low-paid job with a leather firm, then caught on with the Telephone Company and slowly rose through the ranks of its managerial bureaucracy. When, after fifteen years' service, he resigned to run for mayor of Boston, he had reached the job of traffic manager.

During the same fifteen years, he had slowly risen up the political ladder as well. He had put in a two-year term in the State Legislature, six years on the Boston School Committee, and had been an unsuccessful candidate for Congress. After a youthful liaison with former Mayor and Governor James Curley, Tobin broke with the old maestro and defeated him twice running for mayor.

Tobin became mayor at the age of thirty-six, in 1937. After his election, Cecil B. de Mille offered him a movie contract, which he prudently turned down. Tobin was elected with heavy business and Republican support and was ostensibly a reform mayor. But he did no heavy crusading or swashbuckling house cleaning, partly because he was elected under business auspices and partly because he is not an innovator by temperament. However, in a modest way he built up a good record, reducing the city's debt, eliminating the more noisome varieties of fraud, and—by Boston's depressed standards—making a very decent mayor.

In 1944, Tobin was elected governor, thereby automatically becoming the most attractive and ornamental figure to grace that job long monopolized by sad-faced codfish Yankees and overstuffed Irishmen.

As governor, Tobin was a militant champion of labor and social-welfare legislation. He put through some useful bills along this line, including one increasing unemployment compensation to provide extra money for dependents.

But his principal work as governor was as a salesman. (Sales work had been his chosen vocation as a young man.)

He tried to sell Massachusetts to the United Nations as a permanent meeting place, but the Russians weren't buying any Boston Irishmen, thank you. He tried to sell New England business on the notion that it needed to "wake up and live," but New England business preferred to slumber and collect its rents on real estate in Kansas and Chicago. To the Legislature, he tried to sell the idea of civil rights and, after an initial failure, did succeed in putting across a State Fair Employment Practices law.

Tobin, on the whole, was an excellent governor. But the Republicans in 1946 asked, "Had enough?" and the voters, deciding they had not had enough meat, decided to butcher Tobin.

After two years of enforced retirement, Tobin was engaged in a fierce primary scrap when Harry Truman called him long-distance and said, "You can't say no. I've already made you my Secretary of Labor." Tobin held his finger to the wind for a week and decided to take the job. He has never regretted it.

Tobin's sympathies were genuinely strongly prolabor when he came to Washington. But his grasp and detailed knowledge of his Department were a trifle weak when he assumed command Friday, the thirteenth of August, 1948. During his swearing-in speech, he decided to ad-lib a tribute to his late predecessor. That gentleman happened to be the late Lewis Schwellenbach; but it was bustling White House Assistant John Steelman who had grabbed most of the labor headlines, so . . . "I hope that I shall be able to fill the shoes of my late distinguished predecessor, John R. Steelman."

Steelman, still very much alive, looked slightly flustered.

"Schwellenbach," hissed an aide.

"I mean," said Tobin, "Mr. Shellenback."

However, Tobin learns fast. He quickly boned up on the essentials of the Taft-Hartley law and made over one hundred and fifty speeches on the subject in the 1948 campaign. He is a fiery and persuasive campaign orator and also has a most ingratiating radio voice. His solid work in the political field has endeared him to President Truman, with whom he ranks very high.

As a cabinet member, Tobin is somewhat in the position of a man eager to take off, but who finds he has only half a horse. Tobin has scarcely half a department.

Fortunately, it is the pleasant end of the horse: the half with the flying mane, the prancing forelegs, and the loud whinny—not the butt end which carries the work load. The Labor Department has no control over the two biggest and most important agencies in its field, the National Labor Relations Board and the Mediation Service. All the big strikes are handled by the latter agency under able Cyrus Ching, and the day-to-day mechanics of collective bargaining are handled by the NLRB.

When Tobin took over the Department, its personnel had been slashed from a peak of over 7,000 to 3,300, and its annual appropriation had been cut from $32,000,000 to $14,000,000. Tobin had supervised Boston city departments which had bigger budgets than that. (By way of contrast, Charles Brannan administers a billion-dollar budget in the Agriculture Department.) Tobin has managed to revitalize some bureaus and to reacquire the Bureau of Employment Security from the huge Federal Security Agency. But as an administrator he is still little more than a caretaker for the Women's Bureau and the Bureau of Labor Statistics.

Tobin has tended quite naturally, however, to take on another job. Once again, it is a selling job. He is the Fair Deal's No. 1 salesman.

He takes to the road on the average of twice a week. He also speaks widely in his native Massachusetts when he visits his family on week ends. (Tobin is married and has three children, but he has kept them in school in Massachusetts and lives in a small bachelor's apartment in Washington.) Tobin sells the whole administration line, basing it, of course, on Taft-Hartley repeal and on higher old-age pensions and minimum wages. He is a dynamic salesman but in no way the booming Rotarian type. He does not slap backs or overdo the first-name routine. He is graceful, indefinably charming, and suave without being slick.

Tobin has not made much of an impact on Washington. This is partly due to the fact that he runs a truncated department. But there is a deeper reason.

He could grab much more power on labor and economic questions, especially from General Counsel Robert Denham of the NLRB and John Steelman of the White House staff, if he were willing to engage in the savage, behind-the-scenes in-fighting for bureaucratic power which pervades Washington. Tobin does not choose to fight.

He carries out the limited role that is legally his and lets it go at that. Yet he is by nature an ambitious man. The reason for his refusal to engage in jurisdictional combat is that he has his eyes focused on the Massachusetts senatorships which become vacant in 1952 and 1954. He will almost certainly seek one of them, although he steadfastly denies it. He hopes to move into what is every politician's dream house.

Therefore, why make a lot of enemies and hard feeling by struggling for power which will last only a few years? Of course, there is also the thrilling possibility of being the first Catholic President or Vice-President.

His chances are mighty slim. But Tobin is willing.

No office in the government is so much the reflection of the man who holds it as the post of Secretary of Commerce.

This is because the Commerce Department is scarcely a department at all, in any coherent administrative or policy-making sense. The chief function of the Secretary of Commerce, at least in the days before the Hoover Commission report, was to hold hands with the business community and soothe its fevered brow.

That is all very well in the abstract, but it is a little difficult to translate in terms of actual government functions and responsibilities. Businessmen are interested in almost every area of government—taxes, the budget, labor relations, defense procurement, antitrust enforcement, fair-trade regulations, natural resources, conservation, etc. But each of these important subjects is in the hands of an agency existing for that express purpose. In brief, the problem is what agencies can be given the Commerce Secretary so that he will have an official excuse for shaking hands with business leaders and making speeches on business conditions.

This problem has been solved over the years by assigning to the Commerce Department an assortment of miscellaneous bureaus and services. This bureaucratic mulligan stew now includes the Bureau of the Census, Weather Bureau, Coast and Geodetic Survey, Patent Office, Bureau of Standards, and the Civil Aeronautics Administration. Not one of these bureaus has anything to do with any of the others. Not one of them is a policy-making agency. They are functional "service" organizations which perform competently and smoothly regardless of who is Secretary of Commerce. In fact, the less he meddles in their affairs, the better they operate.

These bureaus have no common purpose and therefore no departmental *esprit*. About all the employees in the Department share with one another is the use of the elevators and the cafeteria. They are housed in a huge building known as the "house that Hoover built." As a specimen of his work, the structure proves conclusively that

Hoover was a mining and not a construction engineer. The floors are of some strange composition which makes walking risky and emits a peculiar dull echo. The building is not air-conditioned. And it has a particularly bleak and graceless interior which is like something out of a George Orwell nightmare.

Bossing the incongruous agglomeration in this drab-walled mausoleum is obviously anything that the Secretary of Commerce wants to make out of the job. Up to 1921, nobody did much of anything with it. Then Herbert Hoover came along and greatly expanded the minuscule Bureau of Foreign and Domestic Commerce. He turned it into a huge mill for the collection of business facts, the dispensing of propaganda both economic and personal, and the encouragement of trade associations to standardize products and smother competition. There is no doubt he made a good thing out of it: Hoover became President.

This coup has never ceased to dazzle his successors.

The office, for obvious reasons, languished during Hoover's own occupancy in the White House. Roosevelt's first appointee was the aged Daniel Roper, a nice old man who had supported the Democratic Party in bygone days and who now expected the Democratic Party to support him. The sinecure served as well as anything else and permitted Roosevelt to forget about both Dan Roper and the Department.

But in 1939, Roosevelt retired Roper to Canada as U.S. Minister and installed Harry Hopkins. This was part of a calculated drive to make the ex-WPA chief seem less radical and more palatable to business as a presidential candidate in 1940. Hopkins was even equipped with a council of business advisers headed by Averell Harriman and staffed with what were known as "Harry's tame millionaires." Hopkins' digestive maladies refused to cooperate in the scheme, however, and it had to be junked.

Next to appear was hard-bitten Jesse Jones of Texas. He was already boss of the multibillion-dollar Reconstruction Finance Corporation and very rightly considered that, while Commerce brought honor, RFC brought power. Of the two, Jesse loved power more.

Therefore, Congress obligingly passed a special law permitting Jones to hold both jobs simultaneously. This is what he did throughout the war—and he spent four days on RFC for every day and a half he spent on Commerce affairs. Jones, like Hopkins and Hoover, was receptive to the presidential nomination, but the Democrats were not in the market for pre-Grover Cleveland candidates.

In 1945, Jones had his throat slit by Henry Wallace, who was anxious to follow the Hoover example with a vengeance.

Wallace was running for President from the day he entered the Commerce Department. He took the job as part of a long-range plan to keep in the public eye as the foremost spokesman on New Deal domestic policy as well as on international economic affairs. Already solid with labor and well known to agriculture, he felt all he had to do was to ingratiate himself with American small business and he would be in for '48.

Wallace made a heroic effort to act as if he were administering a rational and coherent department. He talked bravely of an integrated business policy, encouragement of foreign trade, reorganization of the Patent Office, and so on. But long before he committed political hara-kiri over the Russian issue, Wallace had given up on this face-lifting operation. As a political vehicle, the Commerce secretaryship is no jet plane. It is pretty hard to woo businessmen unless one is selling a probusiness program, and Wallace's efforts met the total failure that was implicit in Hopkins' abortive attempt.

It is unlikely that any liberal in the near future will try to go to the White House by being a Democratic Hoover.

From 1946 to 1948, handsome, rich Averell Harriman was Secretary of Commerce. A former investment banker and railroad executive, he had ready entree to the best business circles, but it did not matter much because, like his predecessors, Harriman had his mind on something else. In his case it was foreign affairs, to which he happily returned in 1948 as roving ambassador for ECA.

This produced Cincinnati's silver-haired gift, Charles Sawyer. He entered the cabinet in June, 1948. He was then sixty-one years old. He had spent the preceding forty years, since his graduation from Oberlin College, amassing a large fortune in corporate law and business and persistently burrowing into the outer foliage of political power.

Sawyer in the business world is known as a shrewd, mean, tight-fisted operator. Rather paradoxically, he got his first big boost by the romantic procedure of marrying a very rich woman.

He became attorney for the mighty Procter & Gamble soap interests and for other large enterprises. Both as lawyer and investor, he made a fortune out of the radio industry during its mushrooming infancy in the 1920's. He is a former vice-president of the Crosley Company and still owns radio stations in Dayton and Springfield, Ohio. He is also associated with Crosley as a minor stockholder in the Cincinnati baseball club of the National League.

But, for all his money and business success, Sawyer kept hankering to close his fingers around a healthy hunk of political power. Unfortunately, the very qualities that made him a success in the business world militate against his success in politics.

Sawyer is not the handshaking type. His eyes glitter like a brace of ice cubes. His smile is thin and perfunctory. It is a genuine effort for him to say "Hello," and an undertaking of positively herculean proportions for him to be genuinely cordial. Notwithstanding, he fancied himself a politician.

He had two initial assets. First, he has plenty of money. Second, he has the white hair, erect Boy Scout posture, well-brushed, neatly primped appearance, and vacant intellect that are almost always a sure-fire success in Ohio (as witness the successful careers of John Bricker, Harold Burton, and former Governors Tom Herbert, George White, and Martin Davey).

As a young man, Sawyer was elected to the Cincinnati City Council as a Democrat, and his four-year tenure encouraged him to try for mayor. But he was promptly slaughtered and decided to return to business. In 1930, he ventured forth once more as a candidate for Congress. Time had availed nothing. The results were again disastrous. But this time he persisted, and two years later was elected lieutenant governor. In 1934, he ran against Martin Davey for the nomination for governor. This could scarcely have been an inspiring choice for the voters to make, but, as between the two, the voters took Davey. Four years later, Sawyer junked Davey in the primary, but was himself defeated by Bricker. The electorate that year had the same clear choice as the buying public has between two obsolete mail-order catalogs.

As a reward for his futile diligence and modest campaign contributions, Roosevelt appointed Sawyer Ambassador to Belgium. Sawyer stayed for a year and a half and then packed his grips and came home. His impact on diplomacy had been imperceptible.

This was Sawyer's background when Truman in May, 1948, dug him out of moth balls and put him into the cabinet as Secretary of Commerce. Sawyer immediately left no doubts as to his ideological position. Arriving in Washington, he told his first news conference, "The less government control of inflation or anything else we have, the better. . . . There may be instances where controls are needed to preserve our economy, but I prefer not to go into them now."

The Capital snickered, business applauded, and Mr. Truman appeared somewhat startled. He wasn't quite sure what Sawyer meant, but he strongly suspected it made him look funny.

Sawyer's tenure in Washington has made no change in him. Nothing ever will.

What he is doing in a Fair Deal administration would be difficult to understand if one were not already accustomed to Mr. Truman's habit of saying one thing and doing another. Sawyer is even more reactionary than Snyder; but, since it is so natural to him, he does not bother to boast about it in private as Snyder does.

As Commerce Secretary, Sawyer has devoted himself largely to pressing for corporate tax reduction, for easing up on antitrust enforcement, and for curbing essential social services. He also has grave doubts about the Marshall Plan and expanded foreign trade. As a political factor, Sawyer is a total nonentity. During the 1948 campaign, the Ohio newspaper he owned carried editorials supporting Dewey. His financial contribution, at least the one the Democratic National Committee publicly acknowledged, was meager.

As a public speaker, he cannot be used without danger of bodily harm before any group except Republican-dominated business organizations. His speeches to these affairs are filled with all the standard Old Guard nostrums, and the only connection with the administration is the veiled implication that perhaps Truman is not the s.o.b. his hearers think he is.

Sawyer as an executive has brought none of that highly touted "business efficiency" to the Department.

For a while, his undersecretary was Cornelius Vanderbilt ("Sonny") Whitney, a polo-playing deadhead from the Jockey Club set. Both Whitney and Sawyer are millionaires, but their most characteristic achievement was to set some kind of cabinet record for joy riding at government expense.

Whitney used a Civil Aeronautics Administration C-47 to fly himself and friends to his Little Tupper Lake estate in the New York Adirondacks on week-end fishing trips. The plane would fly them up on Thursday afternoon and then return to Washington so that the crew could spend its week end at home. Then the plane would pick up Whitney on Sunday and fly him to New York City, where he spent the night. The crew, apparently allergic to any part of New York, would then return a second time to Washington, coming back the next day to carry Whitney back to Washington, where he presumably finally got down to work.

These junkets were all at government expense. No public business was transacted; it was purely pleasure tripping for which the taxpayers —who else?—paid the bill.

Whitney has now taken his administrative genius back to the Brook, River, Creek, and Racquet and Tennis clubs, where it still flourishes. But Sawyer continues his own equally flagrant practice of this fine art. He frequently flies home to spend his week ends in Cincinnati.

Again, as in Whitney's case, the pilots come back to Washington to spend their week ends at home, and return to Ohio to pick up Sawyer. In one period of a month, Sawyer made five such trips to Cincinnati. Counting the pilot's return time, this meant ten round trips. Each trip for the DC-3's which Sawyer uses takes five hours at a cost of $100 an hour. The ten round trips cost the government $5,000. It would have cost only $280 for Sawyer to have made these trips by commercial airliner.

Whitney took his expensive jaunts in a government plane because he wanted to show it off like a new-found toy. Sawyer's motivation is different. A grudging nickel-nurser if ever there was one, Sawyer just wanted to save the $280.

Not only has Sawyer been a dud as a public administrator, but he has also flopped even as a pulse taker and exhorter.

He took a much publicized trip around the country in 1949 to survey conditions. In the course of it, he visited New England, the worst hit area of the nation as far as deflation and creeping unemployment are concerned. He spent a couple of days there, nibbled his way through several luncheons, held a press conference, and said, "Things here are generally sound. I found a prevailing tone of optimism. I think local business leadership will be able to handle the region's problems in the usual way."

This burp reminded the thousands of unemployed New Englanders of nothing so much as a stale, putrid breath from out of the Hoover administration. It was this kind of dreary nonsense which did more than anything else to undermine the "confidence" it was supposed to promote in the tragic 1929-32 period.

After two solid years of this kind of diddling around, Sawyer was finally handed some honest-to-God work to do. The President, under his government reorganization authority, assigned the Maritime Commission to the Commerce Department. Since the Department had earlier been given authority over the Civil Aeronautics Administration, the acquisition of the merchant marine paved the way for centralized control of all government activities in the transportation field. The post of Undersecretary for Transportation was set up, and to this important office was appointed Major General Philip Fleming, a shopworn gentleman who long ago forsook the Army for civilian administering.

He has been a familiar figure for twenty years on the Capital cocktail circuit and bureaucratic escalator. Fleming learned all about aviation and the merchant marine as graduate manager of athletics at West Point and as a civil engineer for the Public Works Administration. But at least Fleming is a nice guy over a highball, so there will be one human being running the Commerce Department.

Sawyer fussed and fluttered over his new bureaucratic ducklings like a hen with a nine-day itch. Finally, he sent word to Truman that he did not want any more new bureaus right now. "The Department is not equipped to handle any further expansion at this time," he solemnly reported.

Just as Sawyer was getting his new functions under way, he resoundingly called attention to himself by pulling one of the most morally reprehensible deeds in the long memory of Washington.

All through the spring of 1950, Sawyer had been heckled by Republican Senator George Malone of Nevada on the question of the loyalty of a Commerce Department employee named Michael Lee.

Malone, a mentally muscle-bound stooge for the vicious Nationalist China lobby, tried to cut himself in on Joe McCarthy's publicity by claiming that Lee was a dangerous leftist who was not a Lee at all but a Russian who had changed his name and had used his job in the Department to hold up the shipments of aviation gasoline to Nationalist China. Upon investigation, it was proved that Lee was a Russian, all right—a White Russian, than whom there is none more fiercely anti-Soviet.

Lee was born in Manchuria and immigrated to this country—a sin in itself in the eyes of Malone, whose own family must have come here sometime, unless *he* is only masquerading as an Irishman and is really an Indian. Upon his arrival in this country, Lee dropped his original name. Further, the record showed that Lee, instead of holding back shipments to China, had actually pushed them.

Both Sawyer and his Undersecretary Thomas Blaisdell appeared at hearings of the Senate Interstate and Foreign Commerce Committee and testified to Lee's loyalty and efficiency. "He's one of the best men we've got," Blaisdell asserted.

But Malone kept yak-yaking away like a bush-league McCarthy, and finally Senator Edwin Johnson of Colorado, chairman of the committee, stepped into the picture. Johnson, a Republican who is only masquerading as a Democrat, is no man to let a stray headline go by without making a pass at it.

In late May, 1950, the Johnson Committee summoned Sawyer before it and threatened that if Lee was not dismissed immediately there would be a full-scale investigation of the Commerce Department. Sawyer, no man to stand for a principle when his personal convenience is involved, mulled this over for a couple of days. Then he abruptly capitulated.

He fired Lee—and with him another employee, William Remington, subsequently indicted—but at the same time issued a statement declaring the dismissal was "for the good of the department" and was "not meant to reflect in any way on the loyalty" of the person involved. This silly lie was so absurd as to cast doubt that any sane man could have written it.

Sawyer built a career and made a fortune in private life by pulling just such mean, cheap tricks where there was no one to expose him.

But it is another thing to apply his personal ethics as a responsible government officer.

Washington has seen some unattractive characters and some sleazy operations in its long history, but veteran newspapermen and experienced observers inside and outside the government were of the unanimous opinion that never had they witnessed a more cowardly betrayal of trust, or a more malodorous and degrading deal than that given to his subordinates by Charles Sawyer.

The Korean war-induced industrial mobilization program, in the summer of 1950, forced new responsibilities on Sawyer. Under the administration's emergency bill that was hurriedly rammed through Congress, Sawyer was assigned the task of allocating steel, aluminum, and other strategic materials.

Thus, momentarily at least, it seemed as if he were going to emerge as a major figure instead of being largely window dressing. In fact, the situation became so topsy-turvy that administration spokesmen vigorously dangled Sawyer's name before hostile congressional committees to win their support of the preparedness legislation. An instance of this occurred at a hearing of the House Banking Committee.

Democratic committeemen said virtually nothing; but the GOP more than made up for this silence. Illustrative of their attitude was the questioning by Representative Clarence Kilburn (N.Y.). "What I want to know," he demanded of National Security Resources Chairman Stuart Symington, "is who is going to be boss if we vote these economic controls?"

"The President is going to control the program," replied Symington.

"We're not going to have any Chester Bowleses or Wilson Wyatts, are we?" persisted Kilburn. "That's what Roosevelt did. He brought in Bowles and the rest of those fellows."

"I don't think there is anybody in the government in whom there is more confidence than Secretary of Commerce Sawyer," said Symington soothingly. "And I think the operating responsibility under this bill will be in a large degree under Secretary Sawyer."

Symington, of course, knew better and made this statement tongue in cheek. The plans did not contemplate putting "a large degree" of operating responsibility in Sawyer's hands. But the administration was willing to play him up in order to put through the bill. It was the first time in his undistinguished incumbency that he had served a real purpose.

Sawyer's relative emergence into the forefront, under the temporary industrial mobilization program, is wholly illusory. If and when full-scale mobilization comes, he will be quickly shunted aside. He has not the capacity, imagination, or popular appeal to be a truly outstanding administrator. Sawyer long ago proved that he neither inspires nor creates.

He gave a perfect demonstration of that in a little incident that occurred when he appeared before the Senate Banking Committee on the emergency bill. As Sawyer finished urging enactment of the measure, a young reporter walked up to him and said, "Mr. Secretary. how do you reconcile your being in favor of drafting American boys for military service and not drafting American industry? Frankly, that question means a lot to me. I expect to be called up any day for active duty to be shot at."

This was Sawyer's answer:

"I'll admit that going into the service means that a boy may be shot at. But you mustn't forget this: a businessman can be indicted."

It is a popular game in Washington to compare the Truman cabinet with its Roosevelt predecessor. It is an amusing pastime, but it can't be done. Cabinet officers differ too widely, not only in degree but in kind. There are no standard criteria because there are no traditional policies and no common point of view.

This is especially true of Secretaries of Commerce. All one can say about them is that they are different. Their only common trait is mediocrity. Commerce in the past has hit some pretty deep lows, but there is no doubt that in Charlie Sawyer it has reached the lowest of the low.

RUMBLOSSOMS* ON THE POTOMAC

WASHINGTON society is like lemon meringue pie without the filling: all fluff and a lot of crust.

Any connection between entertaining and fun is purely coincidental. The endless parties, shindigs, and various other gatherings are made up of four kinds of people: those who come to see, those who come to be seen, those who hope to be seen, and those whose job requires that they be seen. And, every once in a while, there are those odd persons who invite people they like. Washington society is thus a mixture of fourth estate, celebrity collector, social climber, and the weary dispenser of expense-account good cheer.

This incredible social merry-go-round has no parallel anywhere else in America, and probably not in the world. It exists in Washington because it is an artificial city. If it were not that the center of the federal government is here, there would be no Washington.

Except for the antique village of Georgetown, which was a small river port in colonial times, there was no settlement in Washington until Thomas Jefferson and Alexander Hamilton struck a bargain over a dinner table one night. Hamilton's acceptance of the unpromising site was part of the deal under which Jefferson agreed to the federal government's assuming the war debts of the states, a trade that proved tremendously profitable to Hamilton's wealthy friends.

Only politics could lure people to the Capital area. It would have been difficult for the Founding Fathers to have chosen a more un-

* A New England colloquialism applied to those who imbibe too freely and acquire red noses. Washington has long been famous for its cherry blossoms. But these can be seen only very briefly in the spring along the banks of the Potomac tidal basin. Washington's rumblossoms are far more numerous and long-lived. They can be seen in the best drawing rooms all the year round.

healthful and unattractive spot, even if they had tried. Raw and dank in the winter, Washington becomes positively inhuman in the summer. It gets hot and humid, then hotter and more humid, then hotter and hotter, and when everyone is certain he can't stand any more, the temperature and humidity rise. This slow broil is punctuated by intermittent days of gray clouds, feeble drizzle, and fetid dampness.

Yet Washington's population increases as inexorably as the national debt. The city has never suffered a loss in population and has nearly doubled in size since 1940. Until 1900, it was little more than a sleepy, unkempt, overgrown Southern river town. But two world wars and the New Deal have transformed it into a huge, sprawling, traffic-choked metropolis and the nerve center of the Western world. Political big shots, foreign kings and potentates, business tycoons and labor barons, the ambitious, the needy, the phony, and innumerable others flock to Washington from three continents. Over a million and a quarter ordinary folk crowd in to work for the government or to serve those who work for the government. This makes the real-estate men happy, but it does not create a genuine city.

Washington is like a giant Grand Central Terminal. People are constantly arriving or departing. There is ceaseless activity, people moving from here to there and from there to here. But despite all this hustle and bustle, all the unending motion and commotion, there is no genuine community spirit, morale, or social pattern. Everything is artificial, pretentious, and fleeting.

The city seems always to retain the graceless, vacant, strictly utilitarian, and almost featureless character of a huge waiting room, where all the seats are taken but everybody sits alone. Even the residential areas are rows of houses, not neighborhoods. Most people look upon them as they do depot rest rooms—places to change clothes and rest their feet. Even people who suddenly discover they have been in Washington twenty or thirty years are constantly talking about leaving and "going home." The reason for all this is the same core of reality that dominates life in a depot: the important thing is what flashes up on the train dispatcher's giant board. The arrivals and departures are important and not the stopover. The people in Washington share in the big events because they buy and sell the tickets, but the nature of these events is determined elsewhere.

For congressmen and their hordes of retainers, the election every two years is the big event. For those in the executive departments, it is the presidential contest every four years. For those in the State Department and the military services, what happens overseas at any time may be decisive. For all these people and their families, the everyday whirl in Washington is "life," but what happens in the hinterlands is the real "reality."

Washington is an extraordinarily middle-class, white-collar town. The myriads of government employees are that middle class. The very rich and the very poor are indirect influences, but they are not decisive. Topping the very rich are the so-called "cave dwellers." These are the aristocratic clump of old families of largely Southern ancestry. They have money with which to entertain, and they are truculently snobbish and inbred. As late as twenty-five years ago, the cave dwellers were dominant in setting the social tone for the upper crust. They gave the town certain airs of a second-rate Charleston. But in recent decades they have slipped irrevocably from the pinnacle. They now lurk in the shadows, and few look to them to set the pace.

Their place has been usurped by wealthy Northerners and Midwesterners who come to the Capital to do business, take a fling at working for the government, or to play the social whirl. They throw around more money than the cave dwellers ever had, and operate in a brassy, big-time way.

At the other end of the spectrum are the city's poor, most of them colored. There is a small Negro middle class, but the vast majority are economically depressed. They work in the service industries and provide a bottomless pool of restaurant and domestic labor and uncommonly polite taxi drivers.

In its race mores, Washington is a Southern city. Segregation is the prevailing pattern. Some Yankees from New Hampshire or the Dakotas who scarcely ever saw a colored person in their lives until they reached the Capital immediately sop up the worst prejudices and stereotypes. But the endless influx of Northerners and Westerners is slowly undermining the structure of segregation.

Back in the days when Warren Harding was President, Negroes went as a matter of course to the back of streetcars. This practice has now disappeared. The legitimate theater was long barred to Negroes, and, in 1948, the sole remaining one closed its doors rather than yield to liberal pressure. Recently, however, the Gayety Burlesque Theater (where President Harding used to watch the girlies from a special box which concealed him from the public) has been converted into a regular theater and admits Negroes. More and more, the Capital's Southern air becomes a stupid affectation rather than a conviction.

Washington's peculiar social make-up, thickly infiltrated with outsiders who expect to leave, or like to think they will, robs the city of civic spirit. This is gravely accentuated by the lack of home rule. Washington is run by three District Commissioners appointed by the President (usually, it would seem, in a fit of absent-mindedness or obscene jesting) and answerable only to God. These three gentlemen are considerably circumscribed by various agencies of the federal government on the one side and by the House and Senate District of Columbia Committees on the other.

These two Committees constitute a City Council, more or less (mostly less). With monotonous regularity, they are headed by men from small-town and rural constituencies. In the Eighty-first Congress, the chairman of the Senate Committee was Matthew Neely of Fairmont, West Virginia; and of the House Committee, John McMillan of Florence, South Carolina. These Committees are postgraduate courses in buck-passing. Even the simplest matters become snarled in their toils. The District of Columbia, for example, still does not have a permanent statute for daylight saving. Every year, Congress has to take time out from national and world affairs to pass a special law on the subject. In 1950, the Senate finally consented to a permanent law, but the House would go no further than a one-year extension. In the ensuing melee, Washington had to continue on standard time for a week until the two chambers composed their differences.

A far more tragic abuse is housing. For fifty years, there has been local clamor and clatter about cleaning up the loathsome slums virtually within the shadow of the Capitol dome. But nothing has ever been done about them. In 1950, the District Commissioners finally wangled the promise of a $2,500,000 allocation from federal housing authorities under the administration's slum-clearance program. It was a pathetically puny start, as twenty-five times that amount would be needed to make a fair beginning.

Only one man has ever been able to pep up Washington's community spirit. He is Bucky Harris. When his Washington Senators baseball team won the American League pennants in 1924 and 1925, the town for once in its listless life went wild.

But Washington is more than listless. It is insecure. Throughout the whole District of Columbia, and from the bleak bungalows of Maryland's Silver Spring, which has become that State's second largest city, to the manufactured colonial quaintness of Falls Church, Virginia, Washington is just one big settlement of camp followers—divided, restless, and uneasy. Rumors run like wildfire. Gossip is incessant. Factions, cliques, coteries spring up, flourish, fall, form, and re-form. Personal feuds and vendettas go on interminably. Men rise or hope to rise, but all is dependent on the turn of the cards at the next election. Even when a party has been in power a long time, a key official may plummet from favor and take his personal "empire" of secretaries, assistants, protégés, and hangers-on crashing down with him.

It is against this background of ceaseless insecurity and fierce competitiveness that the giddy social whirl goes on. For those at or near the top, it has some of the element of the "drink and be merry for tomorrow we die" spirit. Also, since there is no clear social structure, no traditional hierarchy or established social pace setters, each officeholder—or, more important, each officeholder's wife—feels she must put up a big front to prove she and the old man are really right up among them.

"Front" requires only two things—gall and money.

This makes it easy for the ambitious social climber to imitate the real thing and eventually get accepted as part of the real thing. Rich old women with rings on their fingers, time on their hands, and greenbacks in their bank account, lead the chase. Mrs. J. Borden Harriman, a witty and charming octogenarian, frankly calls herself and her rivals "fifty overage destroyers."

The political big shots in Washington's passing parade are usually easy game for the celebrity collectors and the social climbers. They come from out of town, have no roots, no friends, no social ties in the Capital. They begin by accepting dinner bids and cocktail invitations to fill lonely hours and "make contacts"; they frequently wind up by falling for the tinsel and din of the merry-go-round, and ride as hard and as fast as they can.

There is nothing so difficult to dislodge from the scene as a defeated or resigned officeholder who has become an addict of the social whirligig. Washington has enough lame ducks to man practically the entire governmental system. There are ex-officeholders dating back to the William Howard Taft administration. At practically every party the ancients turn up, like specters from another world, stacked three deep at the bar and beneath every potted palm.

Mrs. Woodrow Wilson, looking her usual more-than-generous self, and Mrs. A. Mitchell Palmer, widow of Wilson's Attorney General and famous for her huge chapeaux, still hit the social trail with deadly regularity. Joseph C. Grew, the ageless and ever debonair diplomat, who was Undersecretary of State under Coolidge, is a familiar diner-out, as are eighty-year-old Homer Cummings, who was Franklin Roosevelt's first Attorney General, and dapper Francis Biddle, who was his last. Alice Roosevelt Longworth, the "Princess Alice Blue Gown" of forty-five long, long years ago, continues to crack the whip over her cocktail-table coterie.

In Washington it is an old saying and a true one: "Thousands come and few leave."

What some lame ducks do to keep themselves within elbow-bending distance of the Capital almost surpasses belief. Many become lobbyists. Others sell real estate and insurance. Frances Perkins, Roosevelt's Labor Secretary, syndicated a weekly column to union papers until appointed to the Civil Service Commission. Strangest livelihood of all was that of an aged ex-congressman from the Far West. When he was defeated, he was utterly unable to face the prospect of going back home. He remained in Washington and for many years could be seen daily in his old haunts on Capitol Hill—as a tourist guide. At thirty-five cents a head, he showed them through Statuary Hall, filled with effigies of the great, near-great, and mostly not-so-great.

But the strain is pretty tough on the lame ducks. And the effort is rarely worth it, unless they can hop back within the golden circle of public office. Because, in Washington, it is the job and not the man who gets invited.

Even worse, it is the job and not the personality of the guest which determines his seat at the dinner table. This means that two people may be paired off together who have nothing in common except, perhaps, a mutual dislike. But, boring or not, a guest may be consigned to the same conversational partner at dinner for several or more seasons before death or some other prime cause intervenes to set the official game of musical chairs in motion.

The iron law of precedence operates at its very worst at the White House.

The President and the First Lady traditionally give five formal receptions and five formal dinners each winter. The dinners are for the diplomatic corps; the cabinet; the Chief Justice and the Supreme Court; for the Vice-President; and for the Speaker of the House. During recent years, the Trumans have cut down on this kind of entertaining; first, because of the food-conservation program, and later because they have been living at far smaller Blair House while the Executive Mansion is being renovated. Everyone who is invited attends a White House dinner because such a bid is in the nature of a command. But only fifty to sixty per cent show up for the receptions. The latter are undoubtedly about the most boring, pointless, and frivolous time killers ever devised by the mind of man.

A "reception" consists of a long wait in a reception line to get a chance to shake hands with and nod to the presidential couple, a sip of watery, unspiked punch, and, for those young enough and patient enough, a brief dance in the jam-packed east ballroom. These are white-tie-and-tails affairs for the thousand or fifteen hundred guests who attend. But if the average guest finds this all pretty boring, and God only knows why he wouldn't, for the President and his wife it is sheer, unadulterated torture. Herbert Hoover once had to retreat from the receiving line with a bruised and bleeding hand. Mr. Truman fares better. As a country boy from the farm, he finds the handshaking motion roughly the same as pulling on the udder of a cow. He rests for a minute out of every thirty, but otherwise he pumps his way through an evening with brisk, mechanical efficiency.

Official precedence is so terrifically important at these affairs that it not only dictates who is to sit next to whom, but it also determines what part of the White House a guest may enter. The cabinet and the Supreme Court can use the front door. The lesser political lights come in the south rear door. The great unwashed herd enters by the east wing. Once inside, the same folderol holds true. The cabinet always marches downstairs with the President to the ballroom. The middle-bracket officials then enter to shake hands. The rest just swarm in after that in helter-skelter fashion.

Taking their cue from the White House, private hostesses are haunted by problems of official precedence.

In the old days, there was always a great to-do about whether the Chief Justice and the dean of the diplomatic corps should be invited to the same party, since the two offices are a dead-heat tie on the official precedence list. Formerly, this really wasn't much of a problem, because Chief Justices like Charles Evans Hughes and Harlan Stone rarely dined out. But it would be today, with Fred Vinson holding down the top judicial post. The ebullient Kentuckian clatters around to more shindigs than the hospitality chairman of a lodge of Moose.

Harry Truman cut the Gordian knot, however, by handing down a special edict to the effect that his pal Fred was to get the nod over any imported celebrity.

The present dean of the diplomatic corps, Ambassador Wilhelm de Morgenstierne of Norway, is an amiable old gentleman who drips more medals than a first lieutenant in the Air Force. The Ambassador doesn't seem to mind yielding priority; after all, he could scarcely expect to compete on equal terms with anyone who can sing "My Old Kentucky Home" as movingly as Fred does.

Another precedence problem that set the dinner tables buzzing in 1949 concerned the proper rating to be given Mrs. Max Truitt when she was official hostess for her father, Vice-President Alben Barkley. At first, on the say-so of Mrs. Carolyn Hagner Shaw, veteran arbiter of the social list, Mrs. Truitt was put up with Mrs. Truman as second lady of the land. But then the pundits of protocol at the State Department oracled that she should be shoved twenty notches down the ladder, somewhere between the wives of chargés d'affaires and of the undersecretaries of executive departments. Barkley refused to contest the point, although he was the "Veep."

Twenty years ago, another Vice-President took a less tolerant attitude. Charles Curtis, the bachelor V-P of the Hoover administration, insisted long and loudly that his sister, Dolly Gann, be seated ahead of Alice Roosevelt Longworth, then wife of the Speaker of the House. Nicholas Longworth first stuck up valiantly for his wife, and then resolved the issue by dying. This effectively demoted Alice to the status of widowhood.

Alben Barkley found a happier way out. He married the charming Mrs. Hadley from St. Louis and thus got a dinner partner whose claims to social preferment are undeniable. The Veep is no longer troubled with that problem, and his nickname no longer means "very estimable and eligible prospect."

Unification of the armed forces has broken a lot of hearts among Navy men, but at least on the social front it has been pure gain. In the old days, when an Army and a Navy officer of equal rank went into dinner, the former always got the better seat because the Army was founded earlier than the Navy. Now the length of service of the individual officer determines the issue. This grave problem used to cause great concern to the gentlemen of the Navy.

Those who do the entertaining in Washington fall into certain broad categories. There are the big-timers who make a career of it; the embassies who make a business of it; the proud parents of panting debutante daughters who make a virtue of necessity; and the "young set" who pretend they hate the stuffy affairs but who actually are only in training for more strenuous efforts later.

There are some fifty hostesses in Washington who entertain frequently in what is invariably called "the grand manner." The most prominent of these are:

Mrs. J. Borden Harriman—the grand old lady who set the pattern— as Democratic fund raiser in the 1920's and later as Minister to Norway—that Madame Minister Mesta is trying to follow. Mrs. Harriman, at eighty-two, recently bought a new house in Georgetown because her old dining room was too small to permit her to entertain more than forty guests at a time.

Mrs. Perle Mesta—who is now so busy holding open house for GI's and steel barons in Luxemburg that she keeps only one eye on her old stamping grounds and on her former foremost guest, Harry Truman.

Mrs. Gwendolyn Cafritz—who scheduled her biggest party the day after Mrs. Mesta, her archrival, was sworn in as Minister to faraway Luxemburg.

Mrs. Joseph E. Davies—the former Marjorie Post of the Post Toasties millions, who finally realized her ambition to be the chatelaine of an embassy when she married the Wisconsin lawyer, Joe (*Mission to Moscow*) Davies. Mr. Davies' daughter by his first marriage is the wife of Senator Millard Tydings of Maryland. Mrs. Davies enjoys all the conspicuous success that such awesome amounts of money and political connections can bring.

Mrs. Alice Roosevelt Longworth—the political golden girl of two generations ago, the No. 1 whipcracker of the last, and now a somewhat jaded but still acidulous observer of the passing scene. She prefers to do her entertaining behind silken curtains, but occasionally some of her remarks filter through, such as "Tom Dewey is like the man on the wedding cake."

Mrs. Robert Low Bacon—widow of a very rich Long Island Republican congressman, she hoped to become the queen of Washington society until "the man on the wedding cake" blew his chance and hers.

Mrs. Truxtun Beale—wealthy widow who lives in solitary splendor at historic Decatur House, diagonally opposite the White House. She is proud of two things: her dinners are always served exclusively by candlelight, and, unlike some of her competitors, she never phones her list of guests to the society editors.

Mrs. Lawrence Wood Robert, Jr.—the inimitable Evie who is the daughter of a staunch Republican dowager, Mrs. Harold Walker, and the wife of the irrepressible "Chip," who was once secretary of the Democratic National Committee and is now partner in one of the country's largest contracting firms. Evie was playing up her Republican ancestry in the fall of 1948, but Chip saved the day by sitting up the night of the election with Democratic Chairman J. Howard McGrath. The Roberts are wealthy, daring, and ambitious, but Evie's more effusive friends mourn the fact that she won't stay put long enough to nail down the honors as ranking hostess. She is always off to Palm Beach or Nassau just when congressmen get thirstiest.

When Gwendolyn Cafritz and her husband, a local realty magnate, moved into their big estate at Foxhall, overlooking the Potomac, Mrs. Cafritz called up Mrs. Mesta, who was then living in that swanky suburb. Gwen had met Perle but had never entertained her. So she called her up and very sweetly observed that, now that she had a home in Foxhall, "I suppose we'll be seeing you soon."

To which Mrs. Mesta replied very tersely, "I don't think so."

This anecdote illustrates the difference between the two women. Mrs. Cafritz has the suave, Continental touch and a talent for manipulating even her thorniest opponents, while Mrs. Mesta is the old-fashioned Oklahoma Indian-fighter type who achieves her ends by brute force and gouges the other gal's eye out if necessary.

Gwendolyn Cafritz is the leading claimant for the title of Washington's foremost hostess.

She laughingly denies having any such ambitions. "Heavens," she exclaimed when asked, "why, I'd much rather be on the board of the Smithsonian Institution." But her deeds contradict her, and, after all, as one society writer pointed out, for her to confess such a goal would be "as unrestrained as a debutante advertising for proposals!"

Mrs. Cafritz was born forty-five or more years ago in Budapest, Hungary, the daughter of a wealthy physician named Dr. Laszlo Detre de Surany. As a youngster, Gwen Detre hit the culture circuit pretty hard. She studied and traveled in Budapest, Rome, Paris, Los Angeles, and back to Budapest again before she was twenty. She studied art, learned five languages, and acquired a useful air of cosmopolitan sophistication. She speaks English with a broad "a" and a slight foreign accent.

In the late 1920's, she accompanied her father to Washington when he went there to work for the United States Public Health Service. The somewhat impoverished young European with the large dark eyes, gay smile, and ingratiating manner won the attention of Morris Cafritz, a moderately-well-to-do real-estate salesman on the make. They were married in 1929 and now have four sons. In the last twenty years, Cafritz has built a lot of houses and profited hugely from Washington's bloated size and stringent housing shortage. Now a baldish, sharp-nosed, nondescript man of late middle age, whose most noteworthy contribution in 1950 was to act as a glad-handing prop for the rapacious real-estate lobby, Cafritz has plenty of money to subsidize Gwendolyn's desire to buy her way to the top of the social ladder. They own a magnificent ultramodern house surrounded by gardens and landscaped grounds and equipped with all the necessities for big-time partying, including the inevitable swimming pool.

The Cafritz drawing room is muraled with ancient Egyptian queens. Gwendolyn is undoubtedly eager to play a somewhat queenly role herself. But, like Cleopatra, she occasionally guesses wrong as to the outcome of political battles in this modern imperial Rome.

In the fall of 1948, Gwen figured the Republicans were sure to win, and she was anxious to prevent such old-time elephant followers as Mrs. Robert Low Bacon from getting the jump on her during the Dewey administration. Consequently, the Cafritzes made a fat contribution to the GOP and practically snubbed the penniless Democrats. Gwendolyn also captured every stray Republican within hailing distance and dragged him off to dinner.

But then came the election, and the Cafritzes were out in the cold. Gwendolyn's archrival Mrs. Perle Mesta had not only contributed to the Truman cause but had helped raise money from others. She was in more solidly than ever before. Madame Cafritz spent the whole ensuing winter ruing her bad luck and trying desperately to cuddle up to the Democrats. Finally, when Mrs. Mesta collected a diplomatic appointment as her campaign reward and departed for the pleasant wilds of Luxemburg, Gwen got into high gear again.

The very next day after Madame Minister was sworn in at the State Department and given her credentials, the Cafritzes roared into action. They threw a lavish steak party for one hundred and fifty of Washington's top-flight figures. The affair was ostensibly to celebrate their twentieth wedding anniversary; actually, it was the opening gun in a carefully calculated comeback campaign.

During the 1949-50 season, Gwen made good her ambitious bid. She entertained fiercely and purposefully almost every day in the week. By the end of the year, she seemed to have clinched ownership of the party-giver crown. Toward the end of the spring season, however, Perle Mesta returned from Europe, supposedly to report to the State Department. But her visit stretched on and on for weeks. In the mind of the Capital socialites, she had come back to keep an eye on her rival and maintain a foot in the door.

This soft-shoe jostling for position created difficulties for all the others trying to give parties during this period. It would be most indelicate for both to appear at the same dinner table, or even to run into each other at the same cocktail buffet. Yet, if one were invited and the other were not, the slighted party would unquestionably retaliate. What to do! Hostesses struggled along as best they could. Finally the blowup came.

At a huge semiofficial function in late May, both ladies were invited. They both arrived purposely late—and almost simultaneously. The President and Mrs. Truman were at the head of an informal receiving line. Each contender wished to greet them first. The two ladies edged forward furtively, attempting to maintain dignity and cover ground at the same time.

Mrs. Cafritz, perhaps because she is the younger of the two, beat Mrs. Mesta to the President's side by the margin of an ostrich plume.

She chatted amiably with him and his spouse while her rival cooled her heels at a respectable distance. Then she moved on with head high. Onlookers are convinced that they noticed just a hint of a proud, arch smile flit across Mrs. Cafritz's handsome Grecian features as she turned away.

Gwendolyn Cafritz really has one up on Mrs. Mesta in the race for Washington society's mythical bauble. She is a tall, slender (118 pounds), graceful brunette with dazzling dark hair and eyes. She goes in strongly for low-cut gowns and plunging necklines, and she has something worth plunging to.

Of Mrs. Mesta, it cannot be said that she is beautiful. She does look younger than her age. She could pass for fifty, though she is actually pushing seventy. She is a diminutive five feet tall, has bright blue eyes, wrinkle-ringed and darkly shadowed, and weighs, like her taller rival, about 118 pounds. Her hair is brown without a trace of gray, her jawline is firm, and she smiles readily with lips that are razor-thin and almost nonexistent. As one cat put it, "She *is* remarkably well preserved—considering her age."

Perle Mesta is no fashion plate and makes no bones about it. She fits exactly the crack once made by a writer in *The New Yorker:* "We in New York love to laugh at the dowdiness of women in the provinces. Take Washington, a town notorious for its frumpiness."

But Mrs. Mesta takes the attitude that she is so rich she doesn't have to show it off with diamonds and Parisian gowns like *some* women. "I get a laugh," she says, "when they call me the 'worst-dressed woman in Washington.' I detest fancy clothes. And neither do I need fancy cars." Up to her departure for Luxemburg, Mrs. Mesta continued to use a 1941 Packard.

If Perle Mesta is not fashionable, neither is she witty. She tosses off no bons mots, presides over no political salon. She does have definite ideas on subjects like women's rights, but she couches them in prosaic terms. Her parties are big, loud, long, and expensive. Often she is able to prevail on her guests to perform some eye-catching (and ear-rending) feats. At one of her parties, she inveigled General Eisenhower to sing "Drink to Me Only with Thine Eyes." And, of course, she can get such old hams as former Ambassador Pat Hurley to give his Comanche war whoop and Chief Justice Fred Vinson to sing "My Old Kentucky Home" at the drop of a hat. A unique feat was her persuading Mrs. Cornelius Vanderbilt to whistle a duet with a writer.

Champagne and Scotch always flow freely at Mesta parties, but she herself is a teetotaler and confines her drinking to soft drinks. Her abstinence—she is also a nonsmoker—stems from religious views. Mrs. Mesta is a devout Christian Scientist and contributes heavily in time and money to church activities.

A Mesta menu may not match the unique delicacies of such culinary show places as the French Embassy, but it is pretty flossy just the same. The following is one of them:

Crisp, chilled celery, and olives nearly as large as golf balls.

Salad of mangoes, avocados, midget plums, and blood-red pitted cherries drenched with a tangy lemon sauce.

Thick French white soup, brewed from choice fowl, milk-enriched veal, ham, carrots, parsley, cream, eggs, butter, onions, salt, thyme, and peppercorns.

Suckling pigs, from three to six weeks old, roasted to a succulent turn, gleaming mamey apples in their mouths, cranberries stuck in their eye sockets, their browned carcasses

glazed and adorned tastefully with patterns of pimiento
and green peppers, sprays of water cress, a dressing of
bread, celery, nuts, and sage—all in a pool of sauce made
of vintage wine.

Pheasant or quail basted with smooth Madeira wine and
stuffed to delight the keenest gourmet.

Vegetables prepared in candylike Oriental and European style.

Royal diplomatic pudding, candied cherries and angelica,
wine jelly, and rich, thick cream of fruit.

Perle Mesta has many of the same qualities as the President whose
rise to power gave her her opportunity. Like Harry Truman, she is
vigorous, lively, blunt, and basically plain and ordinary. Entertaining
the low-brow Trumans gave her "the big chance."

She became friendly with them when Truman was a senator. When
he became Vice-President, she took him up in a big way. In the spring
of 1945, she threw a party in his honor that was one of the most glittery in Washington's long history of glittery parties. It had all the
charm of an English court tea, the sparkle of a Viennese ball, and the
razzle-dazzle of a Hollywood premiere. The best names in officialdom
and society attended. Shirt fronts gleamed with star-ruby studs. Evening gowns fairly dripped with diamonds and pearls. Champagne, at
$20 a bottle, flowed in cascades. Kingly delicacies were endless.

Exactly two weeks later, Roosevelt was dead and Mrs. Mesta's guest
of honor was President of the United States. Overnight, society editors
acclaimed her "queen of Washington society."

At long last, she had attained the swooshy throne she had sought so
long. It had been a long, arduous, and expensive pull from the time
she first arrived in Washington in the early 1920's. She had come from
Oklahoma, where her father was oil-rich and where her bachelor
brother is still a well-known figure. She also had the wealth she inherited from her husband, a Pittsburgh tool manufacturer. She came as
a Republican, which was advantageous in that Republican era. In 1931,
a good friend of hers, Vice-President Charles Curtis, the bachelor
brother of the famous Dolly Gann, saw to it that she was presented to
the King and Queen of England when she visited London.

Throughout the New Deal, Mrs. Mesta still remained a Republican, but she steadily broadened her social ties to include many top Democrats, particularly of the "regular" ilk. It was not until the war, when the GOP refused to go along with Wendell Willkie, that she jumped the fence and became a Democrat. Her enemies have ever since derisively called her "Two-Party Perle." Mrs. Mesta is unperturbed. But, while a loyal Democrat, she does not slight her old Republican friends. When she was entertaining in Washington, her favorite "extra man" was House Republican Floor Leader Joe Martin, who for a while showed up at her parties so regularly that he acquired the nickname "Marryin' Joe." The sad-visaged Yankee has remained, however, a wary object of prey.

Naturally, Mrs. Mesta's favorite guest remained Harry Truman. He usually accepted her invitations, and, when he came, he often played the piano. "Mr. Truman," Perle says, "is an excellent musician —for a man who is too busy to practice."

Mrs. Mesta never lacks for willing guests. One year, she opened her home to the public for the benefit of charity. She also served tea to the visitors. As she sat at the serving table, a businesslike man came up to her and remarked briskly, "You give parties and must need extra men. I'm unattached and very agreeable. Here's my name and address."

Turning to go, he added, "I hope you don't think me presumptuous!" Mrs. Mesta had a little difficulty concentrating on her tea for the next few minutes.

Mrs. Mesta had one lively experience in the conduct of international affairs before she became a diplomat. This was the celebrated "Battle of the Brassière."

The controversy arose out of a talk American-born Lady Astor gave before a women's club in Washington, during which she indulged in her favorite indoor pastime of deriding American women. On this occasion, her freewheeling Ladyship complained that American women spend too much time "worrying about uplift."

Mrs. Mesta was present. Her strong sentiments regarding women's rights were outraged, and, springing to her feet, she coldly admonished the speaker as follows, "I'm tired of hearing Lady Astor constantly criticize American women. It is true our women are interested in uplift, but it is uplift of their minds and culture, and not their bosoms."

With that, Mrs. Mesta gathered up her cloak and stalked out.

It was inevitable, of course, that Lady Astor would reply. In fact, the genteel, Virginia-born ex-belle sought out the reporters to make sure that they got her reply.

"Mrs. Mesta," she declared haughtily, "is just a social climber who is using me to get some publicity. I have proof she didn't really walk out. She stayed for every word."

That did it! Then the battle really was on.

Mrs. Mesta insisted that she had really walked out and that her position had been correctly stated in the press.

"Position?" snorted Lady Astor. "Why, she has no position."

To which Mrs. Mesta slammed right back, "Lady Astor's tactics are not surprising. She has made a career of achieving a certain dubious international notoriety by such methods. Lady Astor no longer likes or understands the habits or thoughts of the country from which she expatriated herself a half century ago. I seriously question whether the people of the land of her adoption have ever reciprocated her misplaced devotion. I also question very much if she has ever really understood the American people. It was because of my doubts on these matters that I followed the American privilege of taking a walk."

The delighted reporters dashed back and forth between the two contestants with exuberant enthusiasm and appreciation. It was a tumultuous fracas, and everyone enjoyed it, especially the two ladies.

A local wit once wisecracked that there are three parties in Washington: Democratic, Republican, and Cocktail.

The cocktail party is not just a private affair in Washington. It has been worked up to such an extent that it is a combination of public institution, work of art, and symbolic ritual. The average prominent or semiprominent Washingtonian can, and frequently does, attend an average of three of these a day during the winter season. A cocktail party has no limits as to size. It may range from a half-dozen friends dropping in before dinner to a huge brawl for a thousand guests at a downtown hotel.

Occasionally, cocktail parties still coyly masquerade as "teas." There is nothing so disheartening as to go to a tea and find it *is* a tea. Fortunately, this doesn't happen very often. Sometimes tea is also served, but, whether it is or not, liquor is generally the chief article of refreshment.

During the 1920's, the more law-abiding residents of the Capital used to drink tea in public (saving their bootleg stuff for very select affairs). Recently, the Mayflower Hotel tried to revive tea drinking in the late afternoon. This valiant effort to sober Washington up a little was aptly described as "roughly equivalent to enlisting Jack the Ripper in Gang Busters." One foreign diplomat, a very ginned-up Finn, remarked to a British friend who was with him at the Mayflower on the first day of this epochal experiment, "Very quaint, don't you think?"

"Quite, old man, quite," the Englishman replied, and, with that, they turned and tottered off to the nearby bar.

Every so often someone expostulates about the enormous waste of time and energy expended in going to cocktail parties. On one occasion, Senator Wayne Morse of Oregon went so far as to urge, "Congress should set an example. Simple living and fewer cocktail parties are in order." Erudite Senator Paul Douglas of Illinois echoed this plea, saying, "I would be willing to hold late afternoon and evening committee hearings to escape the people who think a senator's time should be taken up with cocktail parties."

While other senators take a less stern moral attitude, they are equally lacking in enthusiasm about these shindigs. One Midwesterner explained his position privately, "I'm like that old fellow who said 'Ah never troubles trouble, and trouble never troubles me.' I attend precisely the same number of cocktail parties in Washington as I do back home—which is none!" One senator's wife said, "We throw all our invitations in the wastebasket. Why go to them? Nobody has any fun. The average cocktail party is like wading through jelly beans." A third senator echoed her views, "They are a great institution for the free-drink-and-feed fans."

He hit the nail squarely on the head.

For many Washingtonians the cocktail party is THE main activity of the day. Especially popular in recent years is the combined cocktail party and reception running from five-thirty to seven-thirty, rather than the old hours of four to six. These affairs feature a long table running down the center of the room and loaded to the edges with large platters of shrimp, sliced turkey, ham, roast beef, pyramids of sandwiches, stuffed eggs, salads, relishes, nuts, cheeses, and desserts. This "free lunch" has several advantages. It eliminates the necessity for giving formal dinners, to which fewer people can be invited and which are usually expensive and stuffy affairs. At a cocktail party, many guests can be entertained, the food doesn't have to be so fancy, and it is over a lot sooner.

The practice gained great headway during the war. Hostesses discovered that officials working late at the various war agencies could not get away at four o'clock, and when they did quit they were too tired and hungry to be satisfied with a drink and an hors d'oeuvre. Hostesses found they just had to feed them. No free feed, no male guests.

Bigger parties of this type cost around $1,500. Hotel charges range from a flat rate of $4.50 per head to $6 and $7. The liquor is extra and may come to as much as $500 or as little as $175, depending on the quality of the beverages served and the kidney capacity of the guests. (Politicians, as a rule, seem to have excellent kidneys.) Caterers generally figure on three drinks per person. They get fifteen cocktails or twelve highballs to a fifth. Cocktail fashions seldom change. Dry Martinis and bourbon-and-water are the prime favorites, though since the war the Old Fashioned has enjoyed a mysterious spurt in popularity.

Washington laps up three times as much whisky per person as the nation as a whole does. Washington drinks three gallons per person per year.

Attendance at these parties is made up of three elements. First, there are the resident Washingtonians who go because they like a party and think their presence lends distinction to an affair. Although these cave dwellers consider themselves the "creamiest of the cream," actually they are as vapid and banal as the advertisements in a slick-paper magazine.

Congress makes up the second big group in attendance. Certain politicians are vigorous partygoers. Senator Joseph McCarthy of Wisconsin is one of these. He leers at the pretty girls, glad-hands the men, and slurps down Martinis as if they were beer. Senator Millard

Tydings has long been one of the town's most sought-after guests. He is really kept on the go, as both his wife and his mother-in-law are active social whipcrackers. Senator Theodore Green, octogenarian Rhode Island Democrat, is more active socially than many men half his age. But the two Capitol Hill champions are Vice-President Alben Barkley and Senate Secretary Leslie Biffle. During the winter season, they frequently make four cocktail parties and receptions a day.

Congressmen's wives also hit this routine pretty hard. Coming from drab small towns or farm areas, they are dazzled by the ostentation and the glitter. Others come from big cities where they did not cut much of a social figure. Now they suddenly find themselves important and sought after. River Falls was never like this!

The third element which makes up the cocktail party mob is the diplomatic set. There are some seventy chiefs of foreign missions in Washington. All of them keep up a frantic pace. As one of them explained, "We must go everywhere we're asked. After all, that is our business."

The top brass of the cabinet is surprisingly poor recruiting grounds. Secretary of State Dean Acheson rarely goes out, and he has cut his own official entertaining to the barest formal minimum. Defense Secretary Louis Johnson shuns parties. The same is true of Postmaster General Donaldson and Commerce Secretary Sawyer. Labor Secretary Maurice Tobin is practically unknown to the society pages. His wife and family reside in Massachusetts, where he returns each week end. In Washington he lives alone in a modest one-room "efficiency" apartment. The best cabinet bets for hostesses are Attorney General J. Howard McGrath and Interior Secretary Oscar Chapman, and even these are not very active. Agriculture Secretary Charles Brannan usually works late at his office. His mind is full of thoughts of cotton and soy beans, but his wife more than makes up for him by her preoccupation with the social onions.

A new and unconventional source of guests is the august Supreme Court. In the old days, Justices of the tribunal lived in almost monkish seclusion. Those days are gone. Only Justice Hugo Black approximates the old tradition. The rest are all more or less active, while Fred Vinson, Tom Clark, and Harold Burton give and go to more parties than a live-wire lobbyist on an unlimited expense account. No party of any pretensions is complete without them.

Also, no party of any size or pretensions is complete without another species, but a far less welcome one—the gatecrasher.

It is quite easy to crash most Washington parties, since hostesses seldom collect the invitations, though businesslike professionals like Mrs. Mesta do that. Also, a hostess rarely knows all her guests personally. Most gatecrashers do not even take that chance. It is a very simple thing to skip the drawing room, where the reception line holds forth, and go directly to the dining room, where the really important thing is—the buffet table. Gatecrashing is a major activity in the Capital. Many come simply to gape and ogle. Some come to mingle with the great and to feel more important. Others figure it's a wonderful way to save buying an evening meal.

It is a common experience for an embassy or an ambitious hostess to invite five hundred people (of whom it can be safely estimated that at least a third will not come), and have seven hundred show up. Some of the excess is made up of So-and-So's out-of-town guest who was dragged along for want of something better to do with her. But most of the "extras" are gatecrashers, complete strangers to their hostess.

One veteran society columnist gave this graphic description of a "professional" gatecrasher of her acquaintance:

"He is a presentable-looking man of about fifty who sells newspapers in front of one of the big hotels. He consults the hotel's bulletin board daily, and when he sees a notice of an interesting party—provided it does not require tuxedo or full dress—he just walks in. He makes for the bar, casually takes a Martini, and strikes up a conversation with the nearest admiral. He prefers to talk to admirals rather than generals because he's a Navy man himself—seaman, first class, in World War I.

"He says he doesn't get stopped at the door once in a year. Few parties given at the hotels require a ticket. This gatecrasher watches the door for a moment or so, and if tickets are being collected, he skips the party—doesn't want anyone to be embarrassed."

The embassies are great givers of cocktail parties and receptions. The acknowledged champions of "Embassy Row" in this regard are the French.

In the old days before the war, the French were always in the van. But during the war and the immediate postwar era, they were in eclipse. No French vintage wines were served, and the repasts were meager. Now, under the lead of Madame Bonnet, the wife of the Ambassador, the French are once again holding forth with true Gallic brilliance. Their luncheons, banquets, and other soirees are the most exquisite and sought-after in the Capital. They entertain between ten and twenty guests at some kind of function practically every day.

Madame Bonnet is admirably fitted for her role. A talented artist, hat designer, and linguist, she is popular, witty, and astutely diplomatic. Her shapely figure shows off the latest Paris fashions to the best advantage of the French dress industry. To assist her, she has a noted Paris chef. Henri's gustatorial creations are the sensation of Washington. Guests rhapsodize and the local society editors swoon over his culinary masterpieces. Two of his specialties are *potage au velouté de homard,* a thick lobster soup, and gelatin of duck with *foie gras.*

During the '30's, the Russians made a strong bid for social honors. Their receptions, complete with pea-sized caviar, champagne, and Metropolitan Opera stars, were long-remembered brawls. But, since the cold war, the Russians have been largely boycotted by Washington partygoers (a most extraordinary sacrifice, and an indication of the extent to which foreign policy has intruded into private affairs), and the Russians have largely withdrawn from the social arena.

One State Department man who ate at the embassy recently, in the course of business, reports that it was not an enjoyable experience.

"The soup," he says, "was cold, the filet mignon was burned, and all the guests were glum and wary. But the Russians were gay and full of vodka. No caviar, either."

Who knows? Perhaps they discovered the former chef was a "Fascist beast."

In one respect, however, the Russians still have it all over some of the other countries, especially the British. That is in the sartorial department. One society editor recently wrote:

"Some Hollywood pants presser could make a fortune as a consultant to the British diplomatic set. For a bunch that is trying to preserve the Empah and the right to dress for dinner in the jungle, they're sure a lot of sartorial sad sacks.

"It's not that the boys are doing their shopping at the Salvation Army; they still wear the best Bond Street stuff. But some of them look as if they just can't remember to take it off when they go to bed. As a result, you can usually spot 'em a mile away by their rumpled trousers and the pipes, tobacco pouches, old peace pacts, and stray chipmunks spilling out of their jacket pockets.

"It doesn't make sense, but the fashion parade is led right now by—of all people—the Russians. The creases in their pants are as sharp as an OGPU dagger, their jackets are always buttoned in exactly the right place, and their neckties make Adolph Menjou look like something out of the Bowery. With one of those long Russian cigarettes at just the right angle, you'd never take them for the nice, wholesome, postgraduate peasants they really are."

Cocktail parties are given for any and every occasion. One Washington lobbyist, working for government relief of the Navajo Indians, brought four of his clients to Washington and took them around the cocktail circuit. They were rigged out in native costume with moccasins and beads, and they wore their hair knotted at the back of the neck. Various party-going professionals, who adjourn to the nearest free bar the minute the clock passes four in the afternoon, were slightly startled by these strange intruders.

But the "braves" conducted themselves with great decorum and dignity and did not yield to the urge to let out with a war whoop or to drop ice cubes down the hostess's back, as some white guests have been known to do. In fact, the Indians did not do any guzzling at all.

The lobbyist for the Indians put all this under the heading of cultivating good will. In fact, it was not the first time Indians had shown up at swanky Capital functions. The most memorable event of Herbert Hoover's inaugural ball was the appearance of Vice-President Charlie Curtis, one-quarter Indian, with sister Dolly Gann on his arm, entering the vast hall followed by a band of Indians in full regalia.

Another party which was given for the same reason as that of the Indian lobbyist—public relations—was staged by Undersecretary of the Navy Dan Kimball, though in this case the guests were a trifle less bizarre.

It is the custom of the White House Correspondents Association to admit women reporters to all the business privileges of membership but to exclude them from the annual dinner for the President of the United States. This snub has always rankled with the lady reporters. In 1950, Kimball, a rich Californian, decided to assuage their feelings and get a load of free publicity for himself at the same time.

He invited all the women reporters to a dinner at the Carlton Hotel. He made it clear in his invitation that he was not taking sides in the dispute. A decision on that was "for wiser and more foolish heads than mine. All the cables, tackles, tugs, salvage vessels, and beach gear could not draw me into this controversy," he wrote. "My concern is these ladies, underprivileged to the extent of one dinner."

In gushing gratitude, the ladies reciprocated Mr. Kimball's gallantry by each presenting him with a necktie.

Two special types of party are the farewell and the debut.

Whenever an official resigns or an ambassador or military man is transferred to a new post, a contagious rash of "farewell parties" sweeps Washington. The ensuing wear and tear on the departing victim is so exhausting that, at the end, he figures it would have been better to stay, after all—or to have vanished without notice. The wife of one South African diplomat neatly ducked the whole whoop-de-do by sending a note to her friends telling them to skip the parties and instead to send a CARE package to Europe in her name. It worked. But it was not a precedent that was snapped up with enthusiasm.

The debut, or "coming-out party," is a special feature of the Washington social scene. These little events are staged annually for from forty to fifty late teen-agers during the four weeks from mid-December to early January. These affairs cost from $500, for a small tea party at home, to $5,000 for a big buffet and dance at a hotel or the swank Sulgrave and F Street clubs.

These soirees are as stereotyped as a White House reception. The hosts seldom know all their guests. Many of the latter are selected by a lady who stages coming-out parties as a business. Two and a half boys per girl is the prescribed ratio. The social secretary makes up her list from the brothers of the debs and from among their friends. An Ivy League background is highly desirable. The social secretary also guarantees her list of "stags" as "thoroughly nice" and completely wolf-free, within limits.

Debuts have become bigger and louder in the last few years. The decorous tea dance is virtually extinct. Blowouts in large ballrooms, complete with groaning buffet table, well-stocked bar, and a big, brassy orchestra are now the rage, much to the dismay of the cave dweller Old Guard.

The sole purpose of the fracases in Washington, as elsewhere, is to announce that "our little girl" is on the marriage block, boys—come an' git her. The debut usually pays off, sometimes more than the parents expect. Many a Washington debutante winds up taking several trips to the altar.

What is it like to attend a Washington party?

Going to one of these affairs is very much like coming home from work on the subway at the height of the rush hour. Everybody stands up because there aren't enough seats, and they wouldn't sit down even if there were. (If they sat, how would anyone see them?) Also, practically everyone jostles and shoves, sometimes not too discreetly, either, much as the old battle-axes trapped in the back of a bus struggle to get to the door. At a Washington party, however, there are added occupational hazards.

For example, there is always the danger that one's eye will be knocked out by an exaggerated feather or other hat ornament. Or that some lush will pour his drink down your back, although his whisky hand is usually about the only part of his anatomy he does have control of. Most of the jockeying, pushing, and general ebbing back and forth centers about the bar. People are ceaselessly trying to get close enough to it to grab a glass of champagne or get a refill of their highball.

Many would prefer to be businesslike about the whole matter and stay close to the bar all the time. But that is impossible. The traffic is too heavy. Usually it is a small portable bar, three or four feet long and manned by one frantically harried bartender. If three or four habitués attempt to monopolize the path to the staff of life, they are brutally shoved aside. So people are forced to stay at a safe distance; then, without realizing it, the pressure of the crowd pushes them farther off, and when they finally take a swig and find they have nothing left but a soggy lemon peel and the dank remnant of an ice cube bumping the end of their nose, they have to make a concerted effort to return to the bar. Thus, traffic is always moving in two ragged, elongated loops, one toward and one away from the beleaguered refreshment center.

Old-timers, of course, are careful to mask their movements by calling out heartily across the room to distant friends and waving cheerily in the face of total strangers a couple of yards farther on. These "hi, there's" and "hownicetoseeya's" don't really fool anyone. They are not meant to.

Any rational person knows he can't carry on a coherent conversation at a cocktail party or large reception. Making "contacts" is what this form of intercourse is euphemistically called, and most often it is just that—ducking waiters, bobbing, weaving, bumping elbows, a nod, a smile, a handshake, and sometimes a brief and heroic splatter of conversation before the other person disappears in the endless eddy and one's words are lost in the constant din and clatter.

The late Reverend Peter Marshall, Chaplain of the Senate, graphically visualized Washington society when he remarked in the course of one prayer, "Almighty Father, save these, Thy servants, the chosen of the people, from the tyranny of the nonessential, from the weary round of that which saps strength, frays nerves, shortens life, and adds nothing to their usefulness to Thee and to this nation."

The glittery and clever conversational bouts and bons mots which are, theoretically, supposed to characterize Capital society are more often merely mean digs and downright rudeness.

Mrs. Leslie Biffle, wife of the Senate Secretary, is supposed to be noted for her sparkling wit. A sample of it is the following colloquy between her and Mrs. J. K. Vardaman, wife of the Federal Reserve Board member. The two women met at a Mrs. Cafritz party for the Barkleys, and Mrs. Biffle inquired, "Why do you always wear gloves and never take them off during the whole evening?"

"B" Vardaman smiled noncommittally.

Glade Biffle continued sweetly, "I understand J. K. says you always wear them because you've got dishpan hands."

One of the most inane features of Washington parties is the general lack of familiarity among guests. It is true this tends to create an atmosphere of forced heartiness, as each person racks his brain to try to remember whether or not he has met the lady coming toward him with the expectant smile and, if so, what in hell is her name? The strain is very trying.

Mrs. Julius Krug, wife of the ex-Secretary of the Interior, finally lost her patience on one occasion. After a particularly gushy character remarked, "I certainly enjoyed meeting you, Mrs. Krug," the latter cracked back, "Yes, you certainly must. This is the third time you've done it this evening."

Quite often, guests never get a chance to say as much as "hello" to their host or hostess. They arrive, drink, eat, chat with acquaintances and strangers, and leave without ever talking to those who are paying for it all and who, presumably, had some desire to see them.

Mrs. O. Max Gardner, widow of the North Carolina Governor and an active Democratic worker, gave a reception before the 1950 $100-a-plate Jefferson-Jackson Day dinner. Near the end of it, a sad-faced drunk wandered over to another guest and complained mournfully, "As usual, I didn't get a chance to see the hostess."

"That's all right," was the reassuring reply, "for once it's not your fault—she didn't come herself."

Sure enough, the hostess was not there. Mrs. Gardner was too busy working on last-minute details of the big dinner to attend her own reception.

It was the ultimate commentary on the Washington party.

Some people, especially the younger set (which means "under forty-five"), try to jazz up their parties. One effort in that direction is the costume ball. But lately these have been so numerous that hosts are driven virtually to distraction trying to devise new angles.

Mrs. Guy Martin, the former Edith Gould of the ritzy New York family, decided to usher in the 1950 season by giving a party with her guests dressed as political problems. She ingeniously arrayed herself as Mr. Truman's onetime hotly controversial White House balcony. Henry Wallace's daughter, married to a local stockbroker, showed up as the devalued British pound. Others came costumed as the coal crisis (black satin dress, bituminous coal necklace), the Navajo Indian problem (feathers, etc.), and as the Trojan horse (horse's head, of course). But, as Elise Morrow, one of the few society columnists with a sense of humor, remarked, "No one attempted to impersonate the hydrogen bomb."

In addition to the costume ball, there is the Treasure Hunt, which can be made as fantastic as anyone wishes.

Mr. and Mrs. J. Van Cortlandt Wintoun, two active socialites, gave a Treasure Hunt in which twenty-four couples were expected to retrieve: (1) one of Mme. Chiang Kai-shek's chopsticks; (2) an old concert program featuring Margaret Truman; (3) a hair plucked from John L. Lewis's eyebrows; (4) Alben Barkley's left shoe; (5) a can of Leslie Biffle's special tomato juice; (6) one of Senator Tom Connally's white curls; (7) a discarded page of an original Arthur Krock column; and (8) Barnaby's fairy godfather. The prizes were to be a three-wheel automobile for the man and a complete retread job at Elizabeth Arden for the woman. The booby prize was a Dewey campaign button, autographed, and a snippet from his mustache (reputedly acquired after long negotiations with Dewey's barber).

Needless to add, no one turned up any of the "treasures," and the hosts kept the winning prizes. But there was great contention over the priceless snippet of Dewey's mustache. As became anything which had this devout political overtone, the host made a politician's promise: he would acquire a lock for everyone.

Another equally zany affair was staged by the Robert Guggenheims. This was billed as a "leap-year dance." At the dinner preceding the dance, the ladies received cards showing whom they should escort. After the meal, stogies were passed out to the gals. (Madame Bonnet, gallantly carrying Gallic diplomacy to the outermost frontier, endeavored to smoke hers.) The gentlemen, meanwhile, withdrew to the drawing room, leaving the women to talk and smoke over the demitasse. As the men waited, they could admire their corsages.

This is what is described in Washington society as "fun, fun, fun."

One society columnist reported a new game introduced into select circles by none other than Ambassador Lewis W. Douglas, father of the glamorous Sharman. Following is the account of this breathtaking innovation:

"Only equipment needed is a brace of healthy-sized oranges. The guests stand in two lines. Heads of each row tuck orange between chin and chest. The trick is to pass it from person to person, each using chin and chest only. The quickest fruit-passing line is the winner, of course. It's side-splitting to watch gents in stiff shirts, ladies in décolleté gowns concentrating with life-or-death seriousness on chin-and-chesting an orange! It is their postures, rather than actions, which are so startling. Thanks to Mr. Douglas, a number of warm acquaintanceships are due to burgeon this spring in Washington."

This is the game which Ambassador Douglas solemnly reports is "sweeping London like wildfire." Shades of the Marshall Plan!

But, despite the arduous and costly efforts of hosts and hostesses, the rewards of Washington party giving are hazardous and unpredictable. One wealthy lady entertained for a newly arrived South American diplomat and his wife. The couple's English seemed to be quite fluent. At the end of the party, the elegant guest of honor, clicking his heels and beaming, stood in the hallway saying his farewells. In clear, bell-like tones overheard by a dozen other guests, he told his hostess, "Good-by, and thank you so much. It was gruesome. Positively gruesome."

His diminutive wife, standing at his side, did a little curtsey and beamed her thanks. "And greasy," she added, "very, very greasy."

It probably was, too.

THE MONKEY HOUSE

SERVICE in the House of Representatives is one of the greatest frustrations in American life.

New members rush to Washington, panting and eager to get to work, to enact the Fair Deal or to murder it, to cut the budget, scare the hell out of the State Department, and generally put some pep into things. They arrive to find that nobody is the least bit interested in what they think or don't think, that all the important jobs have been gobbled up by party veterans who were here when Calvin Coolidge was a pup, and, after listening to the President's State of the Union message in January, they don't even have a chance to vote on anything for at least three months.

Hotshots at home on foreign policy or taxes, they do not get assigned to the Foreign Affairs or the Ways and Means Committee. They are pigeonholed on the District of Columbia Committee or on some other innocuous group. They turn to the House itself and find that when someone talks nobody listens, and that when a bill worth speaking about does come up, they can't get the floor because the time available is limited and has been parceled out by the bosses on each side.

Thus, frustration breeds cynicism and cynicism breeds irresponsibility.

The House of Representatives does not legislate. That implies debate, reflection, amendment, and free decision. The House does none of these things. It stampedes or it rebels.

Instead of being a deliberative body, it is a cross between a monkey house and a sheep run.

To become influential in the House requires service over a considerable period of time, at least half a dozen terms. In any session, a core of approximately seventy-five men from both parties who have been in the House twelve years or more completely dominates the scene. They possess the seniority and thus control the chairmanships. And that is practically everything in the House. It automatically endows them with a monopoly of prestige and influence.

From this inner circle comes the handful of bosses who crack the whip on the rank and file and who run the House.

On the Democratic side, this is the Rayburn-McCormack-Cox triumvirate. On the Republican side, Joseph Martin, Charles Halleck, and Clarence Brown are the headmen.

The other 350-odd members are largely a shifting crowd who come and go, serve one or a few terms, and depart. During their fleeting sojourn in office, they spend most of their time attending to errands for their constituents.

Congressmen introduce thousands of bills, but very few ever get out of committee. Chiefly, only bills which have administration blessing (and which usually have been written by experts in the executive agencies) reach the floor for action. But it costs nothing to introduce a bill, and it is always good publicity.

Some of these bills are really masterpieces of inspiration. One was brought to light by no less a personage than a Washington society columnist.

She reported in her chit-chat department in February, 1949, that Representative William T. Byrne, New York Democrat, had introduced a bill "to prohibit the transportation in interstate or foreign commerce of bulls with intent to use such bulls for bullfighting and for other purposes." Violators of the proposed law were to be punished by a fine of $1,000 or a jail sentence of six months. The possibilities this opened for commenting on congressional bulls and bull throwing were almost limitless, but the lady columnist restrained herself and took another tack.

"Where there's smoke," she wrote, "there must be fire. Could there be sneak bullfights in Mr. Byrne's district? As an old bullfight *aficionada,* we'd love to see one. *Ole!* Mr. Byrne! *Toro! Ole!*"

Debate in the House is almost indescribable.

It is a shambles of low humor, rank partisanship, incredible dema-

gogery, and wild misinformation spiced with miscellaneous and gro-
tesque irrelevancies.

The House is divided into four sections by a broad center aisle and
two smaller aisles; it is banked like a theater and slopes down to the
Speaker's rostrum in the pit or well of the chamber. Members, perhaps in order to circulate the blood in their posterior regions, periodically get up from the hard, uncomfortable, black-leather benches,
and rush down to the well, wave their arms, bellow some words into
the microphone, and then retire to the accompaniment of good-natured derogatory remarks from front-row colleagues.

Speeches frequently have utterly no relation to one another. A Republican rises to heckle the administration on the potato surplus. A
Southern Democrat thunders against communism. Another member
asks for unanimous consent to "revise and extend my remarks,"
which is a formal way of saying he wants to insert a lengthy—and
usually ghostwritten—harangue into the *Congressional Record* at a
cost to taxpayers of $72.50 a printed page.

Throughout all this, congressmen—there are rarely more than fifty
or seventy-five present—sprawl in their seats, read newspapers, pick
their teeth, and clean their fingernails amid a steady buzz of laughter-
punctuated conversation. Intermittently the buzz swells to a roar. A
frustrated orator asks plaintively, "Mr. Speaker, can we have order?"
The Speaker then taps his gavel listlessly and says in a matter-of-fact
tone, "The House will be in order."

It isn't, but he doesn't get upset about it. It's an old, old story.

Speeches in the House cover every conceivable subject, the juicier
the better. Often these subjects get representatives very excited or confused or something. The following is a one-minute speech, quoted in
full, by Charles Plumley, Vermont Republican and former president
of Norwich University. He spoke during the debate on the 1950 State
Department budget:

> "Mr. Chairman, I wish I had more time in which to get to-
> gether all of the things I think about to talk about a lot of
> things that have been discussed the last few days. Fortunately
> for myself, but probably unfortunately for those who have
> served under me or lived with me, for fourteen years while

I was president of a university. In that group we had homosexuals, but we did not advertise the fact. We did not make it known to the world at large that there were such extraverts and such people as would divert and so divorce themselves from natural laws as to indulge in these unnatural practices to which allusion has been made. I regret very much that it has become so common to discuss to attract the attention of those of high senses, not intellectuals, but of ordinary capacity, to the end that they are induced to know what all is going on among those who divert their attention to the base passions of human nature about which the less said the better. It all sets down to the impossibility of changing human nature, which is not a matter to be accomplished by legislation, if ever."

Representative Dewey Short, Missouri Republican, during the course of debate on the same State Department bill, got permission "to speak out of order." He then proceeded to discuss the Kansas City murder of gangster Charles Binaggio. Short implied that Binaggio had been slain because he differed with President Truman over the choice of a Democratic senatorial candidate.

"I do not know the State Senator from Rolla," thundered Short. "I never heard of him until Harry endorsed him. Mr. Allison, no doubt, is a fine man. But, you know, even thieves will fall out. Binaggio was in the way. So what happened? He was bumped off. . . ."

THE CHAIRMAN: The time of the gentleman from Missouri has expired.

MR. TABER: (Handling the appropriations bill for the Republican minority) Mr. Chairman, I yield the gentleman two additional minutes.

MR. SHORT: Mr. Chairman, I am not going to delve into washing dirty linen here, or run outside of my district just to hunt for trouble. But I have cited incontrovertible facts. I have so many more that I can give, and perhaps one of these days, if I am goaded to it, I shall get an hour's time to recite to you the chapter, verse, and page of one of the most dastardly, the dirtiest, the most corrupt, diabolical, ruthless political machines in the history of this country, that takes its toll from bawdyhouses and gambling dens, and will not stop short of murder. . . .

THE CHAIRMAN: The time of the gentleman from Missouri has expired.

MR. CANNON: (Missouri Democrat handling the bill for the majority and apparently enjoying Short's speech very much) I yield the gentleman thirty additional minutes.

MR. SHORT: Of course, I do not think I can last that long. Had I known it in advance, I would. No; the gentleman from Missouri is a keen student, astute, resourceful, diplomatic. I do not want to tie into him any more than with Jack Garner. Of course there are some important differences between Jack and Cannon. I could take thirty more minutes but I am not going to do it. You are hoping you will give me enough rope to hang myself. I think I have unraveled enough rope to hang many of you this coming November.

Not only are all important bills drafted outside the House and at someone else's instigation, not only are the debates incoherent shambles, but the average member has very little leeway when it comes to voting on legislation. His vote can be predicted on almost every major issue.

There is much talk about the need for a two-party system and for more party responsibility in Congress. Such talk is either superficial or uninformed. In the House there are two parties and plenty of party responsibility—after a fashion.

When the make-up of the House is viewed not as a division of Republicans and Democrats but as a solid Republican-Dixiecrat bloc on one side and a less stable coalition of Northern Democrats, marginal Republicans, and border-state Democrats on the other side, then the confusion about parties and party responsibility vanishes. These two "parties" have a coherent, consistent record. There is little deviation or crossing of "party" lines. Almost any big vote can be predicted.

On the question of repeal of the Taft-Hartley Act, for example, the GOP-Dixiecrat group delivered its total maximum strength and defeated repeal 217 to 203. The same was true on the Lucas amendment to the 1949 minimum-wage law which knocked out one million workers from the protection of the law. The GOP-Dixiecrat phalanx put the amendment across, 225 to 181. On the other hand, Speaker Sam Rayburn and Banking Committee chairman Brent Spence saved the public housing bill, the only major accomplishment of the Truman administration in 1949, by swinging every doubtful border-state vote. They won by the margin of 209 to 204.

In the Eighty-first Congress, the official party division was 261 Democrats and 169 Republicans, with the rest scattered or vacant. There were approximately 143 Democrats from the North and West, including nominal border states like Missouri and Oklahoma. Scarcely one of these 143 voted against the administration on a major policy issue in either session of the Eighty-first Congress. The one or two exceptions were so rare as to attract attention immediately.

Clinton McKinnon of San Diego, elected as a militant liberal, betrayed his pledge and voted with the real-estate lobby against the middle-income cooperative housing bill. So did Representative Abraham Ribicoff of Hartford, Connecticut. But they were striking examples which prove the general rule.

Of the 169 Republicans, all from the North and West, not more than 25 ever differ with Joe Martin and vote for an important administration bill. Thus the 144 Northern Republicans cancel out the 143 Northern Democrats. The balance of power is held by the remaining 115 Democrats from the South.

In this group are included the members from states such as North Carolina, Tennessee, and Kentucky who more frequently vote with the administration than against it on big domestic issues. These middle-of-the-roaders are joined by a handful of lonely liberals from the Deep South: men like James Trimble from Arkansas, Henderson Lanham of Georgia, Hale Boggs of New Orleans, Hugo Sims of

South Carolina, Lindley Beckworth and J. M. Combs of Texas, and Carl Elliott, Robert Jones, and Albert Rains of Alabama.

But this small contingent is decisively outweighed by the preponderantly conservative delegations from Texas, Mississippi, Georgia, Florida, and South Carolina. This cohesive bloc follows the lead of Georgia's Gene Cox and Virginia's Howard Smith. In common parlance, these are the Dixiecrats.

Cox and Smith can deliver 65 to 75 sure antiadministration votes. Together with the 145 "safe" Republicans, this gives the conservatives 210 to 220 votes, enough to control the House.

The basic realities of the political situation in the House were explored in an interesting exchange, on February 16, 1949, between Representative Ben Jensen (Rep, Ia.) and Representative John McCormack (Dem, Mass.) over an amendment offered by Jensen to cut the Interior Department's deficiency appropriation bill:

JENSEN: Mr. Chairman, before speaking on the amendment, I should like to say to the new members . . . and to remind them, especially members from the Southern States, that one of these fine days you will be voting with a number of us members on this side of the aisle when the States Rights bill comes before the House for consideration if it ever gets here. May I say that as one member of Congress I have been with you folks of the South right down the line on States Rights issues. Quite a few of us feel that your states should decide the kind of election laws you want without Government interference, as the Constitution provides. . . .

MC CORMACK: Mr. Chairman, I was very much surprised to hear the gentleman from Iowa [Jensen] make such an open and, if I might politely say, crude appeal to sectionalism that he made just a few minutes ago. I resent it as a member of this body. I resent making a direct appeal to members of this body from the South, and a subtle appeal on civil rights; an appeal to emotions, when he knows that when the vote comes on that question every member of his party will not vote the way the subtle appeal was just attempted to be made. . . . The appeal just made was so open, so apparent, that I could not remain in my seat and let it go by unanswered. . . . Throughout the years, on every matter that has come up, the party of my friend from Iowa has consistently in the great majority voted against progressive measures, no matter what part of the country they affected, particularly the Southland. . . .

JENSEN: Mr. Chairman, will the gentleman yield?

MC CORMACK: I yield, but the gentleman did make an appeal to sectionalism, did he not?

JENSEN: I wonder if the gentleman could tell us when we could expect to have the States Rights bill on the floor of the House?

MC CORMACK: The gentleman is a smart individual, he thinks. He made an appeal to sectionalism, did he not?

JENSEN: I am asking the gentleman a question.

MC CORMACK: The gentleman just a moment ago made an appeal to sectionalism in its crudest form, and that appeal is repugnant to the sensibilities of any decent person and any decent member. The gentleman has been one of the most backward-thinking members of the House.

JENSEN: Oh, is that so?

MC CORMACK: If the gentleman wants to cleanse himself and make an open confession, I will yield. An open confession is good for the soul.

JENSEN: I will make an open confession.

MC CORMACK: Then let the gentleman go ahead and, in his own time, make a free and complete confession, and try to become progressive minded.

JENSEN: Why does the gentleman not answer my question?

THE CHAIRMAN: The time of the gentleman from Massachusetts has expired. All time has expired.

This discussion, unlike most debates in the House, came to grips with the fundamental issue. Jensen's appeal was poorly timed, and, characteristic of him, crassly voiced. But it laid bare the basic strategy on which the GOP-Southern alliance operates.

In passing, it may be noted that Jensen is notorious for his moss-bound reactionary attitude on every issue. He poses as a great econo-mizer. This sometimes makes him leap before he looks.

On one occasion, the Interior Appropriations Subcommittee, of which he is a consistently obstructive member, was hearing some dis-sident Indians testify against the Bureau of Indian Affairs. They were heard in secret session, but the Indians were anxious that their views be published. So they smuggled into the hearing room a "paleface" re-porter disguised as a red man. The Indians really poured it on the government agencies.

"The Indian," they thundered, "wants no federal handouts. He wants only to be left alone."

This was right up Jensen's alley. "This is wonderful," he beamed, "wonderful." As the Indians prepared to leave, he shook each by the hand and thanked him for testifying. As Jensen came to the dis-guised reporter, he said, "Say, you didn't testify. Don't you want to say something?"

"No say," the reporter replied.

"Well, thanks anyway," said Jensen.

"Thank you," the "Indian" replied. "Heap good story."

Congressmen in the old days used to complain that they lost money in Washington. They could not make ends meet. This sad plaint is still heard occasionally. But nobody should be fooled. The boys are just howling for the sake of the record.

Nowadays it pays to be a congressman.

A representative receives a salary of $12,500. That is taxable. He also gets $2,500 for "expenses," which is tax-free. What these expenses can possibly be is a mystery. Almost every legitimate expense is provided for in other ways.

A member of the House gets $500 a year for telegrams and long-distance telephone calls, and $50 annually for air-mail stamps. In ad-dition, he draws twenty cents a mile from his home at the beginning of a session and the same amount to his home at the end of the session. For Westerners, this comes to $1,200 per session. Further, a complete office staff is paid for by the government to the tune of $16,300. This means at least four persons, since no member of the staff can receive more than $5,000.

Not counting railroad travel, which fluctuates with each member, a representative's salary, expense money, clerk hire, telegram, and stamp funds add up to $31,850 a year.

Members, of course, also get free office space and equipment not only in Washington but also in their home town in whatever federal building is available, usually the post office. The Botanical Gardens also furnish free ferns and plants. The government, for some worthy hygienic purpose now shrouded in antiquity, supplies free bottles of carbonated water. (Senators can store theirs in government-supplied refrigerators, but representatives have to rough it and buy their own iceboxes.) Senators also are one up on the House members because they get free shaves and haircuts.

When representatives are ill, they have their own physician with a clinic on Capitol Hill. He is Dr. George W. Calver, who is detached from the Navy but still draws a rear admiral's pay. Not only congressmen but also their families enjoy this free medical care. Dr. Calver's office handles eighty thousand patient-visits a year. This keeps him, an assistant doctor, nine nurses, and three Navy enlisted men busy full time. Twice a year, a congressman can go to a government hospital for a free laboratory checkup. If he is seriously sick, he can go to either the Army's Walter Reed Hospital or the Navy's Bethesda Hospital and get complete care, surgery, and doctors' and nurses' services, all for $9.75 a day, about one-fourth what hospital care would cost in a top-flight civilian institution.

Many a representative, restored to health and vigor at Walter Reed or Bethesda, returns to the House and celebrates his recovery by making a slashing attack on "socialized medicine." Nobody ever laughs.

The aged representative, who cannot get re-elected or who cannot stay awake when he is re-elected, has long been the object of tender solicitude in the House. The toils of the Heaven-protected working girl are as nothing compared to the tribulations of the overaged statesman! Former Representative Clifton Woodrum of Virginia, eager to avoid such a melancholy fate, retired some years ago to become the $35,000-a-year lobbyist for the fertilizer companies (politely known as the American Plant Food Council). Before he departed, he delivered a heartrending account of the broken-down servant of the people: "I have seen," he declaimed, "men come to this body in the heyday of hopeful youth, and stay under the blistering spotlight of public service until those once raven locks were frosted by the passing of many winters, until that agile step had slowed and that eagle eye had dimmed."

As an orator, Mr. Woodrum obviously did not need any fertilizer.

Responding to such appeals, the House finally adopted a pension system. It hastily killed the bill, however, when some cynical Westerners started a "Bundles for Congress" drive along the line of other wartime drives for stricken peoples. But once the uproar subsided, the bill was again trotted out and quickly passed.

It provides that any member who wishes can contribute $62.50 a month and retire when he gets to the age of sixty-two, if he has served three terms. A pensioner who has served only the minimum six years gets $1,875 a year for life. Those who have served longer get progressively higher sums up to three-quarters of their base pay.

Thus the House, which took six long years to pass a bill to increase Social-Security benefits for toilers, managed in swift and sympathetic fashion to take care of itself handsomely.

One of the pleasantest perquisites for representatives is the franking privilege. This lends itself to all sorts of devices and stratagems.

Related to this free postal privilege is the gift of free stationery. About $100,000 in free stationery is distributed to members of the House each year. If they need more, they can buy it at the House Stationery Room at a special discount. This Stationery Room, contrary to its guileless name, is actually like an Army PX. It stocks and sells at discount everything from Christmas cards and typewriters to elaborate desk sets.

Years ago, it was practically a wholesale store and sold almost everything imaginable. But a Southern representative made a spectacle of himself and created a minor scandal by buying women's hosiery and cases of perfume and other articles in large quantities. Whether he had a mistress or was in the retail trade was never made clear, but his actions caused a curtailment of the Stationery Room's extensive line of merchandise.

Representative Edwin Arthur Hall (Rep, N.Y.), under attack for abusing his franking privilege, ingeniously figured out that the average congressman sends out a ton and a half of free mail a year. He solemnly told his colleagues that he rarely exceeded this average. But the explanation was drowned out as they greeted his triumph of mathematical analysis with roars of laughter and hoots of derision.

Representative Ralph Gwinn, one of Hall's fellow Republicans from upstate New York, is guilty of the most flagrant abuse of the franking privilege. Gwinn is one of the most reactionary and crass politicians in Washington. He is generally referred to as "Merwin K. Hart's congressman."

In 1949, Gwinn had three of his own speeches printed and distributed. One was against rent control, one against public housing, and one against federal aid to education. Although Gwinn has only 280,-000 constituents, he had 900,000 copies of each speech printed. These were then folded, stuffed into envelopes, and mailed at government expense. The Post Office estimated it cost $27,000 to mail them. The government also paid for the $1,750 worth of envelopes and the $3,000 in labor costs to stuff the envelopes in the House Folding Room. The actual cost of printing the speeches was $10,000. They were stamped, of course, "Not Printed at Government Expense." The $10,000 came from the Apartment House Owners Association and Frank Gannett's Committee for Constitutional Government.

Thus, what Gwinn did, in effect, was to soak taxpayers almost $32,000 to finance a private lobby's publicity campaign.

Hearing of all these shenanigans, it is not surprising that during the 1949 Christmas season one taxpayer innocently sent a bushel of Christmas cards to Representative Les Arends (Rep, Ill.) with this note:

> "Dear Congressman—I understand you have free mailing privileges. I am sending you all my Christmas cards. Would you be good enough to drop them in the mail for me? Thank you."

One of the darkest blots on the record of Congress is nepotism—packing the public payroll with relatives.

During the Republican Eightieth Congress, members of the House had sixty-two close relatives on their office payrolls, including thirty-six wives. In the Democratic Eighty-first Congress, there were sixty, including thirty-four wives.

Aside from the favoritism, inefficiency, and bad morale which the practice fosters, it is also in reality a flagrant form of chiseling. Most of these family hangers-on never get within hailing distance of their jobs. Some don't even live in Washington. There are exceptions, such as Mrs. Libbie Heselton, wife of Representative John Heselton (Rep, Mass.). Mrs. Heselton has no children and has long worked faithfully and efficiently as her husband's secretary. But it is safe to say that two-thirds of the wives on the congressional payroll do no more than collect the salary.

When a reporter called one office to speak to a woman who was on the official list at $40 a week, the clerk answered, "Oh, she hasn't been to the office in months. She's having a baby."

The title of all-time champion payroll padder is held by Edwin Arthur Hall, Republican representative from Binghamton, New York.

Hall is a politico who has a pronounced penchant for stuffing both feet in his big mouth every time he opens it. He came to Congress in a special election in 1939 when he was thirty, with strong Townsendite support in a rock-ribbed Republican district.

One of the first things Hall did was to appoint his father as his secretary and his mother as his clerk. His mother stayed quietly at his home in Binghamton and never did any government work whatsoever. This went on for several years until exposed by the *Washington Post.* Hall then took his mother off the payroll. His father stayed. Soon thereafter, Hall added his daughter, his two sons, and his housekeeper to his office payroll. Undoubtedly he would have included his wife if he had not been separated from her.

It is fair to conjecture that Hall's office must have been a cozy little place what with Hall, Grandfather Hall, and three little Halls, plus the housekeeper, all crowded into the two-room suite. But appearances are deceiving.

Miss Hall never came to the office because at the time (1949) she

was nineteen years old and was attending college twenty miles outside Washington. The Hall boys did not clutter up the place, either,
because they were sixteen and seventeen years old respectively and
were busy going to high school. Miss Frieda Stein, the housekeeper,
did what every good housekeeper should do—she stayed home and
kept house. Nonetheless, the total "earnings" of Mr. Hall's family
and his housekeeper came to nearly $15,000 a year.

There is nothing illegal in this procedure. The law states only that
a congressman shall appoint his clerks; it doesn't say who they shall
be or that they must work for the money.

J. Parnell Thomas, who had his wife, his wife's aunt, his daughter-
in-law, his secretary's maid, and a couple of other people as phantom
employees, went to jail because it was proved that he collected the
total salary of most of these people as a "kickback"; though he paid
taxes on their salaries, he paid in the lower bracket they were in rather
than adding the extra sums to his own $12,500 income where it really
belonged.

Whether Hall's children and housekeeper kick back their salary to
him would obviously be difficult to prove.

It may, however, help to explain Hall's rise to affluence while serving the public in Washington. Prior to his election in 1939, he never
made more than $2,000 as a clerk in a bank. He had no property what-
ever except for household furnishings and personal effects. Today, he
owns a well-stocked farm near Bethesda, Maryland, and another farm
in Susquehanna County, Pennsylvania, overlooking Quaker Lake,
where he has built a summer home. Meanwhile, he has educated three
children, maintained an automobile and a servant, and supported an
estranged wife.

As the saying goes—it's nice work if you can get it.

Speaker Sam Rayburn has spent his whole adult life studying laws
and making them.

As a youth in Texas, he studied law and practiced briefly; at twenty-
four he was elected to the State Legislature, at twenty-eight he was
Speaker, and at thirty he was elected to Congress. That was in 1912.
He has been in Washington ever since. In 1937, he became Majority
Leader and four years later Speaker of the House.

Rayburn came to Washington a flaming back-country radical. He introduced a bill for the nationalization of the railroads and harassed the Wilson administration by advocating advanced social legislation. But then the militant young Turk slowed down and developed into a party wheel horse.

He was close to his fellow Texan, John Nance Garner, who became Speaker of the House and Vice-President. When the New Deal arrived with a clash and clatter in 1933, Rayburn was a veteran of twenty years' experience in legislative maneuvering. He was the provincial country man who had learned over long years the virtue of patience and the value of entrenching himself.

Constantly briefed and pepped by young New Deal brain-trusters, Rayburn became a tower of strength for the administration.

He pushed through banking legislation and the Securities and Exchange law and had a big hand in other key measures. In return, the administration made him Floor Leader in a close battle with former Representative John O'Connor of New York.

Rayburn is now sixty-eight. He is a bachelor and lives alone in a modest apartment. He has no other interests but his work. He has devoted his life to Congress as a career, is proud of his achievements, and hungers for nothing more.

The years have told on Rayburn. He is not complacent but he is satisfied.

He feels the country's crusading days are over for this decade, at least, and he knows his own are. He feels the postwar period is one of readjustment, when the gains of the New Deal should be consolidated and the country given a rest. There is no one to contradict this view or to alter his mood.

Since 1945, the pressure from the White House has been off. The smug, intellectually arid crowd around Truman does no needling. Only a small leaderless band of young liberals in the House has a militant outlook, and they carry little weight with Rayburn.

It is against this background of intellectual drift, waning vigor, personal self-satisfaction, and the increasing loneliness of old age that a new and crafty element has moved into Rayburn's social atmosphere.

This element is big oil and its big and insidious lobby.

The oil barons know what they want and are persistent, relentless, and well financed in their drive to get it. Big oil wants three things: state rather than federal control of the oil-rich tidelands; removal of federal regulation of the natural-gas industry; and the retention of the scandalous 27½ per cent tax allowance for depletion of oil holdings.

The oil gang has many political henchmen in Washington: rank and filers, leaders, jurists, and socialites. These oil servitors—grasping, wheedling, whispering, laughing, and persuading, over tall drinks and across the poker table, from late in the afternoon till far into the night—have spent many hours working on Rayburn.

For years, oil and Rayburn did not mix. His district is not in the heart of the petroleum country. He did not need the oil barons' campaign contributions, and they could not easily mobilize pressure against him.

His chief foes were the power interests, whom he fought openly in Congress and in Texas. They reciprocated with savage intensity but little effect. But the oil interests—Rayburn did not oppose them or help them. Except for a belated and inept drive in 1944, they left him strictly alone.

But in recent years Rayburn has yielded more and more to their blandishments. By 1948, his indifference had changed to hearty accord. Sam and the oil barons were *simpático*. In 1949 and 1950, Rayburn threw the full weight of his liberal prestige and the great powers of the Speaker's office squarely behind Operation Oil.

Before the President issued his 1950 tax message urging that the oil-depletion tax allowance be cut or abolished, Rayburn argued strongly against this move at a White House conference. Unsuccessful, he truculently took his fight directly to the House Ways and Means Committee and there lined up a solid bloc to kill any revision. The President's proposal never got out of the Committee.

When the Kerr natural-gas "ripper" bill came before the House in 1949, Rayburn rammed it through one Friday afternoon, with virtually no chance for debate and with 103 members absent. Later, when the measure came back from the Senate for final action, he personally arranged for the Rules Committee to give it priority so he could rush it to the floor immediately. He then buttonholed every member he could find to vote for the bill as a special favor to him.

When even this private lobbying seemed unlikely to carry the day,

Rayburn took the floor and made one of his rare speeches. Trading on his liberal reputation of bygone days, he scoffed at critics, saying, "With my long record in this House of Representatives . . . I do not think I can be accused of having any great desire to serve the interests over the people." He then proceeded to make an assertion as bald as his own head: "In my opinion—and I state this to you deliberately; I would not deceive you—you know that; this bill will not raise the price of natural gas to any consumer in the United States one red penny."

By these extraordinary tactics and unconscionable statements Sam finally succeeded in weaseling the grab bill through the House. But it was no credit to him nor to the measure.

The vote was 176 to 174.

It was a great triumph for the oil and gas lobby and a sad blow to Rayburn's once high repute. The President's scathing veto did not remedy the damage.

Unless Rayburn frees himself from the clutches of the oil lobbyists, it seems more and more likely that they will write a dark and greasy concluding chapter on what had been a very honorable and inspiring American career.

Majority Leader John McCormack has made a career of going along.

A tall, gangling Irish lawyer from South Boston, he served in the Massachusetts Legislature from 1920 to 1926, when he came to Congress in a special election. He has always supported the Democratic administration under both Roosevelt and Truman. In domestic affairs, this took no particular courage, since he represents a low-income city stronghold. But McCormack has also gone down the line on foreign policy. That has taken courage, lots of it.

It is not generally realized, but McCormack led the fight for the 1946 British loan, and his name appears with Barkley's as co-sponsor of the original Lend-Lease bill. The Boston Irish have not been notorious for their enthusiasm for such proposals.

McCormack and his wife Harriet lead an almost Spartan existence. They have no children, rigorously shun the cocktail-party circuit, and live quietly and simply in a small apartment. McCormack has no interests outside of his political work. His only indulgence is a cigar. He smokes several a day, and when he is not smoking, he usually carries an unlit one clenched between his fingers.

The McCormacks are profoundly pious Catholics who are active in charity work and have received Papal honors. On many an evening, McCormack returns from a hectic day on the Hill to have a quiet dinner with his wife and some lonely young priest whom they have temporarily "adopted."

McCormack's only vanities are a pride in his oratory, which is loud, fluent, and colorful, and an ancient ambition to be the kingmaker of Massachusetts politics. Since the death in 1947 of the late Senator David I. Walsh, McCormack has some chance of attaining that role.

Paradoxically, his success in the House is based on his close relations with the Southern bloc. Some of McCormack's best friends are Southerners.

He lived at the same hotel as Jack Garner, and they were close associates. McCormack was boosted to the Majority Leadership with Southern votes; whether they will be forthcoming when he runs some day for Speaker is conjectural.

McCormack has sponsored no important domestic legislation and has no militant ideas, which perhaps explains why his relations with conservative Southerners have always run smoothly. He is also genuinely liked and respected by fellow Northerners, particularly from the big cities. He is thus an almost ideal man for his job.

He does that job day after day. Gripping his ever-present cigar and with a friendly light in his blue eyes behind rimless spectacles, he goes along, patient, loyal, intent, rounding up votes and urging everyone to stay in step with the party.

Gene Cox of Georgia is the most potent of the Southerners next to Speaker Rayburn.

Cox is ranking Democratic member of the House Rules Committee. The nominal chairman is eighty-four-year-old Adolph Sabath of Chicago, whose New Deal views put him in a perpetual minority in his own bailiwick, which is tightly dominated by a Republican-Dixiecrat bloc consisting of Democrats Cox, Howard Smith of Virginia, and William Colmer of Mississippi; and Republicans Leo Allen of Illinois, Clarence Brown of Ohio, James Wadsworth of New York, and Christian Herter of Massachusetts. This gives this clique a clear seven-to-five margin. Since the Rules Committee must pass on every bill before it is reported to the floor, this gives Cox tremendous power, which he delights in using.

In 1949, the House loosened Cox's grip somewhat by adopting the rule that a bill could be called up by its chairman if the Rules Committee did not clear it in twenty-one days. But because of the possibilities for endless jockeying and raising of technicalities, this reform is a slow and cumbersome procedure. The Rules Committee continues to blockade bills it dislikes, and it can be dislodged only when a measure has the most intense kind of support both from the public and from the House.

Cox is a fairly characteristic specimen of one type of Old Guard Southern politician. He is an accomplished rabble-rouser and has the histrionic manner, vocal antics, and mobile expression of an old-time vaudeville ham actor.

He has a sharp wit, tells good stories, and is one of the best poker players in the poker-playing Capital. He has narrow, reactionary views and manias on every conceivable subject. He has even been quoted as saying:

"It seems to me that the good Germans were the Nazis who were loyal to the government which the United States recognized at the time, not those who were disloyal."

Tennessee's Percy Priest is the leading contender for the title of ugliest man in the House—and the best liked. He is Majority Whip and a sort of junior partner to Rayburn and McCormack.

Priest is an ex-newspaperman with a gaunt, red face dominated by prominent cheekbones, and a lean, long jaw. He has a shock of grayish hair and perpetually chews gum. He filed for his seat in 1940 after the Democratic primary had closed, and was thus elected as an Independent, defeating the Democratic incumbent. This stain on his escutcheon is one Priest never refers to, as he has a horror of being considered a "deviationist."

Joseph William Martin, Jr., of North Attleboro, Massachusetts, leader of the Republican Party in the House, is one of those strange men in American politics who rise to the top equipped with nothing but deadly perseverance.

Martin has been Minority Leader, Speaker, chairman of the Republican National Committee, permanent chairman of the Republican National Conventions of 1940, 1944, and 1948, and a dark-horse candidate for Vice-President or President at each of these conventions. In 1947-48, when the vice-presidency was vacant and he was Speaker of the House, only Truman's life hung between him and the White House.

Yet Martin has never sponsored an important piece of legislation, has never offered an interesting or constructive proposal, and has rarely been right on a major issue, foreign or domestic, in thirty years. He has neither brains nor wit nor charm. He is actively hostile to abstract ideas, ignorant of economics, inexperienced in foreign affairs, and boring and banal as a public speaker.

Untraveled, unread, unsophisticated, he is one of the four or five most important men in Congress.

Men like Joe Martin are not uncommon in high American politics. They have no qualifications save those possessed by Martin: unswerving party orthodoxy and a threadbare good fellowship.

There was, for example, Charles Curtis, the monosyllabic politician from Kansas. He was in Congress for thirty years, became Floor Leader in the Senate, and wound up as Hoover's Vice-President. Who today remembers Curtis? Joe Martin, two years, or six months, after he is dead, will be similarly forgotten. But as a peculiar phenomenon of American politics, the Joe Martins have never ceased to interest both foreign and native observers.

Henry Adams summed up the type as succinctly as anyone has ever done, as follows:

"Crushed by his own ignorance, the scholar finds himself jostled of a sudden by a crowd of men who seem to him ignorant that there is a thing called ignorance; who have forgotten how to amuse themselves; who cannot even understand that they are bored. The American thought of himself as a restless, pushing, energetic, ingenious person, always awake and trying to get ahead of his neighbors. Perhaps this idea of the national character might be correct for New York or Chicago; it was not correct for Washington.

"There the American showed himself . . . inarticulate, uncertain, distrustful of himself, still more distrustful of others, and awed by money. That the American, by temperament, worked to excess was true; work and whisky were his stimulants; work was a form of a vice; but he never cared much for money or power after he earned them. . . . He was ashamed to be amused; his mind no longer answered to the stimulus of variety; he could not face a new thought. Congress was full of such men; . . . pathetic in their helplessness to do anything with power when it came to them. They knew not how to amuse themselves; they could not conceive how other people were amused. Work, whisky, and cards were life."

This breed has not changed since Adams' time.

Martin, as Floor Leader, has committed his party to a thoroughly negative, reactionary, and obstructionist policy.

He voted against every New Deal bill, whether it was important or unimportant. He was the backbone of isolationism in the House before the war. Ham Fish and other characters like him got the headlines, but it was Martin who, on every issue, delivered the preponderant Republican vote for the isolationist cause. He did not waver a fraction of an inch right up to Pearl Harbor.

Since the war, he has been a grudging and restive supporter of the bipartisan foreign policy. He constantly struggles to hamstring ECA with amendments and starve it with meager appropriations. He has fought bitterly the mild and inadequate reciprocal trade agreements program. He has been found on the side of every Treasury raid, every pork-barrel bill, every tariff steal, every selfish grab of private interests from the power lobby's attempt to capture Muscle Shoals in the 1920's to the Kerr natural-gas "ripper" bill in 1950.

In all this, Martin has had but one motive—loyalty to his party. If the Democratic Party is for a measure, Martin is against it. That is his sole criterion.

The nature of the bill, the circumstances at the time, the situation at home or abroad—none of these has the slightest influence on Martin. He knows but one way for the Republicans to build up a record in Congress, and that is to be against everything the Democrats are for.

Like the men Adams described, Martin has a great awe of money and a profound respect for the rich. But money as a personal possession does not strongly attract him. Martin, unlike some of his colleagues, is personally incorruptible. Nor does he have any bitter, pathological prejudices or deep-rooted convictions on any particular subject. He is simply the amiable, faceless embodiment of partisanship.

No partisan charge is too ridiculous, no proposal is too hypocritical or outrageous for Martin to make with a straight face and a stolid, weary manner.

In March, 1949, he traveled to Ohio and assailed the Truman administration as a "spendthrift government gone wild." Then, in the same week, he returned to Washington and voted for the Rankin omnibus veterans' pension bill which would have cost two billion dollars a year immediately and ultimately one hundred and twenty-five billions.

Martin's private life fits perfectly the dull pattern Henry Adams pictured. Only more so. Martin, a half-bald, diminutive bachelor, does not smoke, drink, or play cards. He only works.

Martin lives today on the very same spot where Henry Adams lived a half century ago. Martin lives in the Hay-Adams House, a quiet but swanky residential hotel. It is located on the site of the house from whose windows Adams and John Hay and the elder Henry Cabot Lodge used to look across Lafayette Square to the White House and make clever, cynical comments on the politicians who came and went there in the 1890's.

Martin, of course, makes no cynical comments. For him, it probably seems more significant that the Hay-Adams also overlooks the national headquarters of the mighty U.S. Chamber of Commerce.

Martin detests parties—except the GOP. He goes to a few out of a sense of duty, but always leaves early. He usually retires at nine P.M. Like Calvin Coolidge, he sleeps easily and he likes to sleep. Unlike his Yankee predecessor, he does not take a two-hour nap after lunch, but Martin hates having his nightly rest disturbed.

The story is told of the 1940 presidential campaign when Wendell Willkie was the candidate and Martin his National Chairman. Willkie, in Washington for a brief stay, decided around eleven P.M. that he would like to discuss an important matter with his National Chairman. He drove to the Hay-Adams, went to Martin's room, and knocked on the door. No response. Finally, after furious pounding had brought no sound of activity, Willkie shouted, "Joe, this is Wendell Willkie. I want to see you." From within came the determined reply, "I don't give a --- damn who you are. Go away and let me sleep!" Willkie went.

Well fortified by such rest, Martin gets up every morning before eight and walks the two miles to the Capitol. Here he breakfasts and begins his day's routine. In the evening, around six or seven, his work done, and no dreary cocktail parties to look in on, Martin customarily walks back to his apartment. These daily constitutionals probably explain in large part Martin's rock-ribbed physical stamina. Somehow, they are also symbolic of Joe Martin and the life he has led.

His mind and outlook are geared to an age which moved no faster than a man could walk or a horse trot.

As he walks down from the Hill, past the foul Negro slums, through the busy shopping district, past the rows of marble-and-granite government buildings, and into the neighborhood of Lafayette Square, Martin can reflect on little in his own or the world's affairs which gives him pleasure. Turning into the driveway of the Hay-Adams, he can see through the trees the outlines of the White House gleaming in the gathering twilight. He once hoped to move across the park and live in the mansion. It was the goal at the end of the road over which he had plodded doggedly for over forty years.

Now there is little chance Martin will ever get there. His face is lined and weary; his manner is increasingly listless. Time has overrun him.

Charles Halleck of Indiana is one of the most thoroughly unattractive men in Washington.

The stubby, curly-haired, bulb-nosed Republican from Indiana was majority leader in the Eightieth Congress and is now Martin's right-hand man. His views on domestic and foreign affairs are of no moment. He has none. He is a screaming reactionary hack who can defend or oppose nothing.

What makes Halleck uniquely unpleasant is the constant odor of self-seeking and vulgar gratification which hangs about him.

Elected to public office as prosecuting attorney the year he got out of law school, Halleck has been feeding at the public trough ever since. He has never had a big private law practice and he has never made over $12,500 in public life. Yet Halleck manages to live on a millionaire's scale.

He is called "Two-Cadillac Charlie" because he owns two limousines which he drives on alternate days. One of these Cadillacs, plus two other automobiles, Halleck acquired during the war when no cars were sold on the open market. He also owns three farms in Indiana and a smartly furnished house in Washington. He has a weakness for high society and is a frequent item in the Washington gossip columns. Halleck both gives and goes to enough cocktail parties to more than make up for Joe Martin's deficiency in this regard.

Halleck is also frantically ambitious. In 1948, he double-crossed Taft and delivered the Indiana delegation to Dewey in return for a tacit promise of the vice-presidency. But then Dewey, to the glee of the Washington press corps, double-crossed Halleck and gave the nod to Governor Earl Warren of California.

Much about Halleck can be explained by the fact that he long ago made himself the darling of the Republican fat-cats.

Men like Joe Pew, Irénée du Pont, and certain members of the New York banking set who have bulging purses and pathetically naïve views of what is politically possible in present-day America, have long looked on Charlie Halleck as a fine type of up-and-coming statesman. Halleck has never done anything to disturb this view. He cemented his relations with these gentry when he was chairman of the Republican Congressional Campaign Committee and was charged with raising and disbursing campaign funds.

Halleck does not limit himself to being agreeable to rich Republicans. When the Kerr bill to rip the natural-gas industry from the control of the Federal Power Commission came before the House, Halleck dutifully obliged the gas and oil lobby, largely financed by Democratic money from the Southwest, by making a fervid speech on behalf of the measure. Since oratory never swung a vote in the House, Halleck did not depend on lung power alone.

Behind the scenes he lined up three Republicans: Paul Shafer of Michigan, Earl Wilson, Indiana, and Henry Latham, New York, who were too timid to vote for the consumer gouge, but who promised to do so in a pinch if their votes were needed. They were. On the first count the Kerr bill was beaten, 178 to 172. The three Republicans, joined by Morgan Moulder of Missouri, who was seeking to curry favor with Speaker Rayburn, then hurriedly switched their votes, and the bill carried, 176 to 174. As Halleck's three stooges trotted down the aisle to change their votes, the Associated Press, in a story printed the next day on the front page of *The New York Times,* reported that a voice from the Democratic side shouted, "How much did you get?"

It was a good question.

Representative Clarence Brown is the GOP hatchet man in the House. The big, bluff, hearty Ohioan can be depended upon to do any dirty work that the party leaders feel needs to be done.

It was Brown, for example, who made the shabby and unfounded attack on young Franklin Roosevelt for his supposed absenteeism from the House. Actually, Roosevelt's attendance during his first full session was above the average, and, since he is ambitious, he works harder than the average, answering more than one hundred letters a day. But it made a subject for a good partisan attack, and Brown is never averse to doing that kind of hatchet job.

He also does not believe in pussyfooting on domestic legislation. Unlike some of his Republican colleagues, who often try to appear more liberal than they feel, Brown says flatly and in a voice that shakes the walls, "If opposing this legislation be reaction, I am a reactionary."

Off the floor, Brown is jovial and companionable. His stories are excellent and he has a legion of friends, including many Democrats. But on the floor Brown makes the rafters ring and the opposition quail.

It is a frayed cliché that Congress does its most effective work in committee. But there is an element of truth in it, even if the remark is not justified by what happens on the floor.

Most committee chairmen are old men, past the prime of their intellectual and physical vigor. Typical chairmen are Robert Doughton, Ways and Means, eighty-six; Adolph Sabath, Rules, eighty-four; Clarence Cannon, Appropriations, seventy-one; John Kee, Foreign Affairs, seventy-six. Harold Cooley, the North Carolina Democrat who heads the Agriculture Committee, is at fifty-three the "baby" of the House chairmen.

Representative John F. Kennedy, Massachusetts Democrat who was elected to Congress in 1946 at the age of twenty-nine, made the pertinent remark, "The House is run by a crowd of old men who would have been pensioned off years ago if they were in private industry."

"Muley" Doughton of North Carolina, chairman of the Ways and Means Committee, is the oldest man in Congress and one of Washington's best-known characters.

He is a deaf, cantankerous old man who has spent much of his life fronting for the big cigarette companies. Doughton's district is in the heart of the tobacco country, and the cigarette tycoons have seen to it that every two years he is elected with little or no opposition and, therefore, no expense to himself.

The cigarette companies are heavily taxed, but this makes no difference to them, as they pass the tax to the consumer. If cigarettes were freed of local, state, and federal taxes, they would sell for around eight cents a package. Over the years, the manufacture and sale of cigarettes has become a monopoly of three big companies—R. J. Reynolds, American Tobacco Company, and P. Lorillard. Since they have such a strangle hold on the industry, it is almost impossible for small competitors to grow, because they cannot pay for heavy advertising and other costs. The only hope for the little fellows is that cigars and cigarettes be taxed proportionately according to price rather than at a flat rate, as they now are.

This would give the smaller firms, putting out cheaper brands, a price advantage. This is the procedure followed with almost all other luxury and semiluxury goods. (A leather suitcase, for example, is taxed twenty-five per cent of its sales price rather than a flat sum regardless of its price.) This graduated tax was followed up to the turn of the century, when the tobacco barons put over a fast one, which they have worked hard to protect ever since. Doughton has been their main defender for many years.

The smaller companies made a determined drive on this inequality in 1935. At that time, they secured the appointment of a subcommittee to study the problem. The subcommittee was headed by Representatives Fred Vinson, now Chief Justice, and John McCormack, now Majority Leader. Out of deference to Doughton's feelings, they killed the matter. Intermittent attempts to revive the issue came to a head in 1950, when President Truman recommended that wartime excise rates be lowered. Doughton lectured witnesses favoring revision and was in a very bad humor throughout the hearing.

Representative Wilbur Mills of Arkansas, Doughton's right-hand man, pulled the *faux pas* of saying, at one point, "Mr. Chairman, will it be all right with you if we finish up these witnesses for the revision tomorrow, and then hear your witnesses on Monday?"

"They are not *my* witnesses," Doughton snapped, "I am impartial in the matter." Mills subsided into crestfallen embarrassment.

Proponents for a graduated tax got a report from the Treasury favoring the proposal. But before it could be made public, the tobacco lobby went to work. The Treasury is honeycombed with North Carolinians and Kentuckians from the tobacco country. With the help of some behind-the-scenes prodding from their great and good patron, Muley Doughton, these officials quickly killed the report and sent up a guileless subordinate to tell the Ways and Means Committee that he knew nothing about the report and that the Treasury favored keeping the existing tax system.

But despite this backstage maneuver, the Committee voted for the lower tax on economy brands by a margin of 13 to 12.

Whereupon, Doughton irately proceeded to stage a sit-down strike.

He would be shocked and outraged at the idea of a sit-down strike among farm laborers or mill workers. He would be aghast at the suggestion that he himself might lead a strike. But that is exactly what he did.

He told his colleagues there was no use considering the tax bill any further. He just wouldn't allow a bill out of the Committee until this odious provision was dropped. The Committee continued to work on the measure, but administration leaders and all Capitol Hill observers agreed that tax legislation was dead for the session.

Old Muley was staging a sit-down strike, and neither tears nor tear gas would dislodge him.

The Committee held another vote to make permanent all the cuts voted up to that time. (The earlier vote had been tentative.) Doughton made a fervent plea. The tobacco farmers of North Carolina would suffer because they would get lower prices for their tobacco. That was rank nonsense and he knew it. The price was already rigidly determined by the tobacco monopolies. A graduated tax might hit these big companies a little but would never even be known by the farmers. But Doughton stormed, thundered, cajoled, pleaded, wheedled, and threatened. Alas, however, to no avail. Again, the champions of reform triumphed, 13 to 12.

Doughton then went to work behind the scenes. He put pressure on Representative Aime Forand, Rhode Island Democrat, who at first held firm. Word was sent to the jewelry manufacturers, who are strong in Forand's district, that there would be no tax cut on jewelry because his stubbornness on the cigarette issue was holding up the whole bill. That did it. Forand surrendered.

When the third vote came up, Doughton was so pleased that he made a little speech. In the course of it, Forand became bored and walked out. Unaware of that, a member dutifully made the motion for reconsideration, and the clerk called the roll. To Doughton's horror, Forand was missing, and the motion for reconsideration lost, 12 to 12. One of Doughton's supporters promptly argued, "Forand was here just a moment ago. I know how he was going to vote, so I will vote his proxy. Forand votes aye."

The opposition objected vehemently. Representative Hale Boggs, leading the fight for economy brands, finally said, "I will put it up to the Chairman. If Mr. Forand gave his proxy to the Chairman, I will not object. Did he give you his proxy?"

Doughton was caught in a quandary. He closed his hands, then unclosed them, stared at the ceiling, and after a hilarious pause of fully three minutes, during which dead silence prevailed, he finally said, "No, I cannot honestly say that the gentleman from Rhode Island gave me his proxy." He then adjourned the meeting in a raging huff.

However, that did not end the chase.

The next day Doughton caught up with the penitent Forand and this time got his proxy in writing.

But the following day another hitch developed. Representative Thomas Martin, Iowa Republican who had supported Doughton up to that time, decided to switch to the other side. Muley heard of this and, hurriedly getting hold of Martin, proposed a deal to keep him in

line. Doughton offered to vote against an increase in corporation taxes
—an increase recommended by the President but opposed by the
GOP—if Martin stuck with Doughton on the cigarette tax.

Martin agreed, and finally, on the fourth ballot, the graduated tax
was beaten, 13 to 12.

Muley's persistence had paid off.

The great American Tobacco Company sent a private note of thanks
to all the Committee members who supported Doughton. None of
them has yet received a communication from a tobacco grower.

Doughton is extraordinarily tightfisted and canny. Scrupulously
honest in a strict money sense, and with no income other than his congressional salary, he has managed by personal thrift to accumulate a
tidy personal fortune. He attended the $100-a-plate Jefferson-Jackson
Day dinner in 1950, although colleagues surmise he must have wangled
a free ticket. "Muley doesn't spend that much money a month," one
colleague observed.

Whether he paid or not, Doughton determinedly made the best of
it. During the evening, he made several trips to a side room where
some surplus cut oranges had been left. After one of these trips, a fellow diner, his curiosity reaching the bursting point, asked Doughton
whether he was eating the oranges.

"Nope," was the reply, "I'm taking them home with me for break-
fast."

The second-ranking Democrat on the Ways and Means Committee
is Jere Cooper of Tennessee. A member of Congress since 1929, Cooper
has a magnificent, rich, deep voice. A colleague remarked of him, "Jere
sure would be a great congressman if he lived up to his statesmanlike
voice."

On the whole, Cooper is a capable, intelligent conservative. He has
been waiting patiently for ten years for Doughton to die or retire. But
the old man refuses to depart. When questioned on the subject of retirement, Doughton declared, "I work six days a week and, as the
Lord says, I rest on Sunday. Every Sunday night, after hours of rest-
ing, I feel tireder than I do any other day. I guess I better keep
working."

One champion of the futile struggle to put across the cigarette tax reform said to Cooper, "Here you are, going along with Doughton on this only because you want to stay on the right side of the old man until he leaves. When I first knew you, years ago, that's what you were doing. Then you had a full head of hair and it was all black. Now you're bald and gray and wrinkled, and Doughton is still chairman. Why, you'll go on doing this for thirty years, and when you die at eighty-seven, Doughton will be only one hundred and fifteen and he'll still be chairman."

The observation was so ridiculous, and so true, that even Cooper laughed.

Meanwhile, he has another worry. He is becoming increasingly nervous about organized labor. It is slowly growing stronger in his district and may eventually oust him. It would be ironic indeed if, after all these years, Cooper should be defeated the year Doughton dies.

It is doubtful if Jere would join in laughing at that one.

Clarence Cannon is the Mr. Moneybags of the House.

The lean, gray-haired, tough old Missourian runs the Appropriations Committee. Everyone has to come to him for funds. To his everlasting credit, Cannon is always fair and does not abuse his power.

He supports the Truman administration as he did the Roosevelt administration—in a workmanlike, unemotional way and by reasoning processes that are sometimes inscrutable to his more fervidly liberal colleagues. Cannon is a wise old hand who knows all the tricks. He started in Washington forty years ago as Speaker Champ Clark's secretary. He then became parliamentarian of the House and wrote several books on parliamentary procedure, including the official *Cannon Manual*. In 1922, he was elected to Clark's seat and has held it ever since.

Cannon's steadfast right-hand man on the Appropriations Committee is very able Mike Kirwan, Democrat from Youngstown, Ohio. Kirwan's reputation as a tough guy in across-the-table bargaining won him a stiff assignment on the day Congress adjourned in 1949.

He was eating a hasty luncheon when Cannon rushed up and exclaimed, "Mike, I need you. You are the only man to do this job. You've got to come with me at once. We have to whip some senators into line."

On the way to the conference room, Cannon explained the situation. The House had included an $8,581 item in a deficiency bill to pay the back salaries of Michael Straus, head of the Reclamation Bureau, and Richard Boke, regional reclamation director in California. But the Senate eliminated the provision, at the demand of Senator Sheridan Downey of California. He had been waging a vendetta against the two officials for several years.

In the conference, Kirwan wasted no time swinging into action. "This is money the government owes," he said, "and it must be paid. These men earned it, and it is ridiculous to refuse to pay them."

"What about Downey?" asked a Senate conferee. "He will filibuster all over the place."

"He hasn't the guts to try it," snapped Kirwan. "All the facts and justice are on our side. A Supreme Court decision held these men are entitled to their pay, and I have a note here from the Comptroller General saying the same thing. That ought to be enough."

"Mike is right," broke in Representative Louis Rabaut, Michigan Democrat. "Nobody is going to filibuster today. There is nobody in the Senate galleries, and not even Downey is going to make a long speech for a few senators and some bored newspapermen."

That ended the matter. The Senate conferees agreed to restore the item, and Cannon beamed at Kirwan.

Representative John Kee of West Virginia is the little-known chairman of the Foreign Affairs Committee.

A short man, with a soft, tired face and thick fringe of gray hair parted in the middle, he wears severe Oxford-gray suits. Modest and sweet-tempered, he is a considerable contrast to witty, histrionic Sol Bloom, who ran the Committee as a one-man show up to his death in 1949.

Kee, seventy-six and in ailing health, is not so effective at cracking the whip as Bloom was. This is unfortunate because by accident the House Committee on Foreign Affairs has the biggest collection of hoot owls under the Capitol dome. Kee himself is a firm supporter of the bipartisan foreign policy. Mrs. Helen Gahagan Douglas, who retired from the House in 1950 to run for the Senate, and able, hard-hitting Mike Mansfield of Montana have been Kee's only effective supporters on the Democratic side. On the Republican side, Jacob K. Javits of New York has been a tower of strength.

But the rest of the Committee is hopeless. It is made up of self-important, self-styled experts like Walter Judd of Minnesota and John Davis Lodge of Connecticut. Lodge's chief qualifications, so far as anyone has discovered, are his grandfather's sins and his wife's Italian ancestry. Judd once lived in China and never got over it. What is worse, he won't let the State Department get over it, either.

The second-ranking member on the Democratic side is James Richards of South Carolina, a mediocre Dixiecrat who gets plenty of support from Omar Burleson of Texas, who keeps trying to turn the foreign-aid program into a grab bag for the farm bloc. The Republicans also contribute generously with deadheads like Chester Merrow of New Hampshire and unregenerate, scalp-hunting isolationists like Robert Chiperfield of Illinois, John Vorys of Ohio, and Lawrence Smith of Wisconsin. The ranking Republican, aged Charles Eaton of New Jersey, is an amiable internationalist who means well but can deliver nobody's vote but his own, and that only when he is awake.

The Agriculture Committee is one of the best-run committees in the House.

Candid, serious-minded Harold Cooley of North Carolina is an efficient chairman, and he has been aided by veteran Stephen Pace of Georgia, who retired in 1950, and genial, vigorous Robert Poage of Texas. The Democrats are also fortunate in having some live-wire freshmen on the Committee, such as Eugene O'Sullivan of Nebraska and able, conscientious Cecil White of California. The GOP delegation is less distinguished, but it is headed by one of the strongest Republicans in the House, Clifford Hope of Kansas, a capable, high-minded, experienced champion of the farmer.

Another excellently conducted committee is the Banking and Currency group headed by the veteran Brent Spence.

A husky, heavy-set Kentuckian whose mental vigor belies his seventy-five years, Spence has served in the House since 1931. A staunch supporter of the administration, he fights like a lion for every major bill coming out of his Committee, whether it be OPA or veterans' housing.

Spence has some top-flight associates on the Committee, among them Wright Patman, the militant Texas liberal who has a long and distinguished career fighting monopoly, Frank Buchanan of Pennsylvania, and Mrs. Chase Going Woodhouse of Connecticut. This trio form the core of a liberal bloc which, unlike many committees where the Democrats have a nominal majority, more than holds its own against the Republican minority.

The Armed Services Committee is a bird sanctuary where everyone sings his own tune loudly and off key.

Chairman Carl Vinson, Democrat of Georgia, is the worst of the lot. He has the moral instincts of a hawk and the modest manners of a rooster. Vinson talks incessantly of civilian control of the military and of congressional responsibilities for national defense. What he means is that Carl Vinson wants to run everybody and everything in the Pentagon.

Vinson was chairman of the Naval Affairs Committee in the days before unification of the Armed Services. At that time, he was a rabid Big Navy man. He still thinks the fleet is his special preserve. His high-handed meddling has harassed every Navy Secretary from Claude Swanson to Francis Matthews. But in recent years Vinson has taken the Air Force under his wing as well. Part of this is a shrewd politician's instinctive desire to be associated with the most popular service; another part is the supersalesmanship of former Air Force Secretary Stuart Symington.

Vinson's opposite number on the Committee is Republican Dewey Short of Missouri, who was an isolationist before the war, an isolationist after the war, and a flutterhead all of the time.

Short's Republican colleagues are less noisy but little more distinguished. The most prominent is James Van Zandt of Pennsylvania. He is a professional veteran who has been National Commander of the Veterans of Foreign Wars. He is now a captain in the Naval Reserve, and his great ambition is to be an admiral.

This ambition made Van Zandt a willing tool of the extremist clique in the Navy during the unification battle. He leaked information for them and spread Navy propaganda no matter what its source or reliability. Van Zandt is also a member of the Joint Committee on

Atomic Energy, where his antics have won him the accolade of "Hickenlooper of the House."

Vinson does have a few strong members on his side of the table, such as Melvin Price of Illinois and wise Franck Havenner of San Francisco. But on the whole the Armed Services Committee is stacked with hacks from the Deep South.

Typical is Paul Kilday, genial Irish politician from Texas. Kilday is the Washington agent for the hard-boiled San Antonio political machine run by his brother, the local sheriff. Kilday holds the seat once occupied by crusading Maury Maverick. Maverick lost caste in Texas because he wrote a book. Kilday doesn't do anything unconventional like that. He sits on the Armed Services Committee because there is vital patronage to be protected at Randolph Field, which is in his district.

The chairmanship of the House Un-American Activities Committee is apparently a standing invitation to sin.

J. Parnell Thomas, the last Republican chairman, is now in a federal penitentiary for payroll padding and fraud. Representative John Wood of Georgia, the present Democratic chairman, has been flirting with a scandal almost since he took over the job.

Wood's difficulty, like that of Thomas's, had its beginning before he rose to the lofty position of public censor of political morals. Back in 1944, Ralph Stanfield of Tate, Georgia, in Wood's congressional district, was hit by an Army truck and seriously injured. Wood promptly introduced a bill in his behalf for $10,000 compensation from the government. At that time, Wood's secretary suggested that Stanfield's father pay part of this sum to the Congressman. But the bill did not pass that session, and the question was not pushed.

Finally, the bill did pass, and Carl Tallant, Wood's law partner, told the elder Stanfield that it was "customary" to pay ten per cent on compensation bills of that kind. That, of course, is not true. All congressmen introduce private claim bills for constituents all the time, and it is a federal offense to collect any part of the money as a kickback. Stanfield realized Tallant's "suggestion" was no casual remark, for he knew that Tallant is not only Wood's law partner but that he is also on Wood's payroll as an office assistant at $7,000 a year. Thus Tallant,

both as law partner and employee, was obviously in a position to speak
for Congressman Wood. When Tallant made out to himself a check
for $1,000 and "suggested" that Stanfield sign it, Stanfield signed.

Columnist Drew Pearson got wind of this transaction and secured a
photostatic copy of the check, dated September 13, 1947. When Wood
heard that Pearson was on his trail, he sent an emissary to Stanfield
and asked for the canceled check, promising to return it in a day or
two. Stanfield gave it to him. It has never been returned.

Wood fiercely protests his innocence. He threatens ominously to do
this, that, and other things. But he has done nothing. Perhaps he is
publicity-shy.

The House Education and Labor Committee in the Eighty-first
Congress is a glaring example of how one man occupying the strategic
post of chairman can disrupt and obstruct the work of twenty other
men.

The late chairman John Lesinski had two overriding loyalties. One
was to the CIO and the other to the Catholic Church. It is probable
that his ardor harmed rather than helped them.

On the Labor Committee, he was surrounded by a roster of some of
the best men in the House, including Augustine "Gus" Kelley of
Pennsylvania, John Kennedy of Massachusetts, Carl Perkins of Kentucky, Hugo Sims of South Carolina, Andrew Jacobs of Indiana,
Thomas Burke of Ohio, and Tom Steed of Oklahoma. But Lesinski
nonetheless managed to confuse and antagonize all his associates and
to mangle the three major pieces of legislation his group considered.

One of these was the aid-to-education bill, in which every conceivable kind of sensitive issue was involved. A smooth, astute chairman
would have found a way through the shoals and charted a middle
course. Lesinski took an extreme position and was not only personally
intransigent in his views but quarreled bitterly with those who opposed him. By the time the wrangling was finished, the education bill
was dead. Throughout the Committee's deliberations, Lesinski took a
dictatorial and unfair approach. At one point, he refused to call the
Committee into session for weeks at a time.

But under the seniority system he was safe. He might well have headed the Committee for the next twenty years. But God intervened near the end of the session, and the Committee got a new chairman.

He is Graham Barden of North Carolina, one of the most conservative men in the House. This bodes no good for either labor or the education bill. Barden is just as much an extremist as Lesinski. He is aggressively and uncompromisingly antiunion and equally militant on the education bill, though on the other side from his predecessor.

Committee chairmen have complete authority over the official records of their committee. They may censor them and delete or alter their own remarks at will. This gives some of these petty oligarchs great scope to pursue vindictive vendettas.

Representative William Whittington, Mississippi Democrat and chairman of the House Public Works Committee, is a fierce foe of the Columbia Valley Authority, although his own State benefits richly from the Tennessee Valley Authority. When Oregon State Senator Vernon Bull appeared before the Committee to testify for CVA, Whittington gave him the works. One excerpt that did not appear in the official record is as follows:

WHITTINGTON: (To clerk taking down the testimony) This is off the record. (Then to Bull): You say you haven't appeared before the Senate Committee?

BULL: No, sir.

WHITTINGTON: Good, then we'll get rid of you fast. Are you in favor of this proposed CVA legislation?

BULL: Yes, sir, I am. I believe that the people of the Northwest . . .

WHITTINGTON: Yes, yes. We've heard all that. Now give us your reasons—one, two, three.

Whittington is also a great champion of economy—except when it comes to pork for his own Mississippi. His State is eighth in getting flood control and river and harbor improvements. Whittington also plays a potent role in shoring up Dixiecrat control of Congress. He can punish recalcitrant colleagues by scuttling their local public-works projects.

Dixiecrat chief Gene Cox finds pal Whittington's hatchet very useful.

Representatives come from all walks of life and represent many diverse shades of American society. In the average Congress, however, 300 of the 435 are lawyers, 50 to 75 are businessmen, and the rest are everything from movie actors and public-relations men to dentists and college professors. Lawyers have the edge in politics because they have a calling they can readily turn to when things go wrong in the political arena.

It is also a profession which they can practice while they are in office.

It is this fact which has led, in recent years, to the development of a flagrant abuse.

Congressmen who are paid by the public to enact laws have, with increasing frequency, been appearing in federal courts to represent clients who have broken laws or who seek to make good a claim under a federal law. This puts federal judges and attorneys in a delicate and difficult position. The congressman is indirectly one of their bosses; he can have much to do with whether or not they are promoted in the future.

Further, and what is even more sinister, he can go to any government agency, ask, as a congressman, to see confidential government files, and then use this information against the government in arguing his case as a private attorney. If he does not appear in the case personally, he can still turn the information over to his law partner and split the fee.

This little-known racket has been going on for many years. The Justice and Interior Departments are the worst sufferers in this milking of confidential files, but no Department is exempt. It is particularly widespread in connection with oil-lease cases, immigration and deportation proceedings, and fraud prosecutions.

The situation was finally spotlighted in 1949 in the case of Representative Earl Chudoff, freshman Democrat from Philadelphia, who attempted to represent a client charged with sending obscene literature through the mails. Judge James McGranery, a former Democratic member of the House, pointed out to Chudoff that he was violating Section 281 of the U.S. Criminal Code, which forbids members of Congress to accept compensation in connection with cases tried before government departments and officers. Chudoff replied that, as a member of the bar for twelve years, he sat ". . . in this courtroom and saw congressman after congressman appearing here, and nobody raised a question." Replied McGranery, "You are right, and I don't care to mention names, but that's no reason why I should allow you to do the same."

One of the representatives both had in mind was Francis Walter, veteran Pennsylvania Democrat, who, early in 1949, collected a $170,000 fee for representing stockholders of the Pennroad Corporation in a successful $15,000,000 suit against the Pennsylvania Railroad.

This action was doubly questionable because the case was an outgrowth of a congressional investigation into railroad holding companies, and because Walter is ranking Democratic member of the House Judiciary Committee. Few members of Congress have more intimate and influential relations with the Justice Department than does Walter. No government attorney or federal judge could look upon Walter as just another lawyer trying a case.

It is not necessary to invoke masculine gallantry to say that the ladies of the House are as distinguished as they are personable. It is a fact.

The nine women representatives are, both individually and collectively, decisively superior to the average male member.

They all work hard, think conscientiously about issues, and invariably display greater initiative, intelligence, and legislative capacity than their male colleagues. None of them ever gets involved in a scandal or boodle grab; they do not make silly speeches, come on the floor drunk, front for a venal lobby or special interest, have flare-ups of bad temper and bloated vanity, or exhibit psychopathic prejudices. In other words, they do none of the things which are so common among the men as to be almost characteristic.

When one of the ladies is formally referred to as "the distinguished gentlewoman," it is—for a change—the honest truth and not the debased coin of fake congressional courtesy.

Until Mrs. Mary Norton decided to retire in 1950, she was the dean of her sex in the House. She has always been a loyal stalwart of the Hague machine in New Jersey, but in the Capital she was a legislator of unswerving integrity, sincere liberalism, great personal courage, and a lively sense of personal dignity.

She was the first woman to head a House committee, when she succeeded to the chairmanship of the Labor Committee in 1937. She fought hard for the minimum-wage law and for other labor and educational legislation. She became a close friend of Mrs. Roosevelt, and the two women had a mutually inspiring effect on each other. In 1947, when Republican Fred Hartley became chairman of her Committee, Mrs. Norton had the character and courage to resign. In a blistering speech in the House, she explained she would not serve under a chairman who did not know his head from a bucket of lard as far as labor problems were concerned and who had the worst record of absenteeism on the whole Committee.

Quick-witted and lively, Mary Norton will be missed in the House. She was always a lady and a stateswoman in the finest sense of those terms.

Mrs. Edith Nourse Rogers is the senior woman on the Republican side. She has been in the House since 1925, when she succeeded to the seat left vacant by her husband. Able, devoted, and high-minded, Mrs. Rogers has made the cause of the veterans the passion of her life.

During the Republican Eightieth Congress, she was chairman of the Veterans' Committee. Unlike some of her male colleagues, she does not champion the veteran as a political gesture; she comes from a rock-ribbed Republican district where nothing could unseat her, short of a political hurricane. If she wished, she could do nothing but draw her pay and still be sure of re-election. But that is not her nature.

Mrs. Rogers toils on behalf of veterans because of a profound concern about them. All during the prewar years, when no one was thinking about veterans or doing anything for them, she was doggedly fighting their battles in Congress, in the Veterans' Administration and everywhere else it was needed. No cause is too complex, no case is too trivial for her to give it her full attention. And when she goes to work on a project, she gets results.

For years, Mrs. Rogers has been the conscience of the Veterans' Administration, and God knows that bureaucratic behemoth needs one.

Thousands of baffled and frustrated vets, exasperated by stupid delays, confusion, contradictions, inefficiency, and unconscionable indifference, have turned to Mrs. Rogers and received heartwarming and hope-restoring assistance. Servicemen, whether they fought at San

Juan Hill, Château-Thierry, Guadalcanal, or in the Bulge, know she is one politician who can be depended upon.

Mrs. Katherine St. George represents the New York district once held by isolationist Ham Fish. Mrs. St. George is a personable woman with genuine talents of a high order. They would stand out more, and make a more impressive record, if she would only stop voting Ham Fish's convictions.

Edna Kelly is a Democrat from Brooklyn, and Cecil Harden is a Republican from Indiana. But they have two things in common besides their sex. Both entered the House in 1949, and both are experienced politicians who know all the tricks the men do—even if they don't make use of them all.

Mrs. Harden is a vivacious, middle-aged ex-schoolteacher. She has been active in the hard-boiled Hoosier Republican machine for twenty years and has been GOP National Committeewoman since 1944. She is a conservative, but a reasonable and intelligent one. She stands head and shoulders above the other Republican members from her State.

Edna Kelly is the widow of a New York City judge. Before her election, she served five years as research director for the New York Democratic State Committee and as a Kings County Committeewoman. A slender, youthful woman who wears her handsome black hair in a boyish clip, Mrs. Kelly accents the boyish touch by wearing severely tailored black suits and four-in-hand ties. But, for all that, she still looks slightly elfin.

Her wit, intelligence, and svelte appearance make her a feminine bright spot in a desert of sagging paunches and bald heads.

Mrs. Frances Bolton is a Republican from Cleveland's "gold coast." She is a calm, common-sense person with a balanced, up-to-date, moderately conservative outlook on life and issues.

She was the only Ohio Republican to vote for rent control in 1950. The year before, she was the only Ohio Republican in the House to vote for public housing. On the Foreign Affairs Committee, she is an able and constructive member with a broad-gauged viewpoint and a level of intellect far above that of her GOP male colleagues on that body.

Connecticut's contribution to the female contingent is Mrs. Chase Going Woodhouse. An ardent liberal Democrat and former college professor and dean, Mrs. Woodhouse's intellectual level is at least five notches above that of most of the men from both parties who surround her in the House. But like the wise woman and astute politician she is, Mrs. Woodhouse tries not to make them too aware of that fact.

Fortunately, as a member of the Banking Committee, her knowledge of economics, one of her strong points, can be put to excellent use. Mrs. Woodhouse can become a figure of major significance in the House if the voters of Connecticut give her enough continuous service to build up some seniority.

Mrs. Reva Beck Bosone, Utah Democrat, is a bespectacled, red-haired widow. A freshman in the House, she had wide public experience in her home State. Mrs. Bosone is a very fine person with terrific energy, sincerity, and personal warmth. She is a conscientious, high-minded liberal and early in her congressional career stamped herself as a representative who is certain to make a contribution of more than ordinary merit.

Mrs. Helen Gahagan Douglas is a prisoner of her reputation.

A militant New Dealer for three terms, she is still better known—outside California and Washington—as the glamour gal of politics.

There is no denying she is glamorous. She is a brilliant, intense brunette with a shapely figure, sparkling eyes, vivid smile, and a thrilling personal presence. But the onetime star of stage and screen has much more than a photogenic presence to contribute to Congress.

Helen Douglas is one of the most outstandingly dynamic, creative, courageous, and eminently statesmanlike figures of either sex in either chamber. Her high caliber as a person, her trenchant intellect, her glowing idealism, her magnetic charm, and her tireless, unstinting, day-to-day hard work have made her one of the six or eight most valuable members of Congress.

She led the fight for public housing and for rent controls on apartment houses.

Another of her great achievements was her leadership of the battle in the House on behalf of price controls. She battled hard and long, both on the floor and on the public platform, for safeguards against runaway inflation. On one occasion, with her inherent flair for the dramatic as distinguished from the merely spectacular, she appeared before a House committee with a huge basket of groceries on her arm.

She illustrated her testimony on behalf of inflation controls by taking each package from her basket and comparing its price under OPA with its price after OPA. It was a stirring demonstration of her thesis and a brilliant personal triumph.

Mrs. Douglas has never stuck to the easy and obvious issues. She studies hard to "bone up" on the intricacies of complex questions such as public power, soil conservation, irrigation, reclamation, and water resources. She has become an expert on the problems of the great Central Valley in California and is the most effective champion in Congress for the program to develop the Valley.

And she knows how to wage her crusades with vigor and wit and marvelous clarity. As an old trouper, she not only always knows her lines, but she writes them herself. She needs neither ghost writers nor prompters when she talks about the present and the future of California.

As a member of the Foreign Affairs Committee, Mrs. Douglas has been a tremendous tower of strength in building a postwar policy to support the United Nations and international peace. She has fought consistently for the Marshall Plan. Almost singlehanded, she succeeded in preventing the plan from becoming a grab bag for special interests and boodlers.

Mrs. Douglas left the House in 1950 to run for the Senate. If she attains her ambition, she will give California its first good senator since the far-off days when the late Hiram Johnson was a fighting liberal. And at the same time California will give the country a senator of broad vision, brilliant attainments, and true national stature.

The House numbers two Negroes among its ranks—Adam Clayton Powell of New York and William Dawson of Illinois. Both are Democrats, but otherwise they are as different as two men could be.

Powell, tall, handsome, light-skinned, is better known as pianist Hazel Scott's husband and as a colorful Harlem pastor who was the late "Bojangles" Robinson's minister than he is as a congressman.

He has served in the House since 1945. Before that, he was New York City's first Negro councilman. Gifted with a superb baritone voice, sparkling eyes, and a strong, mobile face, Powell is a ruthless, brilliant, cynical rabble-rouser. He thunders against both parties, plays ball now and then with the Communists, and makes wild threats and thrilling promises which he can't keep. He feeds upon the misery of his fellow Negroes to satisfy his own gnawing hunger for the limelight.

The tragedy is that in a healthier, better-adjusted society he might have made great use of his genuine talents. But, as it is, he accomplishes nothing in Washington, and his excesses of emotion are a handicap to worthy causes.

Further, Powell is notorious in the House for his absenteeism. One reason for his being away from Washington so much is his private lecturing; but even in this he is notorious for canceling engagements at the last moment. Powell apparently is so busy trying to do everything he can't do anything.

William L. Dawson, who has represented Chicago's "black belt" since 1943, stands midway between the radicalism of Powell and the "hat-in-hand" conservatism of an older generation.

Dawson's predecessor was Oscar De Priest, the first Negro to serve in Congress since post-Civil War days. De Priest as a youth was Booker T. Washington's office boy. De Priest is not much of a hero to the more militant Northern Negroes. He is now retired to Virginia, where he lives the life of a gentleman farmer and carries on some of the agricultural experiments started by George Washington Carver.

Dawson was born in Georgia in 1886 and graduated from Fisk University. He came North to get a law degree at Northwestern University in Evanston, Illinois, and stayed on in Chicago. He served as first lieutenant in the 365th Infantry in France and lost a leg from German machine-gun fire. He was an active Democratic machine politician after World War I and served on the Chicago Board of Aldermen during the 1930's. He is still very much a politician. Autographed pictures of Franklin Roosevelt, Ed Kelly, Bob Hannegan, and other Democratic notables line his office walls.

Dawson's experience as soldier, lawyer, and ward politician has given him a keener grasp of the social realities than De Priest had, and at the same time has saved him from the stormy grandstanding of Powell. Dawson knows he is not going to get the millennium in a day, but, at the same time as he works diligently and quietly to win the half loaves and quarter loaves of the present, he does not sacrifice either the militancy or the idealistic goal which inspires militancy. Dawson also makes a substantial contribution to Negro progress by his fair, dignified, and highly capable handling of the chairmanship of the House Committee on Expenditures in the Executive Departments.

He is a daily example of the Negro's worth and capacity and refutes a thousand hate-filled harangues.

Two of the best-known and most frequently denounced men in the House are also two of the least consequential. They are Democrat John Rankin of Mississippi and Vito Marcantonio of the leftist American Labor Party of New York.

Rankin is a thin little man with a wizened face and a wild head of white hair. He always makes the same speech. It has two punch lines: (1) "The United States is pouring billions into the European rathole"; (2) "Every home that can be reached by the tax collector in time of peace and by the draft in time of war should be reached by a public power line. Let us take care of our own first." Rankin has long been the leader of the public-power bloc in the House and formerly was respected by Northern and Western liberals for his work in this cause.

In recent years, Rankin has made himself notorious for his virulent Jew-baiting and Negro-baiting. The public and the press frequently conjecture why members of the House so rarely contradict or challenge Rankin during his demagogic frenzies. The answer is twofold.

First, if they tried to answer him, they would have to be at it every day. No representative speaks so much or so frequently as Rankin. Secondly, he has become a spectacle and a joke. No one but Rankin takes Rankin seriously. It is ironically fitting that Rankin does not even dimly realize that his daily tirade has lost all effect. He speaks as a prophet; he is heard as a crackpot.

Vito Marcantonio, in his way, is just as malevolent and despicable as Rankin and commands even less support in the House.

Marcantonio has a savage tongue, a crafty mind sharpened by devious dialectical reasoning, and a trigger-quick command of parliamentary tactics and technicalities. No one knows whether or not he is a Communist, but it makes little difference since he knows all their tricks and follows the party line.

He works closely with Republican Leader Joe Martin to embarrass and harass the administration at every turn. The Republicans, of course, always protest their horror of him, but they do not hesitate to deal with him on issues such as foreign aid, veterans' pensions, and repeal of the Taft-Hartley Act.

Marcantonio is a ruthless obstructionist, and it will be a happy day when he is eliminated from the House.

Most Americans, when they think of the House at all, probably have a mental image of the typical representative as a stodgy, conservative Midwestern Republican. This is because Midwest Republican representatives have become almost legendary for their conservatism. It is a reputation that is largely deserved. But certain Eastern Republicans try mighty hard to outdo them. This is particularly true of those from Pennsylvania, upstate New York, Massachusetts, and Ohio. These delegations form a little-known but potent obstructionist bloc.

When Representative Robert Rich of Pennsylvania decided to retire in 1950, "Meat Ax" John Taber lost his staunchest supporter.

Rich is famous for his eternal cry: "Where are you going to get the money?" He raises this refrain at every turn and on every issue. But once his long-suffering colleagues got the chance to turn the tables.

Shortly before he retired, Rich rose in the House one day to request that a $500,000,000 flood-control "pork barrel" bill be increased by $1,000,000 for a project in his district. The House listened with high amusement to Rich's speech, and at the conclusion broke into yelps of laughter and derision. Oregon Republican Homer Angell got up and in his most serious manner demanded of Rich, "Where are you going to get the money?"

The House roared. Rich, furious, turned on Representative Louis Rabaut, the Michigan Democrat handling the bill, and demanded to know why the million-dollar grab shouldn't be included.

Rabaut, smiling broadly, replied, "Oh, consistency, thou art a jewel!"

"You are not making a flowery speech here," thundered Rich. "I want results."

The House gave results, pronto. His pork scheme was turned down by a resounding vote.

Upstate New York has some of the most antediluvian characters in national politics. One of them, Representative Ralph Gwinn, spends a large part of his time running errands for Merwin K. Hart and the real-estate lobby. However, these strenuous pursuits do not prevent Mr. Gwinn from keeping up to date on current economic realities.

When a laundry worker appeared in 1949 to testify before the House Labor Committee on behalf of a higher minimum-wage law, Gwinn told her, "If you don't like the wages your employer pays you, why don't you take in washing at home?"

Any connection between Gwinn and Marie Antoinette is wholly coincidental.

Then there is Representative William L. Pfeiffer, a rich manufacturer, who is State Republican Chairman in New York and a complete nonentity in Washington. Also, Representative James W. Wadsworth, who has been in the House since 1933 and before that served two full terms in the Senate. But alas, experience does not make the full man. Wadsworth voted against the National Science Foundation bill because the $25,000,000 appropriation was too high.

"We have to start economizing somewhere," he argued with characteristic irrelevancy.

Representative Daniel Reed has represented his upstate New York district since 1919. If the Republicans were to resume control of the House, he would be chairman of the Ways and Means Committee. No one would know what to expect of him in such a position, because no one has seen him do anything of importance up to the present.

New England also has its quota of deadhead conservatives.

There are the strait-laced species like Frank Fellows of Maine and Chester Merrow of New Hampshire. But it is Massachusetts that really takes the prize. Beautiful and famed Cape Cod contributes Representative Donald Nicholson, a stunted and warped reactionary of the worst kind in Congress.

Then there is Representative Angier Goodwin. This unknown dragoon voted with the Southwestern Democrats for the Kerr natural-gas grab. Then, in committee, he voted for the bill to hand over the rich tidelands oil resources to private interests. Yet Goodwin represents a tier of cities north of Boston which form a teeming industrial section. It is made up of gas and oil consumers, not producers.

But Goodwin doesn't represent consumers; he represents the mulcters of consumers.

Representative Christian A. Herter of Boston's Back Bay is the most obstructionist of the Republican Dark-Age brigade because he is the most influential as a member of the powerful House Rules Committee.

Herter might, because of his background, be expected to be a source of enlightened leadership. He was born in Paris, educated at Harvard, married into the Standard Oil Pratt family, served as Herbert Hoover's secretary, once edited a magazine, and, personally, is a cultivated and charming man. In Rules Committee hearings, Herter always makes a great show of being "fair." But when the votes are cast, he is always on the side of black and odorous reaction.

When GOP hatchet men Leo Allen and Clarence Brown look his way, Herter, the well-bred Boston Brahmin with the gentle manner and the aristocratic voice, always snaps into line and does their bidding. He never fails them or the vested interests they represent.

Although Herter is from one of the most concentrated apartment-house districts in the country, he has consistently sabotaged rent control and voted against middle-income cooperative housing. He regularly votes with the Gene Cox-Howard Smith-Bill Colmer Dixiecrat cabal against civil rights. In 1950, he supported this clique's attempt to destroy the modest rules reform adopted the year before. He even had the effrontery to defend his shabby stand on the ground that the parliamentary device of "Calendar Wednesday" was an effective alternative. Even the page boys know that, as a vehicle to speed legislation to the floor, Calendar Wednesday is about as speedy as a one-legged goat.

On one subject, however, Herter had to make a hurried about-face. When Theodore Roosevelt, III, founded "HELP" (Holyland Emergency Liaison Program), a pro-Arab organization, Herter became a director. Whether he was inspired by his wife's Standard Oil connections or by his friendship for Roosevelt is unknown. He quickly resigned when word of his indiscretion leaked to Boston.

For Beantown has its Jews and its Micks, but there are no Arabs in Mr. Herter's district.

Another little-known bloc in the House is the "IT&T Club." This select band is made up of those Eastern seaboard congressmen who dash home for three-day week ends—the "in Tuesday and out Thursday" boys.

It is to accommodate them that very little House business is transacted on Mondays and Fridays. And, of course, perish the thought that the House should ever meet on Saturdays.

The two worst offenders on the score of absenteeism are Republicans Kingsland Macy of Long Island and Frederic Coudert of New York City. Out of 342 quorum and roll calls in the Eighty-first Congress, Macy missed 203 and Coudert 202.

Other frequent Republican absentees are Dean Taylor of Troy, New York, Charles Plumley of Vermont, William L. Pfeiffer of Kenmore, New York, and Hugh Scott of Philadelphia. Scott, former GOP National Chairman, is so busy flitting about the country making speeches on "economy" that he can't be present to vote on appropriation bills.

On the Democratic side, the record holder in the IT&T Club is Charles Buckley, from the Bronx. Absent fully two-thirds of the time, he has been dubbed the "phantom congressman." Buckley's secretary has posted an advertisement in his office that she is a registered notary public ready to accept jobs. After all, the poor woman has to have something to do to occupy her time. She rarely sees Mr. Buckley.

In the ranks of the House are a number of able and conscientious men who, were they in a more auspicious setting, would do noteworthy and useful work. As it is, they struggle constantly to lift the House out of its chronic morass, and while they are not too successful, what worth-while work is accomplished is largely due to their efforts.

To these men, often unnoticed in the grandstanding and uproar, goes a brief salute:

ALABAMA: Carl Elliott, Robert Jones, and Albert Rains, a trio of able Democrats.

ARIZONA: John R. Murdock (Dem), a square shooter and hard worker.

ARKANSAS: Brooks Hays and James Trimble, both Democrats. Hays, a devout, serious-minded Baptist, would be liberal if he had been born in the North. As it is, he has risen far above the prejudices of the rural South that bred him. His approach to controversial issues such as civil rights is to pass the shadow and pray for the substance.

CALIFORNIA: Clyde Doyle, Franck Havenner, Chet Holifield, Cecil King, George Miller, John Shelley, and Cecil White, all Democrats. Holifield, forty-seven-year-old haberdasher, has been in Congress since 1942 and is one of the House's ablest liberals. Rugged, personable Jack Shelley, elected from San Francisco in a special election in 1949, hit the town at a dead run and has never stopped going. President of the State AFL, Shelley displays more political savvy and finesse than any three of his average colleagues put together. Slender, bespectacled Cecil White is a wealthy, self-made businessman and farmer. He is also one of the most sincere liberals in Washington. A man of quiet charm and intense moral earnestness, White is far above the House average. Franck Havenner of San Francisco, who was once secretary to Hiram Johnson, is a kindly, tenacious liberal who has taken it on the chin from both the Communists and the reactionaries and has always fought back with both fists.

COLORADO: John Carroll, Wayne Aspinall, and John Marsalis, all Democrats. Carroll is leaving the House to run for the Senate, where he would quickly restore the State's long-dormant fame for enlightened leadership.

GEORGIA: Henderson Lanham (Dem), a sixty-two-year-old lawyer who has been in the House since 1947 and has staunchly and courageously hewed to a liberal line.

ILLINOIS: "Runt" Bishop (Rep), and Democrats Chester Chesney, Thomas Gordon, Peter Mack, Thomas O'Brien, Barratt O'Hara, Mel Price, and Sidney Yates. Of this group, Barratt O'Hara, a fearless Chicago liberal and embattled foe of the real-estate lobby, and bald, stocky, vigorous Mel Price, the onetime sports writer from East St. Louis, are two especially useful members of the House.

INDIANA: Democrats Thurman Crook, John Walsh, Ray Madden, and Andy Jacobs. With the exception of Madden, all of these Hoosiers are freshmen, and they form one of the most promising "classes" in recent years. Jacobs is a bold, hard-hitting labor lawyer with the courage to stand up against anyone, including John L. Lewis.

IOWA: Paul Cunningham and H. R. Gross, both Republicans. Gross, a hard-hitting radio commentator and courageous young Turk from Waterloo, is far above the House Republican average.

KANSAS: Clifford Hope is one of the soundest and most constructive men on the Republican side, and the GOP brains on agricultural policy. If Hope did not have so much important seniority in the House, Kansas Republicans would do well to promote him to the Senate, where his talents would have greater scope.

KENTUCKY: Carl Perkins (Dem) and James Golden (Rep). The latter is a capable, middle-of-the-road Republican. Carl Perkins, a young lawyer, is a genuine liberal and a political comer.

LOUISIANA: Hale Boggs (Dem), elected to the House in 1940 at the age of twenty-six and re-elected in 1946 after wartime service in the Navy, is easily the outstanding member from the Deep South.

MASSACHUSETTS: Harold Donohue (Dem), Foster Furcolo (Dem), John Kennedy (Dem), Thomas Lane (Dem), and John Heselton (Rep). Donohue, a personable, hard-working, redheaded Irishman, has the distinction of being one of the few Democrats to defeat a Republican incumbent in 1946—the Democratic "year of sorrows." Foster Furcolo, an energetic young lawyer who worked his way through Yale washing dishes, and John Kennedy, the millionaire son of former Ambassador Joseph P. Kennedy, are two of the most attractive young men to emerge in New England politics in many years.

MICHIGAN: Louis Rabaut (Dem), John Dingell (Dem), and Albert Engel (Rep).

MINNESOTA: Roy Wier, Eugene McCarthy, Fred Marshall, and John Blatnik, all Democrats. Blatnik, a thirty-nine-year-old ex-schoolteacher, served as a major in the Army Air Corps and the OSS. He parachuted three times into Yugoslavia behind German lines to lead guerrilla fighting. Vigorous and fearless in political life as he was in battle, Blatnik deserves a long and outstanding public career.

MISSOURI: Richard Bolling, George Christopher, John Sullivan, and Frank Karsten, all Democrats.

MONTANA: Mike Mansfield, a dynamic and picturesque New Deal Democrat. Mansfield, in 1917, at the age of fourteen, ran away from home and joined the Navy. He served ten months overseas. Then, to round out his military experience, he served a one-year hitch in the Army and a two-year hitch in the Marines. As a Marine, he served in the Far East, and back in Montana he is still known as "China Mike."

After eight years in the Butte copper mines, Mansfield decided to go back to school, eventully got an M.A. degree, and taught Latin-American history for ten years before he came to Congress in 1943. He turned down the job of Assistant Secretary of State in 1950 in order to remain in active politics. Mike has what it takes: brains, guts, and charm.

NEBRASKA: Eugene D. O'Sullivan (Dem) and Karl Stefan (Rep). Stefan is a former city editor who speaks five foreign languages. Conservative in domestic affairs, Stefan is an informed student of foreign affairs and a hard-working member of the Appropriations Committee. O'Sullivan, sixty-seven, is a genial Irish lawyer and a courageous, stalwart liberal.

NEVADA: Walter Baring (Dem).

NEW JERSEY: Charles Howell (Dem), Clifford Case (Rep), Gordon Canfield (Rep), Peter Rodino (Dem), Hugh Addonizio (Dem), and Robert Kean (Rep). Clifford Case, forty-six-year-old lawyer, is a leader of the younger and more liberal Republicans in the House. Gordon Canfield, ex-newspaperman, was secretary to a congressman for seventeen years before he succeeded to the seat in 1940. Addonizio is a freshman from Newark who has compiled a very fine record, particularly in the housing field.

NEW YORK: John Davies (Dem), Isidore Dollinger (Dem), Chester Gorski (Dem), James Heffernan (Dem), Jacob Javits (Rep), Arthur Klein (Dem), Walter Lynch (Dem), Christopher McGrath (Dem), James Murphy (Dem), Donald O'Toole (Dem), Vincent Quinn (Dem), John Rooney (Dem), Franklin D. Roosevelt, Jr., (Dem), and Anthony Tauriello (Dem). New York, which has the largest delegation in the House, has traditionally sent some of the shoddiest and most mediocre members to Congress. On the Republican side, hard-working, capable Jack Javits is the only one who lives in the twentieth century. On the Democratic side, men like Dollinger, Klein, and Roosevelt show promise, but, on the whole, the Democratic machines are better at producing followers than leaders. Walter Lynch, a quiet, efficient, conscientious tax lawyer from New York City, is a valuable member of the House Ways and Means Committee and a pleasant exception to the rule.

NORTH CAROLINA: Charles Deane (Dem).

NORTH DAKOTA: Usher Burdick (Rep). A grizzled veteran of the once virile liberal Republican movement of the Midwest.

OHIO: Stephen Young (Dem), Walter Brehm (Rep), James Polk (Dem), Thomas Burke (Dem), Walter Huber (Dem), John Mc-Sweeney (Dem), Wayne Hays (Dem), Michael Feighan (Dem).

OKLAHOMA: Carl Albert and Tom Steed, both Democrats.

OREGON: Homer Angell, able, forward-looking Republican who would make a very creditable senator.

PENNSYLVANIA: William Barrett (Dem), Frank Buchanan (Dem), Anthony Cavalcante (Dem), Robert Corbett (Rep), Harry Davenport (Dem), Herman Eberharter (Dem), Daniel Flood (Dem), James Fulton (Rep), William Green (Dem), Augustine Kelley (Dem), James Lind (Dem), Thomas Morgan (Dem), Harry O'Neill (Dem), and George Rhodes (Dem).

SOUTH CAROLINA: Hugo Sims, a miraculously sincere and courageous Democrat who was elected to the House in 1948 at the age of twenty-seven. Sims voted against the overwhelming majority of his fellow Southerners in their attempt, in 1950, to repeal the Rules Committee reform adopted the preceding year. When he walked off the floor after casting his vote, Sims flashed his boyish smile and wisecracked, "Well, you won't see me here next year." He was right. In 1950, his district hugged its prejudices to its breast and voted him out of office.

TENNESSEE: James Frazier and Pat Sutton, both Democrats.

TEXAS: Wright Patman, J. M. Combs, Lindley Beckworth, John Lyle, Homer Thornberry, and Clark Thompson, all Democrats.

UTAH: Walter Granger (Dem).

VIRGINIA: Thomas Fugate (Dem).

WASHINGTON: Hugh Mitchell (Dem), Henry Jackson (Dem), and Thor Tollefson (Rep).

WEST VIRGINIA: Robert Ramsay, Harley Staggers, Cleveland Bailey, M. G. Burnside, Erland Hedrick, all Democrats.

WISCONSIN: Andrew Biemiller (Dem), Gardner Withrow (Rep), Clement Zablocki (Dem), and Merlin Hull (Rep). Biemiller, ex-history professor and labor organizer, is a dynamic liberal from Milwaukee. He stands so far above both the Republican senators from the State that it is an insult to compare them to him. One sure way Wisconsin can retrieve the shame of "Jumping Joe" McCarthy is to replace that blatherskite with a public servant of the stature, integrity, and responsibility of Andy Biemiller.

THE HIGHER PRIMATES

THE United States Senate is every politician's dream house.

Its membership is small enough to permit the ambitious to strut and get some attention for their efforts; its term is long enough to allow the mavericks to flaunt their independence, the demagogues and the arrogant to bulldoze, and the lazy to just plain doze, and all with comparative safety—at least for four years out of six. The patronage and prestige are magnificent.

Also, chances for re-election are usually good, and twelve or eighteen years is practically a lifetime on any politician's clock. The average senator, except when the President stays as long as Franklin Roosevelt, knows he will be around when the present occupant of the White House, cabinet officers, and other big shots in the "downtown" executive offices are gone. This consolation may be a fleeting one, but it gives a tingling glow to senatorial vanity.

With all these attractions, it must be set down to the vagaries of our political system that there are rarely more than a dozen first-rate men in the Senate. Perhaps, like the presidency a century ago, when Webster, Clay, and Calhoun contended in vain for the prize, senatorships are so eagerly sought by rival strong men that it is easier and less disruptive for the state machines to pass all of them over and unite on a mediocrity.

At least money is no longer the predominantly controlling explanation.

Fifty years ago, the Senate was less a democratic assembly than a millionaire's club. Today that is no longer true. Only eight senators fall within the golden circle of millionaires.

But, though the initiation fee is less, the Senate still acts in many other ways as America's most exclusive club. Its traditions are rigidly cherished.

One of these is the right to unlimited debate. The Senate is the last stronghold of thunderous but formal debate, of the freewheeling orator and the unabashed ham. Many liberals gnash their teeth in fury at the Southern civil rights filibusters. Certainly no one quite enjoys a grandstanding filibuster as much as the gentlemen with the well-oiled larynxes from south of the Mason-Dixon line. But many liberals recall darker days when senatorial free and unlimited speech was the only obstacle to a particularly outrageous boodle bill or reactionary coup. Unlimited debate is in loving hands in the Senate.

Even trivial holdovers from the past are retained simply because they emphasize, supposedly, the Senate's strong links with the weighty wisdom and more dignified traditions of ancient times.

Thus, in the pre-Civil War era, senators chewed snuff, and each had a small snuff box on his desk in the chamber. Similarly, the statesmen of yore were accustomed to punctuate their oratory with lusty spats of tobacco juice into a convenient spittoon. The snuff chewers and the tobacco spitters have long since departed to their eternal reward (or punishment), but the Senate clings tenaciously to their heirlooms. The spittoons are kept bright and shiny, and two unused snuff boxes are filled regularly.

But reverence for age is momentous in the Senate in other and more pernicious ways. There is increasingly, today, talk of what to do with the aged when they retire. That is no problem for United States Senators. They don't retire.

Old men and old ideas have an unshakable grip on the topmost places of power and prestige in the Senate.

The escalator called the "seniority system" is the vehicle which slowly and inexorably draws these old men, able or inept, ambitious or torpid, awake or asleep, to the top and keeps them there. Once a committee chairman, always a committee chairman; that is the rule of the Senate. Only death or defeat at the polls—often about the same thing to an aged senator—can cause a reshuffle.

As a result, only three of the fifteen chairmen of the permanent committees are "youngsters" under sixty. The average age is sixty-six. These chairmen and their ages in 1950 were as follows:

Elmer Thomas, Agriculture, 73; Kenneth McKellar, Appropriations, 81; Millard Tydings, Armed Services, 60; Burnet Maybank, Banking and Currency, 51; Matthew Neely, District of Columbia, 74; John McClellan, Expenditures, 54; Walter George, Finance, 72; Tom Connally, Foreign Relations, 74; Joseph O'Mahoney, Interior, 66; Edwin Johnson, Interstate and Foreign Commerce, 66; Pat McCarran, Judiciary, 74; Elbert Thomas, Labor and Public Welfare, 67; Olin Johnston, Post Office, 53; Dennis Chavez, Public Works, 62; and Carl Hayden, Rules and Administration, 73.

A switch to Republican control would make no change. Veterans like sixty-one-year-old Robert Taft and sixty-six-year-old Arthur Vandenberg would succeed their opposite oldster numbers on the Democratic side.

Contrary to the scurrilous rumor started by one frustrated, 50-year-old freshman, the Senate Rules Book is really not subtitled "Life Begins at Sixty-five."

Former Senator Robert M. La Follette, Jr., made a valiant attempt to thin out the mental and physical debris with a comprehensive congressional reorganization bill in 1946. Its core was a provision to limit the tenure of chairmen to six consecutive years. At the end of that time, they would have to yield to the next ranking member.

The anguished screams of outrage that rent the air were so terrifying that this part of the bill had to be knocked out.

After much retching, groaning, and grumbling, Congress finally did pass a reorganization measure. Its chief features were a reduction in the number of committees and the creation of the job of administrative assistant. La Follette spent months pleading and toiling to get this bill through. He thought it so important that he neglected his primary campaign, and Wisconsin voters, in a temporary fit of moral delinquency, rejected him and substituted "Jumping Joe" McCarthy in his place.

The subsequent history of both McCarthy and the Reorganization Act have proved that La Follette made a grievous error of judgment. One good man is worth a dozen reorganization schemes.

Much emphasis was placed on the newly created post of administrative assistant. This office was to be in addition to, rather than a substitute for, that of the senatorial secretary. It carries a stipend of

$10,000 a year, and it was hoped this would attract mature men of wide experience who would take administrative and research duties off the shoulders of senators and give them time to think, insofar as certain of them were capable of that process.

But in the Eightieth Congress, the first to operate under the plan, some eighty-five senators hired administrative assistants, and a spot check revealed that fifty-nine were merely their old secretaries adorned with a prettier title and a fatter pay envelope.

Some senators, like Arthur Vandenberg and Walter George, gave their sons the job. The lofty concept of the "assistant senator" who could do everything but vote appeared to be lost in the grab bag.

Even proponents betrayed the plan. Joseph Ball, Republican of Minnesota and very soon to become ex-Senator Ball, had been one of La Follette's staunchest supporters. When the question was being debated, he told the Senate, "I intend to pick out a young man, just out of law school, start him out at a lower salary, and hold out to him the prospect that, if he delivers the goods, he will receive an advancement in salary."

That was on August 1. In January, Senator Ball appointed his wife to the $10,000 job as administrative assistant.

In the Democratic Eighty-first Congress, there has been a little improvement—thanks to a few outstanding newcomers. Illinois' Paul Douglas employed Robert Wallace, brilliant young University of Chicago Ph.D., as legislative assistant. Senator William Benton of Connecticut selected Laurance Henderson, expert on housing, as his assistant. Henderson was not only *not* a Connecticut man but he had up to that time been working on the staff of Republican Senator Ralph Flanders of Vermont.

Some of the old patronage grabbers in the Senate have never recovered from the shock of this heretical act.

New York's Senator Herbert Lehman went the Reorganization Act one better. He not only employed all the government-paid assistants and clerks he was entitled to, but out of his own pocket recruited an even larger staff and rented a whole floor of a neighboring hotel to give them office space. With the aid of this "little cabinet," Lehman is prepared with up-to-the-minute information on every local and national issue, whether it be barge traffic on Long Island Sound or the Chinese minority in Indonesia.

Few senators, of course, have Lehman's wealth to finance such an organization. But many of them do not have the brains to make the most efficient use of the staff the government does supply them. They impede their own work by using office jobs as plums for hacks and political hangers-on.

Another feature of the reorganization plan was the expansion of the technical staffs of committees. These jobs have in a sense been corrupted into patronage boodle, but this was largely inevitable, since no man can serve two masters.

Staff people can't be just information gatherers; when one of them, for example, is doing delicate liaison work between the departments downtown and a Democratic chairman, in connection with a bill the administration is pushing, he inevitably learns secrets he cannot "objectively" and "impartially" divulge to the Republican minority. Unless he is an emotional eunuch, he sooner or later—and usually sooner—becomes a partisan for or against the bill.

But, once these political realities are recognized, it is still possible for an energetic staff to be enormously helpful in keeping the legislative mill turning.

The Senate Foreign Relations Committee is ably staffed. Both Representative Brent Spence in the House and Burnet Maybank in the Senate have organized high-grade staffs for their respective Banking and Currency Committees. These bodies handle all housing legislation, and much of the credit for the fact that housing bills were the chief legislative accomplishment of the Fair Deal in 1949-50 must be attributed to the effective work of these anonymous staff men.

On the other hand, Senator Pat McCarran turned the Judiciary Committee setup into a patronage pigsty, crawling with hatchet men and incompetents.

At least on one occasion, an anonymous staff member played a decisive role. During the lengthy Senate debate on the original Marshall Plan bill, Senator Olin Johnston of South Carolina announced he would probably vote for the measure, but with little enthusiasm. He told his administrative assistant, "Prepare a speech putting me on record for the bill, but reluctantly so. A lot of folks back home are against it. So when you write the speech, make it favorable, but in the windup put in some good arguments against it. That's to show I have considered all the pros and cons and whys and wherefores."

The speech was written according to instructions. But when the vote came, Johnston voted against the Marshall Plan. The administrative assistant, baffled, asked, "Didn't you give the speech, Senator?"

"I sure did."

"But the speech was for ERP, and you voted against it."

"I know," replied Johnston. "But when I was reading the speech into the *Record* and came to the part listing the reasons for opposing the plan, I was very much impressed. You know, your arguments against the plan were so good, I couldn't help but go along with them. So I voted no."

The incident is also unique in another respect. It is the first objective evidence we have that senators listen to their own speeches.

The Senate chamber is neatly divided into two sections by the center aisle that runs between the tiered rows of small school desks. The Vice-President sits on a rectangular dais at the front of the room. Below him are arrayed the parliamentarian and a quartet of clerks. At the front desks on either side of the aisle sit the Majority and Minority Floor Leaders and their Party Whips. On the left are the Republican members; on the right, the Democrats.

To the visitor in the gallery, it would seem that the Senate is made up of two parties, with the physical separation of the center aisle serving as a symbol of the ideological and political gulf between them.

Never were appearances so deceptive.

The Senate is ruled by a conservative coalition which closes ranks and votes as a unit on every vital question.

It is a coalition indifferent to party labels, party platforms, and party candidates, in or out of the White House. Economic interests and intellectual conservatism transcend the make-believe of political conflict.

For any major issue, the Republican side can furnish this bloc with a solid phalanx of thirty-five votes. The Southern Democrats can marshal fifteen. Together they make up a clear and unbeatable majority of fifty. (Often they can pick up from six to a dozen votes from the jelly-boned, "sixty-per-cent Democrats.")

Since 1938, this hybrid offspring has squatted squarely athwart the legislative road and blocked the passage of all constructive domestic legislation. Only in the emergency area of housing did it give way, and even there it stalled for five long years.

This union between Northern Republicans and Southern Dixiecrats has not been solemnized in any official manner; there are no formal conferences or open fraternizing. It is a common-law marriage based on mutual interests and convenience. In front of naïve, respectable people such as voters, the partners give no hint of recognition, betray none of their connubial intimacy.

Early in 1950, "Honest John" Bricker, Ohio's Mr. Throttlebottom, made a couple of speeches to his brethren, saying in effect, "Aw, come on, fellas. Let's get right with God and make it legal. Everyone knows we sleep with the Dixiecrats. Why not admit it?"

This righteous plea was received with an icy calm which could not have been more profound if he had slurped his soup in polite society. Nothing more was heard of the subject.

It is commonly believed that it is the heavy chain of civil rights for the Negro which holds the Republicans and the Dixiecrats together; that the Northerners keep their Southern allies in line on other bills by the threat to vote for civil rights should they misbehave. That is largely untrue.

It ignores the real nature of the Dixiecrat bosses. They are men like Walter George and Richard Russell of Georgia, Harry Byrd of Virginia, and Spessard Holland of Florida. None of these men is a "nigger"-baiter; none is a hero to the wool-hat boys of the arid hills and the pine barrens. They are smartly tailored, sleekly groomed lawyers and businessmen, indistinguishable from their Northern counterparts. Negro or no Negro, they would be Bourbons.

The fact that the steel mills and banks and power companies they speak for happen to be in Texas and Georgia rather than in Pennsylvania or Ohio is only an accident of geography. The color of their flag is green on green, not white on black.

Nor do the Republicans vote against civil rights legislation as part of a cynical Machiavellian deal. They are not following an astute stratagem. They are voting a state of mind.

Narrow and complacent, they are satisfied with the *status quo*—

after all, it put them where they are, so it must be pretty good, don't you think? Also, they are profoundly committed to the sharp, competitive, dog-eat-dog values of the everyday business world. They don't want any legislation hampering business, and they instinctively vote against FEPC bills, just as they opposed stock-market regulation, wartime price controls, or antitrust laws. The business of America is business, and what is good for business is good for everybody, or at least it will be if those at the bottom will be patient and wait for the benefits to dribble down.

As for human misery and injustice: their social conscience extends only to the giving of a hundred dollars a year to the Community Chest . . . and then, back to work!

There is no doubt, of course, that respectable Southern conservatives like George and Byrd consciously support the racial issue as a means of distracting attention from the real economic controversies and as a blind to hold off unionism. It is also true that much of the lowered moral tone and bad morale of Northern conservatism is due to its being a beneficiary of racial hatreds and antagonisms through this silent political alliance with the Dixiecrats. But these effects of the Negro issue are only secondary by-products. The fact remains that the Republican-Dixiecrat alliance is a natural one.

The real reason Bricker's proposal for a shotgun wedding fell flat was that no preacher will marry a pair of blood brothers.

The Senate in the last twenty years has witnessed a slow but transcendently important revolution. To understand its significance, it is necessary to recall what the political make-up of the chamber was when the Democrats took control in 1931.

The party was completely dominated by a group of able, conservative, Southern politicians led by Joe Robinson of Arkansas, Pat Harrison of Mississippi, and John Bankhead of Alabama. The Republican Party was largely in the grip of an Eastern faction whose ideas and methods dated from the Harrison-McKinley era. The leaders of this faction were such men as Hiram Bingham of Connecticut, David Reed of Pennsylvania, George Moses of New Hampshire, and Jim Watson of Indiana, plus, of course, their stalwart colleague from the Far West, Reed Smoot of Utah and the Mormon Church.

Battling these apostles of high tariffs and old-fashioned Republicanism were a corporal's guard of maverick Republicans from the trans-Mississippi West. The terms "farm bloc" and "sons of the wild jackass" were used interchangeably to describe them.

This was inaccurate, for the farm bloc was actually a larger group which numbered various Midwesterners such as Arthur Capper of Kansas, who always lined up behind farm-relief bills but who otherwise lapsed back into GOP orthodoxy. The true insurgents, as opposed to the foul-weather radicals, were the sons of the wild jackass. At best they never numbered more than ten or a dozen men. But what men they were:

George Norris of Nebraska, Robert M. La Follette of Wisconsin, William E. Borah of Idaho, and Hiram Johnson of California were among the ablest, most indefatigable, resourceful, and genuinely distinguished men who ever sat in the upper chamber. Joining these hardy insurgents were a pair of dissident Democrats, Tom Walsh and Burton Wheeler of Montana.

These Westerners were the brains and guts and fighting heart of the liberal movement of the 1920's and early '30's. They fought not only for the immediate local interests of their farm constituencies. They were on the firing line for public power (Norris and TVA, Walsh and the 1928 power-lobby exposé), for unorganized labor (the Norris-La Guardia Anti-Injunction Act of 1932), for protection of our natural resources (Walsh and the Teapot Dome oil scandal), for honest elections (Norris almost singlehanded prevented William Vare from assuming the senatorial seat he had bought in a fraudulent Pennsylvania election), and against lush tariff grabs (Borah's fight against the Smoot-Hawley Tariff).

Where are these men or their successors today?

They have vanished. From Wisconsin to California, in the whole expanse of the Midwest and the Far West, there is only one progressive Republican senator. Worse than that, there are very few political figures of real moral and intellectual stature in the GOP.

The simple fact is that the heart has gone out of the Republican Party.

There are several reasons for the disintegration of the progressive Republican tradition. One was the foreign-policy issue. It was a sword which cut both ways.

Men like Norris, whose thinking on foreign affairs kept abreast of the times, were punished by their own people, as the Germans of Nebraska punished him in 1942. Lesser men such as Nye and Shipstead, who refused to change, had their vision warped and their hearts poisoned by their long sojourn down what proved to be the dead-end street of isolationism. Many a good Midwestern liberal was killed by the lethal embrace of the America First Committee.

Another factor was the dwindling flame of personal ardor and perseverance. By 1946, Henrik Shipstead and young Bob La Follette were two such tired liberals.

But the fundamental reason lies in the changing nature of the Midwest.

The farm states have become fat, prosperous, and successful. The railroads and the power trust and the grain-elevator companies have become senile, toothless dragons.

Nebraska is now a hundred-per-cent public-power State. The grip of the warehousemen and the grain-elevator operators has been broken, in large part, by the growth of cooperatives. The terrors of droughts and crushing surpluses have been lulled by the government price-support system. Good roads and local airports have banished social isolation and thereby drained off one potent source of psychological discontent in the farm areas.

In many families in Iowa and Kansas and North Dakota, it is not a question of who shall have the family Ford, but whether Junior should have a Piper Cub plane in addition to his Chrysler convertible.

The farm bloc has "arrived." It is one of the powerful interests in the established *status quo,* right up there if not ahead of the oil barons and the Pennsylvania Manufacturers Association.

That is why Norris has been replaced by a brassy tractor salesman named Kenneth Wherry, La Follette by "Jumping Joe" McCarthy, Borah by Dworshak, and Hiram Johnson by Knowland; and also why it is that Iowa's most distinguished contribution to the vernacular of the Truman merry-go-round is the phrase "to pull a Hickenlooper."

With the lone exception of Oregon's Wayne Morse, the Republican liberals, few as they are, come from the East—once the lair of the blackest reactionaries. This is because the only kind of Republicans who can get elected in the heavily industrialized and heavily unionized areas are men who are at least aware of, and sensitive to, current social issues.

Meanwhile, a parallel revolution has been proceeding on the Democratic side of the aisle. The Northern wing of the party has been steadily strengthened until it is now in a slight but nonetheless real preponderance. The subtle shift in the balance of power was symbolized in 1949 when Scott Lucas of Illinois became Floor Leader. Lucas was the first Northern Democrat elected to the floor leadership in the twentieth century.

This change has deeper roots than such immediate causes as the impact of the depression, the rise of trade unions, and Franklin Roosevelt's personal leadership. It also represents the political coming of age of those millions of immigrants who came to America in the period from the 1880's to the opening of the first World War.

The Democratic Party is traditionally the party of what the politicians somewhat patronizingly call the "newer races." At first, these immigrant poor swarmed into the slum tenements of the big cities and gave mighty strength to the urban machines in New York and Jersey City and Chicago and Boston. But they persevered and multiplied, and in the past twenty years they have come into their own.

States such as Rhode Island, Massachusetts, and New York have been changed from Republican to Democratic strongholds. Young politicians have surged to the fore with liberal slogans on their tongues, if not liberal ideas always in their heads.

Robert F. Wagner of New York, elected to the Senate in 1926, was the forerunner of this revolution. Like his friend Al Smith, Wagner started as an errand boy to the Tammany bosses and rose to levels of genuine statesmanship. Brien McMahon of Connecticut, Francis Myers of Pennsylvania, and others have followed in his wake. They are a better breed than the henchmen that the city machines sent to the Senate in the old days, on the rare occasions when that opportunity came to them.

Having a keener feel of the issues, these men make better politicians, too. One of the old-timers who rode to Washington during an early Roosevelt tidal wave was notorious for his ceaseless clamor for WPA patronage. When remonstrated with, he replied, "Boodle got me here and boodle is going to keep me here." It didn't.

THE INNER CIRCLE

Scott Lucas is a man who painfully knows the price of ambition.

Driven by an insatiable desire for power and self-importance, he daily goes through the gestures of being a liberal and the spokesman for a Fair Deal administration. It is his duty, as Democratic leader of the Senate. And he has to be Floor Leader, otherwise he will not be a member of the inner circle and appear to be an important figure.

But doing his duty has ruined his digestion and disposition. It has given him ulcers and forced him to drink milk when he would much rather be drinking Scotch; and it has soured his affable temper and made him cranky and irritable. For Lucas, you see, is no more a Fair Dealer than he was a New Dealer—and that was not at all.

Lucas comes from downstate Illinois where most people, except for some unconverted Southerners, are Republicans. For reasons known only to Lucas and to God, he became a Democrat. Except for one term as district attorney, being a Democrat did not prove to be very profitable or rewarding. So Lucas spent much of his time building up a following in the third party of American politics, the veterans' organizations.

In 1926, he was elected State Commander of the American Legion. The next year he was chosen judge advocate of the national organization. He was consistently renamed to this post, but each year the Legion kingmakers passed him over when it came to national commander. This was Lucas's first great frustration. What, he kept asking friends, has Paul McNutt (who made the grade as national commander) got that I haven't got?

As a matter of fact, that is a hard question to answer.

In a general way, they look much alike. Like McNutt, Lucas has the sharp, clean-cut profile and tanned skin of a country-club Romeo. A broad-shouldered six-footer, he dresses fashionably in double-breasted suits with wide, flaring lapels, and walks with the erect carriage and confident stride of a man who knows where he's going. His brown hair is touched with silver. Under Klieg lights, it goes beautifully with his glittering smile and vigorous gestures.

But what Lucas lacks is not beauty but charm.

Whereas McNutt could butter people up quicker than a popcorn machine, Lucas is a dud at that. He is quick-tempered and irascible. Essentially, he is a cold person who is not interested in others or in their points of view.

Successful politicians have to have an earthy quality—a certain durability which allows them to sit for hours listening to and participating in boring or frustrating or irritating dickering and palaver. As one veteran politico remarked after returning from an exhausting week end of conferences in his home state, "I feel like a fish in the fish market covered with flies." Lucas's trouble is he just doesn't like flies.

Lucas finally received his reward in the 1930's when the Roosevelt landslides began.

One of them carried him to the House and another one re-elected him. In 1938, with the connivance of the Kelly-Nash machine in Chicago, he grabbed off the senatorial nomination from a hapless incumbent named Dieterich and squeezed into office. Six years later, the last of the Roosevelt sweeps carried him through again.

Like his luckier colleague from Missouri, Harry Truman, Lucas hustled after patronage for the machine and voted, at least on final passage, for most of the New Deal bills. He did what he was told by Roosevelt and Kelly. Regularity was his virtue. Enthusiasm was not required.

Before rising to Majority Leader in 1949, Lucas was mostly distinguished for his middle-aged good looks and his fair talents as an old-line party orator. These remain his chief qualifications.

As an intellectual, he has been rated as "ten pounds lighter than a Panama hat." As a parliamentary tactician, he is inept. As a cloakroom wirepuller, he will never endanger the laurels of Jimmy Byrnes or Alben Barkley. On the floor, he vacillates between toughness and timidity, blowing now hot and then cold.

But it is as a liberal champion that Lucas's difficulties really begin to mount. Truman owes his election and Lucas his floor leadership to the Democratic Party's stand on three issues in 1948: Taft-Hartley repeal, farm aid, and civil rights. But Lucas is secretly not in sympathy with the administration's official position on any of these questions.

He has always been cool to organized labor. In 1946, he voted for the drastic Case bill, the predecessor to Taft-Hartley which was killed only when the House upheld Truman's veto. After the Republican triumph in 1946, Lucas came out for a "crackdown" on unions. Only his last-minute about-face on Taft-Hartley the following year makes him at all palatable to the unions.

On the controversial Brannan Plan, Lucas has consistently bucked Truman and taken a straight Farm Bureau Federation position. In the summer of 1949, moreover, he served on the conference committee on the farm bill and worked hand in glove with New Mexico's Clinton Anderson in a partially successful attempt to juggle the parity price system arbitrarily and short-circuit the administration. As for civil rights legislation, Lucas privately looks askance on all of it. Only the potent vote of the Chicago "black belt" keeps him even nominally in line.

Truman has remonstrated several times with Lucas for his failures and bungling.

The President well knows that the 1949 Housing Act, the main legislative achievement of the first session of the Eighty-first Congress, was driven through by Acting Leader Francis Myers of Pennsylvania, a capable and conscientious liberal. Truman tells confidants that he considers Lucas too weak, conservative, and slow-witted to be an effective Floor Leader and would like to ditch him. Lucas takes these open and covert criticisms with bad grace.

In part, he feels that Truman is just the pot calling the kettle black, since the President surrounds himself with a staff of muddlers who are of little assistance in the legislative arena.

Thus Lucas perseveres alone, chewing his tablets and drinking his milk and trying to spoon-feed the Senate with a shaky hand and a bent spoon.

Alben Barkley has performed one of the neatest tricks of the twentieth century.

He has played the role of Romeo at seventy-one to his thirty-eight-year-old lady love, kissed hundreds of babies, beauty queens, and Girl Scouts, and been the jovial funnyman at everybody's laugh fest in and out of Washington. Yet, at the same time, he has never raised a doubt in anyone's mind as to his complete capability to take over the biggest job in the world on a moment's notice and fill it creditably.

The key that unlocks the contradiction is sincerity.

Alben Barkley is not playing a role. He enjoys meeting people, shaking hands, kissing babies of all ages, and saying kind or amusing things to make his listeners laugh. He would do it even if they had no votes, or if he were not running for office. He is gregariousness in person.

As a politician, Barkley has made the Democratic Party his religion. He sincerely and uncritically believes that it is the only true vehicle of the people's wishes. He doesn't go in for any of this intellectual nonsense about wishing the Republican Party were stronger so that the two-party system would work better. Barkley wants to bring everyone within his heavenly fold.

He has personal ambitions, but he is not warped or hag-ridden with them. One reason for this jovial freedom from rancor and bad nerves is that he has had a remarkably smooth and successful career.

At twenty-eight, four years after he passed the bar examinations, Barkley was elected prosecuting attorney. He has never been out of public office in the forty-five years since then.

After four years as county attorney and five as local judge, he was elected to the House in 1912. Here he served six consecutive terms before going to the Senate, to which he was elected four times prior to becoming Vice-President. Barkley has come as close as any politician can to enjoying civil service tenure. Nothing can take credit from the intrinsic warmth of his personality, but many colleagues from more erratic constituencies envy Barkley his secure position.

He is the travelingest Vice-President America has ever had. The following is a list of his engagements during one brief period in the summer of 1949:

> On June 21, delivered commencement address at Miami University in Oxford, Ohio. This, incidentally, was his twelfth stint of the commencement season, and each address was on a different topic.

> On June 25, addressed the Jefferson-Jackson Day dinner in St. Louis.

> June 26, flew to Los Angeles, where he was the chief speaker at dinner meeting of United Jewish Appeal.

On July 1, turned up on the other side of the country as main speaker at the Jefferson-Jackson Day dinner in Columbus, South Carolina.

Next flew to Piggott, Arkansas, where, on July 4, he was principal speaker at the Leslie Biffle Day ceremonies honoring the Senate Secretary.

Returned to Washington for few days and then, on July 15, traveled to his home town, Paducah, Kentucky, where he delivered a speech at the West Kentucky Fair.

On July 23, arrived in Minneapolis, to be Grand Marshal at Aquatennial celebration.

Next day flew to St. Louis, where he lunched with the future Mrs. Barkley and got in some fast courting.

Then returned to Washington, and on July 27 flew to Chicago to address annual banquet of National Association of Credit Jewelers.

Next day flew to Culpeper, Virginia, and crowned and kissed queen of the 200th anniversary celebration and made a "few brief remarks."

Barkley, incidentally, is the man the Truman forces did not want for Vice-President because "he is too old."

Barkley had a unique training for this arduous career. His first wife died a slow, lingering death, and the bills for medical care reached a large figure. To supplement his senatorial salary, Barkley worked in the lecture industry at $750-$1,000 a night. He was extremely popular on the lecture circuits and had all the engagements he could fill. Now that he is freed of this personal burden and his salary, as Vice-President, is $30,000 (which is taxable) plus a tax-free expense allowance of $10,000, he usually declines "honorariums."

Barkley is more than merely one of the principal salesmen of the Fair Deal. He also plays a highly important role in behind-the-scenes maneuvering in the Senate. In fact, he sees the President more, and can influence legislative policy-making more regularly and effectively, than he did when he was Democratic Floor Leader.

After the first year of the Truman administration, relations between the White House and its nominal legislative lieutenants on Capitol Hill deteriorated steadily. During the last twelve months of Truman's first term, Truman all but ceased his weekly conferences with the Democratic "Big Four" of the House and Senate. When they were held, nothing but political gossip and banalities were exchanged. Each side privately felt the other was to blame for the dreary failures the administration was suffering on all fronts, and a mood of silent recrimination hung over the meetings. The smashing 1948 victory cleared the air and restored working efficiency. Barkley no longer has to play by ear and wait uneasily for dissonant echoes from the vicinity of the White House.

Barkley spends much of his time backstopping Truman's wild pitches and Lucas's passed balls. He has an especially strong, triple-thick chest protector to aid him in his work.

He is not only the party's most dependable and venerable wheel horse and work horse, who has served as permanent chairman of one Democratic National Convention and keynoter for three others, but he is also a pretty good liberal. His support for the Roosevelt and Truman programs stems from no coherent intellectual convictions of his own but rather from a strong sense of party tradition and from a warmhearted sympathy and vicarious kinship with "ordinary folks."

Only once did Barkley revolt against White House leadership. In 1944, he huffily resigned the leadership and delivered a stinging speech against Roosevelt's tax-bill veto. At that time, such a veto was unprecedented, although Truman later vetoed three tax bills passed by the Republican Eightieth Congress.

Barkley's insurgency, it is significant to note, came not on a broad positive issue but on a question of strategy. He felt that the tax bill, though it did indeed favor "the greedy not the needy," was the best that could be wheedled out of the Republican-Dixiecrat coalition which writes all tax legislation. The veto, he felt, merely exacerbated an already raw situation and made his work harder. Once Roosevelt capitulated in one of his famous "Dear Alben" letters, Barkley's injured feelings were assuaged and he returned to the fold without rancor.

But Barkley's most effective weapon, surpassing even his long party service, his liberal inclinations, and his legislative savvy, is his genial wit. His delightful sense of humor has lowered many an overwrought senatorial temper. At the same time, it serves as a buffer during difficult or boring situations.

For example, during the five hours that Truman and Barkley stood throughout the inaugural parade, the gentleman from Paducah steadily regaled the President with merry stories. Later, Barkley was asked what they talked about.

"It was," he said, "presidential and vice-presidential stuff and of no possible interest to anybody else."

When his colleagues pressed him, he told the story of the old maid who went to the zoo:

"She paused in front of the hippopotamus cage and asked the keeper, 'What kind of animal is that?'

" 'That's a hippopotamus, Madam,' he said.

" 'Is it male or female?' asked the lady.

" 'That, Madam,' said the keeper, 'couldn't possibly interest anyone but another hippopotamus.' "

The third member of the Democratic inner circle is a man who, like Barkley, has no vote there, and who holds a traditionally unimportant clerical job. Yet this man is a key senatorial figure, a prince of wirepullers, an intimate of the President, the maker of the Vice-President, and the crony, adviser, and drinking companion of senators, lobbyists, Supreme Court Justices, socialites, cabinet members, columnists, brass hats, diplomats, and various other Washington species.

The hero of this shining success story is Leslie L. Biffle.

Les Biffle (the "L" in his name is like the "S" in Harry S. Truman and stands for nothing) is Secretary of the Senate. As such, he is, in effect, the chief clerk of the Senate. Like most other congressional jobs, it is a patronage plum. Incumbency shifts with the tides of politics. The majority party controls the job.

Outside of congressional circles, "Leslie the Biff" was virtually unknown when he became Secretary of the Senate. But he has been a congressional employee for forty years.

Small-statured, wiry, and dapper, Biff is the son of the country store owner in tiny Boydsville (pop. 889), Arkansas. He got his start as the $1,200 secretary of the representative from his home district. Later, Biff shifted to the Senate, where patronage is generally of longer tenure. Through the years, as a result of deaths and other attrition, he slowly rose up the patronage escalator as one of the anonymous group of congressional employees. In February, 1945, after being chief of the folding room of the Senate mail department and twelve years on the sergeant-at-arms staff as Secretary of the Democratic Majority, Biff reached his present pinnacle, following the death of the incumbent.

Biff's present job pays him $12,000 plus a Cadillac and chauffeur. Previously, he never earned more than $7,000 a year. Yet he and his equally charming wife have for several years set a terrific social pace.

They live in a swank apartment house and are members of a number of clubs, including the very ritzy Burning Tree. Biff frequently tosses expensive buffet luncheons and every year distributes cases of "Biffle's Tomato Juice" to scores of friends as Christmas mementos. That sort of tempo costs money in Washington, which has the most expensive living costs in the country. Until their 1949 pay raise, it was a common plaint of cabinet officers and other top figures that they were unable to make ends meet on their salaries. Some went into debt, yet few of them lived on Biffle's scale.

Friends have an explanation for his opulence. They attribute it to shrewd real-estate investments. That is possible. The Capital doubled in size during the 1940's, and handsome fortunes were made in real estate. Through his many political and social contacts, Biffle could well have been advised on smart buys that paid off handsomely—under the capital-gains tax.

In any event, he is obviously well heeled enough to be right up there in the social whirl. His name and picture are fixtures in Washington society columns. It is rare when the name Biffle does not figure prominently on the leading guest lists, often ahead of his nominal bosses, the U.S. senators. Society reporters know their political onions, even if the smell sometimes does not square exactly with the perfumed aroma of orthodox official precedence.

In the press gallery, where Biff is viewed with a mixture of cynical friendliness and indulgent amazement, he is sometimes referred to as the "Perle Mesta of Capitol Hill."

The basis for this frothy bubble of social activity and political prestige is Biffle's chance friendship with Harry Truman.

One of the functions of a Majority Secretary is to steer and counsel freshmen senators. Truman was a particularly shy and hesitant freshman. The mild little Missourian and the soft-spoken little Arkansan took to each other from the start. Both were background figures, had a lot in common in origin and traits, and a cozy friendship developed between them.

Since Truman became President, Biff's friends have told stories about how influential he has been at various stages of Truman's career. Biffle is credited with selecting Truman to head the War Investigating Committee in 1941 and with engineering Truman's nomination as Vice-President in 1944. These and most of the other stories are apocryphal, but the President and Biff have been close enough to give a semblance of truth to the rumors.

The President never fails to drop into Biff's office when he visits on Capitol Hill. And on occasion he has used him for quiet political chores. But the most important fact of all is that canny Biff knows a good thing when he sees it, particularly when it is the President of the United States. Biff has been discreet and adroit about it, but he has played that bull market for all it is worth.

On one notable occasion, he used it to put over a coup on his good friend the President himself.

It occurred at the 1948 convention. After Truman failed to persuade Supreme Court Justice William O. Douglas to take the vice-presidential nomination, Truman telephoned former National Chairmen Frank Walker, Bob Hannegan, and Ed Flynn and asked them to dig up a running mate. Their choice was Wilson Wyatt, former mayor of Louisville and postwar Housing Expeditor. Young, liberal, and from a border state, Wyatt, in the opinion of the three veteran leaders, would be a help to the ticket. Truman agreed—although, the year before, he had allowed Wyatt to quit in disgust.

Secretly, Walker, Hannegan, and Flynn went to work for Wyatt. But while they were busy behind the scenes, Biffle deftly short-circuited them and the President. Biff planted a press story that Alben Barkley was Truman's choice.

The horde of reporters fell for the plant, hook, line, and sinker. The convention had been a wake for newsmen. For days they had been rehashing the same dull stories. Biffle's "inside tip" was the first hot news to come out of the convention, and the bored reporters leaped on it.

Truman awakened the next morning to find the story splashed across the front pages in boxcar headlines. It was a distressing situation. He did not want Barkley, thought him too old, and personally felt lukewarm toward him. Moreover, he had quietly agreed on Wyatt.

But, there it was, in roaring type, that Barkley was his choice. Pal Biffle had done a masterful job. Regardless of Truman's feelings, he couldn't repudiate the story publicly or privately.

Barkley would have been mortally offended and might have thrown his weight against Truman. The President's hold on the convention was too precarious to hazard that. In fact, when he didn't immediately confirm the Barkley story, Southern leaders who were privy to its origin began to talk up Barkley as a substitute for Truman. That threw a real scare into the President.

So he grimly swallowed his chagrin and bowed to the coup his good friend Biff had put over.

Biffle's primary motivation in this extraordinary affair was simple. He was taking care of himself—first. Truman was his friend, but Barkley was his boss.

Being a crony of the President of the United States has its advantages and favors. But Presidents come and go, and in July, 1948, it looked as if Truman were definitely on the go. The Senate, on the other hand, is Biffle's meal ticket. Barkley was Democratic Floor Leader. His patronage had made it possible for Biffle to become Secretary of the Senate. Whatever happened in the campaign, Barkley was sure to remain potently in the Senate picture, either as Democratic leader or as Vice-President. Biff couldn't lose.

Whatever Truman's irritation at Biffle may have been, it vanished in the elation of being re-elected. Victory wiped out past scores, just as it had between Truman and Barkley, and Biff's stock soared sky-high.

There is considerable suspicion that, like certain other kinds of stock, Biffle's is watered. More than one job seeker has discovered that Biff promises more than he will (or can) deliver. An example is the case of former Representative Richard F. Harless of Arizona.

Casting about for a lame-duck job, he decided he would like to be Ambassador to Mexico. Harless talked to Biffle. "We'll take care of it," was the reassuring reply. Harless departed under the impression the "we" meant Biff and his pal Truman. But weeks passed and nothing happened. Finally, Senator Carl Hayden, Arizona's grand old man, took the matter up with the President. It was all news to him. Biffle had not mentioned Harless.

Another instance was a Republican vacancy on the Federal Trade Commission. Biffle managed to give the impression to three different aspirants that he was going to go to bat on their behalf. He didn't lift a finger for any of them.

The similarity of Biff's breezy absent-mindedness in these and similar instances indicates that it was not a coincidence. Whatever else he is, Biff is not fuzzy-minded. One of his proud professional claims is that he is an ambulatory encyclopedia of senatorial lore and legislative minutiae. In these patronage affairs, Biff clearly was the victim of a common political affliction. He just couldn't bear to say no, even though he knew he couldn't deliver. So he said yes and hoped for the best. He was either too smart or too ineffectual to attempt to make good.

These incidents led to quite a bit of private spluttering among Biff's bosses, the United States senators. They consider patronage their exclusive prerogative and did not take kindly to Biff's intrusion.

As a result, they slapped him down vigorously in 1949 when he tried to make his secretary's husband the Sergeant-at-arms of the Senate. This plum went to Joe Duke of Arizona, the candidate of Senator Hayden. Several of Duke's ballots were actually inscribed "Joe Doakes." The Democratic senators may not have known how to spell the name of Hayden's candidate, but they were very positive they did not want to vote for Biffle's.

But Biff goes his merry way, and his office remains as crowded as ever.

It is the favorite hangout of Vice-President Barkley. So many people visit the place, and so much food and drink is consumed there, that correspondents have dubbed it "Biff's Diner."

There are four Republican members of the Senate inner circle.

Robert A. Taft dominates the party Policy Committee; Eugene Millikin presides over the Republican Conference, which is political jargon meaning the Policy Committee plus *hoi polloi;* Kenneth Wherry is Floor Leader; and Arthur Vandenberg serves as the party's oracle on foreign policy.

Each member of this directorate views the others with the leery suspicion of a veteran actress afraid she is being upstaged by a new-comer. Sometimes this nagging fear gets a little out of hand and breaks out in public. It did, for example, at the height of the OPA fight, when Wherry, after glumly perusing a batch of newspaper clippings, took the floor and, waving his arms, bellowed:

"Taft! Taft! Everybody's always talking about what Taft has done to OPA. I'm the fellow that knocked out meat control, and I've done more to that bill than anybody else. Why do they always talk about Taft?"

Nobody answered the plaintive cry. It might have been painfully embarrassing.

For the truth is that everyone talks of Mr. Taft because he is the dominating intellectual figure of the party and is generally about three jumps ahead of Wherry and his cohorts. In fact, most people, even in Washington, often think that Taft leads the party singlehanded.

Robert Alphonso Taft is the unhappy son of an unhappy father. William Howard Taft was unhappy because he was in one place and wanted to be where he belonged. Robert Taft is unhappy because he is where he belongs but wants to be somewhere else.

In the father's case, he was Governor General of the Philippines, or Secretary of War, or President, or in some other executive job, when he wanted to be on the Supreme Court where he belonged. Robert Taft has always hankered for the presidency, although he already has the job he is pre-eminently suited for, as a member of the United States Senate.

Taft is a brilliant and tenacious legislative strategist and floor general. This is not surprising since his whole political experience has been legislative. He has never held an executive job. During the 1920's he served six years in the Ohio Assembly, including one session as speaker. Later he served a two-year stint in the State Senate. This was his sole political background prior to his election to the U.S. Senate in 1938.

Taft, though he would disdain the term, is a member of what is as close to an hereditary Tory aristocracy as anything our rather youthful American society has produced. To be a Taft in Cincinnati is "to belong." This has been true for a century.

His father and his grandfather before him were born into the world of big houses, many servants, the best clubs and schools, the "right" business connections, and the social deference inevitably accorded money. For those who belong to it, it is a warm, happy, secure world. Taft is a strong, self-confident man, and the fact that he comes from a successful and solidly based economic and social environment has a lot to do with making him that way.

But another aspect of Cincinnati's ruling class, important for an understanding of Taft's personality, is that it has lost none of its original entrepreneurial vigor. The drive to run things, to make money, to play an active and meaningful role in business and civic life has not faded out. Few scions of Cincinnati's top-drawer society turn up as "artists" on the Paris Left Bank. Nor are Bob Taft and his friends tired Dodsworths wondering why they did it all in the first place. The Tafts are men of purpose.

Religion is also an important element. Taft's brother Charles was the first lay president of the Federal Council of Churches of Christ. Taft's own religious bent takes a more conventional turn.

He believes strongly in the old-fashioned idea that the rich have a stewardship, a responsibility to take care of the poor and the unfortunate. If direct personal charity is no longer feasible, then the wealthy must assume the burden in the form of paying taxes to the government, preferably the local government, to do the task. He believes as vigorously as any self-made businessman in individualism and the Horatio Alger values of push, tact, and principle. But Taft is distinguished by his instinct for tempering the old laissez-faire ideas, not with humanitarian zeal or emotional sympathy for the underdog but with the historically deep-seated, experienced sense of responsibility for the whole community characteristic of the genuine aristocrat.

Taft's entire career has been in this Cincinnati tradition compounded of inherited wealth, established social position, acquisitive vigor, orthodox conservative religion, and a sense of public duty.

His class and its interests were his interests; its mores were his mores. As a local politician, he took no part in the sporadic crusades for clean government in which his brother was interested and which ultimately led to Cincinnati's adoption of the city-manager form of government. Taft followed an unwritten agreement with the unsavory local machine: it sent him to the legislature—or at least did not oppose his candidacy—and in return he did not attack its vices. In the legislature, his voting record was unvaryingly conservative. He championed the sales tax vigorously. In these years he made several trips abroad, but, as his subsequent isolationist record showed, they did not serve to broaden his outlook.

Cincinnati was his home; it was the focus of his interests; it was the limit of his horizon. That was true in 1925; to a large extent it remains true today.

In 1938, Taft defeated Democratic Senator Robert Bulkley and moved into the political big league. Almost immediately, he became a presidential possibility and an active and decisive figure in the Senate. Yet throughout the swift, shattering, kaleidoscopic events of the years that have come and gone since 1938, Taft remains the same, his convictions, his opinions, and his prejudices virtually unaltered.

At first glance, it is rather difficult to understand the basis of Taft's tremendous reputation and prestige both inside and outside the Senate. Certainly it is not due to any unusual qualities of insight or comprehension of present or portending issues. The record of his miscalculations and errors of judgment and understanding is staggering.

But, despite this, Democratic Senator Paul Douglas of Illinois called Taft "probably the ablest man in the United States Senate," and one hundred Washington correspondents in 1949 voted him the senator "who contributes most to the country's welfare." The bedrock basis of this admiration is the realization that Taft is a responsible man; he never ducks an issue.

Great or small, procedural or fundamental, every public question is a challenge to Taft's sense of duty. He may come up with answers that are as wildly wrong-headed as some of his stands on foreign policy. But at least he will have an answer, and he will be willing to defend it with considerable candor at any time and in any public forum. Laziness and slovenliness are qualities with which he has never become acquainted. Also, he has one of the ablest and best-balanced staffs in Congress, and on top of that he is his own best research man. He gobbles up facts and technical information of all kinds like a combine in a wheat field.

As he sits in the Senate day after day, his deep-furrowed face, the cocksure glint of his eyes, and a half-smile playing about his mouth all exhibit, as Mark Twain would say, "the calm confidence of a Christian holding four aces."

Taft is the most feared and respected figure in the Senate. His mastery of facts, personal courage, and stubborn tenacity have made him the Samson holding up the badly sagging Republican temple. How he would stack up in a Senate which included men like Walsh, Norris, La Follette, Cutting, Johnson, and Borah in their prime is conjectural. But, surrounded as he is by McCarthys, Wherrys, Cains, Jenners, Hickenloopers, and Lucases, he stands out like a giant.

Senator Eugene Millikin of Colorado is a firm believer in the principle that God helps those who help themselves. For thirty years, he has been assiduously engaged in assisting the Deity in that worthy enterprise.

Two years out of law school, he wangled a job as secretary to the governor of Colorado. World War I interrupted Millikin's civic service, but on his return he further exercised his taste for distinguished men by hooking up in a legal partnership with United States Senator Karl C. Schuyler. Their clients were always in the top brackets, and Millikin did his best by them even when, as in the case of Henry M. Blackmer of Teapot Dome fame, the client thought it best to skip to Europe for twenty-odd years to avoid prosecution.

In 1933, Schuyler died and Millikin took over the practice. Two years later, he married Mrs. Schuyler as well.

Two weeks after Pearl Harbor, Millikin was appointed to a Senate seat, its possessor having fortuitously departed for the other world. Millikin's predecessor Alva Adams had been a Democrat, but in name alone; Millikin's succession made no appreciable difference except that he was a Republican who would admit to the fact.

His only previous political activity had consisted of being a campaign contributor. But he rapidly displayed real talent for parliamentary maneuvering. His mastery at delaying tactics, legal technicalities, and economic data made Taft recognize in him a happy kindred spirit. Moreover, in private conference Millikin's fund of ready wit belied the rather solemn impression conveyed by his tight mouth, pince-nez, and round, bald head, and served to make him popular with colleagues who were less intellectual than the senior Senator from Ohio. Millikin quickly became No. 2 man on the Republican Policy Committee, and when the Republicans organized the Eightieth Congress, Millikin had amassed enough seniority to become chairman of the potent Finance Committee. It was pretty fast traveling for a man of only five years' service in the Senate.

Millikin's record has been one to gladden the hearts of the Colonel Blimps in the stodgy Denver Club.

Colorado is an economic colony producing profits and raw materials for Eastern business interests, but, if properly developed, it could be an economic empire in its own right. Millikin, however, has grown rich under the present system and has therefore done nothing to further the industrial growth of his State.

He votes against the Fair Deal program with undeviating consistency and is an unshakable foe of public power, the Columbia Valley Authority, rural co-ops, housing programs, and all antimonopoly legislation. As a champion of tax cuts for corporations and of budget cutting at the expense of welfare services, Millikin has revived the tradition of the 1920's, when the Republican from Colorado was known as "the third senator from Pennsylvania."

In one respect, however, Millikin has been big enough to rise above principle and put his own interest ahead of government economy.

Facing a tough fight for re-election from youthful, liberal Representative John Carroll, he decided that it behooved him to do something for the struggling farmers of western Colorado, because, while they were not quite the sort one met at directors' meetings, they did vote in disconcertingly large numbers. Millikin, therefore, in company with his reactionary Democratic colleague from Colorado, Edwin

Johnson, quietly tacked onto the cotton acreage bill an amendment lowering the acreage restrictions for wheat farmers. This was designed to give the cushion of price support to those farmers in arid, irrigated areas like western Colorado—farmers who had ventured into wheat production during the lush war years and were about to switch to some other crop.

The cost to the government of keeping these uneconomic producers in the wheat business, under the amendment sponsored by these two staunch economy advocates, would be around $100,000,000 a year.

Kenneth Wherry is a self-confident man. He is sure he knows how to lead the Republican Party back to the land of milk and honey. His general approach is, as he puts it, "to return to first principles." These beliefs are so primary as to be almost primitive.

"Move aside," Wherry says to the ghosts of Hanna and McKinley, "and make way for a good man."

Wherry is a bulky, bustling man who is in his late fifties but looks younger. Wherry's official title is Republican Floor Leader. In this capacity, he is somewhat in the role of a fullback carrying the ball on plays which Taft and Millikin have called as quarterbacks. Wherry is no "fancy Dan" in the backfield; nine times out of ten he tries a straight plunge through the center of the line. It's tough and brutal, but battling Ken has the skull for it.

The trouble is, however, he does not always have the line support for such power plays.

The GOP-Dixiecrat block is, of course, firmly in control of the Senate, but keeping the Southern brethren in line and also holding the wavering Eastern Republicans often requires fast footwork or outright concessions, and this invariably leaves Wherry exhausted, baffled, and frustrated. "Taft," he mutters darkly to friends, "sometimes acts almost like a Socialist." And Irving Ives of New York, Wherry laments, is a fine conservative who is the prisoner of the radicals in his home State. "Why, he's got five hundred thousand of those left-wingers in New York City alone," Wherry remarked sadly to one reporter.

But among his fellow Republicans from the Midwest and the

Mountain states, Wherry is happy and at ease. His thinking is in tune with theirs.

He is unalterably reactionary and opposes all social legislation as "thinly disguised government handouts." He was an isolationist before the war and he remains firmly opposed to most foreign commitments. He voted against the Atlantic Pact and sees Anglophiles, Communists, and homosexuals—preferably three in one—behind every State Department desk. He was the chief champion within the Republican inner circle of giving support and encouragement to "Jumpin' Joe" McCarthy's berserk witch hunt in the spring of 1950. Wherry also works hard to gut the Marshall Plan and cut ECA appropriations.

All these various enthusiasms sometimes involve him in extraordinary contradictions that would embarrass a lesser man. For example, one day in February, 1950, he stentoriously demanded that the United States resume shipping arms, supplies, and credits to the corrupt and demoralized remnants of Chiang Kai-shek's government on Formosa, despite all the evidence that billions of dollars in previous aid had been squandered and looted. Then, a few moments later, Wherry resumed his stance as the strident guardian of the Treasury and demanded suspension of all aid to Socialist Britain.

"There is no sense in pouring the taxpayers' money into a bottomless pit," he thundered with a firm voice and a straight face.

But, whether he is spending money or saving it, Wherry is the beau ideal of the Republicans in the Senate. Taft they respect, but Wherry they love.

Wherry plays the role of true defender of the orthodox faith with such zest because he brings to it the militant zeal of the convert. For, if truth be told, he was once something of a radical himself.

It is a subject of conversation which does not stir the Senator to much enthusiasm today. In fact, bringing it up at all is almost as much a social *faux pas* as asking him why he left the undertaking business. ("The practice of law has always been my *main* occupation," he explains with a mixture of insistence and despair.)

But when Wherry launched into politics in Pawnee City back in 1927, it was as an admiring supporter of Senator George Norris. It is true the association was mostly one-sided, with Wherry the wooer. But he kept at it in that persevering, hard-breathing way of his.

In 1930, he decided to run for governor. So he packed a grip, traveled more than a thousand miles to Washington, exchanged pleasantries with Norris for ten minutes, then used the Senator's office to announce to a handful of Washington newsmen that he was running for governor, put on his hat, and returned to Nebraska.

But the voters in the Republican primary were unimpressed, and Wherry was far in the ruck when the count was in.

Undaunted, he next proposed, as a member of the State Senate, to use the State's credit to pay depositors' losses from bank failures. This rather sweeping piece of agrarian radicalism got nowhere in the Legislature, but it aroused the horror of the local business community, which promptly lowered the boom on Wherry in the next election.

Nobody could foretell it then, but that defeat was the end of Wherry the liberal. Thereafter, he swung violently to the far right.

The next decade Wherry spent in the political wilderness, shouting for the defeat of the Democrats, who seemed equally well entrenched both in Washington and in Nebraska. Also, he quit embalming and acquired a tractor agency. Wherry was a star salesman.

Increasingly, he applied to politics the techniques that worked in business. "Republicanism" became to him a product to be sold like any other profitable commodity—fast and snappy, and far superior to anything else on the market. By 1939, he had risen to State Chairman, and in 1941 he was made Western director for the National Committee. The next year he decided to try his luck again and challenged his one-time hero, the now aged and ailing Norris. Wherry won by a whisker, but it was all he needed.

He knew at last he was on the right track, and he has been galloping furiously down the far right-hand side of the track ever since.

As Republican Floor Leader, Wherry is curiously similar to his opposite number, Scott Lucas.

Wherry, too, is trigger-tempered under pressure, slow-witted and heavy-handed. Between him and Lucas the basic test is always who will outfumble the other worst and most. They are a pair of prize stumblebums.

Graphically illustrative of Wherry's distinctive talent for inanity is the following exchange he had on September 7, 1949, with Senator Tom Connally of Texas:

WHERRY: I ask the distinguished Senator if it is not true that since
            1946 General MacArthur has made bimonthly reports on
            the Chinese situation?
CONNALLY: The Senator seems to know all about it. Why is he asking
            me? I do not know.
WHERRY: Because I should like to have the Senator make such re-
            ports available to the members of the Senate. . . .
CONNALLY: We will try to accommodate the Senator. I have not seen
            any of the reports which the Senator says have been
            made every two weeks.
WHERRY: No; bimonthly.
CONNALLY: That is every two months.
WHERRY: No, that is twice a month.
CONNALLY: I said every two weeks.
WHERRY: No; the Senator said twice a week.
CONNALLY: No; I said every two weeks.
WHERRY: Mr. President, will the Senator further yield?
CONNALLY: I yield.
WHERRY: The bimonthly reports I am talking about are two reports
            a month, which have been made since 1946.

At that point, even the Republicans were laughing at Wherry.

Arthur Vandenberg is a man who had a rendezvous with Destiny,
but Destiny didn't keep the date.

Throughout his life, Vandenberg has had a taste for grandeur and
an eye on history. He has longed to be a statesman in the best and most
romantic manner.

As a boy, he reveled in the triumphs of Alexander Hamilton. As a
young man, he wrote three books about him. Later he became a Lincoln worshiper. In the Senate, he thrilled to William E. Borah's
magniloquent oratory and now uses the office and the Senate desk of
the Idaho peer. Even as a man of sixty, Vandenberg was a sucker for
the pompous mystique of General Douglas MacArthur and proposed
him for President in 1944. Finally, when Roosevelt passed from the
scene, Vandenberg prepared to make his big move and play the leading role. For a time, when Congress was Republican and Byrnes and

then Marshall were Secretary of State, he did, to a large extent, make foreign policy.

Then came the Republican National Convention, Philadelphia, 1948. The leading Eastern metropolitan newspapers and magazines hailed him as THE man for the presidency. Republicans of the more internationally minded set panted hopefully. Was this, perhaps, another, slightly overaged Willkie come riding out of the West to sweep all before him and save the party from Dewey's chill grip? Vandenberg deprecated the talk and sat happily on a park bench in the sun posing for photographers. It was all right by him, he said, if everyone wanted him, but he really wasn't looking for it. The next day he made his awaited appearance on the platform to hear the plaudits of the delegates and figuratively hold his finger to the convention winds. The response was so cold and polite as to verge on the unfriendly.

Vandenberg was like a man who had stumbled into a deep-freeze by mistake; he crawled out of the hall all covered with hoarfrost and carrying his nomination chances like wilted posies in his limp hand.

But still there was hope of a Republican victory and the chance to be Secretary of State, or at the very least the administration's chief counselor and No. 1 spokesman. Harry Truman ended all that. The Democratic victory reduced Vandenberg from president pro tem of the Senate and chairman of the Foreign Relations Committee to the status of a mere member of the minority directorate.

Moreover, there came to the head of the State Department, for the first time in many years, an able, vigorous, strong-willed, and highly experienced man in the person of Dean Acheson. Vandenberg's role as unofficial policy-maker dwindled to that of occasional consultant and adviser. And as the beckoning beacon of power glimmered out, the long accumulating burdens of age and fading health descended suddenly upon him with almost crushing weight.

Destiny had passed him by and seemed unlikely to return a second time.

In retrospect, Arthur Vandenberg's career appears to be that of one who waited too long.

Throughout his years in Washington, Vandenberg has been generally considered a political lightweight. His record is too wobbly to classify him as a foe of the administration. But never has he shown the courage to venture outside the party pale and be a truly independent Republican, as were Norris and Borah. He has mostly gone along for the ride, and he looked the part even more than he lived it.

He is known as a man who can strut sitting down. His windy speeches carefully put him on record on both sides of every issue, as witness his classic stand on the conflict between human rights and property rights: "I heartily believe that human rights far outweigh property rights in their value and their challenge, tempered always with the reservation that property rights are among the greatest of human rights and that you can't have the former without the latter."

As one reporter commented, "Every politician has to face both ways occasionally, but few can do it as adroitly as Vandenberg can nor with such classy rhetoric. One of the last of the old-time orators, he can make a retreat sound like a call to arms, an evasion like a declaration of lofty principle."

The tragedy of Arthur Vandenberg is that he longed for greatness but loved respectability more. He mixed timidity with his dreams and was lost.

In the 1930's, he might have been the great leader of his party. Instead, he puffed on his fine cigar and let the Liberty Leaguers lead the Republicans to the slaughterhouse. In the prewar days, he might have had the wit and the courage to buck the isolationist tide, but, eying the presidency, he played it safe and allowed a maverick Democrat to steal the ball from him. On January 10, 1945, Vandenberg made his famous speech pledging cooperation in postwar peacemaking if Roosevelt would deal with the GOP in a spirit of "honest candor." This move made his reputation, even though it was not wholly original with him. In the years since then, as Vandenberg discovered at Philadelphia in 1948, much of his reputation has been the synthetic fruit of newspaper hoopla.

He has neither the power in Washington nor the popular following in the country that has been credited to him.

As the partisan struggle grows more intense, Vandenberg's figure recedes more and more. For him, it is ebb tide and the end. For a man who dreamed great dreams, reality must have proved a paltry thing. It has been too much a tale not of what was but of what might have been.

LOOK AWAY, DIXIELAND

A salient fact always to be kept in mind in analyzing the party make-up of the Senate is that the two-party system exists in the South, but Southern Republicans call themselves Democrats. With the exclusion of Missouri, the thirteen border and Deep South states usually return a solidly Democratic delegation every year. But this unanimity exists mostly on paper.

These twenty-six Democrats were divided as follows during the Eighty-first Congress:

Fifteen conservatives (Dixiecrats), led by Richard Russell and Walter George of Georgia and Harry Byrd of Virginia, and including Tydings and O'Conor of Maryland, Stennis and Eastland of Mississippi, McClellan of Arkansas, Ellender of Louisiana, Connally of Texas, Holland of Florida, Hoey of North Carolina, Robertson of Virginia, and Chapman of Kentucky. Joining these is Kenneth McKellar of Tennessee, who has a superficially liberal record but who is a most serviceable façade behind which conservatives operated during all filibusters and other parliamentary maneuvers when he was president pro tem in the Seventy-ninth Congress.

Opposing this band is a moderate minority of eleven led by Lister Hill and John Sparkman of Alabama and numbering in its ranks Maybank and Johnston of South Carolina, Withers of Kentucky, Kefauver of Tennessee, Long of Louisiana, Johnson of Texas, Fulbright of Arkansas, and, until their defeat, Pepper of Florida and Graham of North Carolina.

On certain local issues, momentary split-ups occur on both sides of this political divide.

Walter George, high priest of the Tories, usually votes for TVA appropriations, and Lyndon Johnson, one of the more liberal Southerners, always bows to the pressure of the Texas oil barons. But barring such minor deviations, the breakdown presented above is an accurate picture of the real alignments behind the universal Democratic label.

If the fifteen Southern conservatives were listed in the Republican column, where they really belong, and the half-dozen Republican "liberals" who often vote with the Democrats were switched to the latter's column, the Republican-Dixiecrat bloc would have fifty votes to the Democrats' forty-six, instead of the nominal division of fifty-four Democrats and forty-two Republicans.

This dominant alliance has existed openly in all but name and has controlled the Senate since 1939. Its grip is further strengthened by the fact that three or four Northern and Western Democrats, such as Johnson of Colorado and Gillette of Iowa, are off the reservation more often than they are on it.

The Southerners of the conservative wing are customarily called Dixiecrats. It is unfortunate for purposes of analysis that this term should be so drenched with racist overtones, because the fundamental division is not racial but economic. Both liberal and conservative Southerners would vote against any stringent civil rights legislation. And many of the staunchest conservatives, such as Byrd and Robertson of Virginia, have not consorted, at least publicly, with the avowed Dixiecrat movement.

The Southern politicians offer a wide, picturesque, and sometimes gamy gamut of personalities. They differ almost as much from one another as Miami does from Charleston or Birmingham from New Orleans.

The real leader of the hard-shell Southern conservatives is handsome, youngish Richard Russell of Georgia. Elected in 1931 at the age of thirty-three as the "boy governor" of Georgia, he still keeps his trim figure and youthful aura, although he is now a hard-bitten veteran of nearly two decades in the Senate.

Russell presides over the Dixiecrat caucus which meets regularly, just as do the Republican and Democratic Policy Committees. He is an able parliamentarian, and under his leadership the Dixiecrat caucus is the most cohesive and effective bloc in the Senate. But the best proof of Russell's astuteness came in the 1948 bolt from the Democratic Party. He could have had the Dixie nomination for President on a silver platter. He shrewdly passed it by.

Harry Flood Byrd is the best-publicized and the most sweepingly overrated of all the Southern senators.

A member of a famous trio of brothers—Tom, Dick, and Harry— he is a scion of one of Virginia's most illustrious colonial families which, until the present generation, had been in eclipse both socially and financially for almost two centuries. Then Tom became a wealthy businessman, Dick became an admiral and began his famous explorations of the Antarctic, and Harry entered politics. He served as governor from 1926 to 1930 and then sat around waiting for one of Virginia's aged senators to die, a demand they were exasperatingly slow in filling. In 1932, however, he guessed right, came out for Roosevelt before the Chicago convention, and was rewarded when Roosevelt promoted Senator Claude Swanson to Secretary of the Navy.

Once in office as Senator, Byrd proceeded to make Roosevelt regret his action.

In seventeen years, Byrd has managed to talk more and do less than almost any other senator. He has introduced no important bills, never made a memorable speech, and has never played a constructive role in shaping any major legislation. His one thin, tenuous claim to self-justification is his work on behalf of economy as chairman of the Joint Committee on the Reduction of Non-essential Federal Expenditures.

In 1950, Senator Hubert Humphrey of Minnesota ripped this pretense to shreds in one slashing speech.

Humphrey showed that this Committee needlessly duplicated the work of the regular Senate Committee on Executive Expenditures, and that it had squandered over one hundred thousand dollars in cash and wasted another quarter of a million dollars in government time and work, in requiring government offices to do all the labor on its reports. Humphrey further showed that the Committee rarely made specific recommendations for budget cuts but contented itself with vague sweeping demands for firing government employees. In brief, the chief function of the Committee was as a publicity vehicle for Harry Byrd.

"This example of inefficiency on the part of the legislative branch," Humphrey concluded with a touch of sarcasm, "is not conducive to the success of our efforts for the reduction of federal expenditures."

Byrd's record is spotted with all sorts of fascinating inconsistencies.

To cite one example: He favors making farm migrant families and other low-income groups pay for the hot lunches their children get in school. Disregarding the humanitarian aspects of this proposal, it is doubtful if the plan would raise five million dollars a year in revenue.

Yet, two weeks after he made this demand, Byrd voted for a bill increasing the acreage allotment for cotton and peanut growers. Since the government already has warehouses bulging with surpluses of these two crops, this bill meant an annual increase of at least one hundred million in the cost of the price-support program.

Voting with Byrd were three other inveterate critics of "New Deal spending"—Walter George of Georgia, John McClellan of Arkansas, and Eugene Millikin of Colorado. But Harry Byrd is the self-proclaimed leader of this "economy bloc"; as such, he can take all the credit for the achievements of this group—the phoniest thing under the Capitol dome.

Millard Tydings resembles Harry Byrd in only one respect. He, also, is a Senator who has two votes.

Tydings' colleague Herbert O'Conor spent the first two years in office, after his election in 1946, voting with and propitiating the Republicans in order to avoid an investigation of alleged vote frauds. The matter was finally dropped, and O'Conor was then presumably free to vote his conscience. But all that happened was that he then voted Mr. Tydings' convictions.

The senior Senator from Maryland (he has been in office since 1927) took this quite naturally as part of the deference due him. For Millard Tydings is one of the vainest men in a body of men scarcely lacking in that quality. It is not that he is unpleasantly pompous or overbearing; his conviction of his own superlative abilities is so natural, so much a part of him, that he feels under no strain to make himself or anyone else uncomfortable about it.

Tydings is undeniably able. He was a daring and brilliant officer in the first World War, winning the Distinguished Service Medal and the rank of lieutenant colonel. He is an adroit and almost unbeatable machine politician. As a straight-out, old-line party orator he has few peers; he is not so warm and eloquent as Alben Barkley, but he mingles cold sarcasm, savage, slashing attack, and well-phrased rhetoric with great effect.

Unfortunately for the Truman administration, his talents are not often enlisted in its support.

Tydings is a hard-shelled conservative with a consistently antilabor record, and was one of the senators who survived the Roosevelt purge of 1938. But he is still very much a party man, for the Democratic Party is the only available vehicle for his vigorous ambitions. Tydings has been known to look in the mirror and see therein the face of a future President. But most of the time he has had to content himself with more modest visions.

When domestic economic issues are absent and his ambitions and party loyalty are given free rein, Tydings can move with devastating effect.

He was a natural choice for chairman of the Foreign Relations Subcommittee to investigate McCarthy's charges of communism in the State Department. He did a suave and brilliant job of driving "Jumpin' Joe" to the wall again and again on every vague accusation or misleading innuendo. McCarthy's only ally on the committee was Bourke Hickenlooper of Iowa. Since he was unable to cross-examine witnesses himself, McCarthy whispered his questions to Hickenlooper. But the Iowan would get tangled up or be crossed up by Tydings, and he would look beseechingly at McCarthy. This prompted McCarthy to describe him privately as "a four-star jerk." After leading the hapless Hickenlooper through the jumps, Tydings would light a cigarette, stretch back with his hands behind his head, rock on the legs of his chair, and let a thin Cheshire smile spread across his angular, lean-jawed face.

He felt almost as proud of himself as if he had sunk a thirty-foot putt on the Burning Tree golf course.

James Oliver Eastland is the closest thing to a Bilbo now in the Senate. What this Mississippi Democrat lacks is not prejudice but daring.

He has befouled many pages of the *Congressional Record* with long, ranting attacks on displaced persons and Negroes, and many of his speeches have anti-Semitic overtones. But he lacks the audacity to write the "Dear Kike" and "Dear Nigger" letters of a Bilbo, and he does not have the tenacity of a John Rankin in making a persistent nuisance of himself.

Eastland contents himself with being Pat McCarran's hatchet man on the Judiciary Committee, and Dick Russell's axman in filibusters against civil rights bills.

"Judge" John Stennis, Eastland's colleague from Mississippi, is of a very different stripe.

Stennis holds the late Bilbo's seat but not his demagogic views. A tall, courtly, conservative gentleman, Stennis comes from the wealthier, more fertile districts along the Mississippi River rather than the poor upcountry areas. He speaks for the plantation owners, the bankers, and small businessmen, rather than the "rednecks" who are lucky if they raise five bales of cotton a year. Stennis is the shrewd, middling-average product of a typical Southern courthouse machine.

He makes much less noise than Eastland but has just as much influence in the Senate—which isn't much.

Walter F. George, at seventy-two, is senior Senator from the State of Georgia and obviously a very distinguished man, though he does not pose for whisky ads.

Among Southerners, George is a revered figure. The rank and file of Dixie congressmen and hundreds of lesser politicos look up to him. He is second only to McKellar in seniority in the Senate. He openly bucked Roosevelt and beat him. He survived the purge in 1938 and had the added satisfaction of having Roosevelt endorse him for re-election six years later. He is chairman of the potent Finance Committee. A great vote-getter, he has never been associated with the demagoguery of the Talmadges. He has won the praise of leading newspapers in the North without swerving an inch from Southern orthodoxy.

But before the mythmakers inject the embalming fluid and erect the pedestal, it might be good to inspect the hero a little more closely.

Walter George is, indeed, chairman of the powerful Finance Committee. This body writes all federal tax legislation. And throughout the New Deal, he openly fought and secretly sabotaged every attempt of the Roosevelt administration to shift the main tax burden from the lower and especially the middle-income tax groups to those in the higher brackets. Much of former Treasury Secretary Henry Morgenthau's reputation for "coldness" and "unpopularity with Congress" stemmed directly from his courageous and unyielding struggles with George and the small but powerful private interests that George speaks for.

When the war started, Roosevelt expressed the hope that it would be government policy to raise enough taxes so that two-thirds of the cost of the war could be paid for, and only one-third passed on to future generations in the form of a swollen national debt. George publicly denounced this policy and balked at raising tax rates to such an extent. He declared that not more than one-third of the cost could be raised.

In the end, as a compromise, something less than half the war was paid for out of current revenues, a huge and inflationary debt was created, and a crop of war millionaires even bigger than that of the first World War sprang up.

For those who have watched George's operations at close range for many years, it is one of the bitterest ironies of the Washington scene to hear him hailed in the conservative press as a "financial statesman" and an "economic conservative." George's tax policies have been reckless, imprudent, and socially irresponsible.

An inspection of Walter George's record on foreign policy is equally instructive.

Throughout the 1930's, George always posed as a great internationalist. But in the summer of 1939, Roosevelt made a desperate effort to repeal the arms embargo and return to the policy of "cash and carry." This would have worked clearly to the advantage of France and England, and it was hoped that it would serve as a warning to Hitler. It was a major step in the administration's eleventh-hour effort to deter Hitler from war by throwing the weight of American backing behind the Western powers. George was fully apprised of these aims, but when the issue came to a vote in the Foreign Relations Committee, he broke a 6 to 6 tie to vote with Borah and the isolationists and killed the bill.

This was the way this great Southern gentleman and statesman vented his spleen on Roosevelt for the attempted purge of the year before. When the chips were down, George put petty revenge ahead of the peace of the world.

In 1941, George succeeded to the chairmanship of the Foreign Relations Committee. But almost immediately the chairmanship of the Finance Committee also became vacant. No truly big man with a sense of history, seeing all the exciting and epochal events of wartime diplomacy and postwar peacemaking looming up before him, would consider giving up the chairmanship of the Senate Foreign Relations Committee. It would be like dropping the curtain before the first act began.

But as head of the Finance Committee, George would be in a more strategic position to do favors for the economic interests who put him in office and who have financed his campaigns. Like the dog on the old-fashioned Victrola, George heard his master's voice. He surrendered the chairmanship of Foreign Relations to stand guard on Finance.

One of George's sons was killed in the war, and during one of the early postwar debates on the UN, he made an eloquent and stirring plea that the sacrifices of his son and other American boys not be forgotten and that, whatever the cost, America see to it that we prevent future wars. But five years later, when asked by a reporter to comment on Secretary of State Dean Acheson's San Francisco speech proposing economic and military assistance to the Communist-threatened countries of Southeast Asia, George replied, "He'd better promise them moral support instead. It's cheaper."

In the disgusting cynicism of that statement, the flame of faith and serious purpose, which had never burned too brightly in the cold and pompous shell of the man that is Walter George, virtually sputtered out, leaving nothing but a greasy wick.

Virgil Chapman is a prime example of what the bad effects can be when any group takes a walleyed stand in politics.

Chapman, a Kentucky Democrat, defeated Republican John Sherman Cooper in a tight contest in 1948 solely because the coal miners followed John L. Lewis's orders and voted for Chapman. During the struggle over Taft-Hartley, Cooper had resisted heavy UMW pressure and voted for the bill. In the election that followed, Lewis made Taft-Hartley the sole criterion for support or opposition. As a member of the House, Chapman had also voted for the bill, but Lewis backed him on the theory that he couldn't be worse than Cooper and at least would be a change.

But it has proved, as almost anyone could have predicted, to be a change for the worse.

Cooper was an unusually able senator with a strong grasp of international problems and, unlike many Republicans, he did not have to depend on Bob Taft to do his thinking for him. On many domestic issues he had liberal views. But he voted for Taft-Hartley, so Old Eyebrows said, "Off with his head!"

His replacement by Chapman lowered the level of the Senate by at least a couple of notches.

Chapman is a briefless lawyer who has been ensconsed in public office practically from the day he left law school. But never once has he emerged from the ruck of party hacks. In the Senate he has continued his negative and reactionary record. A lazy man of mediocre talents, Chapman has a greater liking for gay, convivial drinking parties than he has for serious work.

He is just another "Happy" Chandler but without the clowning.

It may come as a surprise to many Northerners that there *is* another Senator from Florida besides Claude Pepper.

But there is, and his name is Spessard Holland.

Once that is said, he might just as well be forgotten, for that's what the rest of the Senate does. Holland, a slender, white-haired ex-governor of Florida, has been in the Senate since 1946. His main effect has been to cancel out every one of Pepper's liberal votes with a reactionary one of his own. Holland is even to the right of George Smathers, Pepper's successful opponent. Whether he will stand out any more clearly remains to be seen.

The most memorable incident connected with Holland's name occurred during the meetings of the Senate-House conferees on the bill for government aid to rural telephone co-ops by lending them money at two per cent interest. The telephone lobbyists waged a ferocious behind-the-scenes fight against the measure. Representative W. R. Poage of Texas, championing the legislation, was suspicious of a tricky provision in the Senate version of the bill. It read:

> "No loan shall be made unless the administrator shall determine (and set forth his reasons in writing) that no duplication of lines, facilities, system, or services will result therefrom in any area except where existing telephone systems in such area are unable or unwilling to provide reasonable service."

Poage contended this would largely defeat the purpose of the bill, since no one could readily establish what was "reasonable service" and the telephone companies could tie up the government in almost endless court litigation. He offered a safeguarding amendment.

Whereupon Holland got up and announced, "Before a vote is taken on this amendment, I want to show it to a representative of the telephone industry. They are entitled to every consideration in this matter."

Astounded, Poage roared, "I knew all along that the telephone companies wrote that provision. Now I have my proof."

Holland did become a little red-faced but nonetheless trotted out to the corridor to confer with the lobbyist.

Senator John McClellan of Arkansas does not have to go anywhere to confer with a lobby. He runs his own.

McClellan is president of the National Rivers and Harbors Congress, the chief pressure group for bigger pork raids for ports and waterways, which means everything from the Gulf of Mexico to Muddy Creek.

McClellan is also chairman of the Senate Committee on Expenditures in Executive Departments. In this capacity he is a bellowing advocate of government economy. In 1949, he led a stormy attack to force the President to cut all appropriations by five to ten per cent.

But as generalissimo of the Rivers and Harbors lobby, McClellan a few months later sonorously declared, "Flood control and navigation projects call for public improvement expenditures of $50,000,000,-000 within the next two decades." That figures out to $2,500,000,000 a year. By contrast, the Atomic Energy Commission asked for only $260,000,000.

Finally, as a member of the Senate Appropriations Committee, McClellan is a vigorous budget cutter of public-power projects, the Reclamation Bureau, and other Interior Department activities. That this is highly pleasing to the Arkansas Power and Light Company and other utility interests is more than a coincidence. But, again, as president of the Rivers and Harbors lobby, McClellan is the fervent champion of the biggest pork barrel of all, the appropriation fund of the Army Engineers.

In the light of this record it is not surprising to find that the secretary of this Arkansas Democrat is none other than an equally reactionary New York Republican who used to work for isolationist ex-Congressman "Ham" Fish.

Tom Connally of Texas might well serve as a model for Kenny Delmar's "Senator Claghorn."

A loud, garrulous, country-style politician, he has all of Senator Pat McCarran's instincts as a spoilsman but is too shrewd to get caught out on a limb where he might look unduly voracious.

He has been roiling the Washington scene since 1929. He is now chairman of the Foreign Relations Committee. But except for his picturesque appearance, Connally has been largely undistinguished as anything but a broad-bottomed politico with a stock of second-rate stories and a fondness for the limelight.

With the faithfulness and persistence of an ole houn' dawg, he has served the greedy demands of Texas oil interests, and with the keen nose of a beagle, he has scented out every scrap of unexploited patronage for fifty miles around. But as a senator he has been stodgy, conservative, uninspired.

Connally has little grasp of world affairs. He usually follows administration policy, chiefly because the President and the State Department spend a lot of time buttering him up and salting him down. This takes a great deal of effort, but from their point of view it pays off. For Connally has been a help to the administration on foreign policy: in a straight-out party clash, Connally, like Millard Tydings, serves a useful purpose.

Occasionally, Connally has a chance to relapse to his natural level, as he did during this little colloquy with Republican Leader Wherry, the merry mortician from Pawnee City.

WHERRY: Mr. President, will the Senator yield?
CONNALLY: Yes, I yield.
WHERRY: The Senator does so with some reluctance, I take it.
CONNALLY: No, I am always glad to yield to the Senator from Nebraska.

WHERRY: The distinguished chairman of the Foreign Relations Committee has just stated how very difficult it is for anyone to know how any member of the Senate can get it unless he asks the Foreign Relations Committee for it. I have been a member of the Appropriations Committee for two years. I am not apologizing for what we did. The Committee on Appropriations submitted an invitation to General MacArthur to return to the United States and testify. It seems to be a very singular fact that after six years we cannot find time to bring General MacArthur back to the United States of America. I should like to know whether he agrees with the policy of the administration?

CONNALLY: I did not yield for that slam on the desk.

WHERRY: That is one way to drive a point home.

CONNALLY: I feel very much like an old lawyer in my section of the country. He had as his legal antagonist a very loud and enthusiastic lawyer who shouted and foamed at the mouth in addressing the jury, and when it came the turn of the lawyer to answer him he stood up and said, "If your Honor please, bow-wow-wow. Now that I have answered my opponent I shall discuss this case."

WHERRY: Bow-wow-wow-wow-wow.

CONNALLY: Mr. President, I do not like to discuss this question in any but the most serious fashion.

WHERRY: Will the Senator yield for another question?

CONNALLY: Oh, yes.

WHERRY: The Senator's answers are just as clear as "bow-wow-wow-wow"—just as clear.

CONNALLY: Well, I use that kind of language and that kind of explanation—"bow-wow-wow-wow."

Allen J. Ellender of Louisiana is a Dixiecrat with kid gloves.

Ellender does not run off the Democratic reservation during elections or rant loudly about states' rights, but when the chips are down, his vote can always be found in the vest pocket of Leander Perez, the Dixiecrat czar of the Pelican State.

Being front man for a boss is an old story for Ellender. He was in the Louisiana Legislature for twelve years, during much of which time he was either Floor Leader or Speaker for Huey Long. Those were the days when Long boasted—truthfully—that he could buy legislators like sacks of potatoes. Ellender was in charge of lining up the sacks.

When the Kingfish died, Ellender succeeded to his seat in the Senate and has been re-elected continuously since then. After the war, he leaped briefly to prominence as co-sponsor of the Wagner-Ellender-Taft public-housing bill. But by the time the measure had a chance for passage in 1949, Ellender was no longer a member of the committee handling the bill and therefore did not share in the glory.

As a result, he did little to push his own bill, and the next year he voted against the administration's middle-income housing measure.

Alabama is probably the only State in the Union to have two first-rate senators, unless it is that other one-party stronghold—Republican Vermont, which is ably represented by George Aiken and Ralph Flanders.

Both Lister Hill and John Sparkman are topnotch senators. Both are also sturdy liberals.

It is fairly easy to see why curly-haired John Sparkman, the sincere, hard-driving son of a poor tenant farmer who raised thirteen children on a back-country farm, should be a champion of the lower-income groups. But it is not so easy to understand why Lister Hill should be, for he is a scion of one of the South's first families.

For generations, the Hills have dominated southern Alabama, much as the Bankheads ruled the northern half of the State. Although never so openly grasping as to arouse public resentment, the Hill clan managed to accumulate considerable wealth and to supply all the civic leadership that was needed. Mayors, sheriffs, congressmen, and county chairmen in southern Alabama turn out with remarkable regularity to be Hill cousins or married to a Hill or just plain Hills. Lister Hill has broken out of the rut of this conservative, tightly knit plutocracy, as perhaps nobody but a rich and restless young man longing to be independent could do. He has never been disowned, but he has managed to go his own way and always do his own thinking.

This has bred in him a strong strain of caution. He always looks once and thinks twice before he walks; he never leaps. On domestic issues, he usually arrives at the same place as men like Claude Pepper, but without the Wagnerian rolls of thunder and flashes of lightning. Both his caution and his intellectual integrity are masked by an almost overwhelmingly ingratiating manner.

He is a politician who never takes a vacation from his trade. He has already had a long career, though still only in his mid-fifties; he served eight terms in the House before he advanced to the Senate in 1937, to become a worthy successor to Hugo Black.

Hill's power rests on his family's prestige plus a loose network of alliances with the smaller feudal enclaves and local machines scattered through the State. But he is not lacking in the common touch. Faced with a rough re-election fight in 1944 he stumped the State, visited every town of any size and even bus terminals, where he would enter buses, loaded and waiting for departure, and go up and down the aisle shaking hands with passengers.

He won decisively.

Hill is the administration's wheelhorse on the Appropriations Committee, while Sparkman is the liberal catalyst on the Banking Committee.

Sparkman served ten years in the House before coming to the Senate in 1946, and part of that time he was Majority Whip. He has a strong sense of party loyalty, and in 1947 he was the only one of the twelve Democratic senators who had voted for Taft-Hartley who responded to the President's personal plea and reversed himself to support the veto. He is the party spark plug, the vigorous coach reassuring the faithful and exhorting the doubtful.

Working closely together, Hill and Sparkman are two of Mr. Truman's most steadfast legislative aces in a hand painfully short on trumps.

North Carolina's seventy-three-year-old Clyde R. Hoey (pronounced "hooie") is an amiable conservative who is almost a caricature of the old-fashioned senator.

He lets his white hair grow long over his collar, as Tom Connally does, he wears the black frock coat fashionable in the Victorian era, plus a wing collar, high-top shoes, a thin, loosely knotted four-in-hand tie, and a fresh carnation in his buttonhole. He has dark eyes, a friendly smile, and a courtly manner. It is always a pleasant surprise to discover that one who so suspiciously looks the part is not at all pompous or pretentious.

Hoey is an authentic gentleman; a Sunday School teacher all his life, he does not cuss, chew, smoke, or drink. He is unwaveringly conservative, which distresses him somewhat at times, since personally he and Truman get along "just fine."

Hoey carries little weight or influence in the Senate but is esteemed by all his colleagues.

South Carolina's two representatives in the upper chamber represent a happy modification of two familiar species.

Burnet Maybank is the tidewater aristocrat in politics, but he stiffens the breed with a dash of social responsibility. Olin Johnston is the familiar back-country "give 'em hell" orator, preaching a nonintellectual variety of New Dealism.

Burnet Rhett Maybank comes from Charleston, where, as Hodding Carter once wisecracked, "Many are galled and few are chosen." Maybank is one of the chosen. Northerners frequently have trouble understanding Maybank when he speaks on the floor, for he talks with a pronounced Charleston accent. But it doesn't matter much, since speaking is not his forte.

Maybank is one of the wiliest operators on Capitol Hill. It is not generally realized that it was he, as chairman of the Banking Committee, who, with the effective aid of John Sparkman, led the administration's fight for housing legislation.

Personally, Maybank is quite conservative, but he has some of the flexibility and political astuteness that Middle Western Republican conservatives so sorely lack. Maybank will never push for change if left to himself, but when he feels public pressure, he does not try to do an imitation of a stone man. But it is as a legislative operator that Maybank excites the most admiration in Washington. As one colleague remarked admiringly, "You have to get up pretty early in the morning to get a jump on Maybank."

Lyndon Johnson of Texas and William Fulbright of Arkansas have much in common.

Each was a protégé of Roosevelt, who hoped he could inspire them to enlighten the political murkiness of their respective States. Each is an intelligent and well-intentioned man who would be a distinguished liberal if he came from a Northern state. But both seem to lack the spiritual fortitude to rough it alone.

Johnson came to the House in a special election in 1937. He immediately caught the eye of the President, who encouraged him to persevere in his liberal ways. In 1941, Roosevelt drafted him to run for the Senate seat left vacant by the death of Morris Sheppard. Johnson ran against the fierce opposition of Senator Tom Connally, who had a candidate of his own, and against rabble-rousing Governor "Pass the biscuits, Pappy" O'Daniel, then at the height of his power. In the two-man runoff, Pappy won by 1,200 votes. Johnson held on to his seat in the House and in 1948 ran again for the Senate, this time squeaking in by eighty-seven votes.

With this buttery grip on his constituency, it is not surprising that Johnson often votes conservatively. But on public power and a few other issues, he justifies the faith Roosevelt had in him. It would take a George Norris to buck openly the ruling economic forces in the oil-owned commonwealth of Texas, where the dominant intellectual spirit was summed up in the oil millionaire's snort, "If you're so damned smart, why aren't you rich?"

William Fulbright is both smart and rich. It is one of the tragedies of Congress that he hasn't had the guts to live up to his potentialities.

Fulbright is the son of a country banker who used his lending powers to build up a small-scale economic empire in Arkansas. The Fulbright children today own and operate, as a joint family trust, a large variety of business enterprises. Bill characteristically is most interested in the family newspaper.

As an undergraduate at the University of Arkansas, he played halfback on the football team and won a Phi Beta Kappa key. He went to Oxford as a Rhodes scholar and toured Europe extensively. Choosing law as his profession, he took his degree at George Washington University in the Capital and served briefly in the Justice Department on the staff that helped to prosecute the NRA "sick-chicken" case.

Soon after, he returned to his alma mater as president. In 1942, the governor fired him, and Fulbright went into politics to be "vindicated." Actually, however, it was here that his real interests lay, and his ouster only hurried up the inevitable. In 1944, Fulbright was elected to succeed Hattie Caraway in the Senate.

In his first month in office, he drafted a round robin in behalf of world organization, for which he corralled the signatures of sixteen freshmen senators. It was a move to strengthen Roosevelt's hand and was presented to him on the eve of his departure for Yalta.

But then Roosevelt died. Like many others in government, Fulbright, a shy, introspective man, sorely missed the guiding hand and the words of encouragement from the Big Brother in the White House. For a time he persevered alone.

But his independence gradually dwindled under the dead weight of Southern conservatism and inertia. Today, he has lapsed back into the stodgy, reactionary atmosphere from which he emerged in 1942. As time passes, he seems to grow more and more like the run-of-the-mill conservatives.

Fulbright had a golden opportunity to exercise leadership, but he did not grasp it. He may well be counted a flower which would have come to bloom in any other soil save the spiritual wastelands of the Truman administration.

Russell Long of Louisiana is the biggest surprise in the Senate.

When the thirty-year-old son of the late Kingfish was elected in 1948, it was widely expected he would be either a bizarre copy of his notorious father or a pawn of the reactionary Dixiecrat bosses. Long has proven to be neither.

He has carved an independent niche for himself. He has taken the orthodox Dixiecrat position against civil rights and in favor of state control of tideland oil, but he has not tied up with the Southern extremists. Instead, he has compiled an excellent liberal record and won the respect of the best members of the Senate.

Russell Long physically looks very much like a younger edition of the fabulous Kingfish.

He has the same medium height and stocky build, the same black hair, dark-brown eyes, wide, loose mouth, and blunt nose. On the stump, he displays many of his father's oratorical tricks and mannerisms. This is calculated on his part; he practices facial expressions and gestures before a mirror. But in private conversation he is more natural and relaxed than his father ever was.

He still adores his father's memory and speaks frequently of "my old man." But as a senator Russell has resorted to none of the demagogic tricks or wily maneuvers of the Kingfish. He regularly votes with the administration and, except for civil rights, has supported the whole Fair Deal program (including repeal of the Taft-Hartley Act, housing, aid to education, and public power).

Russell has the ambitions of his father but not the ruthlessness. His career may be a liberal success story, or he may prove as erratic as his Uncle Earl. But Long is not the stuff of which dictators are made.

When Estes Kefauver began his campaign for the Senate in 1948 against Boss Ed Crump's stooge, Senator Tom Stewart, the razor-tongued Crump called him "the Communists' pet coon." Kefauver, who is about as sinister as Harry Truman, replied in a vigorous luncheon speech to several hundred paying customers, "I know one thing. I'm not Mr. Crump's pet coon."

With that, he pulled out a large, furry coonskin cap and waved it to the cheering crowd. He wore the cap throughout the campaign. It was his victory symbol. He won by 160,000.

It was a richly deserved triumph. Kefauver during ten years in the House had proved one of the ablest men in Congress. In the Senate he has been equally outstanding. His rather solemn manner and his professorial rimmed glasses hide a friendly personality and a pleasant dry wit. Kefauver would make an eminent Attorney General or Justice of the Supreme Court. He seems surely headed for bigger things.

Of the liberal Southerners, he shows the greatest promise of becoming a truly national figure.

THE DOG THAT IS WAGGED BY THE TAIL

Examining the non-Southern portion of the Democratic Party in the Senate is like examining a geological formation. Each layer represents a different stage in the historical development of the liberal movement of the last twenty years.

At the bottom are the veterans who have been in the arena since the early New Deal, Westerners like James Murray of Montana and Joseph O'Mahoney of Wyoming and Easterners like New York's Herbert Lehman and Matthew Neely of West Virginia. Some elements have been infused into the composition only under the heat of a temporary pressure, like the upthrust of lava from volcanoes now dead. Such an element is California's departing (without loss) Sheridan Downey, leader of the Ham 'n' Eggers and other depression-inspired fringe movements. There are many cross grains and odd spurs like Idaho's maverick Glen Taylor. There is soft shale like New Mexico's devious Clinton Anderson, and hard granite like Illinois' Paul Douglas.

All in all, it is a complex, involved composition which requires much prospecting and blasting to break it down into its constituent parts.

There are about twenty-four Northern and Western Democrats, or about one-fourth the membership of the Senate. The members of this group, though they do not form a conscious, coherent bloc, on the whole support the Truman administration's domestic program far more than they oppose it. It is clear that even when the eleven Southern liberals are added to their ranks, this Northern faction needs to pick up at least a dozen of the marginal seats in New England and the Middle West before it has anything approaching a majority.

For a while in the sparkling 1932-38 period, they held those seats, and the Roosevelt New Deal was the result. Since then, they have been in a strong but perpetual minority position.

The dominant figures in point of service in this Democratic contingent are a quartet of aging Westerners.

Carl Hayden of Arizona is the oldest, least known, and most influential of this group. He came to Washington as a representative in 1911 and has been there ever since. His career spans Arizona's whole history as a State in the Union. Hayden moved to the Senate in 1926, is now chairman of the Committee on Rules and Administration and senior member of the Appropriations Committee.

Gray-haired and thin, Hayden ambles along the Senate corridors like a carelessly dressed, stooped-shouldered clerk, utterly inconspicuous. He prefers it that way. But few men are more influential behind the scenes. Too retiring to play a dominant role, Hayden is a quiet administration stalwart.

The great cross of Elbert Thomas' life is that people are always confusing him with Oklahoma's cotton-speculating, logrolling, gravy-grabbing Elmer Thomas. The confusion does him a grievous injustice.

Elbert Thomas is a wise, scholarly liberal from Utah. He is thoughtful and gentle; personally ascetic, he was once a Mormon Church missionary. The holder of a Ph.D. in political science from the University of California, Thomas taught for several years and has served as vice-president of the American Society of International Law and of the American Political Science Association. He is an authority on the Far East and long before the war was a deeply convinced internationalist. (In 1934, he wrote a book called *World Unity as Recorded in History*.)

Presently chairman of the Labor Committee, Thomas would make a superb head for the Foreign Relations group now saddled with Tom Connally, the Texas Throttlebottom. His seniority on that Committee is high but not high enough, unfortunately.

The wide chasm of competence which separates these two men is in itself a sufficient argument for at least a four- or six-year limitation on any one chairman's tenure.

Tall, Canadian-born James Murray of Montana is one of the richest men in the Senate and one of its most tenacious liberals.

A lawyer and mining magnate, Murray has fought for the underdog throughout his whole political career. He is the Senate sponsor of the Truman health program. Completely lacking in "color" or personal flamboyance, Murray, now slightly stooped with the weight of his seventy-odd years, never has exhibited anything less than the highest principles and the most selfless integrity. To praise him is to gild the lily.

Joe O'Mahoney presents the classic lively Irish contrast to his earnest Scotsman colleague from Montana.

O'Mahoney is a Massachusetts native who went west to Boulder, Colorado, as a fledgling newspaperman forty years ago. With sound foresight, he turned to law and began practicing in Cheyenne. The senatorship is the only office he has ever held, but politics had long been his avocation.

O'Mahoney is an excellent senator, except for an occasional bit of special pleading on behalf of Wyoming cattlemen or the cement and steel industries' price-fixing basing-point bill. Like Robert Taft and various other colleagues, O'Mahoney occasionally hankers to be someplace else than where he is and where he belongs. For example, he used to be a hopeful aspirant for a Supreme Court appointment.

But it will be a sad day for the country, for Wyoming, and for the Senate when the trim, dapper, perky figure of Joe O'Mahoney disappears through the swinging doors of the upper chamber for the last time.

Herbert Lehman, at seventy-two, is only a freshman in the upper chamber, but he already acts and looks as if he were a lifetime member.

The former New York Governor and ex-UNRRA chief is by nature a somewhat solemn and serious man, but he has set some sort of record in his first nine months in the Senate by never missing a roll call or a committee meeting.

Lehman is inherently rather conservative, as his disavowal of the Truman health-insurance plan emphasized. More impatient liberals wish he would display more fighting ardor, but what he lacks in zeal, Lehman more than makes up in the wide experience and solid prestige he brings to the administration. Nor is he entirely lacking in appreciation of lighter things.

During his four terms in Albany, where he was a thrifty, economy-minded governor, he had a dog named "Budget." When it had its first two pups, Lehman accepted a newsman's suggestion and called one "Deficit" and the other "Surplus." It was not recorded which was the larger.

The small, mountainous State of West Virginia can proudly claim two of the ablest and most indefatigable liberals in the Senate. But the similarity between Matthew Neely and Harley Kilgore ends with their voting records. As personalities, no two men could be more different.

Harley Kilgore is a stocky, friendly man who is as easy to talk to as the neighborhood postman, as relaxed and informal as an old shoe. Matt Neely is tall, bald, and autocratic, with the impressive demeanor of a Roman magistrate and the mannerisms of a Shakespearean actor. Kilgore almost never takes the floor to speak unless he has a committee report to deliver or some other unavoidable chore to perform. Neely loves to make long, loud speeches studded with quotations from Browning, the Bible, and the Lake Country poets. Kilgore dresses like a man who obviously had his mind on something else when he was doing it. Neely dresses flamboyantly and takes pride in the rakish cut and the extra-heavy material from which his suits are made. A green shirt or a purple necktie is nothing unusual for him to wear.

Kilgore gets along with almost everyone, even Senator Pat McCarran, whose discriminatory DP bill aroused him to blazing wrath. Neely is irascible and notorious for irately adjourning committee meetings five minutes after they are scheduled to begin if no quorum is present. This habit is deeply resented by his more dilatory colleagues.

Characteristically, when Neely left the Senate in 1940 to become governor, he wrote a letter concerning some of his more muttonheaded colleagues which became public and caused a furor. But he had not exaggerated. He pinpointed every one of them with deadly accuracy.

Neely has two other distinctions.

He is one of the most durable politicians Washington has ever seen. He does not admit his age, though he is actually seventy-four and looks ten years younger; but he has been in public office for half a century. And while most politicians are joiners, few of them can match Neely's record. He is an Elk, an Odd Fellow, a member of United Spanish War Veterans, a past Supreme Governor of the Loyal Order of the Moose, a past Grand Chancellor of the Knights of Pythias, and a thirty-second degree Mason, plus sundry other fraternal affiliations and distinctions.

Kilgore prior to his election in 1940 served many years as a judge. This judicial background, combined with the inherent kindliness of his nature, has restrained him from the assertiveness needed to be a headline senator. But when the battle lines are drawn, Harley Kilgore is always in there firing.

Warren Magnuson of the State of Washington is the Senate's most eligible bachelor and one of Washington's foremost glamour boys.

"Maggie," as he is popularly known, is a husky, athletic-looking Norwegian with blond hair and a handsome face. He has the ingratiating manner of a bonus-winning salesman. He is very frankly a politician looking for votes and representing a conglomeration of special interest groups, among which Dave Beck's teamsters and the seamen's and longshoremen's unions are dominant.

Magnuson makes no claim to having Elbert Thomas' wide and scholarly interests, nor can he rival James Murray's deep convictions and stubborn tenacity of purpose. But judged on his merits as a politician, and compared with the caliber of Republicans his region has produced—reactionary hoot owls like Harry Cain of Washington or mental Charley horses like Guy Cordon of Oregon—Magnuson scores very high indeed.

Guy Gillette of Iowa is one member of the Senate who never expected to be back there. Defeated for re-election in 1944, he ran in 1948 mostly to prevent the seat from going by default. Much to his own and everyone else's surprise, he was elected by the highest majority in the history of the State.

Gillette is a handsome, silver-haired man of seventy-one with a distinguished appearance and fine oratorical presence. His political views are steel-ribbed conservative. At times he supports the administration, but strictly on a pick-and-choose basis. No one is ever sure of his vote until he casts it. That is a fact he is very proud of.

Roosevelt attempted to purge Gillette in 1938 but failed. After he was defeated in 1944, Truman offered to make him a judge on the Customs Court. Gillette declined on the ground he had forgotten all his admiralty law. "Oh, you can brush up on it," Truman urged. But Gillette rejected the sinecure. His indifference stemmed from the fact that he likes to play an active role and be in the limelight.

Like Vandenberg and Neely, Gillette has a broad streak of the actor in him. Staging and performing in amateur theatricals is his hobby. Politics is his profession. They are not unrelated arts.

Robert S. Kerr of Oklahoma might be a great senator if he weren't so anxious to double or triple his $100,000,000 fortune.

Bob Kerr is a rootin'-tootin', hard-driving go-getter who is fond of saying, "They'll only beat me over my dead body—and I don't die easy." A penniless ex-doughboy in 1919, in the next twenty years he hustled his way ahead in the oil business so fast that he acquired $10,000,000, and, as president of the Kerr-McGee Oil Industries, Inc., he is possessor of petroleum and natural-gas properties worth potentially ten times that figure. Turning to politics in 1940, Kerr made just as rapid progress.

In 1940, he picked up the post of Democratic National Committeeman; in 1942, the governorship; in 1944, he was keynoter and temporary chairman of the Democratic National Convention; and in 1948 he became a senator. Kerr, a fire-breathing, hard-shell Baptist, is fond of quoting the Bible, but he doesn't think much of the Beatitudes, especially the one that says: "The meek shall inherit the earth."

During the decade of his whirlwind rise to the political heights, Kerr has not been too busy to forget the oil business.

One of the first things he did upon entering the Senate was to introduce what became known as the Kerr natural-gas "ripper" bill. Its purpose was to remove most of the natural gas producers from the rate-fixing supervision of the Federal Power Commission and thus open the way for a $100,000,000 boost in consumer rates.

Kerr's company would have been one of the lush beneficiaries of this grab.

With the powerful aid of Speaker Sam Rayburn (from oil-rich Texas), the Kerr bill was whipped through the House one Friday afternoon when more than one hundred members were away. But when it came up in the Senate, a stiffer fight occurred. Opponents led by Illinois' Paul Douglas came close to defeating it. Indirectly, they did lick it.

Their attack was so devastating politically that Truman was ultimately persuaded to veto the measure. And with the nip-and-tuck votes on the issue, Kerr and Rayburn didn't dare to try to override the President.

For Kerr, the defeat was more than the loss of a rich haul. The bill branded him once and for all as a grab-bag senator.

Back in the 1930's, Franklin Roosevelt was trying to put an important bill through a recalcitrant and closely divided Senate. One of the doubtful members was New Mexico's Dennis Chavez. A White House aide, after a talk with Chavez, returned with this word, "He wants the promise of another judgeship to vote for us."

"What, again!" exclaimed Roosevelt, "How many times do we have to 'buy' him!"

"Every time, Chief," was the reply.

If this story ever got back to Chavez, it is doubtful if he would do anything more than smile and shrug his shoulders. Politics for him has always been strictly a cash-and-carry proposition—as it is for all New Mexico politicos. Nationally, little is known about the State, but its politics is wholly professional—as hard-boiled and cold-turkey as any in the country. Chavez may be franker than others, but he is no different.

Chavez' spectacular speech debunking ex-Communist Louis Budenz aroused a storm of controversy. Some of his fellow Catholics praised Chavez and some attacked him. But, throughout it all, he remained calm and affable.

Chavez was happy and content to share the opinion of his friends that it was the finest achievement of his nineteen years in Congress.

Clinton Anderson, Chavez' colleague from New Mexico, is less modest than Chavez about the inherent limits that God has set on his capacities. Clint fancies himself quite a statesman.

He gives much thought and worry to his presidential and vice-presidential prospects, even though he hasn't the remotest chance of getting either. However, it must be admitted that for a man of mediocre talents he has done pretty well.

How he has done it is another story. That's why it's a sure bet he will never go any higher than he is now. Another good reason is that Harry Truman has written him off his slate. Anderson was once Secretary of Agriculture in the Truman cabinet, but what the President thinks of him now is not funny.

Glen Taylor once remarked, "So help me, I ran for the Senate three times before I made the grade, and two of those times I didn't know what the salary was."

This half-facetious remark epitomizes Taylor's two salient qualities: persistence and foolhardiness. Taylor often rushes in where wise men would not tread, but he always keeps plugging away. He wouldn't be in the Senate if he did not.

If Taylor's career in the Senate has been undistinguished, erratic, and confused, this was largely foreshadowed by his life up to 1944. He is so deeply scarred by the emotional turmoil and economic distress of the '30's that he is a sucker for anything with a "liberal" or "progressive" label on it, whatever its contents.

Emotionally oversold on his depression experience, naïve, lacking a good education, and rhetorically self-intoxicated, Taylor has accomplished little of sound and lasting merit in his term in the Senate. Yet his tireless energy, sincerity, native intelligence, generous enthusiasm, and flair for the dramatic give him a good potential.

He will never be a great senator, but he could straighten out and be a good one.

Brien McMahon's father died the week of Pearl Harbor. Shortly before he died, he remarked to his son, "I don't mind dying. I think I've lived through the happiest period of this country's history."

McMahon, as he grapples with the twin dilemmas of atomic energy and foreign policy in the age of the hydrogen bomb, often thinks of his father's words. From the relatively simple problems and clear perspectives of his father's prewar America, he has passed to an age which few think will be happy and in which no problems are simple.

The story of McMahon's life has been one of evolution from the simple and the sure to ever greater and more oppressive complexity.

McMahon was born in the small city of Norwalk, Connecticut, in 1903. His father was an Irish immigrant, working hard to get ahead in the world as a small-time contractor. The elder McMahon's world was the America of the 1870-1930 period.

America was growing, and growing fast. There were railroads to be built, farm land to be cleared, coal and iron and gold to be dug, great cities to be expanded to three, five, ten times their previous size. For contractors, great and small, this meant miles of streetcar lines and sewers and new streets and subways and hundreds and hundreds of rows of new houses. The prevailing spirit was borrow, build, and brag for a bigger tomorrow.

There were tough problems, but none that couldn't be licked by simply thinking quicker and working harder, by swinging more picks and shovels and toting more bags of sand and cement. It was an age that simply bred energy and optimism and recuperative drive.

Brien McMahon, moving today in a different and intellectually more sophisticated social atmosphere, is nonetheless still his father's son. A stocky, thickset man with powerful shoulders and a firm jaw line, McMahon brings to current problems the same innate force and drive and aggressive self-confidence.

In 1944, he made his big move. He ran for the Senate against Republican incumbent John Danaher and defeated him decisively. In 1946, McMahon sponsored a bill for civilian control of atomic energy and emerged as a national figure.

The original measure was written by scholarly James Newman, now a member of the staff of *New Republic* magazine. McMahon fought hard for the bill, against the most intense kind of opposition and with little effective support from the administration.

Senator Edwin Johnson of Colorado sparked the fight to give monopoly control of atomic energy to the military, and, of course, in this endeavor he was loudly supported by Lieut. Gen. Leslie Groves, wartime commander of the Manhattan Project and a veritable Colonel Blimp come to life. McMahon and civilian control were defeated in committee, but eventually he fought his way to a compromise which gave him the lion's share of the prize.

In the years since 1946, McMahon, first as chairman, then as ranking minority member, and then again as chairman of the Joint Congressional Committee on Atomic Energy, has been the bellwether on Capitol Hill of the Atomic Energy Commission and the working scientists. He is suave, sure, potent, and effective.

McMahon walks with a confident stride, but he is aware that he is grappling with awesome problems. He knows that over the top of the hill is not a golden sunrise and an open plain but many more dark valleys and perhaps even steeper grades. The way is long and the responsibility is a heavy one, for he is a guardian of his father's heritage and his father's dream.

The story of Hubert Humphrey's life is a Horatio Alger tale as it might have been brought up to date in a version by the WPA Theater Project.

He is the eager, hopeful young man from the small town who is ambitious, works hard, and dreams big dreams. But in the final act he does not invent a better fountain pen, marry the banker's daughter, and become a millionaire. Instead, he goes into politics, has a whirlwind career, and winds up in Washington a famous Fair Deal senator at thirty-seven. Either way it's a good story and a happy ending.

Humphrey is an excellent influence in the Senate, where the liberal forces have so long lacked a brilliant spokesman with genuine popular backing.

Half loaves and easy compromises are not his specialty; he antagonizes the opposition rather than conciliates it, because he tears aside the mask of cant and demagoguery. But by the same token he inspires his own supporters. He has raised the Democratic morale which had fallen to such depths in the Seventy-ninth and Eightieth Congresses.

Best of all, Humphrey can be depended upon to say the many things which need to be said, no matter how unpalatable.

Paul Douglas of Illinois came to the Senate in 1949 as a freshman. But by the end of his first session, there was little doubt that he, together with McMahon and Humphrey, was a member of the Democratic Big Three and that for solid intellectual force he was outstandingly the ablest man in the Senate.

Douglas has to his credit one powerful performance after another. He battered the basing-point bill sponsored by the steel and cement monopolies and, against the Kerr "ripper" bill, delivered a massive, frontal attack which, with interruptions for questions, lasted for three days. As a speaker on the floor, he is the master of his subject and the master of his audience as well. His speeches are formidable but lucid and acute. He speaks with fervor and conviction, yet he does not lose his self-control or his relaxed sense of humor.

Douglas is the closest thing to a synthesis of the elder Robert M. La Follette and George Norris that can be visualized.

Like La Follette, he has a marvelous grasp of economic perspective and technical detail. La Follette always could read a tax bill or a tariff bill and understand it and its implications. But "Old Bob" was temperamentally cast for the role of a lone wolf. Norris had not only the inner conviction but also the ability to communicate that conviction to other men so that they, too, could see it and follow him. Douglas has the same integrity and the same qualities of inspiration.

Like the giants who preceded him, Paul Douglas has already started to place his mark on the shape of our times.

THE PILTDOWN MEN

In 1912, some workmen in Sussex, England, made an impressive discovery. They dug up bones which were of human origin. Charles Dawson, English scientist, examined the bones with great care and finally pronounced them to be the remains of a previously unknown species of man. As they reconstructed him, he seemed to be characterized by "a retreating, apelike chin and thick cranial bones, but an undeniably humanlike cranium."

Long since extinct, he was older than the Neanderthal Man of the Old Stone Age. In honor of the village in which he had been found, the scientists christened him the Piltdown Man.

But the scientists had made one mistake. The Piltdown Man was not dead, though his species should have been extinct and his Stone-Age mentality was obviously incapable of dealing with the realities of the modern world. The Piltdown Men are a hardy breed, and their numbers still walk the earth.

Some of them even belong to the greatest club in the world, the United States Senate.

They are undoubtedly human, though the noises they make are often strange and frightening to the ears of twentieth-century people. Usually childish and irresponsible, sometimes clever with an animal-like cunning, they obstruct the course of domestic affairs and sabotage the conduct of foreign policy.

Numbering a dozen, they explain graphically the sorry plight the Republican Party is in. Most of them come from great and populous states of the Midwest, though the Eastern seaboard contributes a couple. Each has his own idiosyncrasies, but as a group they show certain common symptoms, such as intellectual constipation, verbal diarrhea, and varicose egotism.

Owen Brewster is so customarily referred to as "Pan American Airway's Senator" or as "Dictator Franco's Senator" or as the "Merchant Marine Industry's Senator" that it is sometimes difficult to remember that he is also supposed to be the Senator of the 850,000 people who live in the State of Maine.

It is also doubtful if Brewster himself always remembers.

It is a familiar and legitimate practice for senators and representatives to do favors and represent the various interests in their states. But Brewster does not concern himself with such petty stuff. He rushes about doing errands for big clients who have no connection whatever with Maine, except possibly to spend a summer week end in Bar Harbor.

But the trouble is that Brewster works so hard and so openly for companies like Pan American that there is no fun in exposing him.

Brewster is a member of the Interstate and Foreign Commerce Committee, where he has long been a zealous advocate of one big overseas American airline. This is the pet scheme of Juan Trippe, the boss of Pan American Airways. Pan Am is presently the dominating giant in foreign air transportation, and Trippe nourishes the grandiose dream of crushing all his smaller competitors and getting a government-guaranteed monopoly.

The State Department, the Armed Services, and all his competitors are violently opposed to the scheme. But Trippe is persistent and, through his flock of high-priced lobbyists on Capitol Hill, has managed to corral quite a few congressmen. Owen Brewster and Pat McCarran are his chief spokesmen, and Senate Secretary Leslie Biffle, commonly known as the "Democratic Owen Brewster," is his inside operator.

All this has been common knowledge in Washington for years, but Brewster brought it forcibly to the country's attention when he had the incredible gall to investigate Howard Hughes, one of Pan Am's competitors, for improper lobbying activities.

This black-pot-black-kettle affair brought Brewster's colleague Homer Ferguson into the picture. After the plain talking and tough fighting, Hughes was through with Ferguson and Brewster, the nation was laughing uproariously at both of them, and Ferguson's reputation as a dynamic prosecutor had sagged to gutter level.

Ferguson came with bright laurels from Michigan, where, as a one-man grand jury, he had broken a powerful gambling syndicate. But in the Capital he never gets beyond his own ten-yard line before he falls on his face.

He conducted the Pearl Harbor inquiry but failed to prove it was really Roosevelt rather than the Japs who caused the debacle at Pearl Harbor. He ran the Hughes investigation, and wound up in the ash can. He investigated speculation in the commodity market in 1947, and collaborated with Harold Stassen in turning it into a political brawl. But most revealing of all was Ferguson's shocking handling of the probe of Senator Elmer Thomas' grain-market operations in 1948.

Two weeks after he began, Ferguson suddenly quit cold. The reason for this abrupt change of heart was finally disclosed by Drew Pearson. He published an amazing letter that Thomas had written Ferguson, as follows:

> "I assume that you will not object to me using my private funds to do some investigating of facts, or incidents that are coming to me from all parts of the country. . . . I refer to the Chrysler Airtemp Sales Corporation and to the Charles R. Beltz and Co. [Beltz is Ferguson's son-in-law] and this is to advise that I have rather full information and data respecting your connection with such organization. While you have deemed it in the public interest to investigate my wife—Edith Thomas—and to leave the impression that I have used and am still using her as a 'front' for my private business transaction, I wonder what your friends and constituents in Michigan will say when they learn that the same charge can be made against you.
>
> "I have all the pertinent facts with respect to the said company; the names of the stockholders, the number of shares and the official positions held by each stockholder. . . .
>
> "I assure you that I do not want to be driven to making public, data, in the form of charges against you and your committee. Personally it should be of no concern where you have spent your summer vacations, whom with, who paid the bills, or when and how you have entertained your friends here in Washington. That is your private business—but you must remember that I have private business myself. Swanky parties with all that goes along—including the best of drinks including good champaign [sic]—all paid for by another—is not good publicity at any time—and is especially bad in a personal campaign year. Luckily I am not a candidate this year.

"You will no doubt be surprised to know that among my letters and reports, some not signed—that charges have been made that certain wealthy automobile interests, acting through lady members of their inside organizations, have made gifts of valuable coats, dresses and other items to certain members of your family. . . .

"I have personally written this lingthy [sic] note in order to keep it strictly private. However for fear that I may hereafter need a copy I have had the sheets photostated but I do not plan to make the contents public unless I deem public interest will be served thereby.

Sincerely,

ELMER THOMAS"

After Ferguson's dismal performances in the Pearl Harbor and Howard Hughes fiascoes had raised grave doubts as to his professional competence as a prosecutor, the Thomas episode revealed a certain degree of, to say the least, moral obtuseness. It gave the *coup de grâce* to Ferguson's standing.

He is really nothing worse than a bush-league lawyer with a bad case of political opportunism and headline hunger—but that is not much of a record for a man who aspired to be Dewey's Attorney General.

John Bricker and Harry Cain are the hatchet men of the real-estate lobby.

Whatever kind of axing or scuttling has to be done on legislation which serves the public interest, Harry and John, with a smile on their lips and a song in their hearts, grab their little tomahawks and race to do the job. With Harry and John, the slogan is "Your Realtor Is Our Mentor."

Harry P. Cain is a strange and complex man. Born in Tennessee, he moved as a child to Washington State. After college, he went to work for the Bank of America, which, among other interests, runs the largest small-loan company on the Pacific Coast. In 1940, at the age of thirty-four, he was elected Mayor of Tacoma in a surprise upset. After wartime service in Europe, he returned to win election to the Senate.

His campaign was heavily financed by real-estate operators and apart-ment-house owners.

In the Senate, he has never deviated from the official line laid down by Herbert Nelson, lobbyist for the National Association of Real Estate Boards.

Cain has fought slum clearance, public housing, farm housing, and cooperative housing. Except for an occasional flicker of isolationist opposition to administration foreign policy, he seems to have no inter-est in any other subject. Completely frustrated on the administration-dominated Banking Committee (which handles housing legislation), he switched from that to Armed Services in 1950 and left Bricker to hold the fort alone. But in blatherskite speeches on the floor and in all his public utterances, he has not changed his emphasis from the housing issue.

The Washington press corps which has seen many "characters" come and go is perplexed by Cain. One reporter voiced the consensus as well as anybody could.

"That guy," he said, "is a screwball."

John W. Bricker of Ohio has been called an "honest Harding." This does Harding an injustice. He had a sense of humor.

But, worse than that, it is completely misleading. Harding was a jovial, poker-playing, whisky-drinking, good-natured newspaperman. John Bricker is a sanctimonious milksop.

Almost all accounts of him fail to get across his real essence, because they quite understandably emphasize the deviousness, the hard-boiled reaction, and the cold grossness of his public record, thus implying that he planned it that way. Bricker is intellectually incapable of sus-tained schemes. He can best be compared to a big, soft, white sponge cake. Like a cake, he has mass but not weight, because the mass is made up of countless air holes.

Bricker is all of Sinclair Lewis's small-town characters rolled into one.

Utterly unsophisticated, ignorant of all literature, all complex ideas, he has worshiped one thing—money. Lacking the drive and the ruthless native force to be a successful businessman himself, he trans-forms his admiration into a cloying awe of rich men. He boasts to visitors that he knows Tom Girdler and Ernest Weir and can call them by their first names.

Bricker's narrow, small-bore outlook, rather than any active prejudice, explains why he and many of his supporters are easy marks for the anti-Semitic and anti-Negro propaganda of Gerald L. K. Smith, Gerald Winrod, and others of the lunatic fringe. That is also why it is one of the most ghastly and profoundly disturbing facts of 1950 Washington that a man of John Bricker's mentality should be sitting on the Joint Congressional Committee on Atomic Energy.

But out of it all one happy thought emerges. Bricker will never be President. His golden dream, and one of America's second-string nightmares, is thus over.

Bricker himself recognizes this. He no longer worries about his once statuesque figure, and he can go to town at the dining table. The more the outline of the White House retreats into the limbo, the more his waistline expands. In the last few years he has acquired one of the biggest paunches in the Capital.

Where will Ohio turn when its silver-haired, sweet-smelling, clean-living hero becomes a slob?

Missouri's senior Senator Forrest Donnell is a most respectable man. Indeed, respectability is his creed and he its high priest.

He would far rather suffer the law's delays than advance by one jot the course of human happiness at the cost of a departure from true form and procedure. For Donnell, the question is not is it wise, but has it precedent? Not is it practical, but is it proper?

Donnell is sixty-six years old, a small man with hunched-over shoulders and a disproportionately large head, pale, protruding eyes behind colorless, shell-rimmed spectacles, a long nose, a large mouth, crepy, wrinkled neck, and flag ears that stand out from his head at almost ninety-degree angles.

Donnell speaks always in terms of "legality," "sovereignty," "due process," "unconstitutionality," and other imposing phrases. He seems to wear a mask of weary indifference to the actual nature and results of the legislation he is delaying and obstructing. A non-lawyer character in Dickens' *Bleak House* had the final word on this pose:

"I am not sure, my dear girl, but that it may be wise and specious to preserve that outward indifference. It may cause other parties interested to become lax about their interest; and people may die off, and points may drag themselves out of memory and many things may smoothly happen that are convenient enough."

New Hampshire's Styles Bridges is the shrewd, smooth, hard-boiled Yankee slicker come to the big town.

But Bridges is out for bigger things than peddling tinware and cheap jewelry. He operates with big pressure blocs such as the private power companies, the railroads, and the Farm Bureau Federation. For a country boy he has done very well.

As a senator, Bridges is a very vocal and narrowly partisan conservative. He follows closely on Wherry's heels in every vicious political scalping party. He heckles and yells and nags.

As ranking Republican member of the Appropriations Committee, he serves his old power-trust friends faithfully, struggling year in and year out to cut the heart from public-power appropriations and to sabotage reclamation and rural electrification programs. Although "Meat Ax" John Taber in the House Appropriations Committee got more publicity, Bridges was more effective in the Eightieth Congress in knifing these proposals and compiling the bad record which so alienated public feeling in the West.

Like his illustrious New Hampshire predecessor, George Moses, who years before outraged the West by calling progressive Republicans "sons of the wild jackass," Styles Bridges thus had a lot to do with dragging his party down to defeat in 1948.

No Republican has declaimed louder and longer than Bridges against "labor monopolies" and New Deal "subservience to unions." It came as a great surprise, therefore, when he was discovered taking money through the grace of John L. Lewis. Bridges was Lewis's choice as "public" trustee on the three-man board supervising the United Mine Workers' health and welfare fund, receiving $35,000 a year for the sinecure.

When this fact was revealed, Bridges announced that he had to spend a "substantial" part of the salary to hire lawyers and accountants to aid him in his work on the board. But then it was revealed that the board had a staff and that a Justice Department lawyer had been paid a special fee of $15,000 by the board to advise Bridges. Trapped on that one, Bridges still insisted that he had to spend his own money for expert advice, which, if true—and who would doubt the word of a senator?—must have made him one of the best-advised men in Washington.

When public clamor still continued, Bridges dolefully announced that he was getting off the board "in two or three months, as soon as an audit can be made of the accounts." That put the lions to sleep, and the public forgot about the affair. But months passed and Bridges hung on and on. The pension fund was stalled by dissension and paid out almost nothing to the miners, but Bridges' $35,000 rolled around regularly. It took him a long, long time finally to cut himself off from it.

This Lewis tie-up helps explain two puzzling aspects of Bridges' career.

It helps, in part, to explain how he can afford to live on such a lavish scale on a senator's salary. It also explains why Bridges, rabidly anti-labor, should have suddenly remembered a very important speaking engagement in New Hampshire the week the Taft-Hartley Act came up for repeal in 1949. He thus ducked voting on the amendment to abolish the injunction which Lewis so detests.

Homer Capehart of Indiana suffers from a serious and almost incurable malady. Clinically it is known as pernicious rotundity—fat head, fat body, and fatuousness.

Capehart is a vivid example of what happens when a certain type of businessman goes into politics. In business, Capehart was a whizz-bang and made a million dollars. In politics, he has been like a defective radiator—clanking noisily, hissing spouts of steam, and giving no heat.

Capehart, fifty-three, is a rotund Hoosier with a double chin, black hair, spectacles, a blunt-shaped nose with thin nostrils like slits in a wad of putty, and a swelling paunch. He wears conservative, double-breasted suits and smokes big cigars. To describe his conventionally successful rise in the business world is, as one writer remarked, "to commit a prolonged cliché."

His career in the Senate has been one long frustration.

Completely unequipped to deal intelligently with foreign affairs and the more complex domestic issues, he yet has a crude vitality which keeps him lumbering back again and again, no matter how many times he is made a fool of.

He rushed out on the limb with Bricker and Cain on behalf of the phony antisegregation amendment to the public-housing bill. He got up and shouted boldly, "Who can possibly be against permitting people of all creeds and colors to live in housing which has been constructed by the American taxpayers' money? Who is going to vote against it? Who is against civil rights?" At that point Taft rose and said calmly, "The senior Senator from Ohio is going to vote against the amendment." That lowered the boom on gaping Capehart.

Painfully parochial, Capehart refuses to hide his ignorance. He tangles with fellow senators and attempts to browbeat expert witnesses in every conceivable field. As a member of the Banking Committee, he spent a whole morning one day arguing vehemently with Marriner Eccles of the Federal Reserve Board. At the conclusion, Eccles commented crisply, "The trouble with the Senator is, he doesn't understand money."

Most observers would not limit the field to money.

Sometimes Capehart stands up and just starts talking to reassure himself. One of these heroic efforts was the following speech, quoted in its entirety:

"When I look about me, Mr. President, and see the intelligence displayed on the faces of members in the Senate, and when I look at the members of the House of Representatives and see the intelligence displayed on their faces, and when I meet officials of the administration and see the intelligence displayed on their faces, when I look about me and see so much intelligence displayed, I wonder what, after all, we are thinking about."

One thing is certain. Capehart will never know.

Senator William Jenner of Indiana is at the other pole from his earnest, bumbling Hoosier colleague.

Jenner is a young, handsome, dapper politico who was elected to the State Legislature four years after he graduated from law school, and was Minority Leader when he was twenty-nine. He served briefly in the war, came back to become State Republican Chairman, and in 1946 retired the ineffectual Republican Senator Raymond Willis.

Jenner is the young "squirt," the wiseacre type who never grew up. He perpetually wears a big, loose grin and has a gay gleam dancing in his eyes. Completely irresponsible and intellectually vacant, he regularly comes up with some incredible remark, such as in the spring of 1950 when he solemnly announced that he and the Indiana Republican delegation in the House were holding conferences to decide whether or not to institute impeachment proceedings against President Truman.

As a member of the Judiciary Committee, he always votes with Forrest Donnell, and, on behalf of the real-estate lobby, with Bricker and Cain. He is as isolationist as any man in Congress. And, of course, he stands ever ready to give a helping hand to any know-nothing crusade concocted by Wherry, Bridges, and McCarthy.

Jenner is totally without influence in the Senate, where he is recognized for what he is, a blowhard and a hack.

Senator Karl Mundt of South Dakota has built a whole career defending American womanhood (and "our children's children") from the perils of Red Communism. The tendency of most Washington reporters is to dismiss him as a windbag. This instinct is strengthened by a cursory inspection of Mundt's various activities.

For example, he lists with great pride the fact that he is editor of a speech magazine called *The Rostrum,* and associate editor of another called *The Speaker,* and that he is "co-founder and holder of membership certificate No. 1 of the National Forensic League, of which he is now president." This passion for undergraduate activities on the part of a grown man fifty years of age undoubtedly reveals certain ludicrous aspects of Mundt's character. But he cannot be dismissed.

For Karl Mundt is one of the most ominous figures in Congress.

Mundt, in collaboration with Representative Richard Nixon of California and Senator Homer Ferguson, is the author of a bill to establish thought control and police-state repression of intellectual freedom in the United States.

This bill has been vigorously opposed by the FBI and the Department of Justice. But, of course, Mundt knows more about scenting out Reds than any other man alive, unless it is J. Parnell Thomas, who, unfortunately, has had to curtail his patriotic activities in recent months while putting in time in a federal penitentiary.

As the *Washington Post* commented: "If the Mundt bill actually would accomplish the purpose of forcing the Communists into the open . . . that would be one thing. But should anyone in this day and age be deluded that the really dangerous Communists are those who go by that name and hold party cards? Surely the Kremlin's masterminds are persons who shun party meetings and even are known as anti-Communists. The restrictive features of the Mundt bill would only serve to push beneath the surface the visible portion of the Communist Party, which, like an iceberg, is six-sevenths submerged anyhow."

It is a dangerous era for Americans when they exalt into high places men like Karl Mundt who think with their larynx.

Senator William Knowland of California is making a strong and persistent bid to be a one-term senator.

It is not that he would not like to be re-elected in 1952. But he spends all his time working on behalf of constituents in Formosa and neglecting those who live in San Francisco and Los Angeles. Unfortunately for Bill Knowland, the folks in Formosa can't vote for him.

Knowland is the chief protagonist of Chiang Kai-shek in the Senate. Other Republican politicians thunder about the sorry plight of the Nationalist government cooped up in Formosa, but with them it is only a convenient partisan issue. With Knowland, it is a holy cause. Just why this should be so is a mystery.

It is a mystery not worth troubling to explore. Knowland swings little weight in the Senate, and won't be there long enough to grow to any stature.

Bourke Hickenlooper of Iowa has probably made a more lasting contribution to the American scene than any of his fellow Piltdown men. He has introduced into the language the phrase "to pull a Hickenlooper" as a modern synonym for "to pull a boner."

Bourke Blakemore Hickenlooper is ranking Republican member of the Joint Committee on Atomic Energy and was its chairman during the Eightieth Congress. He achieved this lofty and, apparently for him, dizzying eminence by reason of his long subservience to the Old Guard machine of Harrison Spangler, wartime chairman of the Republican National Committee and long-time kingmaker of Iowa Republican politics. Hickenlooper comes from Spangler's home city, Cedar Rapids.

Hickenlooper is a thin man, around medium height, with thinning brown hair, a high forehead, pale eyes behind spectacles, and a weak, receding chin. He presents a generally mousy, nondescript appearance. His only concession to cosmopolitan sophistication is the use of a rakish, Rooseveltian cigarette holder.

The trouble with the Iowa Republican is simply that he is confused by Washington. At every turn, for the first time in his life, he is confronted with some first-class minds.

As a member of the Foreign Relations and Atomic Energy Committees, he tangles with Democrats such as Millard Tydings, who was mauling better men than Hickenlooper twenty years ago; or with shrewd old Senator Theodore Green of Rhode Island, who was masterminding party caucuses when Hickenlooper was in high school. The poor, confused bumbler from Cedar Rapids is just an upstream trout in a sea of sharks.

During his first four years in the Senate, Hickenlooper generally kept his mouth shut and avoided undue notoriety, as became his mental stature. But in 1949, he decided to try his hand at the kind of hoopla hit-and-run attacking specialized in by Wherry and Mundt. He issued a statement charging Lilienthal with security leaks and "incredible mismanagement" of the Atomic Energy Commission. The show was on.

But it didn't last long. All of his blatherskiting blew up in his face. Hickenlooper wound up in even lower esteem in the Senate than before, and that was pretty low.

Senator Joe McCarthy has been pushing himself forward all his life. He has never hesitated to cut corners if a moral short cut would get him there quicker.

McCarthy, at forty-one, is a square-shouldered, sturdily built Irishman with thinning black hair, light-blue eyes, black eyebrows, and a small scar just to the left of the bridge of his nose. He has a surprisingly light, youthful voice, more to be expected in a college undergraduate twenty years his junior. McCarthy has a quick, alert air, as if he is constantly looking for someone or is expecting to move from where he is to where he isn't. Extraordinarily gregarious, he astounds people by his capacity for remembering names and personal details. This is not accidental.

While campaigning for the Senate, he kept a wire recorder in his automobile, and after each talk or at the end of the day, he would dictate the nicknames, family connections, and other pertinent details of the people he had met. These recordings were typed up by his campaign staff, and he referred to them whenever he returnd to that area, or when he sent out campaign literature. It is quite likely that he continues the practice in Washington.

Some writers during the McCarthy uproar were so stampeded by the sensational impression he was making that they began to describe him as "equal to the late Huey Long." That was silly. McCarthy is not in Long's class at all.

Long had a razor-sharp mind and could have become a millionaire had he chosen to practice corporate law. Justice Holmes described Long as one of the best attorneys ever to practice before the Supreme Court in his time. No one would ever say that of McCarthy.

He is only a mean shyster with no claims to legal ability, no grasp of social issues, no visions or long-range plans. He is just a low-grade operator involved in something 'way over his head and too stubborn to have gotten out while he still could. He has courage of a sort—the kind of ruthless determination which many a street-corner "tough" exhibits when he has been backed against the wall by a bigger and better man.

Guys who use brass knuckles often have brass nerves.

At heart, McCarthy is very insecure. He has a constant and insatiable mania for headlines and personal publicity to reassure himself that he really is "on the ball"; that he is, as Studs Lonigan would say, "the real stuff."

At the height of the State Department investigation, a correspondent visited McCarthy's office. During the conversation, the phone rang and McCarthy said, "No, no, I can't see you now. I am tied up being interviewed by two newspapermen." This caused the lone reporter to look over his shoulder, but McCarthy was not fazed by the exaggeration. He has for so long felt the need to bolster his confidence with a web of small lies and needless exaggerations that he is now accustomed to it.

He is a pathological liar. Like the character in *Alice in Wonderland,* McCarthy feels he must run very fast just to stay in the same place. It was when he felt himself slipping in the topsy-turvy world of politics that McCarthy reached down and came up with the charge that he knew there were 57 (or 81 or 205) Communists in the State Department.

McCarthy and his antics reflect in heightened and distorted form every facet of the Piltdown thinking of the Republican know-nothings.

They are as morally obtuse as Brewster and Bridges, as irresponsible as Jenner, as fatuous as Capehart, as moronic as Hickenlooper, and as sinister in aims as Mundt. Like Bricker and Cain, they have long been subservient to the real-estate lobby.

McCarthy is thus the ultimate of the breed of political Stone-Age men now darkening the Washington scene. (It is bitterly ironic that McCarthy, a Catholic, should be a leader of this faction, considering the Ku Klux Klan views privately held by several of his colleagues.)

Ignorant, insecure, reactionary, ruthless, intolerant, and frightened, they go roaring around, borrowing the methods and repressive ideals of Russian terrorists to fight their opponents at home and to obscure their incapacity to deal constructively with that Russian menace itself. In one way, they are objects of pity and a spectacle for derision. But in a larger sense they are far more ominous than this. The power they hold is too great and solemn for pity or derision.

In this desperate hour, it is the American people, who pay for their ride on the merry-go-round, who should be the true objects of pity.

THE MUTES

In the spring of 1950, the Senate was engaged in the long and furious debate over the Kerr natural-gas "ripper" bill. One day, at the peak of the controversy, someone called the Senate press gallery and inquired, "What's doing today?"

"Gas again," replied the clerk cryptically.

"I know," said the voice on the phone, "but what are they talking about?"

The Senate of the United States is the great stronghold of free speech; rhetorical gas is never under any regulation or restraint there. But in this august and verbose assembly there is a group which rarely participates in the verbal orgy.

They are what are known as the Mutes.

They come to Washington, sit in their plushy offices in the Senate Office Building or at their small desks in the Senate chamber, and, day after day, year after year, either say nothing or, when they do speak, still say essentially nothing. In most cases, they also do nothing. For the silence of these Mutes masks not the silence of wisdom but the emptiness of the void.

Some Mutes know nothing but, unhappily, are not aware of it. They occasionally rise to rend the air, but it doesn't matter since they never say anything.

There is, for example, Republican John Williams of Delaware who can deliver four hundred words a minute, the fastest rate in Congress and so rapid that the official stenographers cannot catch it all for the *Congressional Record*. But neither the *Record* nor the Senate misses anything.

Then there is James Kem, the docile reactionary from Missouri, who broke a lengthy silence to rise and deliver a vigorous speech against, of all things, the Kerr gas bill. Even though the press gallery knew he was under heavy pressure to do so by the crusading *St. Louis Post-Dispatch,* the newsmen practically toppled over the railing when Kem made his unprecedented plea.

No party or section of the country has a monopoly on the Senate Mutes.

Delaware, in addition to its Republican Mute, the thin, bespectacled, forty-six-year-old chicken-feed dealer Mr. Williams, has a Democratic member of the group, J. Allen Frear, a milk dealer and fertilizer sales-man who was drafted to run, against his own wishes, when no other Democrat would serve. Delaware has traditionally made a kind of specialty of being the only State to have two Mutes.

The Democrats also have Mutes such as Herbert O'Conor of Maryland, John Stennis of Mississippi, and Spessard Holland of Florida. But since the Democratic species have been discussed previously, this section will deal only with Republican Mutes. In addition to those already mentioned, these include:

Hugh Butler, Nebraska
Zales Ecton, Montana
Arthur Watkins, Utah
Henry Dworshak, Idaho
Andrew Schoeppel, Kansas
Edward Martin, Pennsylvania
Leverett Saltonstall, Massachusetts
Robert Hendrickson, New Jersey
Alexander Wiley, Wisconsin
George Malone, Nevada

Some Irishmen in the Capitol, when feeling particularly low, speculate dolefully on why it is that the race for the prize as the dumbest man in the Senate should be a flat-footed tie between two big, husky Irishmen, Joe McCarthy of Wisconsin and George Malone of Nevada. It is more than likely that Hickenlooper of Iowa should really be given the booby prize, but there is little doubt that Malone is a serious contender.

George "Molly" Malone lists himself as an "engineer." Actually, the only thing he ever engineered was his own election to the Senate in 1946; considering the raw materials he had to work with, it was quite a feat.

Malone is an ex-prize fighter who has spent most of his life on the outer fringes of the Western mining industry in various promotional activities, such as "public-relations counselor" and "economic consultant." For years he hung around Washington as a lobbyist for the silver bloc and various other special interests. He is the founder, and for fifteen years the sole director, of an organization known as the Industrial West Foundation, which is self-described as a "nonprofit industrial and business research organization." The Foundation, now defunct, was a front group for the forces fighting public power development and was largely financed by the private utility companies.

During his first three years as Senator, Malone was largely a tool of the man who was nominally his administrative assistant, Dr. John B. Crane.

Although the government provides Malone with a suite of offices, he continued to operate principally from a downtown office run by Dr. Crane. The rooms were the same as those previously used by the Industrial West Foundation. Indeed, that was still the name on the door. Also on the door was the name of a firm called Transportation Analysts, Inc. This is an economic consulting outfit working for private airlines. It was headed by Dr. Crane, who at the same time drew his salary as Malone's aide.

Malone's excuse for continuing this, to say the least, peculiar arrangement was that his government office was "overcrowded." Malone has one of the worst records for absenteeism in the Senate. When he does vote, it is invariably in accord with the interests of the various clients Dr. Crane represents and whom Malone formerly served in private life.

In 1949, Crane resigned as Malone's assistant, and he and his wife left for Germany, where they went to work as "contact agents" for various large German cartels. In January, 1950, Malone offered in the Senate a petition prepared by Crane demanding a halt to further dismantling of German war plants and the rearming of Western Germany. Whenever Malone does speak in the Senate, it is to urge this line or to re-echo a few stock isolationist arguments he gleaned from an old *Chicago Tribune.*

He has the dubious distinction of being one of the handful of diehards who voted against all Marshall Plan appropriations and against the North Atlantic Pact. Curiously, although professing great hatred of Communists and Russia, Malone's record on these votes parallels exactly that of New York's avowed party liner, Representative Vito Marcantonio.

Malone is absent so frequently, and cloaks his every action with such a veil of silence and secrecy, that Washington is at a loss to figure out whether he is sinister or merely stupid. Those who knew him in his pre-senatorial era, in the old days when he was a lobbyist and frequenter of the Press Club bar, tend to think the latter.

But there is no doubt in practically everyone's mind that he is one of the most worthless of all the senators.

Malone broke part way out of his cocoon in the spring of 1950.

First, he led the scalping party which stampeded Commerce Secretary Charles Sawyer into firing two government employees. Then Malone and his wife, who is even more reactionary than he, if that is possible, held a big "'steak roast" for 175 guests. There may have been some relation between the two events, as the party occurred the same week as the scalping. Perhaps it was meant to be a victory celebration.

The Malones had staged steak parties in other years, but this was an orgy that surpassed all others.

One society columnist wrote that the 175 who attended were "very hand-picked guests." They were hand-picked all right, and how! Every member of the Republican-Dixiecrat goon squad was there— Joe McCarthy, Joe Martin, Owen Brewster, Karl Mundt, Bill Knowland, Dick Russell, Chip Robert, Walter George, Harry Byrd, Kenneth Wherry, Harry Cain, etc., etc., *ad nauseam*.

Those two ghosts from the completely unlamented past, Dolly Curtis Gann and Alice Roosevelt Longworth, also showed up. Joe Pew, the oilman and GOP sugar daddy, flew down from Philadelphia. Colonel Robert R. McCormick arrived from Chicago. Mr. and Mrs. William Randolph Hearst, Jr., attended; and, just to make the gathering complete, the Ambassadors from the only two countries this crowd feels is worth America's attention in foreign affairs—sleek Wellington Koo of nonexistent Nationalist China, otherwise known as Formosa-by-the-Sea, and paunchy Felix de Lequerica of Fascist Spain—both put in an honored appearance.

But even more extraordinary than the guest list is the intriguing problem of figuring out what the Malones had to do with their own party.

The raucous shindig was held at the suburban estate of Mr. and Mrs. Peter Miller, publishers of the Washington *Times Herald*. Mrs. Miller is a niece of Colonel McCormick. The 2½-inch steaks were contributed by William Moffatt, Nevada cattle king. The party "favors" were contributed by Nevada gambling clubs.

Apparently all the Malones did was send out the invitations.

The gifts and favors are a story in themselves. The men received sterling silver tie clips to which were attached tiny silver ten-gallon hats branded "Harold's Club, Reno." The same little hats were made into pins for women. They also received gold pencils and key rings hung on scarlet plastic dice. These were branded "Golden Nugget," the name of a Las Vegas gambling club reputed to be the biggest in the world.

(Note: Highlight of the party was a roping contest. The prize was a miniature roulette wheel.)

There is nothing mysterious about Zales Ecton of Montana. A jovial, sandy-haired, red-faced livestock farmer, he is an amiable party minion. Further, he pretends to be nothing but what he is.

The only subject that really interests Ecton is the stillborn Missouri Valley Authority plan, which he strongly opposes. He is an undiluted utility spokesman. Occasionally he will orate about "regimentation," "government centralization," "Washington controls and the loss of our local liberties," and all the other claptrap he has read in utility propaganda bulletins, but after a short time it gets to be too much for him. So, with a merry twinkle in his eyes, he lumbers off to the Senate to listen to the great men debate and to vote Kenneth Wherry's convictions.

Arthur Watkins of Utah takes himself and his work seriously. That is of no consequence because nobody else does.

Wiry and diminutive, Watkins has to work hard not to be overlooked completely. In private, he is garrulous and provocative in his judgment of affairs and issues, but he succeeds only in boring and irritating his Republican colleagues, with whom he is quite unpopular. On the floor he is meek and silent. His isolationist and reactionary vote can always be found in Floor Leader Ken Wherry's vest pocket.

Henry Dworshak of Idaho, now serving an interim appointment, is like a man caught in a revolving door. He keeps whirling around and around, now outside in the cold of defeat, now inside in the warmth of public office. But Dworshak keeps hanging on; he's been in Washington since 1939 and he just hates to let go.

Even after his resounding defeat in 1948, he didn't leave Washington. Neither did he stop acting as if he were still a senator. Although his term expired December 31, 1948, Dworshak remained in Washington and sent out considerable quantities of mail at government expense under his old free postage frank. Many of the letters, on the stationery of the Senate Appropriations Committee, of which he was once a member, lobbied against the proposed Columbia Valley Authority.

Dworshak is personally a genial and friendly sort of small-town fellow. He is quite candid about his views. They consist principally of an almost obsessive hatred of union labor, an unswerving fealty to private utilities, and an unyielding hostility to all forms of internationalism. He also detests Governor Thomas Dewey, who studiously ignored him throughout the 1948 campaign.

Dworshak is an admirer of Taft but privately confesses that the man he most esteems in the Senate is John Bricker of Ohio. Counting Mrs. Bricker, that makes three.

Nebraska's Hugh Butler is something which, by definition, could scarcely be said to exist. He is a reactionary Republican who is more reactionary than Kenneth Wherry. It is a truly prodigious achievement.

But Butler takes it in stride. He has known all along that he was a pretty smart cookie.

Butler is a very rich Omaha grain dealer. As a tough and driving operator, he spent decades amassing a large fortune. Then, like the wealthy man satirized in so many novels of the 1920's, he felt called upon to acquire a thick veneer of respectability. He became a heavy contributor to all the conventional good causes—Boy Scouts, Community Chest, YMCA, Salvation Army, the college he went to in his youth, etc. In a word, Butler became a pillar of society. But that somehow was not enough.

He turned to politics. The Republican Party in Nebraska in the 1930's was in a parlous state. Butler took over as National Committeeman and proceeded to revive the patient with heavy transfusions of greenbacks. Teaming up with Kenneth Wherry, who was State Chairman, Butler played the role of Old Moneybags while Wherry served as barker.

The act paid off. Butler came to the United States Senate in 1940. Wherry followed him two years later.

Smug and self-confident, Butler has been a perfect dodo in his ten years in the upper chamber. He talks occasionally about economy and then always votes for all the pork-barrel grabs. He is an isolationist from the darkest corner of Colonel McCormickland. He votes always with Taft except when the Ohioan goes "Socialist" on matters like public housing.

But Butler, like Democrat Bob Kerr, has not been so preoccupied with the weighty problems of statecraft that he can't find time to put over a fast one for his old friends in the grain business—his own large firm being one of them.

Butler doesn't have quite Kerr's gall to do the job himself and out in the open. Instead, he wheedled Senator Ed Thye of Minnesota into offering a loosely drawn amendment to the Commodity Credit Corporation extension bill of 1950, requiring the agency to use private storage facilities for all its surplus grain holdings. This would have frozen out the cooperative grain elevators and meant a lush profit for the private operators.

However, the boodle graft didn't get far. Under a withering fire from Agriculture Secretary Brannan and Commodity Credit officials, the amendment was killed in committee. Butler didn't have the courage to offer it on the floor, and Thye refused to do so.

Even Butler is aware that he is a cipher as a statesman, and he is eying a new role which would give him power without the glare of public responsibility.

He talks privately of surrendering his seat in 1952 to ambitious Governor Val Peterson, in return for Peterson's support of one of Butler's business protégés for governor. This deal would unite the two factions and give Butler, through the governorship, an iron grip on the Republican State machine. In that new status, no one would criticize him for the vast, if somewhat ornate, silence he keeps on all issues. A Warwick is supposed to keep his mouth shut.

In one way, Alexander Wiley of Wisconsin is a relief from Hugh Butler. Wiley has a sense of humor. In fact, he is a regular good-humor man; all he needs is a white apron.

Wiley collects jokes as a hobby and collects dust as a senator.

The Wisconsinite has been in Washington since 1939 and is seeking a third term. This makes him one of the senior Republican senators. But even seniority cannot endow Wiley with importance and prestige.

He is a large, shapeless man, devoid of ideas, convictions, and enthusiasms.

Throughout the spring of 1950, Wiley quaked and quavered on the political hot seat. "Jumpin' Joe" McCarthy, his junior colleague, was running amuck discovering Commies behind every desk and file case in Foggy Bottom. Wiley could not make up his mind whether to come out for McCarthy or whether to criticize him for his excesses.

It was not a problem of trying to make up his mind on the questions involved; it was simply which tactic would win the most votes. Wiley decided to play it safe and lie low.

He said not a single word about McCarthy throughout the whole 1950 session. In private, he would occasionally join in with a little yelp to the effect that "they shouldn't be kicking Joe around so hard." But when Mrs. Smith made her "declaration of conscience" speech socking McCarthy, Wiley was second only to Senator Lehman of New York in the line of colleagues who shook her hand.

Edward Martin of Pennsylvania is the traditional variety of Joe Grundy stooge thickly wrapped in the aura and military glamour of a retired major general.

Martin takes great pride in the fact that he has served in all grades of the military service from private to major general, and his publicity always makes a great point of his high rank. Behind this there lies a story.

When the Pennsylvania National Guard was mustered into service, Martin was called to duty as brigadier general in command of the 28th Division. After an initial training period, the 28th went to Louisiana to participate in maneuvers. The resulting confusion was almost too horrible to contemplate. Soon thereafter he was promoted to major general and retired. That was in the spring of 1942, just in time for the off-year political campaign. The GOP machine, which had never considered Martin anything more than a dutiful and uninspired minion, promptly nominated him for governor and put him on the stump as, of all things, a "war hero." The General thought it was great and played his part with gusto. A portly old gentleman, he has at least some of the frozen manner and good posture of a general.

He looked very military at political rallies, standing between a keg of beer and the flag.

At that, he barely made it, squeaking in by only 10,000 votes. At Harrisburg he found life much easier than in the Louisiana bayous. Mr. Grundy was chief of staff, the Pennsylvania Manufacturers Association did the G-2 work, and General Martin was content to sign the order of the day. It was the happy ending to a story of long and faithful service.

In 1946, "Fighting Ed" was advanced to the Senate, where he has been sitting quietly ever since. But Martin has one virtue as a statesman. He does not snore in public.

The story of Leverett Saltonstall of Massachusetts is a tale of the decline of a reputation.

Few men come to Washington with bigger advance notices than Saltonstall when he arrived in 1945. His six-year tenure as governor was the longest since post-colonial times. He had given an honest and competent administration, in contrast to the venality and fumbling that had preceded him. Also, as a Willkieite, he had been an early supporter of Roosevelt's foreign policy. Saltonstall seemed headed for a distinguished role as a senator and as a potent leader in the revitalization of the Republican Party.

In 1945, his first session in the Senate, Saltonstall showed some glint of this promise. He voted for the Reciprocal Trade Agreements Act, a marked departure from the high-tariff orthodoxy of New England Republicanism. But soon the darkness fell all around him. The Senate met and the Senate adjourned. Great and solemn issues vexed the world.

But from Leverett Saltonstall no word came to break the silence of the night.

Years passed. And, alas, all had to confess that Saltonstall was a Mute. (Was it perhaps because he had nothing to say?)

The Boston Brahmin sat in the ranks with the chicken-feed salesman from Delaware and the grain dealer from Omaha. Wherry and Bricker and the other Piltdown men had nothing to fear from him.

He, too, voted with the utility lobby against TVA and against rural electrification. He, too, voted for Bricker's "quickie" amendment to kill rent control in 1949. He, too, voted with the Southern Tories to deprive 750,000 people of Social Security benefits and to deny a minimum wage to 250,000 retail employees. He, too, voted to exempt insurance companies from the antitrust laws.

So, because he was so docile and "regular," they rewarded him— with a seat on the Policy Committee and the designation as Party Whip.

But his silence is still unbroken.

Saltonstall remains, of course, a most honorable and kindly gentleman with impeccable manners, a fine family (one of his daughters is married to Senator Byrd's nephew), and a big "gentleman's farm," to which he would probably retire altogether were it not for the inflexible sense of duty that keeps him in public life.

GOP MAVERICKS

There are nine Republicans in the Senate who may loosely be classified as "liberals." These nine have only one thing in common. They are all independents.

With one, independence is erratic and personal; with another, it is based on keen political intuition; with a third, it is the servant of ambition; with others, it flows from quiet decency and courage. Each is proud that he wears no man's collar; several scarcely wear the Republican label. All are generals and none is a private.

As individuals, the Republican liberals include some of the most able and attractive men in Congress; as a group, they are weak, divided, and ineffectual. They do not work together, have no common program and no accepted leader. Each fights alone, and the Devil and Bob Taft take the triumphs.

Wayne Morse of Oregon is the most brilliant, audacious, and only genuine liberal of the Republican mavericks.

He has a mind like a buzz saw, a tongue like a lash, and the fighting guts of a bantam rooster. With the ability to cut to the heart of an issue and a masterly grasp of the essential realities, Morse is the scourge of both parties.

Imperturbably impartial, he pounces caustically on the bungling and moral flabbiness of the Truman administration, and just as devastatingly exposes the Wherry-Bridges leadership when it tries to sneak over a reactionary fast one. Most Democrats suspect he really isn't a Republican, and most Republicans wish he weren't. Morse goes his own way.

The story of Wayne Lyman Morse and his family is the story of restless Americans who kept going West until they came to the last frontier on the edge of the Pacific. Descended from Congregationalist New England Yankees who fought in the American Revolution, Morse was born in 1900 on a 300-acre farm near Madison, Wisconsin. He went to the University of Wisconsin in the years from 1919 to 1924, when Progressive Republicanism was riding high and old Bob La Follette was in his prime. Naturally, Morse imbibed deeply of this heady politico-economic brew.

In 1929 he went to the University of Oregon as an assistant professor of law. Two years later, at the age of thirty-one, he was dean of the Law School, one of the youngest law deans in the country. He also established a wide reputation as a legislative consultant and labor arbitrator. In 1944, he made his first try for political office and won. He was elected to the Senate, defeating one of the worst of the Piltdown men—reactionary, bumbling, isolationist Rufus Holman. Morse and Roosevelt both carried Oregon in 1944, Morse winning by a better than 3 to 2 margin.

As a senator, Morse has been a tower of strength to the liberal cause. In fact, he has been a more vigilant and constructive liberal than most of those nominally enlisted on the side of the administration. Morse hasn't been content merely to compile a decent and enlightened voting record. He gets right in there and claws and battles for unpopular issues.

In the summer of 1949, the antediluvian Republicans joined hands with oil-smeared Robert Kerr and his fellow Democrats from the Southwest to destroy the career of one of the ablest and most conscientious public servants in Washington, Leland Olds, who was up for confirmation to another term on the Power Commission. He had committed the heinous crime of denouncing Kerr's "ripper" bill as a boodle grab. So Olds was butchered, 58 to 15. Morse not only fought and voted in his behalf but, after the battle was over, aggressively insisted on placing in the record a tribute to Olds written by the staff of the Power Commission. Similarly, in 1948, Morse and Langer of North Dakota were the only two Republicans to vote against the vicious Gearhart resolution which deprived three-quarters of a million people of Social Security protection.

It is this moral courage, this willingness to stand alone in defense of the right, no matter how unpopular, which gives Wayne Morse a strong claim as heir to the great tradition of Norris and La Follette.

But his intrepid qualities have made Morse a lonely and isolated figure among fellow Republicans. They look on him the way Stalin looks on Tito. Morse frightens his old-fashioned brethren in the Senate not only because he is liberal but because he is an ambitious and daring man. Worst of all, he compounds his sins by being right.

In 1946, after Representative Carroll Reece, Taft's choice, had been elected National Chairman, Morse declared:

> "The meeting of the Republican National Committee at the Statler Hotel last night was a grand flop. If [this] program is to constitute Republican policy during the next two years, the Republican National Committee will re-elect Harry Truman in spite of everything he is doing to defeat himself.
>
> "We listened to the same old clichés and reactionary nostrums *ad nauseam* which have produced Republican defeats since 1932."

Two years later the voters proved Morse right.

But with the Stone-Age Republicans, it is scarcely a virtue to be right or to have the majority of the people with you. Wayne Morse will have to do a lot of tugging to lead the elephant out of the salt mines.

Senator Irving Ives comes from New York. That fact is at once his boon and his cross.

It is his boon because it has given him the national publicity and reputation which his very ordinary talents and achievements would not otherwise have merited. It is his cross because it forces him—a conservative by instinct and background—to take consistently more liberal positions than he wants to.

Ives's career before he was elected to the Senate in 1946 was devoted to banking, insurance, and to small-time politics. He served in the

New York Legislature for sixteen years, totally undistinguished. But toward the end he acquired fleeting prominence because his name was on the Fair Employment Practices bill drafted and passed by the Dewey administration and as sponsor of a State School of Industrial Relations at Cornell. In Washington, Ives has had a tough time living up to his greatly exaggerated advance billing as a liberal.

Had he just been an insurance man and Republican politician from Topeka or Yankton, nobody would have expected much, and he would have been free to vote his conservative instincts and let it go at that. But, coming from New York, he is the object of attention of the great metropolitan press, national magazines, the powerful trade unions in the garment industry, and the leaders and pacesetters in a hundred different domestic and foreign causes and projects. He has been forced to take stands and make speeches on a vast array of subjects from labor relations and racial practices to ECA and the recognition of Franco. Who knows what Schoeppel of Kansas or McFarland of Arizona thinks on these matters, or whether they even think about them at all?

Ives is no better nor worse than these run-of-the-mill backbenchers, but he is always in the limelight—to his great distress.

He betrays this gap between private inclinations and public statements, between natural abilities and public expectations, by his verbosity in private conversations with constituents and newspapermen. He talks continuously and too much, because he has an uneasy conscience. He betrays it also in the curious shifts and contradictions in his voting record.

On labor issues, as the representative of an industrial State, he is expected to take a more intelligent view of this complex problem than rural yahoos like Butler and Ecton. Ives lived up to expectations as best he could by voting in the Eightieth Congress for every crippling amendment offered by the liberals to the Taft-Hartley bill, and then, when the amendments failed, by voting for adoption of the bill. Then, in the Eighty-first Congress, he turned around and voted to repeal the bill.

He also voted to deny minimum-wage protection to 250,000 workers previously covered by the law.

On aid to education, Ives supported the bill on final passage, but first voted for all the hamstringing amendments proposed by its foes.

Similarly, on taxes, he voted both in 1947 and 1948 for the Knudson bills, which reduced federal revenue by five billion dollars and caused a budget deficit. On December 20, 1948, Ives told a press conference, "I certainly had my fingers crossed when I voted for it. In a time of high national income you certainly shouldn't cut taxes."

"Then why did you vote for it?" he was asked.

"I voted for it as a loyal member of the Republican Party," replied Ives. "The reason that made it a party issue was that so many Republican members of the House had made it a campaign issue to reduce taxes."

Ives has thus used all five classic techniques of the hypocritical politician.

He has switched from one side of an issue to the other in succeeding years; he has voted with one side on amendments and with the other side on final passage; he has knifed bills in the secrecy of committee which later he voted for in public; he has straddled an issue by refusing to take a stand at all; and he has taken refuge behind the shield of party loyalty.

President Truman has a word for such ersatz liberals. He calls them "jellylegs." Ives is indeed a jellyleg but, withal, a pleasant, personable fellow.

If only all those damn people up in New York didn't insist on his being a liberal and a statesman!

Margaret Chase Smith of Maine is the only woman in the Senate. Her career and her voting record may be explained much better by referring to the simple fact of her sex than by attempting to hang any ideological dog tags on her.

Margaret Smith comes from Skowhegan, a small town of 7,000 situated along the Kennebec River. She is in many ways the typical, pleasant, small-town woman, the kind who works hard, is well informed but not gossipy, bakes pies for the church supper, nurses sick neighbors, serves on the school board or runs the post office in a pinch, and is liked and well thought of by everyone. Cheerful, hardworking, and good-natured, Margaret Smith has none of the stale neurotic ambitions and the bitter prejudices and fixations which beset so many of her masculine colleagues.

In the Senate, Mrs. Smith's chief accomplishment so far was her ringing speech against McCarthyism. It was a major triumph.

The address was a happy blend of forcefulness and tact and exhibited a healthy, clear-eyed perception of the central issues. She closed with a "declaration of conscience" which was a strong warning to her Stone-Age Republican colleagues. Their only response was to churlishly nickname Mrs. Smith and her six co-signers "Snow White and the Six Dwarfs."

Alexander Smith of New Jersey and Ralph Flanders of Vermont have one thing in common. They are generally classed as Republican liberals, but if their party were not weighed down by an overabundance of deadheads and reactionaries, both would be recognized for what they are: honest, well-informed, and responsible conservatives.

Unlike Ives, they do not pretend to any phony liberalism; it is simply the political setting that makes them look like liberals.

Smith's specialty is foreign affairs; Flanders' chief concern is the domestic economy. Both are distinguished by a wealth of experience and the wide knowledge which each brings to any discussion in his respective field. Both men are seventy years old, and both turned to politics only after putting in rich, full lives in other areas of activity. But here the similarity ends.

Flanders is a piquant and aggressive figure. Smith tends to be overly cautious in his thinking. Flanders is picturesque in speech and bold in his thinking. He considers mass housing for low-income families one of the great challenges that private enterprise has not met. No one is a more vigorous champion of government action in this field. On other issues, such as labor, he is not a standpatter, but his views diverge considerably from those urged by unions.

Basically, what distinguishes Smith and Flanders from their Stone-Age colleagues is that they have had broad, practical experience in actually running things. Most of the reactionaries have had no actual important experience in running either domestic or foreign affairs. They are salesmen like Wherry and Capehart or second-rate lawyers like Bricker and Donnell. To Flanders, "free enterprise" is a mechanism to be operated and constantly improved; to men like Mundt and Jenner, it is a shibboleth to be jabbered about on the platform. Similarly, Smith has a polished and cultivated mind richly informed on foreign affairs by years of study and travel. Characters like McCarthy and Knowland are ignorant, prejudiced amateurs who wouldn't know the Treaty of Rapallo from the ILO covenant.

Flanders and Smith are not rip-roaring crusaders. But they are gentlemen, and they stand out because they have something simple, something almost unique, which all those trying to doctor the Republican Party frequently overlook—brain power.

William Langer of North Dakota illustrates graphically one part of the story of what went wrong with the insurgent movement of the Republican farm states. Big, bluff, hearty Bill Langer is a crafty political free lance who has worked both sides of every street for thirty-five years.

As a senator, Langer has an almost perfect New Deal voting record on domestic issues. On foreign affairs, he constantly plays to the grubby isolationism of his strongly German constituency.

Langer has a brilliant mind and undeniable personal charm and force. He wrote a minority report on the Mundt-Nixon bill which was a masterly summation of the evils of that vicious measure. What Langer tragically lacks is a moral anchor.

For example: He is a militant crusader against congressional nepotism and is the author of a bill prohibiting the appointment of relatives "related by consanguinity or affinity within the fourth degree computed according to the civil law." In a magazine article, he assailed nepotism as "one of the worst practices in American public life." He boasted that "as Attorney General of North Dakota, as Governor of that State, and as U.S. Senator, I have never appointed a relative to a job under me."

But a scrutiny of the federal payroll disclosed that Langer secured a $12,000 job on the U.S. Court of Customs in New York for his nephew, and that he put his son-in-law's sister on the payroll of the Post Office Committee (of which he is ranking Republican member) as minority clerk at $11,000 annually.

But more ominous than this indiscretion is his stand on foreign policy. Langer is not merely an intransigent isolationist. His pro-German proclivities have strong Nazi and anti-Semitic overtones.

He writes regularly for *The Broom*, an anti-Semitic gutter-rag published by a man who was indicted for sedition during the war. He pressured the Alien Property Custodian into reopening a case involving the daughter of a Nazi agent sentenced to death for treason in Hawaii during the war. He worked very hard to arrange a parole for a woman serving time in a federal penitentiary for harboring Nazi spies in her Detroit home during the war. He was a violent foe of liberalizing the displaced-persons law.

Langer is the kind of German who exemplifies Mr. Dooley's remark, "Wanst a German, always Dutch. . . . A German is niver an American excipt whin he goes back to Germany to see his rilitives."

Charles Tobey of New Hampshire would be a great senator if his head were as sound as his heart.

The tall, bald, bespectacled Yankee has a warm, fervid, emotional nature which is constantly going up and down like a barometer in stormy weather. His heart is attuned to high purposes and generous enthusiasms, but his mental processes are erratic and vagrant.

One of the more impassioned isolationists, he switched and became an internationalist in 1941. Then, a week after Pearl Harbor, he wanted to call off the war for a couple of months so the Senate might find out what really happened at Pearl Harbor. On the labor issue, he voted for Taft-Hartley in 1947 and to repeal it in 1949. He sponsored a sweeping, $3,000,000,000 housing program in 1949. The next year he opposed the administration's middle-income cooperative housing bill because its $2,000,000,000 authorization was "inflationary"!

Some observers contend that the last man to talk to Tobey before he goes into the Senate is the one who gets his vote. But at other times all the talking in the world cannot change his vote.

Tobey comes from, and identifies himself with, the hard-scrabble, individualistic Yankee farmers of New Hampshire, who have a conservative social pattern but no particular vested interest in the economic *status quo*. Tobey, unlike most politicians, can help his neighbors with the haying and look as if he really likes it. He enjoys leading group singing or "calling" a square dance, and he can deliver a rousing, hellfire-and-brimstone sermon on Layman's Sunday.

Tobey is rural and parochial but authentic.

Too quixotic to be either a dependable leader or a loyal follower, Tobey remains the genial, impulsive, candid Eagle Scout of the Senate.

Henry Cabot Lodge is the openly avowed candidate for the leadership of the small band of maverick Republicans.

In speeches and magazine articles he has urged that the party take a forward-looking stand, accept the welfare state, revise the Taft-Hartley Act, and champion civil rights. But he has never gotten anywhere in his quest, and his record may explain the reason.

When he came up for re-election in 1942, Lodge told a group of constituents privately, "I am a member of the radical wing of the Republican Party." It is difficult to discover his radical actions.

In 1937, he was one of sixteen senators to vote against the slum-clearance bill. In 1938, he twice voted with the Southerners against cloture during an antilynching-bill filibuster. In 1939, he was one of four senators to vote against the confirmation of William O. Douglas to the Supreme Court. In the same year he voted against an increase in the WPA appropriation bill, and the proposal lost by one vote. In 1942, he was one of only four senators to vote against an amendment to the Social Security Act increasing appropriations for the care of crippled children.

His only liberal stand in six years was his vote for the Wage and Hour Act, but in view of the intensity of feeling in New England against "unfair" competition from cheap Southern labor, this was scarcely a "radical" sortie.

As the grandson of a chairman of the Foreign Relations Committee and the ambitious heir apparent to Vandenberg's leadership of the internationalist Republicans, Lodge has always prided himself on his insight into foreign affairs.

But when war broke out in September, 1939, he declared, "The fight in Europe is not our fight. It is theirs. If the British and French empires cannot stand without our help, then they deserve to fall." In the two years that followed, Lodge pursued a vacillating course. *Time* magazine summed it up this way:

"He voted to limit use of United States forces to the Western Hemisphere, to restrict transfer of naval craft, to make a two-billion-dollar loan instead of Lend-Lease. Then he voted for Lend-Lease, then to retain the neutrality act, then to declare war, thus taking all sides."

In February, 1944, he resigned his seat to go on active duty with the

Army. He returned in 1946 to take away the other Massachusetts Senate seat long held by isolationist David I. Walsh. Where Lodge stood at that time on foreign policy was rather difficult to establish. As the *Christian Science Monitor* cautiously observed: "On the controversial question of handling Russia, he has postponed a decisive answer. 'My views on all questions regarding foreign policy and national defense,' he said in a communication to the *Haverhill Gazette,* 'would almost inevitably be subject to drastic change because as a Senator I would possess information not now available to me as a private citizen.'"

Even veteran politicians found this masterpiece of straddling rather breath-taking.

Since his return to the Senate, Lodge has been a fairly consistent and substantial supporter of a strong, bipartisan foreign policy. In domestic affairs, he acquired considerable prestige as co-sponsor of the bill creating the Hoover Commission on Government Reorganization and as co-author of the constitutional amendment to revise the electoral college. Both proposals are eminently worth while and eminently safe.

On more controversial issues, he voted for Taft-Hartley in 1947 and to repeal it in 1949. Although he is a strong advocate of a Republican-run welfare state, he voted in 1948 to take 750,000 people out from the protection of the Social Security system. He opposed the federal aid-to-education bill as a "subsidy" from the rich states to the poor ones. He tried to kill the bill by tacking on an antisegregation amendment, but he was defeated by a bipartisan coalition headed by Taft.

This was precisely the same tactic followed by Bricker on the housing bill, but in Bricker's case it brought down on his head a storm of public censure because of his duplicity. Lodge somehow escaped criticism for using the same strategy.

Lodge supported public housing. He also supported Bricker's motion to kill rent control.

On the basis of his public record, it would be hard to say that Senator Lodge's views are either conservative or liberal. Perhaps flexible might be a better word.

It would be hard to imagine a sharper contrast between two men than that which exists between Lodge and another liberal-minded New England Republican, Vermont's George Aiken.

Lodge is a tall, elegantly groomed aristocrat with a Harvard Square "a" and a strong interest in foreign affairs. Aiken is an easygoing, rumpled farmer of medium height with a friendly, homely face and a close-knit head of cottony white hair. He speaks with a slow Vermont twang. Aiken before the war was a nonranting isolationist; now he is a silent supporter of administration foreign policy. In both phases, he has never left the slightest doubt that domestic affairs are the chief concern of his heart and brain.

Aiken and his fellow liberal Yankee Republicans were always close to the Roosevelt administration. They are less in rapport with the Truman gang. In the eyes of these members of the GOP, it is no sin to be a Democratic fellow traveler, and a considerable number have received federal appointments.

In 1949, Governor Ernest Gibson of Vermont became a federal judge. His wartime predecessor, William Wills, was appointed to the Federal Communications Commission by Roosevelt in 1945. The late John Winant, onetime Republican Governor of New Hampshire, was wartime Ambassador to England; and Francis Murphy, Republican Governor of New Hampshire from 1937 to 1941, openly campaigned for Roosevelt in 1944.

In fact, the unshakable Republicanism of Maine and Vermont is a deceptive thing. If the nation really went as Maine and Vermont sometimes go, Kenneth Wherry would drop dead.

Aiken is a versatile man. He is the only senator to sit on both the Labor Committee and the Agriculture Committee. Most politicians see a conflict of interest between these two great power blocs. Aiken does not. He is generally the friend of both organized labor and the small farmer.

Aiken also carries on the best traditions of town-meeting democracy. He champions the right of everyone to be heard. He speaks out on behalf of Negro and sharecropper, of every minority group, every oppressed people.

Of the handful of Republican liberals, Aiken is best qualified to be the leader.

Wayne Morse is so outspoken and so daring that he has been put in quarantine by his fellow Republicans. Henry Cabot Lodge, operating more from intuition than conviction, is caught in the maze of his own ambitions. Ralph Flanders and Alexander Smith are too old and too inexperienced in political guerrilla tactics. William Langer has deeply compromised himself in the field of foreign affairs. Irving Ives of New York is unequipped, uninspired, and unconvinced. And neither Mrs. Smith of Maine nor Charles Tobey of New Hampshire has the personal weight and standing to take a decisive role. This leaves Aiken to carry the torch.

But merely calling this roll delineates clearly his difficulties. Also, Aiken is himself not equal to the task. He has the moral stature, the inner conviction, and the tenacity of purpose. But he lacks the spark of fire, the crusading zeal to lead the way.

To topple or seriously to curb the Taft-Wherry-Bridges leadership requires more ruthless fighting qualities than the kindly, reflective, high-minded Yankee liberal usually displays.

Perhaps he is waiting for time, like rain on a Vermont hillside, to erode them away.

FIVE-PERCENTERS—AND UP

> "Contrary to tradition, against the public morals, and hostile to good government, the lobby has reached such a position of power that it threatens government itself. Its size, its power, its capacity for evil; its greed, trickery, deception, and fraud condemn it to the death it deserves."
>
> HUGO L. BLACK

> "Nearly every activity of the human mind has been capitalized by some grafter with headquarters established for this activity in Washington."
>
> SENATOR THADDEUS CARAWAY

> "Lord, we are ashamed that money and position speak to us more loudly than does the simple compassion of the human heart. Help us to care, as Thou dost care, for the little people who have no lobbyists, for the minority groups who sorely need justice. May it be the glory of our government that not only the strong are heard, but also the weak; not only the powerful, but the helpless; not only those with influence, but those who have nothing but a case and an appeal. . . . Amen."
>
> REVEREND PETER MARSHALL
> *Senate Chaplain*

LIFE in Washington is in many ways like a fairy tale.

Once upon a time, there was a powerfully built but plodding ox plowing a field. A gnat came along, circled around, and dived for the ox's ear, then his neck, then his buttocks, so much so that the ox was kept busy tossing his head, swishing his tail, and twitching irritably, and could scarcely do any plowing. This seemed to please the gnat greatly.

A second gnat came along and began stinging the ox on the flanks, all the time buzzing loudly. This made the animal grunt and sweat and struggle to get away from the annoyer. This seemed to please the second gnat greatly.

Finally, a third gnat came along and landed on the nose of the ox. It was a very well-behaved insect and did no buzzing and stinging. It seemed happy just being up front. Whenever the ox would get to the end of a furrow, however, this gnat would buzz about loudly and excitedly for a moment or two. To all the world, it announced proudly, "The ox and I plowed the field together."

In this little parable, the U.S. government, as represented by the two branches of Congress, is the ox. The gnats are the politico-biological species known as lobbyists. These gnats are of three varieties:

First, those who try to harass, obstruct, confuse, and defeat the great animal of government in order to protect some special or vested interest. Secondly, there are the gnats who want the ox, which is Congress, to move with the speed of a gazelle, or they want to prod it out of its course. Lastly, there are the gnats who sonorously call themselves "expediting engineers" and "special consultants," but who are more commonly known as "five-percenters" and "influence peddlers." These pernicious insects usually do nothing.

Their whole secret is to do nothing, but to convince others that they are doing everything. Since they deal with stupid or very nearsighted people who come from out of town and cannot seem to see or feel the ox for themselves, the gnats make a great impression by just riding up front and doing a lot of buzzing.

This would just be an amusing parable except that there is a vast host of people depending on the ox who rarely, if ever, see it at work and who do not know about the gnats. These people make the story grimly important because they own the ox and the field. These people are known as taxpayers.

The chances are very strong that you are one of them.

The ratio of three gnats to one ox is not an allegory. There are a total of 531 members of Congress—96 senators and 435 members of the House. But there are never fewer than 1,500 active lobbyists in Washington and frequently upwards of 2,000. Thus, for every congressman there are three or four lobbyists trying to put pressure on him. For sheer weight of numbers, if for no other reason, it is not surprising that the lobbyists frequently win out.

Lobbying, next to politics, gambling, and the society racket, is Washington's biggest business.

Organizations of every conceivable nature admittedly spend more than $10,000,000 a year lobbying Congress, and probably spend much more than that, camouflaged as "legal fees," "public relations," and "miscellaneous." One pressure group alone, the American Medical Association, officially reported it spent $1,523,000 in 1949 fighting low-cost national health insurance. The uncrowned "king of the lobbyists," Purcell Smith of the National Association of Electric Companies, gets $65,000 a year, which is almost five times the pay of a congressman. Lobbying is lush business.

The lobbies of the first type—those trying to kill, obstruct, or delay government action of some kind—include the private-power industry, the real-estate gang, the American Medical Association, the U.S. Chamber of Commerce, the National Association of Manufacturers, and assorted business-front outfits such as Dr. Edward Rumely's Committee for Constitutional Government. These interests are virulently active because they are both defensive and hungry. For years they have been shrieking "socialism," "regimentation," and the "hand-out state" against every proposal for social reform, no matter how modest or how long overdue.

At the same time, they are also on the make. The power companies want to grab off the cheap electricity produced at government-built dams whose construction they originally violently opposed. The real-estaters want to siphon off hundreds of millions in housing profits by attaching themselves to the federal Treasury in a variety of ways.

Sometimes it seems as if practically everybody and everything has a lobby.

There are lobbyists from the cradle to the grave—the National Institute of Diaper Services and the American Cemetery Association. In between, to cite a few, are the Lighthouse Keepers Association, the Peanut and Nut Salters Association, the Apache Indian Tribes, the Wine Institute, the Airline Pilots Association, the Plant Food Council, the Third Class Mail Users Association, and the New York Stock Exchange.

One rather obscure outfit really got some pressure up. This was the carbonated-water lobby. This group may be said to have put the fizz into things—for a while.

The soda-pop makers wanted the production of sugar increased—sugar is their chief ingredient—so that its price would tumble and they could save money. To obtain their end, they bombarded Congress with demands for a big boost in sugar crop quotas.

This high-powered campaign was making considerable headway when it was spiked by the Agriculture Department. The Department sent a letter to all farm-state senators pointing out that sugar reserves were more than adequate and that the price of the commodity had already declined. The Department also shed this revealing light on the machinations of the lobby:

> "In view of the number of complaints that you may be receiving from bottlers and others as to a sugar shortage, you may be interested to know that these appear to be resulting from a highly organized propaganda campaign rather than from the facts in the sugar situation. . . . There is enclosed a copy of exhibits submitted at the recent sugar hearings showing materials being distributed throughout the country by the Washington office of the American Bottlers of Carbonated Beverages. You will note that these statements call for the holding of local luncheon meetings and include copies of press releases and speeches to be made by local leaders, *even to the point of suggesting what should be said while dessert is being served.*"

It takes plenty of crude gall to be a success as a lobbyist. Most of the Washington operators have it. They are not above attempting to browbeat a British Prime Minister or to buy a United States senator.

When Winston Churchill announced he was coming to the U.S. in 1949, the National Association of Real Estate Boards cabled asking him to speak at their annual convention. Churchill turned down the invitation. Undeterred, and characteristically, the lobby promptly resorted to pressure. Insistent messages rained down on Churchill's friends both here and in England. Still no results. So the realtors discarded the velvet glove and tried brass knuckles.

Herb Nelson, their $25,000-a-year Washington storm trooper, went to the British Embassy and demanded that it prevail on Churchill to unbend. Thundered Nelson, with a minimum of tact, "We are the largest taxpaying group in the country, and the appearance of Churchill at our convention might constitute some small compensation for money the United States has spent abroad."

The Embassy took the admonition calmly. So did Churchill. He did not address the real-estate lobby.

One of the boldest lobbyists on Capitol Hill is Vernon Scott, registered agent of the National Tax Equality Association and campaign manager of former Senator Joseph Ball, Minnesota Republican.

A supercharged lobbyist, whose mission is to tax farm cooperatives, Scott has used every trick in the book to secure backing for NTEA's proposals. On a number of occasions he has tangled openly with senators and representatives who have resented his tactics. But it wasn't until late in the 1949 session that Scott met his equal in Senator Milton Young.

Pressuring Young to permit NTEA to reprint a private letter, Scott offered to raise $10,000 for Young's 1950 campaign from the private utilities which had fought the North Dakota Republican in the past. The ensuing explosion is graphically recounted by Senator Young himself:

"When Scott called on me in my office last August, he walked around my desk, examining it closely.

"'What are you looking for?' I asked, astonished.

"'I want to make sure you don't have a wire-recording machine,' was the frank answer. 'I don't want this conversation recorded.'

"Scott then offered to raise ten thousand dollars for my 1950 campaign, if I permitted NTEA to reprint a private letter sent me by a North Dakota farmer. I refused and told Scott to get the hell out of here and stay out."

Who are the people who do lobbying?

First there are the lawyers, thousands upon thousands of them. Washington is a lawyer's paradise. There are old lawyers and young lawyers, Republican lawyers, Democratic lawyers, and "nonpolitical" lawyers, lawyers who practice in court and lawyers who consult only in offices, lawyers who work only for other lawyers, and lawyers who work for the government and at the same time for themselves on the side.

Washington lawyers make more money than do their colleagues anywhere in the country. The average income of lawyers in the whole country is $7,500 a year; Washington lawyers average $14,000. In California, the average is $10,000 annually, and in New York, $9,000.

Washington lawyers are in an enviable position because they are close to the center where the federal laws are made, enforced, and, ultimately, interpreted. They are close to men in government and in Congress on a personal and intimate basis. Under the pretense of giving legal "advice," they can put "the fix" on and get away with it.

As one observer remarked, "The myth has been built up that anything a lawyer does for his client is on the same high plane as what a doctor does for his patient. A lot of bon-ton legal abortions get performed that way, for fancy fees. . . . Low-paid government lawyers try to figure out ways to enforce the laws, while high-paid private lawyers figure out ways to obey or evade them or to get clients out of trouble if they have broken any."

Where lawyering stops and lobbying begins nobody knows. But it is a fact that the best and most successful lobbyists are usually lawyers. Aside from the general lawyer-lobbyist category, lobbyists fall into three special categories:

> The Close-up Men
> The Lame Ducks
> The Inside Men

The Close-up Men are public officials who deliberately quit office to capitalize on their experience and contacts. The most recent striking example of this group is Clark Clifford.

The handsome, magnetic, golden-haired St. Louis attorney spent four years on the White House staff as Mr. Truman's personal counsel. For this important and exhausting work he was paid $12,000 a year. (At the very end of his tenure, Congress raised his salary to $20,000.) Clifford decided he could make ten times that amount in private law practice if he got out while Truman was still in the White House. He resigned in January, 1950, and his first six months of business showed he had figured it right. So many big clients rushed to hire him, they practically jostled one another going in the door.

Clifford celebrated his arrival in the promised land by buying a swanky Maryland estate.

Another prominent figure among the Close-up Men is Max O'Rell Truitt. Affable, jovial Max is a Close-up Man on three counts. He is a former chief counsel and former commissioner of the U.S. Maritime Commission; he is a son-in-law of Vice-President Alben Barkley; and he is a member of the firm of Cummings, Stanley, Truitt, and Cross. Head of this firm is eighty-year-old Homer Cummings, one-time chairman of the Democratic National Committee and Attorney General in the first Franklin Roosevelt cabinet. Other partners are A. O. Stanley, Cummings' first assistant when he was in the Justice Department, and Albert Reeves, a Republican ex-congressman from Missouri.

Truitt has almost a dozen shipping companies on his list of clients. He and his associates are also registered lobbyists, at $30,000 a year, for Franco Spain, as well as for an Argentine shipping combine, the tidelands oil lobby, Dictator Trujillo of the Dominican Republic, and Standard Oil Company.

Most Close-up Men are recruited from the executive agencies, but occasionally a member of Congress decides to retire and cash in his chips. Clifton Woodrum, a veteran Virginia Democratic congressman, gave up his safe $12,500 seat to go to work for the fertilizer interests at $36,000.

Most congressmen who resort to lobbying do so involuntarily, however. They are the Lame Ducks who are rejected by their constituents. The thought of going home is too painful to consider. They decide to stick around the Capital. Their number is infinite.

One of the most enterprising and best paid is ex-Representative Wesley Disney, Oklahoma Democrat, who now lobbies for thirteen different clients ranging from the Western Oil and Gas Association and the Talc Mining Group to the American Hotel Association. Disney's assorted activities net him $45,000 a year.

Other lame-duck lobbyists include ex-Senator Burton K. Wheeler, Montana Democrat, who gets a $1,000-a-month retainer from the tidelands oil lobby, in addition to his lush private law practice; ex-Senator John Danaher, Connecticut Republican, who represents the Fuller Brush Company as well as getting $25,000 annually from the Revere Copper and Brass Company; ex-Senator Kingsley Taft—Ohio Republican and distant relative of Robert A. Taft—who served two months of an unexpired term in 1946, and who now represents the Holstein-Friesian Association (the "cow lobby"); ex-Senator Edward Burke, Nebraska Democrat, who bolted to Willkie in 1940, formerly worked for the Southern Coal operators, and now lobbies for Hawaiian statehood; and ex-Senator Felix Hebert, Rhode Island Republican, now the agent for ten different insurance companies.

A special group are brass-hat Lame Ducks. These are high-ranking military men who have gone to work for corporations. One of the most prominent is Oliver Echols, retired Air Force major general, who headed the War Department's Civil Affairs Division and is now lobbyist for Aircraft Industries, Incorporated.

An ex-congressman or ex-senator has a very special value as a lobbyist. He retains for life certain privileges of congressional membership. He can, for example, visit the private congressional cloakrooms and go on the floor of the House and Senate to visit with his former colleagues, something no other member of the public can do.

Some congressmen do very effective work for special interests without waiting to be retired to lame duckdom.

Ex-Representative Carter Manasco, Alabama Democrat, now a registered lobbyist, really did his best lobbying while a member of the House. When the Full Employment bill came before his committee in 1945, Manasco privately informed a number of business groups that he was having a hard time defeating the measure. He urged them to supply him with information and hostile witnesses. Donaldson Brown, at the time a vice-president of General Motors and on the board of the National Association of Manufacturers, hired a lawyer to help out Manasco. The lawyer lined up a list of witnesses and assured Manasco they had all been primed to testify in the right way. Manasco was satisfied.

Senator Harry Cain, the real-estate lobby's senator from the State of Washington, was in harness from the day he was nominated. Ward A. Smith, Tacoma, regional vice-president of the National Association of Real Estate Boards, wrote the following letter to the Washington national office on June 4, 1946:

"We are vigorously supporting the former Mayor of Tacoma (Cain) for the Senate on the Republican ticket to replace Hugh Mitchell, and if he is successful, I believe that we will have a champion of our thinking. I am very close to him and have a great deal of confidence in his ability; and if, in anticipation of his success you feel that I can be of assistance, I will be happy to serve on the Washington contact committee.

"His last official act on Saturday, when his term as Mayor of Tacoma expired, was to appoint me as Chairman of Tacoma Emergency Housing Committee; which is some evidence of his thinking on the matter of our housing problem."

It was excellent evidence indeed. Need more be said?

Lobbyists have many different techniques. The two oldest and simplest are to buttonhole a congressman personally and give him "the pitch"; and to flood him at crucial times with home-town mail.

The first approach is, of course, constant and often successful, but usually it needs to be supplemented by other tactics. The "mail campaign" is still used, but through abuses it has become a doubtful device. Politicians have learned to read their mail with a critical eye and can quickly discern what is a genuine letter and what is lobby-inspired. This letter technique reached its peak and passed it in 1935 when Howard Hopson, late utility manipulator, arranged to have hundreds of thousands of telegrams descend on Congress at the time the Holding Company bill was nearing a vote. Hard-hitting Senator Hugo Black, now a Justice on the Supreme Court, conducted an investigation which revealed that most of the names signed to the telegrams were copied from telephone books or were wholly fictitious.

Instead of letters and telegrams, lobbies now go in for quick, flying visits from important people back home. Business groups have used this tactic with increasing frequency in recent years. It is a particular favorite of the power-industry and real-estate interests.

The utilities periodically fly groups of vice-presidents to give talks to press breakfasts and to buttonhole their representatives in Congress. The real-estate boards have set up a so-called "Washington Committee," with at least one member from each congressional district who is supposed to know his representative on a first-name basis. This pattern is duplicated by all the subsidiary real-estate lobbies, such as the National Retail Lumber Dealers Association.

This decentralized form of lobbying—with the Washington headquarters pulling the wires and calling the shots—offers various advantages.

It opens the way for circumventing the Lobby Registration Act with no risk of being caught. It also provides the lobbies with undercover "safety men" who can be used to kill legislation at the local level or to spearhead campaigns to elect sympathetic congressmen. Herbert U. Nelson, of the National Association of Real Estate Boards, fascinated by the tantalizing possibilities of such lobbying in depth, bluntly presented the case for it in a private letter to Ted Maenner, former president of the NAREB and a close friend of Senate Republican Floor Leader Kenneth Wherry of Nebraska:

"It doesn't do too much good to increase activity in lobbying congressmen after they are elected. Even if we could spend millions, we could not change the votes of men who owe their election to the CIO or AFL. We must develop ways of meeting the attack in the field before it is too late."

One lobbying technique which until recently was thought to be passé is that of plying congressmen with wine, women, and song. However, during the war, businessmen scavenging for lush cost-plus contracts revived the practice of entertaining members of Congress, Army and Navy officers, and government officials.

These expenses had the double advantage that they could be charged to the government as part of the cost of the product being manufactured or else deducted from income-tax payments as a "necessary business expense." Almost every big corporation leased a house or an apartment in Washington during the war to put up guests from out of town and to entertain local celebrities. Much of this still goes on.

This whoop-de-doo-ing at taxpayers' expense was brought out graphically in 1947 during the Senate War Investigating Committee's probe of the Kaiser-Hughes flying-boat contract.

This committee was the peacetime heir of the old and distinguished Truman Committee. But in the Republican Eightieth Congress it had fallen into the hands of those two old-time gravediggers, Owen Brewster of Maine and Homer Ferguson of Michigan. They were outraged that That Man had beaten them four times straight, and they were determined to rake up something they could use to jostle his corpse. To their great delight, they discovered that one of the many Army and Navy officers entertained by Johnny Meyer, Howard Hughes's publicity man, was Elliott Roosevelt, then a general in the Air Force. Excerpts from Meyer's testimony went as follows:

FERGUSON: Now, we will take the next item [on Meyer's expense account]. What is the item on your sheet after the $106.50 for the three night clubs?

MEYER: The next item is liquor. . . .

FERGUSON: One hundred and fifteen dollars?

MEYER: That is right.

FERGUSON: Now what apartment was that?

MEYER: The Ritz Tower Apartment.

FERGUSON: And who stayed with you in that apartment?

MEYER: I don't know.

FERGUSON: Did Colonel Roosevelt?

MEYER: I don't think so. He might have slept there. I don't think he stayed with me.

FERGUSON: Did he occupy the same apartment?

MEYER: Yes, but I always had big apartments.

FERGUSON: I realize that.

MEYER: Sometimes there were four and five bedrooms.

FERGUSON: I was not talking about his staying in the same room. I was talking about the apartment.

MEYER: I am not sure he did. He might have had an apartment on another floor.

FERGUSON: Do you know that as a matter of fact?

MEYER: No; I can't remember. . . .

FERGUSON: But at least, you took to the apartment at that time $115 worth of liquor?

MEYER: That is not too much, because liquor was quite expensive.

SEN. PEPPER: [Dem, Florida]: Colonel Roosevelt did not drink all of this either, did he?

MEYER: I am quite sure he did not.

FERGUSON: Now, the next item?

MEYER: It says: "Presents for girls, $75."

FERGUSON: How many girls?

MEYER: Two.

FERGUSON: Could you tell us more about that? Who were the girls? Do you know?

MEYER: I haven't any idea.

FERGUSON: Was there anybody with you in New York at that time?

MEYER: No.

FERGUSON: You have another item for $200 above there for presents for four girls; and then there is this item for presents for two girls, $75. Would they be girls eating at the same dinner?

MEYER: Certainly, certainly. Positively.

FERGUSON: Pardon me?

MEYER: Positively.

FERGUSON: Now will you read the next item?

MEYER: The next item is the next day.

FERGUSON: Yes, the twenty-fifth.

MEYER: That is Miss Emerson [Faye Emerson, then Roosevelt's fiancée, later his wife], lunch at the Madison Restaurant.

FERGUSON: How much?

MEYER: Seven and a half.

FERGUSON: The next item?

MEYER: That afternoon, some nylon hose that I bought Miss Emerson as a present, $132.

FERGUSON: And the next item? Do you want to see my copy?

MEYER: No, I can see it. It says: "Miss Emerson, Cash to travel home, $20."

FERGUSON: Now can you tell me why you were charging up to [Hughes] Aircraft $132 for nylon hose for Miss Emerson?

MEYER: Because she had been very charming.

FERGUSON: Very charming.

MEYER: Girls are very pleasant.

FERGUSON: What has that to do with aircraft production?

MEYER: They just went along. Every company in business did it. We were no different.

FERGUSON: You say because she was very charming you charged up this item of $132 to the production of airplanes?

MEYER: That is right.

FERGUSON: Now, would you tell us why you gave her $20 to go home, and charged that up to the company, if she was very charming?

MEYER: Well, you topped me. That is very good. I will concede that.

FERGUSON: You do not have an answer to that last question?

MEYER: I do not. I must admit that you topped me.

FERGUSON: The next day what happened?

MEYER: Do you want to continue with the question as to why I gave her $20?

FERGUSON: Oh, yes, let us settle that point. I thought you did not have an answer.

MEYER: I think I took Miss Emerson to the airport, and when she was getting on the plane she discovered that she did not have any money, so I kindly consented to give her the $20 which I thought was very gracious of me.

FERGUSON: All right. The next day? This was quite a week end, was it not? Or was this a normal week end?

MEYER: I'd say this was quite a one.

FERGUSON: Now the next item?

MEYER: It says: "Elliott Roosevelt in the Jungle Room, Carlton Hotel, four people, $15."

FERGUSON: That would indicate that you joined Elliott Roosevelt in the Jungle Room in the Carlton Hotel in Washington, would it not?

MEYER: That is right.

FERGUSON: Why did you come to Washington? . . .

MEYER: Well, I would say I came here to continue my acquaint-
              ance with Elliot Roosevelt.

FERGUSON: And that is why you were charging it up to the aircraft
              productions?

MEYER: But I also saw Jack Frye [president of Hughes's TWA]
              while I was here.

FERGUSON: And why did you continue with Elliott Roosevelt?

MEYER: Because he was head of the photographic reconnaissance
              mission.

FERGUSON: And you wanted to entertain him?

MEYER: That is right.

FERGUSON: You wanted to continue the entertainment. At that time
              did you know when he intended to return to the front?

MEYER: I don't think so, no.

FERGUSON: Now, what is your next item?

MEYER: The next item is Saturday night. It says, "Some girls at
              hotels late." They obviously didn't have dinner.

FERGUSON: How much did you pay?

MEYER: Fifty dollars.

FERGUSON: What do you mean "they didn't have dinner" when you
              paid $50?

MEYER: No, they joined us at the Statler at the Embassy Room.

FERGUSON: How do you account for the $50? What is the $50?

MEYER: Probably some presents.

FERGUSON: Well, what does it have to do with the production of air-
              craft?

MEYER: I charged it to the Hughes Aircraft Company.

FERGUSON: But what did it have to do with Hughes Aircraft?

MEYER: Those were my orders.

FERGUSON: Well, now, just look at the first sheet. Colonel Roosevelt
              and the week end cost about $1,500, did it not?

MEYER: If that is what it totals up to.

FERGUSON: What is the next item? . . .

MEYER: Dinner at the Twenty-One Club, five people, Colonel
              William Irvine.

FERGUSON: Who is Colonel William Irvine? . . . Did he have anything to do with the mission?

MEYER: I don't think so. He was just another of the thousand and one Army and Navy people I entertained during the war, among which Elliott Roosevelt is just one.

One lobbyist in present-day Washington added a new feature to the wine-women-and-song routine. Samuel P. Haines, registered agent for the National Committee to Reduce the Twenty Percent Cabaret Tax, was found to have a gaming room in his home.

The fascinating chamber came to light when an investigator for the House Lobby Investigating Committee became curious about a $3,500 item for "furniture" in Haines's expense account. The lobbyist explained it was to "equip my home office." Puzzled, the investigator went to Haines's home. In the basement he found the gaming room, equipped with a dice table, large pool table, and three slot machines, one of which paid off with remarkable regularity.

Haines's equally intriguing arrangement with the Cabaret Tax Committee was uncovered in a letter from Chicago hotelman Otto K. Eitel. It promised Haines a $10,000 retainer and $15,000 expenses, plus a graduated scale of larger payments according to the effectiveness of his lobbying. This could amount to as much as $100,000—if he went to town. Eitel's letter, an illuminating insight on lobbying operations, reads:

"In accordance with our agreement, you are to be paid a retainer of $10,000 and in addition, the sum of $15,000 for expenses in order to bring to the attention of Congress the necessity of a reduction in this cabaret tax.

"In the event you are successful in bringing this matter to Congress' attention by an amendment, rider, or proposed legislation, there will be advanced to you an additional sum of $25,000 for expenses to further guide and assist in any manner which you deem necessary the successful passage of this legislation on both the floor of the House of Representatives and the Senate.

"In further accordance with our agreement in the event you

are successful in having passed legislation that will reduce
the cabaret tax from the present 20 to 10 per cent, you are to
be paid the sum of $35,000 for your services. In the event
the tax is reduced to five per cent, you are to be paid the
sum of $50,000."

The four most powerful lobbies in Washington are the veterans,
the farm bloc, the numerous business groups headed up by the U.S.
Chamber of Commerce and the National Association of Manufacturers, and the labor unions.

Except for the Alaskan Eskimos and the professional white-collar
people, every American may be said to be a member of one of these
four. This is their peculiar strength. Their spokesmen have, or claim
to have, the right to speak in the name of great masses of voters. And
to politicians, that voice is the voice of God.

The veterans' lobby is indisputably the most potent in the Capital.
The American Legion, the Veterans of Foreign Wars, Amvets, Dis-
abled American Veterans, the American Veterans Committee, and
sundry other organizations have representatives in the Capital. Anything these organizations seriously want—they get. Sometimes they
get something even when they are not all united or wholeheartedly
in favor of it, as in 1949, when the House passed the multi-billion-
dollar Rankin pension bill despite the heated objections of many veterans.

Since "veteran" is the modern "open sesame" in Washington, the
big struggle in recent years has been the effort of other pressure groups
to line up veterans' support for their particular pet scheme. In a very
real sense, the other lobbies lobby the veterans' lobby.

For example, it was a crushing blow to the real-estate gang when
the American Legion grudgingly and belatedly, but nonetheless decisively, swung in favor of public housing. Similarly, in 1950, several
conservative House Republicans, such as James Van Zandt of Pennsylvania, voted for middle-income cooperative housing solely because the
Veterans of Foreign Wars had endorsed it.

On the whole, however, the veterans' lobby, and especially the
American Legion, has lent itself as a vehicle for reactionary business
propaganda. General policies are supposedly laid down in the platform

adopted by the national conventions, but these platforms, like most others, are vague and ambiguous, and it is very easy for a conservative-minded legislative representative to interpret them in a way which commits his organization to something he wants to commit it to—like antilabor laws.

The three most powerful farm organizations are the American Farm Bureau Federation, the National Farmers Union, and the Grange—in that order. When they act together, their strength is second only to that of the veterans.

In recent years, however, they have had increasing difficulty in working together. The word "farmer" does not mean the same thing in all parts of the country. Farmers include corn-and-hog men in Iowa, wheat men in Kansas and the Dakotas, cattlemen in Wyoming and Texas, cotton sharecroppers in Georgia, fruit and vegetable raisers on the West Coast, sugar-cane growers in Louisiana, and dairy farmers in Wisconsin and New England. It is difficult to retain the façade of a united front for all these disparate elements.

The oldest of the farm groups is the Grange, the official name of which is the Patrons of Husbandry. The Grange was founded in 1867, largely as a secret fraternal order with the purpose of lifting the pall of drabness and social isolation from the lives of farmers. In the '70's, '80's, and '90's of the last century, it was a potent political force in American life. But since the turn of the century, it has tended to develop hardening of the arteries. Its crusading vigor has waned. But it still has almost a million members scattered over the country— members with a strong sense of institutional unity—a rich tradition, and many "service" features such as special life-insurance policies.

Present head of the Grange is sixty-eight-year-old Albert Goss, frail, white-haired, with a white mustache and a quiet, self-contained manner. He comes from the State of Washington, where he had a varied career as a bookkeeper, miller, country storekeeper, grain-elevator operator, wheat rancher, telephone-exchange operator, dairy farmer, and, for the last thirty years, professional farm-organization man and self-taught economist. During the first seven years of the New Deal, Goss was Land Bank Commissioner, but he resigned in 1940 in the course of a bureaucratic struggle for control of his agency. In 1941, he became Master of the National Grange. Goss takes a conservative approach to most public questions and is a frequent orator on the subject of economy and "bureaucracy."

In most of the Midwest and South, the Grange has been supplanted by the American Farm Bureau Federation. This organization had its start in 1914, when Congress authorized cooperative agricultural work between the Department of Agriculture and the state agricultural colleges. The connecting link was the county extension agent. Most states set up county farm bureaus to carry on the work and to receive the federal and state money.

Usually such bureaus were recognized only if they had enough members, and therefore the county extension agent saw to it that enough members were recruited, since, quite naturally, he wanted his county to get all the state and federal money that was coming to it. In effect, this made a government officer—the county extension agent— an organizer for the Farm Bureau. When this network of bureaus was amalgamated into a nationwide organization, a veritable government-fed behemoth was created.

The American Farm Bureau Federation has never ceased to profit from its intimate connection with the dispensing of government money and information through the county agent. The extension bureaus in most states are still an integral part of the Federation. Extension agents collect Farm Bureau dues and, sometimes, discriminate in the service they render growers, depending upon whether or not they are Farm Bureau members. The Grange, the Farmers Union, and the Department of Agriculture have struggled for years to disentangle the government extension service from the clutches of the Federation, but without success.

The Federation traditionally works both sides of the political street. It matches the political coloration of its presidents to the administration in Washington.

Throughout the New Deal, Federation moguls kept Ed O'Neal, a jovial Southern Democrat, as prexy. In 1947, when it appeared the Republicans were going to return, O'Neal retired and was succeeded by Republican Allan Kline of Iowa. Unfortunately for the Federation, the Republicans did not come back in 1948. Since then, Kline, an unusually bull-headed operator, has managed to involve the Federation in a dangerous duel for power with his archenemy, Agriculture Secretary Charles Brannan.

The Federation is so powerful in Congress and in certain Midwestern states that it is more than a lobby; it is a dictator; but it may be riding for a fall.

The chief competitor of the Federation is the young and rapidly growing National Farmers Union, headed by smart, able James Patton. The Union is oriented to the problems of the small-family farmer and to the Far West; its headquarters are in Denver, and Patton, like Brannan, comes from Colorado.

The Union has been the traditional champion of the Farm Security Administration, the New Deal agency set up to aid marginal and small-scale agriculture. The Federation, on the other hand, has always sought to sabotage FSA. Brannan spent his whole government career in FSA, and his appointment in 1948 was a great triumph for the Union. Patton and his followers have also traditionally been the spearhead of the struggle to unite the farmer with organized labor rather than with business elements. The Federation, except in Ohio, always takes a strong antilabor, pro-big business line.

It is a significant political fact that the farm bloc in Washington now has the strength for internal quarrels. Thirty years ago it was an eager and beseeching pleader for any kind of government succor.

The AFL, CIO, and the Railway Brotherhoods speak for big labor in Washington. Labor units hold occasional press luncheons and congressional cocktail parties, but never on the scale of business groups. Business interests reported spending $3,300,000 for lobbying in Washington in 1949; labor spent $260,000. Labor does not rely on sweet words and cozy conferences to attain its ends. By its very nature—a coalition of huge, sprawling, mass organizations—labor is committed to direct action. It does its effective work on the home-town political level.

The old Gompers principle, "Reward your friends and punish your enemies," has been brought up to date to read, "Elect your friends and try to prevent your enemies from ever getting there."

The "Big Two" among the business lobbies are the U.S. Chamber of Commerce and the National Association of Manufacturers.

The Chamber of Commerce is an aboveboard pressure machine

dedicated to business first, last, and always. It has several different "departments," but the principal aim of the Chamber for twenty years has been to cut taxes and government regulation of business. In 1950, it sounds pretty thin and shrill, but it is unquestionably sincere.

The National Association of Manufacturers is less important, directly and openly, in Washington than is the Chamber. But NAM swings great weight in shaping the public mind, especially the mind of rural America, on current issues.

Professor Stephen K. Bailey of Wesleyan University, author of *Congress Makes a Law,* declares that NAM serves as a "holding company for a variety of seemingly independent pressure groups and as a conditioner of rural opinions." Bailey told the House Lobby Investigating Committee, "It seems highly significant to me that the National Association of Manufacturers sends editorial material all ready to go to print to 7,500 rural weekly newspapers, and that it maintains a service called *Farm and Industry*—a release which it sends to 35,000 farm leaders."

In any discussion of Washington lobbying, it is necessary to distinguish the foregoing groups—the farm, labor, chamber of commerce, and veterans' lobbies—from all other types. The spokesmen for each of these four pressure groups represent millions of Americans. They have tangible economic interests and usually seek quite specific economic goals, but they are so large and so diverse that—within broad limits—it is plausible and permissible for them to identify their own interests with the welfare of the nation.

These are the good, the socially justifiable lobbies. The bad lobbies, from society's point of view, are those whose objects cannot by any normal stretch of the imagination be identified with the welfare of the country as a whole. These undesirable lobbies speak for financially powerful but numerically small interests. Often only one or two mighty corporations, a small clique of financiers, or a handful of large stockholders benefit from the legislation and favors so loudly and vigorously pursued by the lobby corps.

The good and bad lobbies can be distinguished by their methods as well as their objectives. Pressure groups such as the farmers and the labor unions depend heavily on their mass voting strength. They feel that if they can get their argument across to the public they will win.

Therefore they welcome publicity, openly announce their views, and generally conduct themselves in a manner that indicates they have nothing to hide. But the lobbyists for the special vested interests act differently. Lobbies such as those for the aviation, oil, natural-gas, real-estate, and private-utilities interests generally discourage public scrutiny of their activities. Frequently they hire "public-relations experts" to camouflage their work and put out propaganda. These lobbies operate not by appealing to the latent popular following, which in their case does not exist, but by lavish partying, distortion of the facts, undercover force and intimidation, manipulation of fake "front" organizations, and outright bludgeoning of the opposition.

It is fairly easy to account for the differences in working methods. The undesirable lobbies reveal themselves on examination to possess bad consciences. It is not that the leaders and spokesmen are themselves aware of any guilt complexes. Rather it is that these lobbies have situations in their fields which will not stand the full light of public examination. For example, the real-estate interests know that they are not meeting, at a decent price, the housing needs of the mass of middle-income Americans, and they endeavor to conceal that fact. The same is true of the oil kings who are just out for an unconscionable grab, at the expense of the consumer, which they know they cannot defend on its merits. Similarly, the shipping and aviation lobbies occasionally let off a bad odor, and their lobbying always comes with a poor grace because their operations reek with inefficiency, favoritism, and politically dictated subsidies. And so it goes. The most objectionable lobbies in Washington are that way because, morally at least, they are leading not from strength but from weakness. Their huckstering has to be ruthless and often unprincipled if they are going to succeed in selling their case.

One of the most noisome and obnoxious of these lobbies is that of the petroleum industry. At one point during the 1950 session of Congress, there were more registered lobbyists working for the oil and natural-gas interests *than for all other lobbies combined*. This, of course, was part of the struggle to put through the Kerr natural-gas "ripper" bill.

Working in close partnership with the natural-gas interests was the older and equally rapacious tidelands-oil lobby, which seeks to get Congress to waive the government's legal title to these enormously rich resources and turn them over to the states, which are notorious for their easy acquiescence to exploitation. This two-headed monster lobby had the backing of a number of senators and of the entire Texas delegation to the House. But Texas, for all its vaunted wealth and its minions strategically located in high places in Washington, cannot carry off this plunder operation without help.

That is why many an Eastern and Western congressman in both parties received a telephone call in the 1948 election campaign in which the friendly inquiry was made, in a pleasant Southern drawl, "How are you fixed for campaign funds, Fred (or Joe or Tom or whatever the congressman's name happened to be)? There is a lot of money down here in Texas and I can get you some if you need it. Just say the word. I've already helped out some of the other boys who are in a tight spot."

The congressman, if he was honest and politically experienced, turned down this tempting offer. There was, indeed, plenty of Texas money floating around in 1948, and there still is. But that money is oil money, and oilmen are not in the business of philanthropy. In their usual crude fashion, they are out to buy votes for so much cash on the barrelhead.

The American Medical Association lobby differs in one fundamental respect from the other vested-interest pressure organizations. The AMA has employed outside, professional public-opinion molders to do its dirty work.

These "experts" are slick, brazen Clem Whitaker and his wife, Leone Baxter. They got their training for the AMA job by directing the campaign in California which defeated Governor Earl Warren's tepid proposal for a State system of medical insurance. To do AMA's hatcheting, the Whitakers are charging $8,333 a month. This and other lavish outlays are financed from a $3,500,000 fund raised through a $25 assessment of the 140,000 doctors who belong to AMA.

Whitaker's propaganda creation, the "National Education Campaign of the American Medical Association," now has the medical lobby field to itself. For a time, however, it had a competitor, until publicity drove it from the battleground. This was the clumsily concealed "National Physicians Committee."

Formed in 1946 and folded in '49, this outfit described itself as "a nonpolitical, nonprofit organization for maintaining ethical and scientific standards and extending medical service to all the people." Actually, NPC was a front for drug interests working to defeat the health-insurance plan. Not a single physician contributed to the National Physicians Committee, but forty-two companies in the drug and medical-supplies business did, in a big way. Eli Lilly and Company and the Upjohn Company each gave $30,000. Abbott Laboratories of Chicago kicked in with $20,000. Parke Davis and Company contributed $15,000, and the following firms chipped in $10,000 apiece: E. R. Squibb and Sons, American Cyanamid Company, and Mead Johnson and Company. McKesson and Robbins gave $2,500, while a long list of small drug houses gave $1,000 each.

What was the motive in all this? Certainly it had nothing to do with the drug companies' tender solicitude for the patient-family doctor relationship nor with the abstract question of "personal liberty" so dear to the heart of reactionary politicians. It might have had quite a bit to do, however, with the fears of the pharmaceutical business that a government-supervised medical-insurance plan would bring down by one-third or more the highly inflated price of drugs and medicines.

Practically every important figure in British medicine who visits the U.S. confirms the success of the British health program. Does that faze AMA? Not for a minute! Reliable, resourceful, hard-working Clem Whitaker has an answer to that one. In an ingenious question-and-answer pamphlet concocted by him there is this exchange—Question 30: "Why are some prominent British visitors here reluctant to comment on how socialized medicine is working in England?" Answer: "Criticism of their Socialist Government would jeopardize American loans to that Government. Every thinking American is aware of this."

Any other questions, folks?

Another depressing aspect of AMA's tactics is the way its self-appointed leaders browbeat and intimidate their own people—the doctors. This goes far beyond merely hijacking unwilling physicians into giving $25 to the "cause," whether or not they want to. More sinister is the attempted coercion and suppression of opposition or middle-of-the-road views.

The late Nate Robertson, a working reporter of great courage and ability who for many years was chief of the Associated Press staff covering the Senate, told the following story concerning a close friend. This man was a well-established figure in the medical field and a professor in his specialty—pediatrics—at a state university. Early in 1949, this doctor joined with 135 other doctors from all over the country in issuing a statement protesting the AMA's collection of its $3,500,000 slush fund and suggesting that the money might better be used to improve medical treatment.

AMA rulers furiously resented this public rebuke. They proceeded to go to work on the doctors involved. Here is what happened, as related by Robertson:

"AMA did its dirtiest work privately. The pediatrician, for instance, had been invited by a professor at the University of Arkansas to give a postgraduate lecture to practicing physicians at Little Rock on the subject of the feeding and immunization of babies. As a pediatrician, he was an expert in the field. A few days after the public protest signed by the doctor and others was made public, the announcement of his forthcoming lecture was published in Arkansas. One of the leaders of the Arkansas Medical Society is a member of the AMA Committee handling the $3,500,000 propaganda campaign against the President's health program. Within a few days, the pediatrician got this letter signed by the State Health Officer of Arkansas:

'Dear Dr. ——:

'This letter is being written to you as a result of a special request made by the Arkansas State Medical Society and the Pulaski County Medical Society with reference to your appointment as a special consultant in pediatrics for the Arkansas State Board of Health for the postgraduate pediatrics course to be conducted at the University of Arkansas School of Medicine, Little Rock, during the period March 10th to 12th, inclusive, 1949.

'The Arkansas State Medical Society and the Pulaski County Medical Society have been advised through authoritative sources that you were one of the 136 signers of certain papers and documents severely criticizing the American Medical Association. Through this action on your part, the Arkansas State Medical Society and the Pulaski County Medical Society request that you not appear on the postgraduate pediatrics course to be conducted on the above referred dates.

'This department sincerely regrets that this most embarrassing situation has arisen and further regrets that it is necessary to cancel your appointment as special consultant for the Arkansas State Board of Health.' "

Who did you say was injecting politics into medicine?

In recent years the power-trust lobby has done a series of quick-change routines, but the act is still the same.

In its present stage of evolution, the lobby is suave, dignified, and outwardly as friendly as an inner sanctum powwow at the Bankers Club in New York. The chief spokesman for the utilities is Purcell L. Smith, representing a "united front" lobby known as the National Association of Electric Companies. He works closely with another group called the Edison Electric Institute.

Smith's amiability and outward candor is no accident. By nature, he is friendly and good-humored. His subordinates swear by him as a "good boss." But there is a great deal more to it than that. Smith's geniality is as much an integral part of the power-industry's *modus operandi* as it is of his character.

This disarming openhandedness is a carefully conceived and earnestly nurtured stratagem. It's ingratiating window dressing for a distinct purpose.

Although the power trust's greed and gall remain unchanged, seventeen years of New Deal cuffing has taught it one thing: that dissimulation, in the guise of good manners, is a lot more effective in dealing with the public than the rough and tough methods of previous times.

Actually the basic practices are the same. But they are employed more discreetly and adroitly. Now they "kill 'em with a kiss" instead of with a meat-ax.

The power trust learned this lesson very painfully.

In the roaring '20's, utility lobbying was crude and crass. Those were the days of lush back-room parties, limitless expense accounts, and innumerable hushed scandals. Legislators were plied with wine, women, and money, newspapers and newsmen were bought, teachers and college professors traduced, textbooks poisoned with propaganda, and critics mercilessly smeared as "Reds" and "radicals." The industry's sinister and far-flung web of intrigue and control reached from the cradle to the White House.

Montana's late Senator Tom Walsh, a renowned constitutional lawyer, finally succeeded in detonating the first charge under this juggernaut.

Walsh offered a resolution for a sweeping Senate probe of the industry. A fierce battle ensued, with utility-controlled senators of both parties violently opposing the proposal. To help them, the industry flooded Washington with one of the greatest swarms of lobbyists it had ever seen. But Walsh's resolution evoked tremendous popular support. So pronounced was this sentiment that the industry was unable to dragoon the votes needed to kill the investigation. The issue had become political dynamite. Certain senators became so scared that no amount of pressure could line them up for an outright rejection.

So the industry concocted a neat subterfuge to save its hide and theirs. Its Senate spokesman offered a "compromise" to shunt the investigation to the long-moribund Federal Trade Commission.

It was a slick trick. The FTC had never made such a probe; its powers and resources were limited; and, above all, Walsh and his justly feared inquisitorial talents would be bypassed. The trust again appeared to have won. Antiutility forces were very doleful.

But both sides miscalculated. Neither reckoned on the FTC's chief counsel, the late Judge Robert E. Healy.

A New England Republican, he was no liberal in the accepted sense of that word. If he had been, he'd never have gotten the job. But Healy was an honest, decent, public-spirited American who abhorred corruption and monopoly. Quietly and relentlessly he went to work.

Over a period of several years, he exposed the power industry's machinations in all their sordid and vicious infamy. By the time Healy completed his historic investigation, in the early '30's, utilities were the popular choice as Public Enemy No. 1.

But despite the evil repute into which the industry had fallen, it was still unregenerate. It still adhered to strong-arm methods. When the New Deal in 1933-34 brought out its famous "death sentence" Holding Company bill, the industry again stormed Washington with a mob of goon lobbyists.

Headed by Philip H. Gadsden, the lobby set up headquarters in the Mayflower Hotel and, apparently with unlimited funds, went to work on Congress, the press, and the public. But again the industry's crudeness backfired.

A horde of faked and lobby-inspired telegrams pulled the trigger and led to another investigation, this time by the Senate itself.

Senator Hugo Black demanded the probe, and the Senate approved it forthwith by a voice vote. The Alabaman was as great an investigator as Walsh had been. Within a few months, the Gadsden lobby was as dead and odorous as the proverbial mackerel in the moonlight.

The requiem of the lobby's unlamented demise was sounded by the enactment of the Holding Company bill.

Apparently, this mauling finally taught the industry something. Throughout the remainder of the New Deal, it avoided Washington like the plague and confined its feuding to the courts—where it had equally little success. The Holding Company Act is still intact on the statute books.

But once Roosevelt was out of the picture, the power trust lost no time in returning to the Capital.

In July, 1945, exactly three months after he had been laid to rest and as World War II was drawing to an end, a new lobby was organized. This lobby is as well heeled, aggressive, and powerful as its malodorous predecessors. But its trappings have undergone a significant change.

In name and furbishings, this new lobby is in keeping with the times—suave, sonorous, and beguiling.

"Percy" (as he is known to intimates) Smith is an important part of this plastic surgery. By nature and method of operating, he is a fitting choice for head of the National Association of Electric Companies, the disarming nom de plume of the lobby. He is heart and soul a utility man, but it is his theory that the till can be filled more safely and abundantly by the gloved hand than by the blackjack.

As "king of Washington lobbyists," Smith disdainfully eschews such unkingly antics as buttonholing, back slapping, office hounding, and whoopeeing. He leaves such activities to lesser lights: local utility executives and the like, who are brought to Washington for this purpose. Smith doesn't even entertain much. He drinks little and gives and goes to parties rarely.

Smith confines his $65,000-a-year services to masterminding. He is the commanding general of the power lobby. He rallies it, plants its bills, plans its strategy, and directs its operations and propaganda. He likes to compare himself to a football coach.

"I plan the strategy and direct the moves," he explains, "but it is our company executives who carry the ball."

Under Smith's deft, behind-the-scenes handling, local power moguls infiltrate into Washington, lobby their representatives, senators, and any others they think they can influence, and then quietly depart. This has a double advantage. It keeps down their number at any one time in the Capital, and it neatly nose-thumbs the Lobbyist Registration Act. Also, it enables Smith to keep out of the limelight.

That is a key feature of his system. He is no Gadsden. Twenty-four hours after he arrived, everyone in Washington knew Gadsden was in town. Smith is still an almost unknown figure.

And that's exactly the way he wants it to be, for the kind of role he considers his to be. This role covers a wide range of activity.

In addition to drafting and planting power bills, all designed to thwart public-power development, grab off more natural resources, reduce power taxes, and/or wreck government controls, Smith also is the industry's Washington outpost, stage manager, propaganda manipulator, and chief of staff. During an average session of Congress, Smith sends out detailed reports on more than three hundred bills "of interest to the public-utilities industry." These range from a measure giving the Virginia Electric Light and Power Company perpetual use of two strips of land in the Norfolk Navy Yard to labor and tax-reduction bills. Next to waging relentless war against public power, Smith's major passion is tax cutting.

"We believe," he declares, "that there has been too much tax discrimination and too much government competition against privately owned companies."

Smith lays great stress on keeping a steady flow of influential local power officials rolling into Washington. It is not uncommon for a score of such "witnesses" to be testifying before three or four congressional committees at the same time. Before they say their pieces, all are carefully "briefed" and their statements either prepared or edited. Smith once flew all the way to Oklahoma for an advance meeting with a group of witnesses he had assembled for an important committee meeting. And before each of these lobby henchmen leaves Washington, Smith gets a personal fill-in from them on their private talks with senators and representatives.

Smith is unquestionably one of the best-informed men in the Capital on congressional sentiment, peccadillos, habits, and soft spots.

But riding herd on Congress is by no means the greatest of Smith's problems. He has some tough ones in his own camp. One of his biggest headaches is keeping his utility cohorts within bounds. Some of the old-timers are inclined to be impatient of discretion. They can't get away from old habits of slug-'em-and-buy-'em.

These self-important moguls are not easy to control. Big shots in their own realms, they have their own ideas of how to get things done.

One of these is C. Hamilton Moses, president of the Arkansas Power and Light Company and onetime law partner of the late Senate Democratic Floor Leader Joe Robinson. After the latter's death, Moses toyed with the thought of running for the Senate. But the power label, apparently, was too great a load to carry even in Arkansas, and Moses reluctantly subsided.

On one occasion during the postwar shortages, he boiled into Washington and sent an assistant poking around congressional offices asking women clerks their stocking sizes. But the prized accessories were never delivered. Before they could even be bought, Drew Pearson got wind of the affair and exposed it in his column.

Privately, Smith was not unhappy over the incident. It gave weighted point to his oft-repeated admonition that the industry must operate "above reproach"—at least outwardly.

Smith is sensitive about his connection with the notorious Insulls. He claims it was due only to the fact that he happened to be an official of North American when the Insull brothers, Sam and Martin, bought forty per cent of the company's stock.

But Federal Trade Commission files tell a somewhat different story. According to these records, Smith took part in the reorganization of North American that brought the Insulls into the company. Further, he was treasurer of the utility under the Insulls for three years. Also, Senate records reveal a $1,500 check to a newspaper signed by Smith, as North American treasurer. The check was in payment for an unsigned page in the paper furiously denouncing governmental interference in business. The article appeared on the eve of a utility investigation.

Buoyant and jovial, Smith is a bundle of energy. He sings while shaving, bounds up steps two at a time, works late hours, and talks animatedly and fluently. He dresses well but quietly, and his wavy black hair, streaked with gray, is always carefully combed. His employees are very enthusiastic about Smith, say he is never petty or ill-tempered.

When Smith first set up shop, his right-hand man was Ted Crosby, brother of the mellifluous Bing. Crosby was paid $15,000 but apparently wasn't active enough to suit Smith. Smith gave him the six-months' notice stipulated in Crosby's contract and let him go.

Smith on occasion has also had the services of two New York University men. They are Professors Herbert B. Dorau and J. Rhoads Foster. They were hired to prepare a $75,000 study of "taxation of electric utilities" which Smith presented to the House Ways and Means Committee during its hearings in the Eightieth Congress on the income-tax-reduction bill.

Well oiled with money, neatly integrated at the city, state, and Washington levels, and smoothly manipulated by the deft Mr. Smith, the "Private Utilities Express" is the snappiest vehicle on the Capitol lobby run.

The real-estate lobby is in many ways the crudest of the big lobbies. The "realtors" do all the conventional things: high-pressure members of Congress; instigate write-to-your-editor and write-to-your-congressman campaigns; produce fake letters and telegrams when necessary; operate an elaborate network of local and state committees which apply the squeeze on congressmen and senators in various ways, some of them as fragrant as an outhouse; and, finally, the real-estate lobby entertains frequently, lavishly, and boisterously.

There is little the real-estate lobby won't, and hasn't, stooped to, to gain its hoggish ends.

The lobby is an amalgam of a number of special-interest groups. It includes the builders, lumber interests, building-supplies dealers, real-estate operators, bankers, mortgage brokers, architects, and apartment-house owners.

Sometimes these elements have different or conflicting interests. The architects, for example, refused to go along with the rest of the industry in the fight against public housing. But as a general practice the rule of these groups is, "All for one and one for all—and to hell with the public."

Their chief lobbyist is the Herbert U. Nelson already mentioned. Nelson gets $25,000 a year for his work for the National Association of Real Estate Boards (NAREB). He achieved immortality in the spring of 1950 when investigators for the House Lobby Investigating Committee produced a letter he had written to the president of NAREB, as follows:

> "I do not believe in democracy. I think it stinks. I believe in a republic operated by elected representatives who are permitted to do the job, as the Board of Directors should. I don't think anybody but direct taxpayers should be allowed to vote. I don't believe women should be allowed to vote at all. Ever since they started, our public affairs have been in a worse mess than ever."

Nelson is also the author of the breath-taking gem that there was no housing shortage after the war, only "overconsumption of space." Apparently, if three or four families would only double up and put grandma in the garage, the whole housing problem would be solved in a jiffy.

Nelson's chief assistant is Calvin Snyder, who makes $12,000 a year plus expenses. Other real-estate lobbyists include Douglas Whitlock for the Building Products Institute, Joseph King of the National Retail Lumber Dealers, Frank Cortright of the National Association of

Home Builders, John Owen of the National Apartment House Owners Association, and assorted representatives of the American Bankers
Association, the U.S. Savings and Loan League, the Architects Society,
the General Contractors Association, and the National Home and
Property Owners' Foundation.

The head of the latter organization, which spent almost $250,000 lob-
bying against public housing and rent control, is a certain Arthur W.
Binns. In 1949, in Philadelphia, where Binns is a big real-estate man
and former president of the local Real Estate Board, he was hauled
into court on charges of being the "worst operator of firetraps and
health menaces" in the city.

The chief of Housing and Sanitation told the court that the condition of houses operated by Binns "shocked even hardened inspectors
by their filth and squalor; many of them are rat-infested and overrun
with vermin, and many lack any water supply or sanitary facilities.
Despite repeated warnings to Binns, these conditions have gone un-
corrected for two years."

Other tactics of the Apartment House Owners Association indicate
a similar high moral standard.

In 1948, a Mrs. Anna Ward of Akron, Ohio, wrote identical letters
to Senator Robert A. Taft and Democratic Representative Walter
Huber of Ohio. In her letters, she said: "For the last seven years I have
rented a house here in Akron for $18 a month. It should rent for $35.
The Federal Rent Office will give me no relief in spite of higher costs
for improvements. I am a widow and need a few dollars profit from
this house. Can you help me?"

Investigation in Akron revealed that not only had Mrs. Anna Ward
not sought an increase from the Rent Office but that she did not own
any property in the first place. The Akron rent director later discovered that the real author of the letter was Dr. C. F. Wharton, president
of the Apartment House Owners Association, in whose home Mrs.
Ward worked as a maid.

Greed and selfishness are nothing new. No one would object if the
realtors took their pound of flesh and let it go at that. But what is
retching is to hear these sharpers, oozing unctuous self-righteousness
and self-esteem, come to Congress and testify before committees.

Everyone in Washington knows to what an extent the real-estate crowd is gulping at the public trough. Yet they have the gall to moan and bellow that public housing and slum clearance are "an invasion of the field of free enterprise" and "unfair use of the taxpayer's money to compete with private business."

For ten long years, from 1939 to 1949, this pack blocked all government action in these desperately needed fields. In all that time, the real-estate industry never made the slightest effort to lower its costs or to produce mass housing for the low-income groups. Even Senator Robert A. Taft pointed this out when he co-sponsored the administration's public-housing bill. The response of the realtors to this tragic problem was that of Mr. Binns of the Philadelphia Real Estate Board: Let them live in fearsome, vermin- and rat-infested dumps, and we'll collect the rents.

The same outraged shrieking has been raised every year since the end of the war, in a frenzied effort to kill rent controls and open the way for mass gouging of helpless tenants.

These anguished cries redoubled in the spring of 1950 when the administration proposed the Spence-Maybank bill for cooperative housing for middle-income groups. Under this plan, people in roughly the $2,000 to $4,500 income category could join together in cooperatives and erect their own housing with government loans. Sweden, Denmark, and other enlightened democracies have used this method with great success. But the real-estate lobby raged against it, and, with the votes of the ever-willing GOP-Dixiecrat cabal, killed the legislation.

To rob the public is bad enough; piously to croak a sermon while doing it is something that only the real-estate harpies would descend to.

Probably the tawdriest of all the lobbying rackets in Washington is that of the "influence peddlers."

These so-called "five-percenters" have developed many ingenious shakedowns, all based on gall, hokum, and gullibility. The racket of these bunkum operators is not new; the only surprising thing is that they continue to find so many suckers—often in the most respectable business quarters. It is incredible the number of businessmen who are shrewd and hard-headed in Boston or Sioux City but who come to Washington and fall for the phony fronts and lines of the five-percenters.

As one astute observer of the Washington scene wrote:

"Persons visiting Washington on business are very frequently the dupes of impostors with which the city abounds. These scoundrels . . . offer their services to facilitate business in any way that lies in their power, for which they ask a sum which varies with the nature of the business, or of the service they propose to render. Such men are simply impostors, who are constantly on the watch for strangers, out of whose simplicity and ignorance of public affairs they expect to reap a rich harvest. It is best to decline all offers of assistance in Washington, whether gratuitous or for a stated compensation, unless the party making the offer is known to you to be a man of integrity, and capable of carrying out his promises."

This is wise advice. It was written in a book called *The Sights and Secrets of the National Capital,* by John B. Ellis, in 1869.

The late Senator Thaddeus Caraway of Arkansas, a brilliant and caustic crusader in his day, used to take great pleasure in pricking the bubbles of the five-percenters and their half brothers, the so-called "organization counselors." In the course of a speech, he summed up the latter and their numerous stratagems, as follows:

"Ninety per cent . . . are fake associations for the sole purpose of profit for those who are at Washington, and are engaged in obtaining money from those who live away from Washington under the belief that they are promoting some theory of government in which they are interested, or protecting or advancing the interests of some business in which they are engaged. Ninety-five dollars out of every hundred that the public pays to these alleged associations go into the pockets of the promoters of these fake associations. It might be safely said there is not a penny paid to these associations that is not worse than wasted."

But, again, it is the more "respectable" lobbies and the interests they represent that are responsible for the success of these professional promoters. Too many businessmen are ready to resort to any and all tactics to get what they want. This includes the using of spurious "fronts" which, in their way, are as devious as any concocted by the Communists.

When the Georgia Savings and Loan League, an element of the real-estate industry, was fighting the low-cost housing bill, it did not send out literature under its own name. Instead, it mailed thousands of postcards signed by the "Georgia Taxpayers' League." Ed Hiles, an employee of the Savings and Loan League who directed this campaign, admitted the Taxpayers' League was merely a letterhead front with "no charter, no bylaws, no nothing."

Lobbies are an ancient evil in the American political system. Since the earliest days of the Union, lobbyists have been at work. Their sordid record befouls the pages of every era of our history. Wars, depressions, booms, crises come and go, but the lobbies go on unendingly. Countless investigations have taken place, and innumerable sensational exposés have shocked the country.

The lobbies remain unvanquished.

There are a number of reasons for that. One is the fact that members of Congress are extremely reluctant to curb lobbying because many of them derive favors of various kinds from this source and also because they may be forced to turn to lobbying as a livelihood. The lobby is the principal lame-duck employment agency.

Another, and even stronger, factor blocking decisive reform is the combined interest of the powerful economic groups which have special and vested interests to protect and advance. Lobbies are of great value to them, and they fiercely resist any effort to curb such activities. It is only in recent years that liberal and labor groups have set up counterlobbies to oppose these special commercial interests, and even then these liberal lobbies are weak and puny compared to their old and entrenched adversaries.

Lobbying in Washington is, in essence, a highly skilled and highly paid trade serving a roster of powerful clients. It is a business which waxes stronger every year. Its capacity to checkmate forward-looking measures, to block congressional action, and to hamper and evade the controls and supervision of regulatory agencies is more thorough and all-embracing than it has ever been.

Past administrations, and particularly the Roosevelt administration, counterattacked the lobbies by staging aggressive and well-publicized investigations. Ferdinand Pecora's spectacular and devastating exposé of Wall Street in 1933 was the spearhead that cleared the way for the New Deal's law regulating securities and the stock market. Hugo

Black smashed the opposition to the Utilities Holding Company Act with his solar-plexus investigation.

The Truman administration has done nothing remotely comparable to this. It has thought about and made a few feeble gestures in that direction, but they have been too slow-witted and innocuous to resemble anything that might be called a counterattack.

In 1949, the House finally created a special Lobby Investigating Committee. Headed by Representative Frank Buchanan, a conscientious and liberal Democrat from Pennsylvania, the Committee wanted for nothing. It had all the power it needed and adequate funds.

All it lacked was the will and drive and imagination to use these resources.

There are several reasons for this. One is that Buchanan, whose intentions are the best, simply is not a Hugo Black or Ferdinand Pecora. A second reason is that the Republicans deliberately loaded their part of the Committee with three of the worst reactionary obstructionists in the House—Representatives Charlie Halleck of Indiana and Clarence Brown of Ohio, two veteran hatchet men, and Joseph O'Hara of Minnesota.

This trio was put on the Committee by the GOP command for the express purpose of stalling and hamstringing its probing. They have succeeded so resoundingly that the Committee has had virtually no national impact. It took the Committee six months to get under way, and then its public hearings amounted to very little. The only big lobby tackled was that of the realtors, and then only the surface was scratched. Nelson and a few other front figures were interrogated, but not one of the real masterminds of the rapacious and ultrareactionary lobby was put on the witness stand.

And no move at all was made to probe the medical, power, airline, and other ruling lobbies.

Large quantities of sensational evidence were dug up by the zealous and able staff, but the evidence never got out of the Committee's files. It is still buried there.

The only lobby curb of any kind written into the law was the Lobby Registration Act of 1946. It requires lobbyists to register and state the source of their income. But the law is vague and badly in need of tightening. Not more than one-fourth of all actual lobbyists comply with its provisions.

At various times, it has been suggested that a possible remedy for the evils of lobbying would be the creation of a permanent joint House-Senate lobby-investigating committee to police the lobbies. The idea has merits—certainly as a partial solution.

But its chief weakness is the same thing that was wrong with the Buchanan Committee. That Committee had everything needed to smash the lobbies—except the brains and guts to do it. The establishment of a permanent joint committee would not automatically ensure any better results than those of the Buchanan Committee. A coterie of Hallecks, Browns, and O'Haras would be all that would be needed to scuttle the joint committee.

And you can be sure the lobbies would leave no stone unturned to see to it that a gang of their bully-boys was firmly entrenched in the committee to prevent it from doing anything. In Congress, it isn't the form that counts, it's the substance. Congressional committees are no better than the members who sit on them—and who muzzle them.

So far in U.S. history, nothing has curbed the lobbies for long. It doesn't appear probable that anything ever will.

RIDERS IN THE SKY

> "I knew that the Constitution was not to blame and that the Supreme Court as an institution was not to blame. The only trouble was with some of the human beings on the Court."
>
> FRANKLIN D. ROOSEVELT.

THE United States Supreme Court looks today like an elderly woman who is slowly reacting from the effects of a full course of treatments at Helena Rubinstein's.

The temporary appearance of modernity and youthful vigor is waning. The wrinkles are reasserting themselves, the crow's-feet are creeping back, the pouches and the paunch are noticeable once more, the silhouette sags. She doesn't look quite as warped and frazzled as she did before she took the "youth treatment," but she is definitely showing signs of old age.

The Court, in other words, is steadily reverting to its old self—a frowsy, dowdy old woman decked out in yesteryear's fashions.

Taking a youth treatment had never been the Court's idea in the first place. The whole business was forced upon it by That Man. In 1937, Roosevelt proposed that a new justice be added for each justice over seventy who did not retire. This proposal, even though defeated, so panicked the tribunal that one old-timer did quit, and several others hurriedly revived themselves sufficiently to act and vote as if they were living in the present century, after all.

In the end, however, this trend was irresistible, and even half-hearted concessions by Chief Justice Charles Evans Hughes and Justice Owen Roberts could not block it. By the time Roosevelt died, he had had the opportunity to appoint seven of the nine justices. The remaining two departed within a year of his death.

The seven newcomers effected miracles in the appearance, vitality, and outlook of the Supreme Court. It was truly a revolution. But slowly the inevitable drift backward took place. The new flush of youth began to vanish.

First, the new Justices started arguing among themselves: a little squabbling and a little personal backbiting. Then suddenly a scorching feud broke out, so irreconcilable that it will never subside until one side or the other goes to the grave. Then the counterrevolution struck. President Truman appointed one conservative, then a second, then two more almost simultaneously. They stuck together as conservatives always do, and it was easy for them to pick up reinforcements from New Dealers now grown old and disaffected. Thus, the effects of the great revolution, having long since been devitalized, yielded more and more to the pressure of the counterrevolution.

Today the process is almost complete. The Court is back to normal. Not the normalcy of the black and defiant reaction of the early 1930's, but rather the twilight days of the 1870's and '80's—days of limited significance and influence, of stodgy mediocrity in its membership, of lack of creative thinking and leadership on new problems, and of gray, drab dullness and boredom.

It had been a silent revolution. Or, rather, the sounds of the upheaval had been lost in the deafening roar of global war.

Felix Frankfurter and William O. Douglas joined the bench in the spring of 1939, but the country's attention was focused anxiously on the silent streets of Prague where Nazi armies tramped, crowds wept, and freedom died. In January, 1940, when Frank Murphy replaced Pierce Butler, night had fallen over all Europe. Eighteen months later, the Nazi and Soviet armies locked in a wild and savage death grapple. In Washington, Lend-Lease was months old and defense preparations were a feverish reality.

Almost unnoticed in those days of approaching Armageddon, Charles Evans Hughes, of Olympian mien and sculptured beard, the last guardsman of the old era, resigned and slipped into seclusion. Harlan Stone ascended to Chief Justice, and Robert H. Jackson was appointed to the Court. By the time of James F. Byrnes's arrival, departure, and subsequent replacement by Wiley Rutledge, the news of a Supreme

Court shuffle had been relegated almost, though not quite, to the wilderness of the want ads.

As the new crew took over and quickly and quietly set to work, many cherished conservative precedents were jettisoned and sank without a trace. First to go was the narrow, strait-jacket interpretation of the commerce clause that had been used to smother a number of New Deal reforms.

In *Mulford* v. *Smith* (1939), the Court legitimized the sweeping and complex production controls set up by the second AAA. From this decision, a whole new line of precedents sprang to life. Within three years, a unanimous Court, in *Wickard* v. *Filburn,* upheld the Agriculture Secretary's power to penalize a farmer who exceeded his wheat quota, even though the extra wheat was to be eaten by the farmer's own family. As Justice Jackson pointed out, the wheat filled a need which otherwise would have had to be met by purchases on the open market. Thus wheat that never moved off Farmer Doe's own land was still in competition with the crop which moved in interstate commerce.

In the Opp Cotton Mills case, the question of the unconstitutional delegation of power—the same key issue that had killed the NRA in the famous Schecter ("sick chicken") case—once more came to the front. But this time the Court held differently. It ruled that the broad powers of the Wage and Hour administrator were not too vague or too sweeping. The "sick chicken" bit the dust; the old Blue Eagle was revenged.

The infamous *Hammer* v. *Dagenhart* decision, sanctifying child labor, was reversed. The right of Congress under the commerce clause to regulate conditions of work was found to extend not only to children but also to employees, such as janitors and repairmen, who worked not for a manufacturer in interstate commerce but for a local realtor who leased the building to the manufacturer.

The nine young men also reinvigorated the authority of the states to protect the health and welfare of their citizens, under the so-called "police power." The old Court, by drawing a labored distinction between businesses which were "affected with a public interest" and those which were not, had, for all practical purposes, entombed the police power of the states. The new Court restored it to full life.

But few Americans paid much attention to the Supreme Court as it hacked away the legal deadwood that had accumulated since the Civil War. Occasionally an anguished conservative would let out a protesting yelp, but it went unnoticed. The attention of the nation and of the world was centered on more pressing problems.

But at the very time the Court was writing this spectacular legal history, a highly significant trend was slowly taking form within the ranks of the liberal majority.

More and more the Court seemed to break down into three component parts: Justices Black, Douglas, Murphy, and Rutledge opposing Justices Frankfurter, Jackson, and Roberts, with Chief Justice Stone and Justice Reed acting as "swing men," now shifting the tribunal one way, 6 to 3, next shifting it the other way, 5 to 4.

Many of the legal issues in dispute between the two groups are not easy to summarize and describe. A variety of labels have been applied. Some have called the Black group the "judicial activists," and the Frankfurter bloc, the advocates of "judicial self-restraint." Others have used the phrases "tender-minded" and "tough-minded." Partisans of Black and Douglas usually just say "liberals" and "conservatives."

The matter of labels is more than merely an argument over terminology. It is important because the terms in which an issue is stated often predetermine who wins it.

Rationalizers for the Frankfurter point of view put the emphasis on the role and function of the Supreme Court in the governmental system. The Court, they say, should be restricted as much as possible, because it is the arm of government farthest from control of the people. Let the state legislatures and Congress be supreme. Opponents of this view are "activists," eager for power and overly anxious to impose their ideas on the country. This eagerness, contend the Frankfurter defenders, stems from being too tender-minded about social abuses and inequalities. Of course, we feel sorry about these things, too, say the Frankfurter men, but we are tough-minded and put the principle of orderly government procedure and judicial self-restraint ahead of our own convictions about social evils.

Supporters of Black and Douglas object vehemently to stating the argument in these terms at all. They hotly deny that they want to expand the Supreme Court's power. Neither do they have any desire to impose their political and economic ideas on the country by judicial edict.

All the chatter about activism and self-restraint, they assert, is a smoke screen. Every judge tries to take into account what the law-making body had in mind when it framed a law. Every judge has opinions about economic and social problems, and these opinions obviously have a strong influence on the way he looks on a case. Thus, whatever decision he arrives at, a judge is "legislating" in favor of some and against others. A Justice of the Supreme Court can no more "restrain" himself from exercising his authority than a member of a baseball team can "restrain" himself from taking his turn at bat.

Of course, it might be more desirable, were we back in 1787 and starting from scratch, not to give the Supreme Court the sweeping power it now has. But under the American federal system as it has in fact developed, we can no longer choose. Time and history have closed the option.

That is the core of the Black-Douglas view. To them, the basic question is not the role and function of the Supreme Court. It is whether the economic and social ideas which every judge holds are liberal or conservative. That issue is what Black and Douglas consider the crux of the matter.

Black and Douglas are liberals; their opponents, they feel, are conservatives who have betrayed the New Deal beliefs they once professed to support—and which put them on the Court.

The curious pattern of conservative opinions and dissents evolved by Frankfurter and Jackson poses a serious problem in self-justification for these two men who were flaming liberals prior to their elevation to the tribunal.

Jackson defends his position in terms of the immediate issues before him in each case. He is aware that social effects will flow from his decision, and he argues bluntly that they are the right effects. As one of the most facile writers on the bench and the uneasy owner of an irascible temper, Jackson often seems to confuse judgment with morals, implying rather unpleasantly that his adversaries are not merely wrong but wicked as well.

Frankfurter, ever enamoured of the wily and devious approach, never engages in such straight-out battling. He has evolved a mystique by which he conjures himself away from the arena of personal feelings and interests. "In the Frankfurter concept," as one of his friendlier critics remarked, "the judge triumphs over self to declare law."

Frankfurter himself described the act in one of his numerous dissents,* as follows: "Were my purely personal attitude relevant, I should wholeheartedly associate myself with the libertarian views in the Court's opinion. . . . As a member of this Court I am not justified in writing my private notions of policy into the Constitution, no matter how deeply I cherish them."

And so exit liberalism.

" 'Tis not what I would but what I must!" cries Felix as he pirouettes offstage. Critics will be pardoned if they catch a certain note of relish in his melancholy cry.

The New Deal revolution on the Supreme Court has followed the historic pattern of every preceding revolution. Once the barricades were down, the rebels stopped attacking and began arguing with one another as to what it had all been about.

At the same time that their own internecine strife grew louder, their numbers dwindled. Two of their number, Wiley Rutledge and Frank Murphy, have died. Justice Reed, the cautious, kindly swing man, is in delicate health and keeps his dangerous high blood pressure down by living on a rigid diet of rice and dried fruit. Justices Black and Frankfurter, though both in excellent health, are in their sixties.

President Truman has had the opportunity to make four appointments. Each of his selections has turned out to be decisively to the right of center. Usually these four are more steadfastly conservative than even Frankfurter and Jackson.

* In the famous flag-salute cases, Frankfurter contended that the children of Jehovah Witnesses should be compelled to salute the flag, even though they regarded it as repugnant to their interpretation of the Bible. The central issue in these cases was not the specific doctrinal beliefs of these children but rather the fundamental question of how far legislative bodies—in this instance a school board—could go in setting limits to the exercise of the liberties guaranteed in the Bill of Rights. Once again, Frankfurter trotted out his pet theory of legislative supremacy. He piously protested that he would vote against requiring a flag salute, but as a judge he had no choice but to defer to the legislative body elected by the people.

This sudden rightward landslide has apparently startled Frankfurter into at least temporary remorse.

In the search-and-seizure case decided in the spring of 1950, he noted, in a querulous dissent, that he, Black, and Jackson were in the minority against the new conservative phalanx. Rather sharply, he added that the case would not have been decided along this line if it had not been for recent changes on the Court.

This bitter, futile observation was the final touch to the passing of the old era. No two had battled more fiercely than Murphy and Frankfurter. Considering the way in which Frankfurter had gossiped about Murphy's legal competence and how rarely he had voted with him, his posthumous accolade was profoundly ironic—and characteristic of Frankfurter.

Conceivably, it might be possible for Black, Douglas, Jackson, and Frankfurter to close ranks and see eye to eye more frequently. But it will never happen.

Outstanding members of the tribunal are liberals or conservatives chiefly in terms of the peculiar institution in which they find themselves. In another framework their views might be largely indistinguishable. For example, it is almost certain that if Black, Douglas, Jackson, Minton, and Frankfurter were in the U.S. Senate, they would vote much the same on most questions. But they are not senators, free-lancing in a relatively large, informal forum. They are members of a select team: nine players and no substitutes.

They must work and live in a small, artificial world, seeing one another every day, sitting together every day, arguing out cases in a highly secret conference once a week, reading, checking, commenting on, revising, or refuting one another's written opinions all the time. They are sealed off from all outside pressure; there are no "orders" or "appeals" from the White House; no one conducts "Wire Your Supreme Court Justice Today" campaigns. Each knows that he and his "brethren" will be there for the rest of their natural lives, if they so desire.

So, having no constituents and no superiors, save God and their consciences, they commit their cause to the sternest taskmaster of all, History. Some also gesture to what they perceive to be the demands of a symbolic intangible called "the Law." Since neither History nor the Law has any other visible steward, each Justice feels he must fulfill this duty and be his brother's keeper. It should be no wonder, then, that, looked at as an organization of humans, the Supreme Court often exhibits the intellectual pride of a debating team, the conscience-driven self-dedication of a tribal priesthood, and the taut emotions of a barnstorming road company on perpetual tour.

The life of a Supreme Court Justice was made for sin or senility; there is no happy middle ground.

Hugo La Fayette Black is an austere, dedicated, arresting personality.

At sixty-four, he has a trim, youthful figure, his clear gray eyes are untroubled, his angular smile urbane, his voice soft but incisive, his manner graceful, sure, and relaxed. He still plays a rattling good tennis game and can turn in a sixteen-hour workday when necessary. Black is closest to the Nine Old Men of an earlier era in his almost total abstinence from the Washington social whirl.

His life is a thrilling story in self-education.

He was born in 1886, the son of a storekeeper in Harlan, Alabama, a small town in the hill country of the upland South. Black was educated in the country schools and at Ashland College, a local academy. After two years at the State University Law School, he passed the bar and began practice in Birmingham. The twenty years that followed were punctuated by eighteen months as a police judge, three years as a crusading prosecuting attorney, and a year's service in the Army in World War I. In 1926, in a campaign that carried him to every backwoods whistle stop, he was elected to the U.S. Senate. Six years later he was easily re-elected.

The pattern is a familiar one in American politics. Black was the poor boy who came from a struggling farm area (Clay County was proverbially "poor-man's country"), moved to the city, built a successful practice, enjoyed a local reputation, served in minor political offices, was an Elk, Knight of Pythias, Baptist Sunday School teacher, and for a time an inactive member of the Klan.

But Black was too strong an individual to be caged in a conventional pattern. As a lawyer, he fought for the underprivileged, the injured workman, the embattled labor union. As a prosecutor, he cleared the docket of petty cases and thus knocked the bottom out of the fee racket of the jailers who victimized both the taxpayer and the defendant.

As a senatorial candidate, he decked himself out with the grandiloquent slogan: "Hugo Black, the Candidate of the Masses." But he rarely resorted to the moonlight-and-magnolias rhetoric of the professional Southerner, and never did he advocate anything less than strict justice for men of all races. In the Senate, he kept as far away from Tom Heflin, his Catholic-baiting colleague from Alabama, as he possibly could.

Gradually Black came under the influence of the two great old men of the liberal movement—George Norris of Nebraska and Tom Walsh of Montana. Norris educated Black in the subtleties of the fight for Muscle Shoals and made of him a militant supporter. In his first session, Black defended Walsh's proposed investigation of the power industry, an undertaking he himself was to carry out in dramatic fashion years later.

Meanwhile, Black put himself through a rigorous reading schedule built on the firm foundation of his life-long admiration for the writings of Thomas Jefferson. As the depression came and deepened, Black read omnivorously in the works of the leading economists. His special favorites were two of the less orthodox thinkers, Stuart Chase and Thorstein Veblen. Eventually, Black decided on the thirty-hour work week as a thoroughgoing single solution to the unemployment problem. Years later, after he had gone on the bench, Black's bill, after a long detour by way of the NRA, finally became law in modified form as the Wage and Hour Act of 1938.

In the early Roosevelt years, Black emerged as among the most brilliant of the Senate liberals.

In a series of devastating investigations, he unmasked fraud and collusive bidding in the granting of air-mail contracts, punctured the balloon of propaganda sent up by the public utilities in the holding company fight in 1935, and exposed the true nature of the "grass-roots" organizations working against the New Deal in 1936.

Black was one of the mightiest investigators in the history of Congress. This was due to the same qualities that have made him a great judge.

He has deep emotional convictions and a granite will, harnessed to relentless industriousness and an unwavering perception of the central issues. His speeches and judicial opinions are always grounded in solid factual knowledge. Before his elevation to the Supreme Court, no one but Roosevelt surpassed Black as a warm, smooth, persuasive speaker.

When Roosevelt appointed Black to the Court in July, 1937, the conservatives howled in anguish. "A rank partisan," "no judicial experience," "unqualified," were some of the angry shrieks. "Cheap," shrilled Dorothy Thompson. Though he was confirmed, Black took office under many handicaps.

On the eve of his first session, his old Klan affiliation was tardily revealed; this created a short but embarrassing sensation. Further, Black became the associate of a group of judges he had assailed only a few months before, when he was one of the floor leaders and backing the "court-packing" plan. Finally, he had to serve under a Chief Justice against whose confirmation he had voted seven years earlier. Black's first year on the Supreme Court was the most rigorous ordeal in the education of Hugo Black. And none knew this more clearly than the man from Clay County.

Black met the challenge in the only way he knew—by tireless hard work and by reliance on a courteous but aloof and self-contained manner. (Even in his days as a political campaigner, Black never dealt in the devalued coin of easy familiarity. "You might call him Hugo," one intimate remarked, "but you'd never think of slapping him on the back.")

That Black won this memorable battle is a story now well known. The early scorn changed to grudging compliment and finally to undisputed respect and far-flung acclaim. Foes and friends alike agree that he stands high among the great creative thinkers of American jurisprudence.

In every field from patent law to interstate commerce, Black has made a powerful impact. On civil liberties, he has taken a particularly strong position. The man who was so long taunted for his brief political flirtation with the Klan has proved a tower of strength in the struggle for equal freedom.

Back in 1940, when the liberal revolution within the Court was still at flood tide, Black wrote a majority opinion in behalf of equal protection for Negroes that is a legal classic. The case was *Smith* v. *Texas.* A Negro had been convicted on a rape charge, but Black overturned the conviction because no Negroes had been on the grand jury which issued the indictment. There had been a few Negroes on the grand jury lists, but they had always been passed over when a jury was selected. Black pointed out that chance alone could not have brought this about, and he concluded: "If there has been discrimination, whether accomplished ingeniously or ingenuously, the conviction cannot stand."

Tall, bald Justice Stanley Reed, with pince-nez glasses and a slow, placid manner, is now rarely thought of as a New Dealer. Yet in January, 1938, when he was appointed, the belief was widespread that he was a sure vote in the administration's vest pocket.

For three years, as Solicitor General, he had served as the administration's legal spokesman. Before a hostile Court, he had defended a long series of liberal measures and had done so with high technical proficiency. As a Justice, Reed has demonstrated the same legal skill but nothing approaching liberal fervor or clear legal philosophy.

Reed lacks emotion, for nothing ever happened in his life to get him much excited.

As the son of a prosperous Kentucky physician, he knew a secure and happy childhood. In due course, he took his A.B. at Yale, his law degree at Columbia, and spent a postgraduate year at the Sorbonne. After this leisurely preparation, he returned to his home town and put out his shingle. Business came to him at a regular, satisfactory rate. His district sent him to the legislature for two terms, and his fellow Young Democrats elected him their State president.

As a legislator, Reed introduced "radical" bills calling for a workmen's compensation law and a ban on child labor. But these products of a naturally kindly nature were only fitful gleams in an emotionally sedentary career. His over-all record was safe enough to win him two good jobs from the Hoover administration: the first as counsel of the futile Farm Board, and the second as top legal adviser of the Reconstruction Finance Corporation. It was in this latter berth that Roosevelt found him in 1933, and from which he was elevated to Solicitor General in 1935.

It has been a long, quiet, honorable career. Through the whole monotone length of it, Reed has never, to anyone's knowledge, made a genuine enemy.

As a Justice, he decides each case in an apparently *ad hoc* manner, much as a mechanic looks at a battered old car, shakes his head, mutters an occasional "hmm," and sets to work tinkering on it. Reed has exactly the same kind of technician's feeling for detail and an impersonal fondness for the law as an end in itself. Characteristically, his specialty is the dull but important field of administrative law. His opinions on this subject are learned and authoritative, and he expresses them in a severely plain literary style.

Reed is a good man. Period.

When Roosevelt appointed Felix Frankfurter to the Court in 1939, most liberals tossed their hats into the air.

Frankfurter, the intellectual godfather of the New Deal, the defender of Tom Mooney, the champion of Sacco and Vanzetti, had at last received his reward.

In the eleven years since then, those exultant cheers have died away. Bitterness, disgust, and bewilderment have supplanted enthusiasm.

The key to Frankfurter's career as a jurist is that he is a congenital dissenter with nothing now to dissent from.

His entire pre-Court career had been spent as the spokesman of the minority viewpoint. His great hero was the prince of dissenters, Justice Oliver Wendell Holmes. But when Frankfurter himself came to the Supreme bench, he came not as a lonely rebel fighting to hold a bridgehead. The old idols he had railed against were toppling all about him. The goals Holmes and Brandeis had spent a lifetime fighting for were realized. Frankfurter was a prophet with all prophecies fulfilled, a battler with all battles won.

Being what he is, only two alternatives remained for him. He could attempt to rule his colleagues and give all major opinions the flavor of his personality and his views. Or he could shift his ground and find new bases for dissent. In the end, Frankfurter was to do both.

One of the first things he discovered on the Court was that the

Saturday-morning conference was a much tougher arena than the Monday-morning class.

Justices Douglas and Murphy, previously friendly though not intimate with Frankfurter, reacted coldly to his efforts to bludgeon or cajole them into his way of thinking. Black and the late Wiley Rutledge never lost their suave urbanity, but when voting time came they consistently went their own way. Alone of all the New Dealers, Robert Jackson, driven by gnawing personal animosities and frustrations of his own, came under Frankfurter's sway.

On the other hand, his machinations were more successful with the conservatives and middle-of-the-roaders. Owen Roberts, Hoover appointee and now Dean of the University of Pennsylvania Law School, was strongly influenced by his "radical" little colleague. But Roberts eventually succumbed to a growing mood of weariness and hopelessness, and he finally quit in 1945. In his last year, he became so morose and suspicious that he lunched alone and avoided any contact with his colleagues.

Before the deaths of Rutledge and Murphy, in the summer of 1949, altered the complexion of the Court, Justice Reed consistently acted as swing man; that is, on close decisions, his vote often was decisive. Court attachés tell the story of passing Frankfurter's open door one day when he was on the phone talking to Reed. The words which floated out to the corridor were: "Now, Stanley, don't let your vote be influenced by those ——s."

Frankfurter's Machiavellian decisive influence is nowhere better illustrated than by the role he played in the famous Jackson-Black controversy.

It was Frankfurter who was at the bottom of this tragic affair.

Jackson had long been openly ambitious to succeed Harlan Stone as Chief Justice. When the latter died in the spring of 1946, while Jackson was away at the Nuremberg war-criminal trials, his hopes skyrocketed. It was known that Truman had spoken of Jackson as one of the ablest men on the bench. But "dope stories" began to filter out of Washington to the effect that Truman was now hesitant about appointing Jackson because of his lack of tact and obsessive feuds with other Justices.

These press reports were well founded. Truman had cooled toward

Jackson as a result of information imparted by retired Justices Hughes and Roberts. They had visited the President while he was deliberating on the problem and had bluntly advised against Jackson's selection.

Jackson heard these stories and rumors with growing anguish. He fretted and brooded that he should be marooned in far-off Germany at such a crucial time. At this point, Frankfurter wrote him that Black had gone to Truman and declared that he would not serve under Jackson.

That accusation was a lie. There was not an atom of truth in it. Black had neither said nor done anything to influence Truman's decision. The story was solely the product of Frankfurter's scheming and devious imagination.

But to Jackson, seething and raging in Nuremberg, Frankfurter's letter was like putting an acetylene torch to a powder keg. All of Jackson's hates, resentments, and frustrations centered on Black and exploded in a shameful letter of unfounded denunciation.

In his endless efforts to dominate his associates, Frankfurter resorts to various devices.

Conversationally, he has personal charm when he cares to exert it. He also has an imposing knowledge of legal details and of history, a fact which he never fails to make clear to his opponents. But his favorite tactic is to ask questions from the bench to get an attorney to make a point Frankfurter wants to put across.

Frequently these are not questions at all, but lectures for the benefit of his colleagues.

Many high-priced lawyers have sweated and silently cursed under these endless interrogations but have felt it impolitic to give vent to their feelings. Not so, one obscure attorney from Florida who had never appeared in the High Court before. After he had been repeatedly and lengthily interrupted by Frankfurter, the harassed counsel, to the undisguised delight of Felix's foes both on and off the bench, said in a quiet but firm voice, "Your Honor, I'm not going to answer that last question. You've taken up a lot of my time already, and I would very respectfully like to call your Honor's attention to the fact that the time on my side of the bench seems to run a lot faster than it apparently does on your side of the bench."

Frankfurter scowled but subsided.

Despite his devices and ceaseless intrigues and machinations, Frankfurter has got nowhere on the bench or off it. His hungry quest for power has been frustrated. As a result, more and more, he has reoriented his intellectual position so as to cast himself in the role of a chronic dissenter. He dissents solely for the sake of dissenting.

This reorientation has been so pronounced as to justify the suspicion that Frankfurter was never a liberal. Those who know him best attest to this fact. Judge Learned Hand once remarked, "Felix's influence is always divisive. Wherever he is, he likes to stir things up."

This quality made Frankfurter a stimulating teacher, but it has been a corrosive influence in the compact, intimate world of the Supreme Court.

The disparity between his public reputation and his judicial record is most apparent in the field of civil liberties. Here Frankfurter has done an almost complete about-face. Except for one ringing dissent in a case involving unwarranted search and seizure, he has taken an extraordinarily regressive stand.

Supported by Jackson and the Vinson-Burton-Clark trio, Frankfurter has consistently refused to move beyond the reactionary position of the Court of the 1890's on the issue of right to counsel. This issue is one phase of the losing struggle waged by the Black group to prevail on the Court to return to the authentic interpretation of the Fourteenth Amendment.

When adopted in the Reconstruction era, this amendment was expressly designed to make the limitations of the Bill of Rights, which already protected the people from arbitrary action by the federal government, apply to the state governments as well. Through a series of interpretations, the Supreme Court, however, distorted the intentions of the framers and said only certain parts of the Bill of Rights applied while others did not. Frankfurter has steadfastly refused to join in overturning this reactionary concept.

As a result, it is still true that in a state court, in a case involving a crime less than murder, a defendant too poor to hire a lawyer can be tried without one. If the judge is charitable, he may assign an attorney whose fee will be paid by the state. But he does not have to do so, for the right to have legal counsel is one which the Court decades ago picked out of the Bill of Rights as not applying under the Fourteenth Amendment.

Vain, paunchy, sharp-witted, and sharp-tongued, the ex-professor has had a career that is a chapter from the great American saga. Frankfurter knows it and is proud of it.

He came to New York from Vienna in 1894, at the age of twelve. He did not know a word of English. Eight years later, he graduated at the head of his class from the College of the City of New York. He went to the Harvard Law School, where he became a *Law Review* man, the School's top distinction. From there he joined a Manhattan law firm which boasted a select clientele of top-bracket corporations. But within two months he was drafted by the ambitious young U.S. Attorney for Southern New York to serve as his assistant. The U.S. Attorney was a stripling Republican lawyer named Henry L. Stimson.

Frankfurter served under Stimson when the latter went into Taft's cabinet as Secretary of War. In 1914, he joined the faculty of the Harvard Law School, where he was to remain, with one exception, for the next quarter century. The exception was in 1917, when the war brought Frankfurter back to Washington as counsel to the President's Labor Mediation Commission. He ended up as chairman of the War Labor Policies Board, one of whose members was the youthful Assistant Secretary of the Navy, Franklin D. Roosevelt.

In the Hoover days, Frankfurter helped Stimson, by now Secretary of State, to staff his Department. When the Reconstruction Finance Corporation came along in 1932, Frankfurter channeled a number of his bright young protégés into that agency. But it was the Roosevelt New Deal which really boomed business at the Frankfurter employment bureau. Whether the problem was revaluing the dollar, reducing crop surpluses, putting electricity in every farmhouse, or what have you, a Frankfurter-trained lawyer ("hot dog") was on hand to give the final word on its legality.

Meanwhile, Felix was content to stay in Cambridge and occasionally commute to the Capital to inspire, conspire, cajole, bully, adjust, and arrange.

Gay, witty, crafty, indiscreet, passionate, a brilliant conversationalist with a weakness for dazzling solo flights, Frankfurter was the fabulous autocrat of a politico-intellectual empire. Many anecdotes cluster about his name. His own favorite concerns a very noisy party he attended in Washington. The host came over and apologized for the uproar. "Noise?" said Frankfurter, "Why, I like noise."

"Yes, dear," broke in his wife, "but this is other people's noise."

In 1949, Frankfurter and Chief Justice Fred Vinson, along with a throng of other notables, attended the special exhibit of Austrian art at the Washington National Gallery. Each of the two Justices reacted to the masterpieces in a different but very characteristic manner.

Frankfurter, a native of Austria, talked incessantly in German to one of the Austrian curators acting as a guide. The curator got no chance to tell Frankfurter anything. Frankfurter told him—in a voluble flow of German.

Kentucky-born Vinson said nothing until he came to a display of large and voluptuous Rubens nudes. Then he burst out with a loud and enthusiastic "Wow!"

Frankfurter did not abdicate as a political wirepuller when Roosevelt appointed him to the Supreme Court.

It was he who was responsible for Roosevelt's spectacular surprise in bringing Frank Knox and Henry Stimson into the cabinet in June, 1940. Throughout the war, Frankfurter was a regular visitor to Stimson's suite in the Pentagon. On his recommendation, Stimson chose Judge Robert Patterson as Assistant Secretary. When the Pearl Harbor disaster came, Frankfurter proposed Justice Owen Roberts to head the Pearl Harbor inquiry. Roosevelt named Roberts. Frankfurter early in 1942 was a strong Donald Nelson booster for the job of war production boss, principally because he feared the President might choose Justice Douglas, with whom Frankfurter was already feuding.

As the war intensified and the New Deal wave ebbed, Frankfurter scented the shifting winds of power with the sure instincts of a hound dog. Almost unconsciously, he saw less and less of his bright young men. The old clan, founded on the inflexible law of mutual help among all good Frankfurter men, broke up.

Most spectacular was the rift between Frankfurter and Tom Corcoran, which developed when Frankfurter blocked the brilliant braintruster's appointment as Solicitor General.

Frankfurter rushed on unconcerned. He built up a circle of friends among top-drawer admirals and generals. He cultivated Wall Street alumni such as Averell Harriman, John McCloy, and Lewis Douglas. He wooed big-name figures in the press and became a confidant of visiting Britons, both Laborites such as Ernest Bevin and Harold Laski and Conservatives such as Lord Beaverbrook and Viscount Halifax.

Never a recluse, Frankfurter hit the cocktail-party circuit harder than ever. His daily appointment list was often longer than the President's. His office became so crowded that attachés nicknamed it "the barbershop" and solemnly averred that each caller received a slip with a number to designate his turn.

When Truman came to the White House, he brought with him the righteous belief that Frankfurter was one disturbing influence he was going to eradicate. Truman failed. Frankfurter is doing just as much hectic politicking and wirepulling today as he did ten years ago. And he is doing it despite the fact that Truman has sealed off Frankfurter's direct access to the Executive Office.

Franklin Roosevelt could have told Truman why.

At one period in the late '30's, Roosevelt became weary of Frankfurter's machinations, and a definite coolness developed between them. Roosevelt was shocked, therefore, when a high-ranking New Dealer asked him one day why he didn't root out Frankfurter's influence.

"But I haven't seen Felix for months," protested Roosevelt.

"Mr. President," was the reply, "you see Frankfurter a dozen times a day. Not the man himself, but through his protégés, his friends, and his stooges, you see, hear, and read Frankfurter continually."

Roosevelt smiled and acknowledged that was true.

When Truman named Kenneth Royall as Secretary of the Army, he perhaps did not know that he was elevating a close friend and former student of Frankfurter's. Also, Secretary of State Dean Acheson is another Frankfurter intimate. It was Frankfurter who recommended him for his first Washington job as Undersecretary of the Treasury way back in 1933. And when David Lilienthal was made head of the Atomic Energy Commission, Frankfurter spent more time lining up votes to confirm him in the Senate than did the members of the White House staff.

The effect of all this extracurricular activity on Frankfurter's judicial work has been pronounced. His work on the Court has suffered materially.

His output of opinions is the lowest, with the exception of Justice Burton's. While Black and Douglas produce as many as twenty-six opinions apiece in a term, Frankfurter rarely produces more than six or seven. His persistent procrastination has more than once incurred the displeasure of Chief Justice Vinson, and of Stone before him. Each year Frankfurter delays until the spring on finishing up his assignments, and inevitably this means that his "brethren" have to take up the slack for him. On occasion, he has even voted a dissent and blandly announced he would file a statement later.

As a result, while Frankfurter has tossed off scores of "quickie" dissents, he has written few notable opinions. He is just too busy exercising his energies and talents being a hotshot in other orbits.

For those who have studied Frankfurter's career, these extrajudicial antics are wholly in character. For despite all his professions of love for the law, he lacks the one quality whose absence he is always deploring in others: Frankfurter does not have a judicial mind.

Deciding cases is not enough to feed the hunger within him. His deepest instincts are those of the political operator. He yearns for power, to manipulate men and events.

He might conceivably have had a political career in his own right. But after a few years as Stimson's assistant, he turned his back on the rough-and-tumble of law practice and forsook the possibilities of politics in New York. Again, in 1933, he could have become Roosevelt's Solicitor General and participated directly in shaping the New Deal. But he preferred to remain on the side lines, sending little notes to the coach, rather than carry the ball himself.

The academic life is a proud career and a happy one for the man whose political interests and ambitions do not go beyond the desire to fulfill the responsibilities of an intelligent private citizen. But Frankfurter's political instincts are too supercharged to be tethered in the academic pale. So, on the border line between the two worlds, he built a political career of sorts.

He manipulated events by long-distance. He sent other men out to fight the battles and shared their triumphs vicariously. His has been a career built on quicksands.

It rests heavily on the adoration and youthful enthusiasm of his law students of the 1920's and early '30's, whose feelings and views inevitably change as they grow older and more experienced. It involves cultivating the good will of other men, many of whom he rightly considers his inferiors. As one of Frankfurter's colleagues at Harvard Law School observed, "Felix is an intellectual whore; on the side of righteousness, of course, but still a whore."

His appointment to the Court only brought him closer to the center of power, thus whetting his appetite and embroiling him more directly in the day-to-day squabbles of his adherents, without in any way increasing his own power (and responsibility) personally to do anything decisive. The result has been broken friendships, bitterness, feuds, increased dissipation of his time and talents in politics, and missed opportunities to do historic work as a judge.

Drunk with desire, Felix Frankfurter, the would-be political master, has learned that to mix the champagne of power with the brandy of irresponsibility is to savor neither.

Justice Robert H. Jackson is an unhappy figure.

He climaxed a brilliant and meteoric career with the almost unbelievable aberration of his public attack on Justice Black. This blighted forever his consuming desire to be Chief Justice. It also stained his record with the smudge of a whiner and a grudge bearer.

Jackson's only hope now is to recoup his position; he can never advance it. From the occasionally intemperate attitude he displays, it is unlikely he will get anywhere on the first effort, either.

It is ironic that Black and Jackson should be pitted as antagonists. Their careers have much in common. Both are aggressively self-made men.

Jackson, like Black, was born in comfortable but far from affluent circumstances. After high school, he went for a year to the Albany (N.Y.) Law School, read law with an older lawyer (in keeping with an American tradition which seems very quaint and far away today), and then began practice in the small city of Jamestown in upstate New York. For twenty years, on into middle age, he lived in Jamestown.

He built up a successful general practice, served briefly as corporation counsel, and became a respected local figure. He lived as a gentleman farmer outside the city limits, maintained a stable of trotting horses, and seemed headed for a quiet career as a kind of local squire. Then came the New Deal.

Jackson, a Democrat by heredity in a Republican wilderness where Democrats never won, had been barred from State office. But Franklin Roosevelt, as governor, had an eye for upcountry Democrats and knew Jackson. Early in 1934, Jackson was called to Washington as general counsel of the Bureau of Internal Revenue.

Under friendly boosting and steering from the brain-trusters, he blossomed quickly in the political hothouse of the New Deal.

He was drafted by Corcoran and Cohen to help defend the Holding Company bill. Then he became Assistant Attorney General in charge of the Antitrust Division. This put him in the very front trenches (and publicity) of Roosevelt's attack on the "economic royalists." In the next three exuberant years, promotions flowed in rapid order: to Solicitor General, Attorney General, and the Supreme Court. Each swing of Fate's spiral seemed to bring him ever higher, to more dazzling vistas of opportunity.

Jackson even began to dream of the White House, or at least of becoming Chief Justice.

The four war years were an unavoidable hiatus, of course. But the role of chief prosecutor at the Nuremberg trials, for which Roosevelt, before his death, selected him, ended the waiting period and seemed to presage a resumption of the upward climb of the Jackson curve. Thus within five years he had skyrocketed from an obscure, middle-aged country lawyer to an eminence where the most thrilling prizes of American politics and the American bar were either already his or were within his grasp.

It is perhaps not too surprising, therefore, that Jackson's hopes were inflamed and his judgment distorted. He felt cruelly disappointed when his dream castles crumbled overnight.

First, Roosevelt's death destroyed any chance for the White House. The Nuremberg trials proved only a mixed success and added nothing to his legal repute. Then Stone died, and Truman's choice of the relatively vigorous Vinson slammed the door on any possibility of Jackson's ever becoming Chief Justice. It was against this background of failure and frustration that Jackson unleashed his senseless spoilsport attack on Black.

Jackson today is a lonely, isolated figure. Except for Frankfurter, all his colleagues keep their distance from him.

He has grown heavy, the firm jaw line has sagged, and the once full, smooth face is creased and puffy. Only his glib literary wit and sharpness have not lost their edge. Dissenting from a majority opinion written by Black, Jackson quipped, "The undertones of the opinion . . . seem utterly discordant with its conclusions. The case which irresistibly comes to mind as the most fitting precedent is that of Julia, who, according to Byron's reports, whispering, 'I will ne'er consent'— consented."

But literary virtuosity is cold comfort for an ambitious man. Jackson is in the unhappy position of a man who has said and done all the big things he will ever have the chance to do.

Harold Burton has one qualification as a Justice. He looks the part.

Sitting on the bench in his black silk robe, he fits the tourist's preconceived conception: the high, broad forehead beneath the thin crest of silver hair; the dark, shadow-rimmed eyes; the firm, straight mouth; and the whole well-molded face bearing a sober, dignified appearance.

But that is as far as it goes.

After five years on the Court, Burton is still only a picture-postcard judge. In quality and quantity he is the sad sack of the tribunal.

In his first year, he wrote only three opinions. The next year, his output climbed heroically to five, but in 1948, it fell back to four. Burton and Frankfurter regularly run neck and neck for the dubious distinction of low man on the Court.

Friendly, easygoing, and cautious-minded, Burton is inclined to put off until tomorrow what requires some exertion today. He is well liked by his colleagues and is on cordial but not intimate terms with all of them.

Burton's principal distinction as a Justice is as one of Washington's most inveterate partygoers.

He hits the society pages almost every day. No function, whether it be a small cocktail party or an elaborate diplomatic soiree, is really complete without him.

This is the continuation of a lifelong practice. When he was Mayor of Cleveland, he was such a stellar performer on the luncheon and banquet circuits that someone jestingly paraphrased the Bible to the effect that "wherever two or three were gathered, there was Burton."

Recently, at a Washington party, Burton ran into an ex-senator whom he had not seen since both were in the Senate together. The old friend asked, "Well, Harold, which do you like better, the Senate or the Supreme Court?"

"Well, to tell you the truth," replied Burton, "I liked being Mayor of Cleveland best of all."

This anecdote is the key to Burton's character. He is a pleasant, affable, smalltime politician enjoying the security and prestige of his lifetime job on the Court but bored and bewildered by the work it entails.

New England- born and -educated, Burton devoted most of a long career in private law practice to the service of public utilities. As an Ohio State legislator, mayor of Cleveland, and U.S. senator, he was fair and conscientious but never a disturber of the *status quo*.

As mayor, he was the pet of big-business interests and metropolitan newspapers. So alert was he as a fence mender that often he "would climb the steps of newspaper offices at night to deliver in person statements he had written out in longhand." In the Senate, he was an obscure member of the Truman Investigating Committee, and he and Truman became fast friends. Burton was one of the first to profit from the largesse of a friendship-minded President.

Burton, however, was not the first Republican whom Truman considered for the Supreme Court vacancy.

Warren Austin, the sententious and legalistic Senator from Vermont, would have been named except for his advanced age. Undersecretary of War Robert Patterson, a former federal judge in New York, was offered the post and accepted. But before the announcement could be made, Truman's advisers frantically warned him that Patterson would be desperately missed during the difficult days before victory and demobilization. Truman hurriedly dispatched Attorney General Tom Clark to plead with Patterson to give up the cherished appointment. Quiet and high-minded, the very epitome of the good soldier,

Patterson took the setback good-naturedly. Without hesitation he agreed to Truman's request.

Finally, in this confusion, Burton got the call and emerged from the wings.

So far he has missed every cue.

William O. Douglas is a spectacularly exciting and complex personality.

He enjoys untangling the subtleties of a Wall Street deal down to the last nonvoting minority stockholder; he also enjoys leading a pack of howling tribesmen in a wild ceremonial dash on horseback across the plains of Persia. He taught law at Columbia and Yale but shows not the slightest trace of pedantry.

When he stands hip-booted in a mountain trout stream or when he swings his legs up on his desk, cocks his tousled head, and breaks into a boyish grin, Bill Douglas looks like a homespun, small-town fellow. He is indeed a homespun person with a terrific gusto for life and an earthy, old-battered-hat quality.

But he also possesses one of the most acute, daring, and dynamic intellects in contemporary America.

Douglas was born on the wrong side of the tracks. His father, a circuit-riding Presbyterian preacher from Nova Scotia, died when Douglas was five. His mother moved with her two boys to the town of Yakima, Washington, where Douglas grew up.

When he was twelve, Douglas was stricken with polio. His doctor prescribed a fifteen-minute massage every two hours for weeks.

"Mother kept a vigil," Douglas writes.* "She soaked my legs in warm salt water and rubbed it into my pores, massaging each leg muscle every two hours, day after day, night after night. She did not go to bed for six weeks. The fever passed; but the massages continued for weeks thereafter.

"I vaguely recall the ordeal. I lay in bed too weak to move. My legs felt like pipestems; they seemed almost detached, the property of someone else. They were so small and thin that Mother's hands could go clear around them. She would knead them like bread; she would

* William O. Douglas, *Of Men and Mountains*, (N.Y., Harper & Bros., 1950.)

push her hands up them and then down, up and down, up and down, until my skin was red and raw."

Weeks later, Douglas was able to stand, eventually to walk. He began a systematic program to strengthen his leg muscles by hiking in the neighboring mountains. In his years along the mountain trails, he found fear and loneliness and hunger but he found searching challenge and warm fulfillment as well. "At last I felt released, free to walk the trails and climb the peaks and to brush aside fear."

Most lawyers write as if they were wielding a shovel instead of a pen. Not Douglas. He writes with grace and informality and great descriptive power. His vivid autobiography is a broad-gauged, free-swinging book. Campfire recipes and rules for dry-fly fishing, the lore of Indians and sheepherders and the incisive wisdom of generations of mountain men are all graphically related in his story.

Recovered from his near-fatal illness, Douglas sold newspapers and hawked junk to help his mother make ends meet. At seventeen, he left Yakima to go to Whitman College in Walla Walla. As an undergraduate, he picked fruit with migrant workers and lived in a tent. Along this rugged path he earned a Phi Beta Kappa key.

As a boy, Douglas used to slip into local courtrooms and listen to the judges conduct their trials. "There seemed to be a goodness in these judges. I sensed they knew where the truth lay and that no force on earth could deflect them from it. O. E. Bailey, an insurance man, had been to Washington, D.C., and seen the United States Supreme Court in session. He said the same was true of it. He said there was no appeal from its rulings except to God."

Douglas decided to go East and become a lawyer. He had no way to travel save to "hit the rods." He went East on a freight train, with a load of sheep as his traveling companions part of the journey. In New York, he spent three difficult years at Columbia Law School, where he made a brilliant record by day and eked out a living at night by writing textbooks for the International Correspondence School. He graduated second in his class and was promptly asked to join the faculty. He accepted.

A few years later, he quit when President Nicholas Murray Butler selected a new Law dean without consulting the faculty. From Columbia, Douglas went to Yale and from there to Washington, where he has been ever since. After a history-making career cleaning up Wall Street, as chairman of the Securities and Exchange Commission, he was named to the Supreme Court in 1939. Douglas was then forty, the second youngest Justice in history.

When Douglas came to the tribunal, his illustrious predecessor Louis D. Brandeis said to him, "I am glad. I wanted you to have my place."

It was a simple and eloquent tribute from one of the giants of American jurisprudence.

As a Justice, Douglas has kept faith with the Brandeis tradition. Like his predecessor, who originated the concept of sociological jurisprudence, Douglas has a deep interest in economic problems, an abiding respect for the live and controlling social facts of cases rather than for dead precedents, and a keen and searching mind which cuts to the core of every judicial technicality and constantly presses forward to new legal frontiers.

Douglas is an intimate friend and comrade in arms of Hugo Black and shares his profound devotion to civil liberties and the ancient American tradition of the right to dissent. On economic questions, particularly corporation and patent law, Douglas is the bulwark of the Court.

He wrote the majority opinions in 1950 in the Texas and Louisiana cases in which the Court confirmed ownership of the immensely oil-rich tidal lands to the federal government rather than to the states.

Almost from the day Douglas put on his black robes, his friends have been trying to get him to take them off and return to active politics. He has never sought office. Several have been offered him, but he has turned them down.

He was not eager to become war production chief in 1942, and was glad when Roosevelt did not insist on drafting him for the post. In 1946, he turned down a Truman bid to become Secretary of the Interior, and again, in 1948, declined strong importunities to run for Vice-President. Like almost every other able-bodied male in Washington, he would not reject the presidency; but Douglas is genuinely indifferent to his periodic rises and falls in the political dopesheets. He never lifts a finger on or off the bench to forward such ambitions. Because of his pre-eminence, however, Douglas can never be quite unaware of his importance as a political factor, and he pokes fun at himself in wry anecdotes.

In 1948, he visited Montana to address the State Bar Association. His host was Representative Mike Mansfield, an old friend and an inveterate Douglas-for-President booster. In the lobby, before he went in to make his speech, Douglas chatted with a group of local lawyers. Someone mentioned that Mansfield was up for re-election and faced a hard fight. Spontaneously, Douglas expressed the opinion that Mansfield was a fine congressman and he hoped his old friend would be re-elected. One of the bystanders spoke up sharply, "Mr. Justice, I don't think it's right for you to be electioneering for anybody."

"Who are you?" asked Douglas.

"I'm Judge ———," was the reply, "and I'm the Republican candidate for Congress in this district. I don't think it's fair of you to be boosting Mansfield when I'm running against him."

Looking the Montanan straight in the eye, Douglas cracked, "Judge, as a man on the bench, you ought to be keeping out of politics."

During the war and especially the troubled postwar years, Douglas, without discussing a single specific issue or participating in any campaign, made a profound contribution to American political affairs.

It was he who stepped into the vacuum caused by the death of Roosevelt, the aberrations of Henry Wallace, the ineptness of Truman, and the consequent confusion and demoralization of liberal opinion. In a series of clear, incisive, intellectually coherent addresses, he met the need, as he himself expressed it, "to reassess our political achievements and redefine our political responsibilities."

Before the war had ended, he drew a fundamental distinction in a little speech called "Freedom *From* and Freedom *For*."

"The moral," he said, "is clear: Negative freedom is precious and indispensable. But it is not enough. It is idle to deplore the fact that the military war can win us no more than a military victory. We should thank God that high success on the fields of battle has come to us. . . . But we must not expect force to yield us more than force ever can— freedom from violence and slavery, freedom from dependence on force, the freedom to become free."

In his famous Yulee Lecture at the University of Florida in March,

1948, Douglas outlined the challenge at home and abroad in more explicit terms.

The basic choice, he said, "is not between war and appeasement, for neither will solve the problem that confronts us." Communism is a political program and the answer to it is "a dynamic and vital political program on the democratic front. . . . At home we must put an end to the shameful practice of branding everyone a Communist who espouses a liberal reform or promotes a program for the underprivileged. We should no more ban the study of Communist literature than we should bar medical students from studying cancer." If democratic government is effective at home, it "can remove even the pretense for saying that there are insoluble differences between the classes or groups within the nation."

Turning to foreign policy in the days when the Marshall Plan was a yearling and Point Four unheard of, Douglas urged that we not "fashion our foreign policy merely in terms of anticommunism. We will fail miserably if we do no more than that. . . . If we want the hundreds of millions of the peoples of the world in the democratic ranks, we must show them the way with practical programs of social reconstruction."

Douglas, almost alone among the old New Dealers, not only saw the new issues clearly but articulated a faith adequate to meet them. In a tragic hour, he restored to American liberalism its moral fiber.

In the summer of 1949, within the space of a few weeks, Black and Douglas lost their two staunchest associates. Frank Murphy and Wiley Rutledge served relatively brief terms on the Court, but they won for themselves high and honored places in its history.

Wiley Rutledge was a Midwesterner who fitted all the pleasant traditions a Midwesterner is supposed to fit. He was friendly, good-humored, unaffected, hard-working, and high-principled.

He knew his law intimately from years as a professor and dean in Colorado, Missouri, and Iowa. He did not come to Washington until 1939, when he began a brief tour of duty on the Circuit Court of Appeals for the District of Columbia. He thus came to the Supreme bench uncommitted in the various personal feuds which had raged in the New Deal days. To the subtleties of judicial interpretation he brought a healthy instinct for doing the obvious common-sense thing.

For example, in the Williams divorce case, he dissented from the decision which gave North Carolina the option of holding Nevada divorce decrees invalid, and he attacked the semantic mumbo jumbo that underlay Frankfurter's majority reasoning. "Once again," he wrote, "the ghost of 'unitary domicil' returns on its perpetual round, in the guise of 'jurisdictional fact,' to upset judgments, marriages, divorces, undermine the relations founded upon them, and make this Court the unwilling and uncertain arbiter between the concededly valid laws of sister states."

But Rutledge's dissent involved no judicial legislating. The only rule it imposed was that the people who went to Nevada and other easy-divorce states should have their decrees automatically accepted everywhere else. It did not lessen variety; it merely required the forty-eight varieties to accept one another at face value.

This stand was characteristic of Rutledge's lifetime philosophy. He never forgot that law is a social instrument. In his old days as a law school teacher, he used to ask his students, "Of what good is the law if it does not serve human needs?"

It's still a good question.

Death could scarcely have surprised Frank Murphy. It was not that his heart condition in the spring of 1949 was worse or better than it had been for the preceding five years. Rather, he had an Irishman's sense of fate.

Prompted perhaps by some inner security he could not analyze, Murphy from boyhood had created a personal mystique, a sense of pervading, inexorable destiny which had sustained his faith in himself and in his darkest hours had reassured him that defeat was a momentary illusion. He would triumph, he would be a success.

In his last year or two as a Justice, Murphy began to admit to himself that he had gone as far in life as he would ever go; the uphill path had ended and he was on a plateau—a high one, but still a plateau. There was nothing for him to do but to enjoy it. His personal sense of destiny was played out, the motif was complete. Thus, he who had never known blank, empty ease could scarcely have been surprised to meet Death so soon thereafter.

Frank Murphy began battling upward almost from his birth, in 1890, as the son of poor immigrant Irish parents.

Three years out of law school, he was a captain overseas in the AEF. The day he was released from active service, he was sworn in as assistant district attorney in Detroit. Then followed a dozen exciting years as a dynamic prosecutor, a crusading judge, and the popular "poor-man's mayor" of Detroit during the three harrowing years at the bottom of the depression. In 1933, Roosevelt sent him to the Philippines as Governor General. After three years there and one term as Governor of Michigan, Murphy came to Washington as Attorney General. In twelve months, 1939-40, he and his staff sent Moe Annenberg, Tom Pendergast, and the smelly heirs of the Huey Long dynasty to various federal penitentiaries. He also resuscitated government interest in federal protection of civil liberties and created a section in the Justice Department dedicated to their protection. In January, 1940, Murphy was elevated to the Supreme Court.

Long interested in civil liberties, Murphy made the issue his dominating passion as a judge.

Whether those involved were Negroes, anti-Catholic Jehovah Witnesses, Japanese, Indians, or defendants detected by wire-tapping or third-degree methods, Murphy rose to their defense. Often he carried the Court with him; more often, in his closing years, he spoke in dissent. There was never a more ardent and dedicated champion of human freedom on the Supreme Court than Frank Murphy. Writing in a case concerning a conscientious objector, Murphy declared:

"The law knows no finer hour than when it cuts through formal concepts and transitory emotions to protect unpopular citizens against discrimination and persecution."

It was Frank Murphy's finest hour, too.

Chief Justice Fred M. Vinson is a man with a mission.

President Truman appointed him for the express purpose of acting as peacemaker and composing the differences within the Court.

That is an old role for Vinson.

The canny, genial Kentuckian has always been an adroit and effective middle-of-the-roader. During his years in the House of Representatives, he was often used by Roosevelt as a trouble shooter. Midway through the war, he was recalled from a quiet berth on the federal bench to handle the blazing-hot job of Director of Economic Stabilization. After the bitter clash between Jesse Jones and Henry Wallace, Roosevelt made Vinson Federal Loan Administrator, for which the Senate had refused to confirm Wallace. Next came Vinson's promotion to head of the Treasury Department.

He is well qualified for the various chores in political and judicial diplomacy that have come his way.

His instincts are conservative, but he has a shrewd and flexible mind. He never gets marooned in bitter-end impasses. He has a sturdy self-confidence which enables him to be at ease with intellectuals and with strong-willed men in a way that Truman never is.

Men who worked under Vinson in his various executive positions unanimously praise him as a deft administrator. He is patient, amiable, likes to hear different points of view, and always asks tough, searching questions which go to the core of an argument. He does not act on whim, prejudice, or superficial impression; he respects facts and wants to know a situation thoroughly before making a decision. Once he makes up his mind, he has the courage to defend himself and his subordinates.

Like most conservatives, Vinson would like to re-establish the fiction of a united Court. His immediate predecessor made little effort to do that. The late Chief Justice Stone was resigned to diversity.

On one occasion, he attended a meeting of prominent Amherst College alumni at the home of Amherst President Stanley King. Stone was at that time chairman of the board of trustees. In the course of the evening, King made a little speech outlining the program he was going to submit to the trustees the following day. Then, turning to Stone sitting in the front row, King remarked, "I hope the board gives this plan its unanimous support."

With a straight face, Stone wisecracked, "The boards over which I preside are not accustomed to coming to unanimous decisions."

Vinson follows a tactic reminiscent of Chief Justice William Howard Taft. He tries to "jolly" his colleagues along, not ride herd on them.

He has a ready wit and an imperturbable manner, and his soft touch has been successful in restoring at least superficial harmony among the "brethren." Of course, much of this is due to the feudists' wearing themselves out and just naturally subsiding, but Vinson's finesse has played a useful part.

He has also been eminently fair in his assignment of the work load. Naturally, some cases are easier or more interesting than others, and he has tried to see to it that everyone gets an even break. There is little he can do to speed up an incompetent judge like Burton or a dilatory one like Frankfurter, but within limits he has lightened somewhat the burden on Black and Douglas, the two work horses on the bench.

But being presiding officer is only half Vinson's job. He is also called upon to do the normal work of a Justice. As a judge in his own right, his record is far inferior to his accomplishments as "Chief."

His output of opinions is low. In four years, he has written majority opinions in only four important cases. Further, his legal draftsmanship is slipshod, his outlook prosaic, and his literary style dull and uninspired.

Above all, Vinson has revealed himself far more conservative on the bench than he was in the midst of the hurly-burly of politics. Clearly, relieved of the spur of day-to-day pressures, he has reverted to his natural standpat instincts.

On major economic issues, Vinson has been consistently right of center. In labor law cases, for example, he always votes to restrict the right of peaceful picketing. On a number of civil-liberties issues, he has come out on the wrong side. His stand on illegal search and seizure, on the right to counsel, and on free speech is the most conservative of any man on the Court today and is as grossly reactionary as that of the late and unlamented Butler-Van Devanter-McReynolds cabal.

Illustrative of Vinson's die-hard stand on free speech is the Stowe Spinning Case decided in 1949. A union attempted to hire a hall in a mill town dominated by three textile companies. The firms owned all the halls and refused to give the union a place to meet. One of the halls, however, was used regularly by a fraternal organization, which first agreed to sublet to the union and then, under company pressure, reversed itself. The National Labor Relations Board declared this was unfair labor practice and took the company to court when it refused to obey a cease-and-desist order. The majority of the Supreme Court, in an opinion written by Justice Murphy, upheld the action of NLRB.

Vinson, however, joined Justice Reed in a dissent which took the view that a union had no right to the use of a hall or any other company-owned property that was not used directly by the company in its business operations. Just where, under Vinson's reasoning, workers in a mill town would be able to get together and talk in privacy was something the pontificating Chief Justice left unexplained.

On only one issue has Vinson taken a forthright liberal position. This is the question of equal protection for minorities, specifically the Negro.

One of his few major opinions so far is the one he wrote denying legal enforcement to restrictive real-estate covenants aimed against Negroes. At the close of the 1950 session of the Court, he also wrote the unanimous opinions in the Texas and Oklahoma cases which declared the segregated facilities afforded Negro students were not equal to those of the whites. He joined in the decision outlawing segregation in interstate dining cars.

It is not necessary to go far to uncover the motivation for these incongruously liberal decisions. Vinson served two ends very neatly—he hopes.

First, he got his pal Harry Truman off the hook with Negroes for failing to put across his civil rights program in Congress. Secondly, Vinson feathered his ambitions as a presidential possibility. The anti-segregation decisions would help to cancel out his many conservative decisions in other spheres and make him more palatable to labor and liberal opposition.

Vinson has long been a very ambitious man. He and fellow Kentuckian Vice-President Barkley have been covert rivals for years. When the Clark Cliffords opened the 1950 social season with a big shindig in honor of the Barkleys, Vinson, who almost never misses a party, decided to stay home.

Barkley will be seventy-five in 1952; Vinson, sixty-two. Neither is a spring chicken, but both have their eyes eagerly cocked on the White House.

Sherman Minton and Tom Clark have one thing in common. Both are personal friends of Harry Truman. Minton also is a competent judge.

It is well known that Clark was about to be fired from his job in the Justice Department, because of incompetence, when Roosevelt died and Harry Truman promoted him to the cabinet instead.

Clark is a professional Texan with a big, loose grin, a hearty handshake, and an incurable itch to be in the spotlight. He is fifty-one but looks much younger and carefully cultivates an air of youthfulness, which is not difficult, considering his level of intellectual adolescence. He is also a snappy dresser with a penchant for bow ties, and has dark, wavy hair touched with gray.

Clark was born into a prosperous middle-class family in Dallas, Texas, and graduated from the University of Texas and its law school. He practiced law for a time and was secretary to Senator Tom Connally and district attorney of Dallas County before joining the Justice Department in 1937. Here he soon became a special assistant to Attorney General Homer Cummings. Later, Clark shifted to the Antitrust Division, where he became known as "Trust-busting Tom." In professional circles he was less favorably known for filing suits which he never fought through to a conclusion.

In fact, about the only thing Clark ever really busted was headlines on the front page.

After Pearl Harbor, he was alien enemy coordinator on the West Coast in charge of the resettlement of the Japanese. When this job was reasonably well in hand, he returned to Washington, where he became chief of the war-frauds unit. This threw him into close contact with the Truman War Investigating Committee. Clark made a point of cultivating its chairman—as he does all people who might conceivably do something for him. In Truman's case, the cultivating paid off in a big way.

As Attorney General, Clark let his Department sag to the lowest level it had reached since the days of Harry Daugherty.

Clark kept himself busy "fighting juvenile delinquency" by playing golf with Bing Crosby and other Hollywood celebrities. He continued his grandstanding act of making a lot of noise about enforcing the antimonopoly laws but actually did nothing concrete. Within the administration, he invariably lined up with the reactionary elements, and all the time he angled furiously for the vice-presidential nomination.

Clark's appointment to the Supreme Court was engineered by Chief Justice Vinson. According to one account, Vinson wanted Clark on the bench so there would be at least *someone* who knew less law than he did. But this story is doubtless apocryphal because it overlooks the presence of Justice Burton, beside whom no one could feel embarrassed.

The real reason Vinson wanted Clark was more substantial. Clark provided Vinson with a handy and useful extra vote.

Caught in the middle between the Frankfurter-Jackson clique on one side and the Black-Douglas-Rutledge-Murphy quartet on the other, Vinson had only his own vote and those of Burton and Reed to manipulate in his own "center bloc." The death of Murphy gave him a chance to pick up another safe vote and to make his own faction the largest single element.

Truman had previously told intimates he intended to wait a month or more before making up his mind about a successor to Murphy; that this time he was going to make a really distinguished appointment, probably an experienced judge from the lower court. But when Vinson vigorously pressured him for the extra safe vote he needed for his pacification mission, Truman capitulated and gave him Clark.

Clark accepted in a flash and has not failed his patron.

In 107 cases decided during the 1949-50 session, he differed from Vinson only twice.

Clark is slightly more productive than Burton, but otherwise he makes the Ohio conservative a perfect teammate. There is always the possibility, of course, that Clark will grow. But it seems unlikely that he or anyone else will live that long.

Indeed, Clark's main distinction is his perpetual air of youthfulness, complete with all the gaucheries that usually accompany the young. At a Scout meeting in Washington, he was introduced as "the oldest Eagle Scout in America."

It was a perfect characterization.

Sherman Minton is a man of passionate and indomitable loyalties. His heart is always in the right place; the only question is what he has hitched his faith to at any given moment.

Minton is an Indiana Hoosier with a big, friendly face dominated by a pair of sad, dark eyes and a sharp lantern jaw. He was elected to the Senate in 1934, at the age of forty-four. Up to that time he had spent a placid career in private practice. But there was nothing placid about his career in the Senate.

Minton's fierce loyalty to President Roosevelt and the administration quickly made him a leader of the most militant New Deal faction in Congress and won him the job of Democratic Whip of the Senate. He fought his hardest battle in support of Roosevelt's futile effort to "pack" the Supreme Court. In the course of this struggle, he made his famous remark, "You can't eat the Constitution."

Minton sought re-election in 1940. He campaigned not only as a militant New Dealer but as a forthright internationalist. As a youth he had been a devoted admirer of Woodrow Wilson, and he was always an avowed champion of the League of Nations. The rabidly isolationist *Chicago Tribune* has considerable circulation in Indiana, and much of the time Minton seemed to have two opponents—the Republican Party and Colonel McCormick. Minton waged a fiery campaign and assailed "that unspeakable *Tribune, the Chicago Tribune* that even the newspapers themselves condemn." Roosevelt in 1940 was carrying out the pose of the commander in chief too busy to campaign, and he did not visit Indiana.

It is possible that this omission was fatal for Minton, who lost by a wafer-thin margin.

Roosevelt rewarded his loyal supporter with an appointment as one of his "anonymous assistants." A few months later, he named him to the federal Circuit Court of Appeals. It was feared the Senate might not confirm Minton because of the many enemies he had made there. But on the showdown no opposition developed.

Minton was a very capable and successful judge. He handled a number of difficult cases, including the criminal aspects of the A&P antitrust suit, and very few of his decisions were overturned by the Supreme Court.

As soon as Truman became President, Minton's name began to figure prominently every time there was a vacancy on the high tribunal. The two men were known to be close friends, having entered the Senate in the same year and sat together at adjoining desks in the rear of the chamber.

When Murphy died in the summer of 1949, Minton happened to be in Washington visiting a married daughter. He talked to the President at that time, and Truman brought up the question of the Supreme Court vacancy. He told his old friend that he was not going to appoint him because his health might be endangered by the strain of Supreme Court work. (Minton is a diabetic.) Next, the President remarked he was going to take plenty of time to consider the matter and make a very good appointment. Minton, though more than willing to take the risk to his health, did not press the matter.

Almost immediately thereafter, he was shocked by Truman's selection of Tom Clark, who was not a "very good appointment" by anybody's standards. Shortly afterward, when Justice Rutledge died, Minton received the designation—much in the nature of an acknowledgment by Truman that he had not kept his promise in the way he had filled the earlier appointment.

Minton delineated himself and his attitude toward his new post in a letter he wrote the Senate Judiciary Committee which considered his nomination. Some conservatives raised the question of his rabid support of the 1937 "court-packing plan," and Minton was called to testify in his own behalf. Instead, he wrote a letter in which he defended his support of the measure, as follows:

> "You will recall that at the time the bill in question was under discussion I was Majority Whip and, understandedly, I strongly supported those legislative measures recommended by the Administration. . . . As Majority Whip of the Senate I was a strong partisan and supported the Administration. I do not deny this. . . .
>
> "When I was a young man playing baseball and football I strongly supported my team. I was then a partisan. But later when I refereed games I had no team. I had no side. The same is true when I left the political arena and assumed the

bench. Cases must be decided under applicable law and upon the record as to where the right lies."

Minton was unanimously confirmed.

He remains a loyal team player.

He is an enthusiastic and wholehearted player on the team of which Fred Vinson is the captain. Minton is profoundly grateful to Harry Truman for giving him this great opportunity, and he is loyal to Vinson because he considers him Truman's spokesman on the Court. He also feels Vinson, by boosting him to the President, had something to do with his appointment. For these reasons, Minton wants very much to be a credit to Truman, to represent his concept of the Supreme Court in so far as that is possible, and to cooperate in every way with "the Chief"—as he refers to Vinson.

That explains why Minton has consistently voted with Vinson and the Court's conservative bloc. He has voted differently from the Chief only six times out of 107 cases, which is but four more times than Clark, Vinson's alter ego.

It had been generally anticipated that Minton would line up fairly regularly with Black and Douglas, the sole surviving members of the Court's liberal element. This expectation might have come true had there been one of the old liberal stalwarts like Holmes or Brandeis or Cardozo on the bench. Minton would have revered such men and considered it an honor to vote on their side in close cases. He naturally feels no such reverence for Black, with whom he served in the Senate, or for Douglas, whom he knew as a young SEC chairman.

Moreover, as a study of his opinions as a circuit court judge reveals, Minton, though a political liberal, is an intellectual conservative.

That is, he is conservative in the sense that he always tries to hew to the line of precedent as laid down in past cases. This gives him a natural tendency to gravitate toward Frankfurter, with his facile fondness for the "majestic consistency" of the law, and toward precedent-worshiping Burton, "who tries interminably to match cases, as a woman shopper matches colors."

Minton, however, has distinct potentialities as an able Justice.

He far outranks Clark and Burton in brains, judicial experience, and professional competence. He is extremely conscientious and hard-

working. In the 1949-50 session, he turned out a dozen majority opinions, a record figure for a freshman member.

Eighteen years ago, the authors of *More Merry-Go-Round* wrote
about the conservative Court of that era:

"If, miracle of miracles, an enlightened President should fill their
places with liberals, still nothing would be changed fundamentally.
. . . A few years may see a new President, a different-tempered Senate,
who would plug up other vacancies with 'safe' appointees and the old
march of exploitation would be resumed. It is a simple matter for the
Court to reverse itself. It has done so repeatedly in the past. A restored
majority would unquestionably do so again in the future."

In essence, this passage forecast accurately the story of the Truman
Court. An "enlightened President" did appoint a group of liberals, but
since 1945, a new President has filled new vacancies with "safe" appointees. Worse than that, Truman has not only tilted the Court
steeply to the right but he has loaded it with mediocrity. Perhaps it
is too much to say that the "old march of exploitation" has been resumed, but it may be noted that, in the 1950 session, the oil-rich Texas
tidelands were decreed as belonging to the federal government by the
bare margin of 4 to 3.

Certainly the drift to monopoly through manipulation of key
patents and restraint of trade, the constriction of the right of peaceful
picketing, the serious setbacks in many civil-liberties cases all indicate
that a backward, conservative sweep is under way in all fields and is
steadily gaining strength.

In the dark, reactionary days of a generation ago, the phrase
"Holmes and Brandeis dissenting" recurred again and again in the
records of the Court. Today, the phrase "Black and Douglas dissenting" is increasingly common.

It is the lonely dirge of liberalism's lost battle.

FOGGY BOTTOM

As the Potomac River sweeps down to the sea past fashionable George-town and absorbs the waters of Rock Creek, it makes a sharp bend. This bulge of land, bounded by the Potomac on the west and south, by Pennsylvania Avenue on the north, and by 17th Street on the east, is small in size but great in the power it cradles. This area was until recent years the gashouse district of Washington. The fumes from the gas plant blended with the natural odors of this low, swampy, malarial marshland to create a thick swirl of eye-stinging smog which won for the region the nickname "Foggy Bottom."

Today, the fog and smoke still exist, and the area is as feverish as ever, but the smog and tumult are of a different origin. Foggy Bottom is now the home of the U.S. State Department.

Foggy Bottom's rise in the world dates from 1913, when Congress chose one corner of it as the site of the majestic Lincoln Memorial. This structure was completed in 1922. In the years that followed, Constitution Avenue was extended into the region, and numerous imposing government buildings were laid out along the broad boule-vard. A few glass-and-steel apartment houses also emerged above the sordid slums that dominated the area. Then came the U.S. Army.

It erected a huge rectangular, yellow stone office building. But when the project was half completed, it was abandoned for a still more grandiose structure across the river in Virginia—the labyrinthine Pentagon. Thus it came about that the discarded building in Foggy Bottom was eventually turned over to the mushrooming State Depart-ment.

In the spring of 1947, the gentlemen who guide the destinies of our foreign affairs took up residence in Foggy Bottom, halfway between the Lincoln Memorial and the gashouse.

Here, in the district where Irish and Italian youngsters used to roam the cobbled streets, swim in Rock Creek, hunt for water snakes on the present site of the Lincoln Memorial, where the neighborhood baseball team was called the Emerald A.C. and the football team the Irish Eleven, and where two-fisted Marty Gallagher, the later conqueror of Two-Ton Tony Galento, learned the art of boxing by practicing it on the street corners—here several thousand diplomats, lawyers, economists, research specialists, foreign-language experts, propagandists, and speech writers carry on the art of American diplomacy which sometimes uses both fists—and sometimes does not.

Bedecked and bemedaled, and often beturbaned as well, the foreign diplomats drive through the streets of Foggy Bottom in gleaming black Cadillacs on their way to seek counsel, military support, and financial aid. Seventy nations now have diplomatic missions in Washington. The State Department has six thousand employees on its rolls, while nearly sixteen thousand more speak for the United States in various parts of the globe.

America has come of age, and the State Department struggles to keep up with it.

Gone is the leisurely pace of yesteryear. No longer can officials come in at ten and go home at four-thirty, after having spent two hours at the Metropolitan Club for lunch. A Department which was more accustomed to, and in tune with, the age of lamplighters and horsedrawn hansoms has experienced a succession of convulsive metamorphoses in an effort to adjust to the jet-plane-and-hell-bomb era. The Department has had five Secretaries in six years, gone through four major reorganizations, and expanded to five times the number of employees it had in 1940.

But the pressure never lets up. Rather, it gets more intense all the time.

Conducting foreign policy in a cold war poses a constant tension between good and evil.

Secretary of State Dean Acheson has been familiar with this subtle interplay since the moment of birth. His father was an Episcopal bishop and his mother was a whisky heiress.

Acheson was born in 1893 in Middletown, Connecticut. His father, a native of England and educated in Canada, was rector of the local Episcopal Church. Later in his career he became Bishop of Connecticut. Dean's mother, Eleanor Gooderham, was the daughter of a wealthy Canadian distilling family.

Young Dean enjoyed a rowdy, carefree boyhood. He played the usual games and got into the usual boyhood scrapes. He was an overly tall, sturdy, red-haired youngster with bright, merry eyes, a quick temper, and a mischievous tongue. To prepare for college, he was sent to Groton Academy in Massachusetts, an exclusive school where many sons of the Eastern well to do, including Franklin Roosevelt, went.

After Groton came Yale. Here Acheson did somewhat more partying than studying. His undergraduate career seems to have justified the remark of Chancellor Robert Hutchins of the University of Chicago, who used to teach at Yale, that "Yale is just a finishing school for boys."

Acheson rowed on the freshman crew, but he was too light to make the varsity. He was a member of several undergraduate social clubs, including the Turtles and the Grill Room Grizzlies. His sharp wit made him one of the stars of these campus get-togethers. When it came time to graduate in 1915, Acheson had achieved a moderately good academic record and was tapped by Scroll and Key, one of the swankier secret honorary societies. But his classmates remember him chiefly as a delightful dinner companion and a very dapper dresser.

Acheson chose law as his profession and entered Harvard Law School, where he drew as a roommate a lighthearted Midwesterner who seemed to be better at ragtime than at habeas corpus. The fellow's name was Cole Porter.

Acheson came into his own during his years at Harvard. He found that the law was the right forum for his quick-tempered combativeness, and that it gave his sharply honed intellect something more substantial to work on than merely cutting out conversational bons mots.

During these years he underwent other changes. In 1917, he joined the Navy as an ensign, but he was, to his acute displeasure, never sent overseas. In the same year, he married a pretty girl from Detroit who had been his sister's roommate at Wellesley. In a way, this choice of a wife is symbolic of Acheson's personality.

He had always loved a good time and a good party, without ever becoming a playboy or a mere "good-time Charlie." It was natural that, when he came to marriage, he should choose a girl of impeccable family and close personal connections. Acheson is a warmhearted, witty, personable, versatile, and highly sophisticated man, but he always moves within the broad but clear limits of proper breeding and good taste.

When the war was over, he returned to Cambridge and finished the remaining year of his law course. He graduated in 1920, the fifth-ranking man in his class. Felix Frankfurter, one of his professors, recommended him as a law clerk to Associate Justice Louis D. Brandeis. The illustrious jurist accepted the suggestion, and Acheson spent two busy, crucial, and intensely happy years in Washington.

Brandeis' closest friend on the tribunal was Justice Oliver Wendell Holmes. The youthful law clerk came to know both men very well; he was an intimate member of Brandeis' Monday evening "at homes" and regularly paid a monthly visit to Holmes. Coming from a normally conservative, upper-class background, Acheson had little in the way of social outlook or coherent philosophy when he came to Washington. But his close association with these two older men clarified his outlook and shaped his thought.

From Brandeis, who had a profound respect for the determining facts and a militant belief in social justice, he absorbed a sturdy liberal faith. Subsequently, Acheson spent many years in the practice of high-paid corporate law, but he remains a convinced antimonopoly liberal of the older Wilson-Brandeis school, and he retains a stubborn conviction that, despite his personal well being, all may not be for the best in this best of all possible worlds.

From Holmes, a wise old man of glittering intellect, trenchant wit, and sophisticated skepticism, Acheson learned something of patience, tolerance, and contempt for cant. As much as any man in public life today, Acheson represents the introspective, detached, self-critical tradition laid down by Holmes and Brandeis.

In 1921, Acheson entered private law practice, joining the Washington firm of Covington, Burling and Rublee. Four years later, at the age of thirty-three, he was made a partner. He specialized in appellate court work before the federal circuit court and the Supreme Court. He also developed a lucrative side line handling knotty tax cases, and his income rose into the $100,000-a-year class.

When the New Deal came into office, Roosevelt appointed Acheson Undersecretary of the Treasury. Acheson greatly enjoyed the liberal atmosphere and intellectual vigor of the early New Deal and became a strong admirer of the President.

But he was dubious about some of Roosevelt's more ingenious solutions for economic problems, particularly when they involved juggling the price of gold in order to raise the price level. Acheson conceded the short-run advantages of this scheme, but felt the long-run effects might more than outweigh them. When the issue came to a head, less than six months after his taking office, he offered to resign. Roosevelt snapped him up on it and told reporters about it before notifying Acheson.

It is significant, however, that Acheson went out with his head high and his mouth shut. He issued no ringing pronouncements and wrote no articles sputtering with personal bitterness. He continued to support the administration and backed Roosevelt in 1936 and again in 1940.

By contrast, his good friend Lewis Douglas, who was then Director of the Budget and who declared privately, when the United States went off the gold standard, "This means the end of Western civilization," stayed on a year longer and then left as a carping foe of the administration. Douglas went over to Landon and the Liberty Leaguers in 1936, and four years later supported Wendell Willkie. And, of course, the hordes of others who left office emitting thunder and lightning against That Man is almost beyond counting.

Acheson's poised behavior had several explanations.

As a well-bred gentleman, it is not part of his social code to blow his top in public. Roosevelt, an old Grotonian himself, did not fail to note this observance of good form and to remember it.

Further, Acheson, who is not by nature unusually patient, has learned, for his own good, to restrain his feelings and take the long view. In part, this is something he imbibed from Holmes's worldly detachment and sense of perspective on trivial human affairs. In part, also, it is the reverse side of his instinctive quick wit. Because he is so eager and impetuous himself, he knows how exasperating and effective it can be to seem unaware of the other fellow's explosiveness.

Acheson's brother tells a story which illustrates this trait in his personality. When Dean was a teen-ager, the family regularly went to the country for the summer. One year, a new family moved into the house adjoining theirs. Dean's sister went out to watch the neighbors move in. A few minutes later, she returned breathless and eager to relate what she had seen. She came up to Dean, who was sitting comfortably in a chair and deeply absorbed in a book, and remarked excitedly, "Dean, do you know what? There is a new family moving in next door, and they have six horses, four carriages, a coachman, and two footmen. What do you think of that?"

Dean made no reply.

She repeated insistently, "But don't you think it is wonderful that they have six horses . . ." and she rattled off all the rest.

Dean still made no reply.

Finally, she asked, "Well, what would *you* do if you had six horses, four carriages, a coachman, and two footmen?"

Replied Dean, "I'd start a livery stable."

He quit the New Deal with his superb self-possession completely intact and returned to his law practice. But he was not forgotten in administration circles. Roosevelt was personally rather angry at him, but many of the President's closest advisers kept praising Acheson's sterling qualities and tactfully suggested he could well be used in some post. Finally Roosevelt capitulated.

Late in 1940, he confessed to one of his assistants, "You know, I guess I made a mistake about Dean. I am going to bring him back. I talked to him today and offered him his choice of Solicitor General or Assistant Secretary of State. I think he's leaning toward State."

The President was right, and in February, 1941, Acheson re-entered the administration as Assistant Secretary under Cordell Hull.

Acheson had had a long and steadily growing interest in foreign affairs throughout the '30's. In 1940, he became an active leader of William Allen White's Committee to Defend America by Aiding the Allies. In the summer of that year, he and some associates wrote a long letter to *The New York Times,* pointing out the legal grounds which would justify the President's giving destroyers to England in exchange for bases, without seeking congressional approval. This was a very helpful trial balloon which led the way for Roosevelt's historic move a few weeks later.

In the State Department, Acheson was handed the task of coordinating all the economic work. This involved him in innumerable jurisdictional disputes with other agencies, particularly Henry Wallace's Board of Economic Warfare. In these imbroglios, he held his own and came through without leaving his antagonists with permanent feuding scars. Also, the constant jousting, both within and without the Department, gave him an intimate view of many dark corners and moldy patches of bureaucracy and a working knowledge of the day-to-day abilities of large numbers of career employees at the lower and middle levels.

No other Secretary of State in history has ever come into office with such detailed experience and such first-hand knowledge of his agency and his subordinates.

Acheson did not participate in any of the Roosevelt-Churchill or Big Three conferences. While a lot of other people were whispering over the vodka, he was doing a huge amount of tough, vital, but unglamorous work. He put in long hours on the planning and organizing of various international economic agencies such as the World Bank, UNRRA, and the UN Food and Agriculture Organization. He drove himself tirelessly and rarely failed to get matters settled in a way that satisfied him.

His passion for orderliness and precise thinking had some interesting side lights. During the conference which organized UNRRA, he urged that a phrase in one section be changed from "expectant mothers" to "pregnant women." "A maiden aunt of fifty-one told me once that she was an expectant mother," he told the foreign delegates. "What you mean here is 'pregnant women.'"

The delegates made the change.

In November, 1944, Cordell Hull finally retired and Roosevelt appointed Edward Stettinius. Stettinius fired several top officials and brought in six new ones who were to form his "team." He did not fire Acheson, but neither was he especially eager to have him stay on. He followed the circuitous method of shunting Acheson from his important economic work to the brackish backwater of "congressional relations."

Again, Acheson did not do the expected—lose his temper and walk out.

Instead, he crossed up Stettinius and all the observers by accepting the new assignment and quickly making a resounding personal success of it. He put on his hat, grabbed his brief case, and marched up to Capitol Hill to sell the administration's foreign policy. He talked to senators and representatives with refreshing candor, was alert and vigorous in answering their queries and pushing their requests, and built up a wide circle of friends. As any of his Yale classmates could have foretold, he was a special success with the Southerners.

Old-timers like Tom Connally, Millard Tydings, and Alben Barkley have a bottomless stock of stories and an almost equally bottomless liquor capacity. Acheson can both hold his whisky and tell funny anecdotes. For hour after hour, he would sit in Connally's office drinking bourbon and trading quips and tales. This sociability, plus his extensive inside knowledge of the Department, made him an "ace" on the Hill.

Considering his tremendous personal popularity when he held this job, it is incredible and deeply ironic that Senator Joe McCarthy and certain segments of the press should later succeed to a large degree in foisting on the public the idea that Acheson is cold and snobbish and cannot get along with Congress. In 1949, when he first became Secretary, Acheson had a survey made of what could be done to improve the State Department's relations with Capitol Hill. Again and again, the report kept coming back, "Send another guy like Acheson up here. He was a regular fellow and we could talk to him. If he can't come himself now because he's too busy, then the thing to do is find another man like him."

While Acheson performed his daily work and seemed outwardly the most affable and jovial man in sight, he labored under lengthening shadows of worry and personal sorrow.

His daughter Mary, then working as a code breaker at the War Department, was stricken with tuberculosis. Mary and her father were very close. They were in the habit of spending a half hour together each evening in the kitchen, with a bedtime glass of milk, talking over their problems and exchanging views. Mary's illness forced her to go to a sanitarium in Saranac, New York. She was there for more than a year. Every evening during that period, Acheson sat down at the hour he used to talk with her in the kitchen and wrote her a long letter. To cheer her up, he started off each letter with a joke he had heard that day. To relieve his own mind, he took up gardening.

Late in 1945, Mary returned home. But four years later she suffered a relapse and returned to Saranac. In the spring of 1950, at the height of the McCarthy attacks, Mary underwent a series of difficult operations. Acheson, with characteristic self-restraint, said nothing of this, and it was only through the remarks of family friends that there was any public knowledge of the matter.

It was while visiting Mary at Saranac in the summer of 1945 that the next big turning point came in Acheson's career. James Byrnes had replaced Stettinius as Secretary of State, and he urgently requested Acheson to become his Undersecretary.

Acheson, however, had decided that, with the war nearing its end, he could return to private life. But Byrnes called him long-distance and told him that President Truman was equally insistent that he stay, and that they had already dispatched Truman's personal plane to bring him back. Acheson surrendered and returned to Washington to take up his new job.

Byrnes attended a large number of foreign conferences during his eighteen months' tenure as Secretary of State. He was out of the country for 245 of the 562 days he was in office. This meant that Acheson was Acting Secretary during most of 1945-46 and that he made most of the day-to-day decisions.

During this period, Acheson took a leading part in all the inner policy talks that led to the adoption of the "get-tough-with-Russia" program. He always had, on purely intellectual grounds, a profound distrust of the Soviet totalitarian system, but he shared Roosevelt's belief that the West should explore every avenue of approach before giving up on the Russians. When that failed, he was one of the first top men in the administration to press for forceful action. Having come to the decision slowly and carefully, he is now not easily lured by false hopes and intriguing schemes for "fixing things up" with Stalin in a jiffy. Acheson fully backed the adoption of the Truman

Doctrine to contain Russian imperialism in Greece and Turkey, and it was he who, in the early months of 1947, first proposed the aid-to-Europe concept which subsequently became known as the Marshall Plan.

Another significant Acheson contribution during his tenure as Undersecretary was the formulation of the American plan for international control of atomic energy.

Acheson was chairman of the Department of State's Committee on Atomic Energy which included Vannevar Bush, James Conant, General Leslie Groves, and John J. McCloy. This Committee worked with a select panel of expert consultants headed by David Lilienthal and J. Robert Oppenheimer. This Acheson-Lilienthal report, without any substantial changes, was the basis of what became known as the Baruch Plan.

After the publication of the Acheson-Lilienthal report, Acheson addressed a luncheon meeting of the American Society of Newspaper Editors. Byrnes introduced him glowingly, praising particularly Acheson's work on the atomic energy report. Disclaiming the bouquet, Acheson said his appointment to the Committee had reminded him of the Baltimore *Sun's* comment when he was named Undersecretary of the Treasury. The new Undersecretary, observed the *Sun,* not so sunnily, came to his post unfettered by any previous acquaintance with the problems he would have to handle.

Acheson was not always busy wrestling with solemn problems. His status as Acting Secretary meant that he was forced to do much of the entertaining that normally falls on the shoulders of the Secretary.

On one occasion, he was tendered a reception by the members of the Department's Foreign Service. It was an incredibly stuffy affair. Finally, Acheson was called upon to say a few words. His opening sentence immediately washed away the starch and brought the party to life. "All that I know," he began, "I learned at my mother's knee and other low joints. . . ."

Acheson continued as Undersecretary to George Marshall for six months, but he finally resolved he had to leave to recoup his depleted personal fortune. It was with the greatest regret that he departed.

Acheson is reputed to have remarked privately, "I have known two great men in my life and one who was near great. The first two were Justice Holmes and George Marshall, and the other was Louis Brandeis."

Why Acheson rates Brandeis a half step below the others is something he has not explained. But it is easy to see what he admired in, and learned from, each of these three mentors. The classic influence of Holmes and Brandeis is well known. Acheson, like everyone else who knows him well, admires Marshall for his selfless devotion to his duty as he sees it, his utter lack of personal vanity and ambition, and his impregnable integrity.

These are qualities, especially the first and third, which Acheson, a more complex and passionate man, has approximated in the course of his own public career.

Acheson returned to private law practice in July, 1947, after six and a half years in government service. He enjoyed the freedom and mobility of private life, but he was restless for the activity which public office demands. A close friend, who has himself spent long stretches in public service, remarked, "Dean has always thought it was both more fun and more important to work for the government than to pile up money for himself . . . and I consider that a good measure of his intelligence."

Acheson varied his private practice by taking on some civil liberties cases which paid him little or nothing. He also consented to serve as vice-chairman of the Hoover Commission task force studying the reorganization of the State Department. He thus got—while nominally retired—an intensive briefing on the internal problems of the Department he now heads.

The day after President Truman was re-elected in 1948, he suddenly turned to a friend and said simply, with a beaming smile, "Now I can have Dean." Acheson simply could not turn down one of the highest honors that can come to anyone in public life, and he was sworn in as Secretary of State the day after Truman was inaugurated.

The intimate relationship which exists between the two men is one of those puzzlers which defies ready analysis.

One explanation is that Acheson is an exceedingly charming man whom the President has always found easy to get along with. Also, Acheson is extraordinarily well versed in foreign affairs and can explain them simply and graphically. At the same time, he genuinely respects the President because the latter never meddles in the State Department or tries to bypass him. Acheson also has a surprisingly strong sense of party loyalty as a Democrat.

He was the only official of cabinet or sub-cabinet rank who showed up at the railroad station in 1946 to welcome Truman back to Washington after he had received his disastrous shellacking from the Republicans in the congressional elections. It was Acheson who wrote the conciliatory statement, promising cooperation with the Republican Congress, that Truman read at his first press conference after the election.

When Acheson took over as Secretary of State, he moved into the Secretary's office on the fifth floor—a great barnlike affair which was described by Robert Patterson, who occupied it briefly as Undersecretary of War, as resembling "nothing so much as the anteroom to a Turkish brothel."

At one end of the room is a large oil portrait of former Secretary Henry L. Stimson, and beneath it a massive table. One side of the walnut-paneled chamber is lined with tall windows. Here Acheson customarily works at an enormous mahogany desk bathed in dazzling sunlight. On one side of his desk is an unabridged dictionary, and on the other is a globe of the world illuminated from within. This impressive prop is an inheritance from General Marshall's days. Against the farther wall, facing Acheson's desk, is a towering grandfather clock. In the remaining corner are a smaller table and a cluster of easy chairs.

This whole king-sized mausoleum is like something from Berchtesgaden, but, short of ripping out the walls and putting in partitions (Acheson does fancy himself an amateur architect), there is nothing he can do about it.

Visitors to his office find him tall, broad-shouldered, well proportioned, and slim-waisted, with a full head of brown hair and a lighter, reddish-brown mustache. He has a strong nose, bright eyes, moderately heavy eyebrows, and a big, flashing smile. He does not wear glasses except when he reads, when he dons a pair with "flesh-color" rims. He dresses very well, with a conservative distinction that borders on the elegant. He favors blue and medium-brown tweeds which are custom tailored; gay ties, including butterfly-yellow bows and Chinese print four-in-hands; and shirts with broad candy-stick stripes and detachable white collars. He almost always wears a vest and, for street wear, a Homburg.

He runs neck and neck with Labor Secretary Maurice Tobin as the best-dressed man in public life.

Acheson's mustache is the subject of much ribald wit and opposition ridicule. He began it when he was an undergraduate at Yale, in imitation of his father's. Unlike the Bishop's, however, which was a droopy walrus variety like that of a British Colonel Blimp, Acheson's mustache is well trimmed and has no movie-villain twists or curls. It is straight and trim, like that of a British guardsman.

Acheson is very popular with the correspondents who cover the State Department. (Reporters are called "correspondents" in Foggy Bottom.) Like Franklin Roosevelt, he looks upon his press conference as an opportunity rather than a burden. He is candid and direct and invariably exhibits an extraordinary grasp of both the broad outlines and working details of the Department's affairs. Best of all is his sense of humor. It is a rare conference when he does not bring forth a few chuckles from the newsmen.

On one occasion, he was asked if there had been a change in a certain policy. Replied Acheson, "There is no change. I think the expression is 'backing and filling.' I've never known, though, what 'filling' meant."

On the problem of the switch-over from military to civilian control of Germany, Acheson told the newsmen, "Well, it sort of warms up and cools off. I don't know whether this is a warm day or a cool day."

Reporters at the State Department sometimes get even more involved in their language than do the diplomats they deal with. One day, a correspondent put a question which ran something like this: "May we attach any particular significance to the fact that in reviewing the German question you didn't comment on the omission of any reference to the currency situation as a condition?" Acheson, affecting an air of complete bewilderment, answered, "You are too subtle for me. If you will bring it out into the open, please."

Acheson is a great storyteller. When the going gets too rough, he reaches into his grab bag and comes up with one. Pressed one day to comment on something he wasn't ready to talk about, he said, "I'll tell you a story.

"My old law partner, Judge Covington, once went to an oyster roast down on the Eastern Shore of Maryland and had a fine time eating those wonderful oysters, until he was handed a red-hot one. The oyster must have been two hundred and seventy degrees Fahrenheit. Old Judge Covington took one look at it and said, 'A man would have to be a damn fool to swallow *that* one.'"

Dean Acheson has perforce had to swallow more than one red-hot oyster during the course of his stormy tenure, but always he has comported himself with courage, dignity, and integrity.

Of him it can be truly said: He is a gentleman and an officer—without the need of an Act of Congress.

Also, that he is the greatest Secretary of State since Henry L. Stimson.

The Department Acheson took over in Foggy Bottom in January, 1949, had the reputation of being too often literally foggy in outlook and close to bottom in efficiency. It was called the worst-run Department in Washington.

To the extent that this was true—and there was considerable substance to both charges—three factors could be blamed: history, Cordell Hull, and the Russians.

The history of America up to 1933 was such as to keep the agency in charge of foreign affairs largely in the ruck of public attention. Cordell Hull, Secretary of State in the '30's, when the changing tides dictated that the State Department play a larger role in the government, was incapable of strengthening the Department or even of controlling it as it then existed. Once the postwar era arrived and Hull had finally departed, the Russians kept the Department under such pressure that neither Byrnes nor Marshall had the time to deal with the machinery of the greatly expanded agency.

The result was that Acheson inherited a Department which included good men but which, on the whole, was badly run, divided against itself, shaky in morale, and, to say the least, possessed of an indifferent standing and prestige with Congress and the public.

Any study of the merits and demerits of the State Department must begin with the career men of the Foreign Service. It is not that the Foreign Service is by itself the whole story. But it is the core.

The Foreign Service was created in 1924 by the Rogers Act, which merged the old Consular and Diplomatic Services and gave members of the new unit career tenure and civil service protection, but outside the regular Civil Service system. Actually, the law, in a large measure, merely regularized what already existed. The majority of diplomatic jobs below the rank of minister and ambassador traditionally did not change with a shift in administration in Washington. They were held by men who made diplomacy a career and whose professional rise or fall might depend on whether they were members of the party then in power, but whose jobs did not.

In most cases, their livelihood definitely did not, because most of them were men of independent means who had entered the diplomatic service because it was a "gentleman's career."

Here precisely was the difficulty and the curse of the career diplomats.

It was not merely that they were, or became, snobbish, inbred, and highly skilled at logrolling for one another. Nor that men without personal wealth and the right connections found the way to promotions mysteriously blocked. These things were bad enough. But what was worst of all was that the service attracted young men who were primarily interested in being "gentlemen."

Very rarely were such species possessed of native force and driving ability. In a crisis, they lacked the capacity to represent their country either wisely or well. They might be loyal, even industrious, but they were not imaginative, decisive, or vigorous. They stuck to precedent, clung to routine, passed the buck, wrote the weasel-worded cable, and took another glass of sherry.

They were all too truly "cookie pushers," in game as well as in name.

Essentially, this was not so much the fault of the careerists themselves as it was inevitable in the nature of United States history. For example, most career men who were in office when Cordell Hull took over in 1933 had entered the Department in the years between 1900 and 1915. Those were the years of the Progressive crusades, of Teddy Roosevelt's Bull Moose jeremiad, of Wilson's New Freedom, and of a hundred other different blood-quickening movements—in politics, muckraking journalism, social work, education, and the arts. What comparable movements and challenges existed in the field of foreign affairs?

Except for some relatively minor scrapes in the Caribbean area, there was nothing going on in the world which intimately or importantly affected American interests. Diplomacy was taken up with piddling disputes over boundaries and the collection of banker debts from Haiti. No young man of brains, vigor, and ambition would turn his back on the exciting and kaleidoscopic American scene in order to occupy himself with the tedious negotiations and arid trivialities that passed as "American foreign relations."

The surprising thing is not that only rich men entered the foreign service but that anyone entered it at all.

The same held true throughout the '20's. The good men, both rich and poor, tended to work at domestic matters.

It was not until 1930 and after, when the growing menace of Japanese militarism, German, Italian, and Russian totalitarianism, and the general collapse of world order made the foreign scene both darker and more meaningful, that young men of genuine ability began to seek careers in the State Department. The worse things got abroad, the greater was the need for capable people, and the greater was the opportunity for them to do big and useful things.

Viewed in proper perspective, the old-fashioned "career" diplomat was a period piece like Calvin Coolidge—something an easygoing, self-absorbed America could tolerate, but which is too expensive a luxury for these grimly urgent days.

The career men for decades wielded great power. They still do, though not so much as previously. They know their own area, whether it be Scandinavia or Arabia or South America, they know the "ropes," they know one another, and they know all sorts of little tricks to protect one another and to cover up deficiencies. Time and time again, they have outwitted their politically appointed bosses, the Secretaries and Assistant Secretaries, and they have used their expert knowledge to make their superiors captives.

Almost every President and every Secretary of State learned, through painful experience, to distrust and despise the Foreign Service clique. For forty years, men in Congress and in the White House have talked about "cleaning house." But it has always been difficult to recruit new men who were capable and reasonably acquainted with the various complex problems involved in the work of the Department. Foreign Service men, both before the Rogers Act of 1924 and after, were roundly cursed as a self-serving caste, as dilettantes, as "striped-pants boys" who wore white spats and carried canes and were more interested in what the British Foreign Office thought than in what the American public wanted. But nobody effectively rooted them out.

Meanwhile, the Foreign Service men carefully nurtured the half-truth that they were indispensable and selfless public servants who wanted only to serve their country. Nobody else, they hinted, would be willing to go to Guayaquil or Cambodia or Archangel on practically a minute's notice and stay in these unhealthful and uninteresting places for years. Every time a member of the "club" was promoted to minister or ambassador or to some high policy-making job in the Department, they trumpeted it about as a great triumph for the principle of career service.

The truth, of course, was that, while a fair share of the men in the Foreign Service were motivated by a genuine interest in foreign affairs and had a laudable desire to serve their country, there was a large element which looked upon their jobs as a convenient way to make a soft, easy living.

They could play the role of "gentlemen" and enjoy all the dignities, perquisites, and amenities of important men of affairs without doing any work that was very time-consuming or intellectually very arduous. They coasted along on America's rising power and prestige and lorded it over the coolies and natives of far-off countries. They used their official status as a passport to the best foreign and colonial society. In the language of the GI, they were "gold bricks" who played at being "big-time operators."

Most U.S. diplomats away from home "never had it so good."

The tradition about the selfless career man who will go wherever he is ordered at a moment's notice is like a lot of other traditions: one part fact and nine parts myth.

Career diplomats can put on the most furious display of wirepulling and pressure politics when threatened with assignment to an unappealing post. Most of them, in such personal crises, exhibit an energy and ingenuity which they would never dream of devoting to the conduct of normal public business. Political friends in their home state, members of Congress, society pals, fellow logrollers in the Department, and even members of the press are lobbied and importuned to help the threatened esthete.

A classic example was Frederick Sterling, who, in 1937, was made Minister to Latvia. He had no taste for going to the dull, tiny Baltic country—and his wife even less so. She happened to be the sister of Mrs. Juliette Leiter, who at that time was one of the biggest whip-crackers in the Washington social whirl. Mrs. Sterling, who is a very determined woman, shipped her husband off to Latvia, but she returned to Washington and enlisted her sister's support in a concerted drive "to get Fred something better."

Her aim was to get him the ambassadorship to Sweden. Stockholm has frequently been called "the Paris of the North" and, next to the top places in London, Paris, and Rome, it is looked upon as the most desirable assignment in Europe. The social life is excellent, and the problems of Swedish-American relations are, to put it mildly, not taxing.

Mrs. Julie Leiter was only too willing to help her sister, and for four solid months her big, swanky house at Dupont Circle rang from early till late with the sounds of gay cocktail parties, dinners, receptions, and balls. Everyone who was anyone in the State Department was invited. At the end of the four months, Mrs. Sterling had her prize.

"Fred" was appointed to Sweden.

The idea that the promotion of career diplomats to choice ambassadorships and to top policy-making jobs as Undersecretary or Assistant Secretary is somehow a great triumph for better government, is another cherished myth that does not stand the light of day.

Top diplomatic posts both in the field and in the Department are executive positions. They should go to men of proved executive ability, men with vigor and imagination and fresh ideas. Bureaucrats who have advanced because of their skill at inside logrolling, or because of their breath-taking talent at sweeping problems under the rug, are not "better qualified" to run the Department.

Moreover, the posts of Undersecretary and Assistant Secretary are political jobs in the best sense of the word. That is, they require men who can take the long view, who can properly gauge the public temper, and who understand the broad framework of the administration's world policy and can make the political choices that best support that policy.

Career diplomats are wedded to routine; they turn instinctively to the policy which worked in the past and which is "safe"; they have little interest in advancing the policies of a specific administration, because they are primarily concerned with protecting themselves and their associates, all of whom will still be around after the administration is gone, and who, therefore, have nothing to gain from going out on a limb. Lastly, they are wholly unfit for making the political and moral decisions necessary to implement the policies of a liberal democratic country.

Most of them come from the well-to-do or the upper-middle class, and the few who do not, quickly take on the coloration of their colleagues, since that is the "right" and the "expedient" thing to do. As a matter of course, these people turn almost instinctively to the most conservative elements in foreign countries, even when those elements are also decadent, obstructive, and bitterly hated by the local people. Our career diplomats cooperate easily with the spokesmen of finance, business, and the cartel makers abroad; they fumble and shy away from governments which are controlled by laborites and liberals.

The United States has been voting for liberal, New Deal candidates and policies for twenty years, but a large bloc in the State Department's Foreign Service is still operating on the discredited prejudices and misconceptions of the Liberty League.

The appointment of political hacks or big campaign contributors to prize diplomatic jobs is shameful, but the striped-pants boys are not the only alternative. Filling policy-making portfolios need not be a choice between political spoilsmen and civil service doctrinaires.

Overseas assignments below the rank of minister and ambassador are the monopoly of the Foreign Service. That is, no one is appointed consul or first secretary in an embassy abroad who has not passed the exams and been admitted to the Foreign Service. This requirement automatically sets these officials above the majority of State Department employees. It makes them a rigid caste.

The majority of departmental employees who are permanently stationed in this country used to be called, rather quaintly, "drafting officers." That is, they drafted the notes and instructions which were cabled to officers in the field. There are still large numbers of employees who do precisely this kind of work, and they make up a vital part of the Department's staff. But in the last ten years an army of technical experts and specialists has been added to the Department.

It includes scientists, economists, agronomists, laborites, historians, public-relations men, cultural-affairs authorities, etc. The swelling ranks of these experts, and the wide range of subjects they represent, illustrate graphically the ever-expanding scope and complexity of American foreign affairs. International law and an acquaintance with proper protocol are no longer the sole items of knowledge needed by an up-to-date diplomat. But the new army of specialists, like their old-style colleagues, the drafting officers, are barred from getting overseas assignments.

Some of the permanent stateside officials shrivel and become bureaucrats of the worst order.

One of the most notorious of this type is Mrs. Ruth Shipley, the indestructible chief of the Passport Division. "Old Mrs. Bottleneck," as she is unaffectionately known, has been squatting on her present preserve since 1928. No office in Washington carries such impenetrable armor. She has frequently been under heavy fire, but she always comes through unscathed.

From her ballroom-sized office, Ruth Shipley has almost life-and-death power over American businessmen's postwar work abroad. Importers and manufacturers and investors have flooded Washington since 1945 with requests for passports. Mrs. Shipley consults her conscience and her confidential files. Then, by giving or denying a passport, she decides who does business where.

She also has the final authority over what government officials and private individuals may go abroad. Since her political views are considerably to the right of Herbert Hoover's, it is frequently suspected that to be a subscriber to *The New Yorker* magazine is sufficient condemnation in Mrs. Shipley's eyes. Her only explanation for refusing an applicant is the terse line, "This trip would not be in the public interest."

Executives turned down by her scream to the high heavens, but no one has yet been able to get a President or a Secretary of State to agree that the Passport Division is "no place for a lady."

Her soft voice and the gracious way she offers a cup of coffee are ladylike, but sweet femininity plays no part in Mrs. Shipley's incorrigibility. Devoid of all professional or social ambitions and completely convinced of her own immaculate righteousness, Mrs. Shipley has an H-bomb confidence in herself.

There is nothing wrong with Mrs. Shipley that a little decentralized authority would not fix. As it is, she may ask outside counsel on a passport case, but, once she has an opinion of her own—that's all, brother; you're finished, unless you can get the President or the Secretary of State to go to bat for you.

Says Mrs. Shipley crisply, "In every case I do exactly as I think the Secretary of State would do." And as for her critics, "At my age, one either has a nervous breakdown or poise enough to ignore criticism."

No one in Washington thinks Mrs. Shipley lacks poise.

The State Department which Cordell Hull took over in 1933 did not differ substantially from what it was in 1898 when John Hay became Secretary. Tyler Dennett, veteran diplomatic historian and Hay's biographer, described it as an "antiquated, feeble organization, enslaved by precedents and routine inherited from another century, remote from the public gaze and indifferent to it. The typewriter was viewed as a necessary evil and the telephone was an instrument of last resort."

Cordell Hull assumed command of this moribund hulk and promptly initiated a vigorous policy of sitting on his hands.

He writes in his autobiography, "I carefully investigated the character and fitness of officers of the Department, especially those in key positions. Although I weeded out an official here and there who for one cause or another was not equipped to perform the most efficient service, I retained the seasoned, experienced persons in key positions."

In other words, he did nothing, and the inside word went out: All deadheads will stand by for further procrastinating.

Hull was probably one of the most bumbling and inefficient Secretaries who ever held the reins of the Department of State. His sole distinction was that he held them for a longer period than anyone in history.

Hull was profoundly ignorant of world affairs, querulous and ill-humored, slow-thinking, jealous, and viciously petty. His only contribution during eleven long years of international crisis was the Reciprocal Trade Agreements program, which was in the nature of using a lawn sprinkler to fight a four-alarm fire—all very well in its place, but scarcely adequate for the emergency at hand.

Hull was selected by Roosevelt and kept in office for so long for two reasons. First, he was a veteran Democrat and former chairman of the National Committee who had to be rewarded for past services. Secondly, he made an imposing, white-haired front. He was a dignified and innocuous façade behind which Roosevelt could run foreign affairs as he pleased.

Hull had sufficient brains to find this out pretty early in the game, and if he had had any genuine self-respect, he would have resigned. But he deeply relished the semblance of power, even if he did not have the substance, and he had a naïve vanity which was easy for Roosevelt to play upon. It did not take much to persuade Hull that he was "indispensable"—which indeed he was, though not for the reputed reasons.

Throughout most of Hull's eleven-year tenure, there were two Secretaries of State—and neither of them was Hull.

One was Sumner Welles. Welles was a brilliant diplomat who had spent twenty years in the Department. In many ways he fitted the stereotype of the career clique. He was a rich, well-dressed, suave, and somewhat frigid scion of an aristocratic Eastern family. He had gone to the best schools and had the best social connections. His rise in the 1930's was aided by the fact that he was a personal friend of Roosevelt and was a generous campaign contributor.

But Welles was a lot more than that. He was one of the few of his set who happened to be endowed with a twentieth-century mind. He had not only a detailed grasp of affairs in his special bailiwick—Latin America—but he had a stimulating imagination, a tough will, and a belief in the potentialities for liberalism in American foreign policy. In other words, he knew what the score was, in ideological as well as power terms.

The other Secretary of State in fact, if not in name, was James Clement Dunn, now Ambassador to Italy.

Dunn, equally suave and equally well to do, is a deep-dyed reactionary. In the 1930's he was the dean of the career clique. He wheedled his way into Hull's confidence and in rapid succession became chief of the Division of Western European Affairs, special assistant to the Secretary, chief, in 1937, of a new European Division encompassing the whole continent, then he was upped to Political Adviser to the Secretary and, in 1942, added the job of chairman of the Committee on Political Planning. With the aid of Carlton Savage and other picked associates from among the ranks of the careerists, Dunn masterminded as much of the policy-making as he and Hull were able to keep their hands on.

Sumner Welles's chief strength, aside from the personal backing of President Roosevelt, was the core of able assistants he had built up in the Division of Latin American affairs. The most important of these was the late Laurence Duggan.

Duggan entered the Department in 1930 as a non-career appointee. His first job was as a divisional assistant at $3,200 a year. His ability was so outstanding—particularly in the murky gloom surrounding him—that within five years he was promoted over the heads of dozens of Foreign Service "old-school-tie" men to be the head of the Latin American Division at a salary of $8,000. This put him in rank just below an Assistant Secretary. But, as Duggan was to discover later, mere brilliance was no guarantee of lasting success in Foggy Bottom.

The backstage feud between the Welles faction and the Hull-Dunn group came to its first climax in 1937.

At that time, the post of Undersecretary became vacant, and Roosevelt wished to promote Welles. Hull insisted the job go to Walton Moore, a crony whom he had brought into the Department as an Assistant Secretary four years earlier. Moore, then seventy-eight years old, was a decrepit Virginia politico who had served in Congress from 1919 to 1931 and had a long record as a lawyer and lobbyist for railroads and steamship companies. His capabilities as a diplomat were not discernible.

Roosevelt "solved" the problem with a typically Rooseveltian solution. He promoted both.

Welles was made Undersecretary. For Moore the defunct position of Counselor was re-established. This gave him equal pay and rank with the Undersecretary, except that, in the absence of Hull, Welles served as Acting Secretary. Of course, in this way, Roosevelt also kept tabs on the fight from both sides and keenly enjoyed the conflict and intrigue.

As the war drew closer, Roosevelt took the initiative more and more into his own hands. He relied directly on Welles and, later, on Harry Hopkins to perform important missions. Ambassadors in foreign trouble spots were encouraged to keep the President informed directly by phone, rather than by sending cables to the Department. Roosevelt was not only impatient with the slowness of the career boys but distrustful of them as well. It was not unusual for Department division chiefs to edit or suppress cables they were not anxious for Roosevelt to see.

Hull hobbled along in a grudging and irascible attempt to keep the Department abreast of current problems. But he was utterly unwilling and incompetent to strengthen his organization sufficiently for it to meet the manifold problems which the coming of the war and the war itself piled up.

William Harlan Hale, in an article in *Harper's,* summarized the situation succinctly: "Not even this [Roosevelt's bypassing the Department] taught Hull his lesson, though, for after America finally entered the war his staff was still unready to carry out such vital crisis jobs in foreign affairs as propaganda (which therefore went to OWI), economic warfare (which therefore went to the special Board of Economic Warfare), inter-Allied commerce and supply (which stayed under special lend-lease administrators), and the planning of occupation programs (which therefore fell increasingly into the hands of the Army, the Joint Chiefs of Staff, and, of all people, the troubleshooters of Mr. Morgenthau's Treasury)."

Instead of grappling with the burdens that should have been his, Hull was too busy sniping and feuding with his assorted subordinates.

Cursed with a venomously petty and vindictive streak, this meansouled old mountaineer created endless personal tangles by his obstructionism and recriminations. Things drifted steadily from bad to worse. By the middle of the war, there were no fewer than five separate and distinct factions in the Department, no two of which spoke to the others except when official business absolutely required it.

All potshotting and back stabbing came to a climax in the summer of 1943.

For weeks, Hull leaked vicious personal gossip about Welles to Arthur Krock, chief of *The New York Times* Washington bureau. This vendetta-ing at the lowest personal level created an intolerable situation, and Roosevelt was forced at long last to choose between the two men. After going through an agony of indecision, he let Welles go.

The controlling factor in Roosevelt's mind was the necessity of getting the postwar peace plans, including American entry into a new League of Nations, through the claws of an unpredictable Senate. Haunted by the memory of Wilson's tragic failure, he felt compelled to put Hull's popularity with the Southerners and with conservatives generally ahead of Welles's competence.

But, at the same time, Roosevelt decided to install as the new Undersecretary a man who would be personally devoted to him and who would act as his agent in cleaning up the mess in the Department. His choice for this assignment was Edward R. Stettinius, the silver-haired "boy wonder," who was then serving as Lend-Lease administrator.

Stettinius knew nothing about foreign policy, but he was affable and persuasive and might be expected to reconcile conflicting elements. He was also an experienced executive who could chart a new plan of organization, and a master of public relations who could sell administration policies.

Stettinius, however, failed to do the job.

He put through a fairly sweeping reorganization, but he did not have the authority or the thorough grasp of details to prevent it from being largely sabotaged and short-circuited by the vested interests affected.

In late 1944, bad health at long last forced Hull to quit. Stettinius was his successor.

He promptly shunted Acheson to the congressional liaison job, ousted several other men, and brought in six new assistants. These were installed to the accompaniment of a mass rally for departmental employees, complete with music from the Marine Corps band. It was announced that even bigger things were in store. The New Era was here. The Managerial Revolution had come to the State Department.

It was all talk. Nothing changed.

Stettinius' much-vaunted "team" was the oddest and most diverse assortment of talents and nontalents to descend on Washington in a long time.

One was none other than the ineffable Mr. Dunn himself—which was comparable to starting a revolution with Herbert Hoover playing the role of Lenin. To the Undersecretaryship was named Joseph C. Grew, who had been in the Foreign Service since 1904 and was so much the high priest of the clique that he made Dunn look like an acolyte. With Grew wielding the broom, it was certain from the outset that it wouldn't sweep very clean. It didn't.

The other four members of Stettinius' team included Nelson Rockefeller in charge of Latin American affairs, William L. Clayton in charge of economic affairs, Archibald MacLeish for public relations, and Julius Holmes in charge of administration. Rockefeller was a wealthy dilettante; Clayton was a tough, brainy businessman, a type which was to become increasingly familiar in the State Department in the next few years; MacLeish was the brilliant poet who had reorganized the Library of Congress and written some of Roosevelt's better speeches; and Holmes was a cookie-pushing general who sat out the war on Eisenhower's staff and who is now Minister to England, ranking second to Ambassador Lewis Douglas.

This variegated crew never had much of an opportunity to show its wares, if it had any. Within six months Roosevelt was dead, Stettinius was out, Byrnes was in, and everyone but Will Clayton resigned.

Byrnes upped Acheson to Undersecretary and installed Donald Russell, his own law partner, as an Assistant Secretary, and Ben Cohen, the brilliant brain-truster of the Corcoran & Cohen combination, as Counselor.

Thereafter, in the next four years, changes came fast and furious to the Department of State. But they were superficial changes. Fundamental reforms were not achieved, and the prime reason was that no one had the time to give any consistent thought to the subject of basic reorganization.

Acheson, the only top official of the Byrnes-Marshall era who had the necessary experience, knowledge, and courage to do the job, was too busy making policy to have time for it. He did get rid of some of the worst deadwood. Illustration: He exiled Jimmy Dunn to Italy as Ambassador, where he still is. Most of the reshuffling, however, Acheson left to Russell, who was Assistant Secretary in charge of administration.

Russell was painfully unfamiliar with the job that had to be done. Also, he seemed to have a constant itch to change names and titles while leaving the substance of things unchanged. Professor Graham Stuart of Stanford University wrote about one minor but fairly characteristic example of Russell's technique:

"It must be confessed that the [Department's] new intelligence agency did its best to baffle any attempt to follow up its organizational nomenclature and administration. For example, on January 1, 1946, the Division of Geography and Cartography was abolished, its functions transferred to the Office of Research and Intelligence, and its name changed to the Division of Map Intelligence and Cartography. On May 1, 1946, the Division of Map Intelligence and Cartography became the Division of Map Intelligence, and on August 20 it once more became the Division of Map Intelligence and Cartography. On February 4, 1947, it again changed its name to simply Map Division, and two days later it was transferred to the Office of Information Collection and Dissemination. Here it remained until December 29, 1947, when it was transferred to Central Intelligence Agency, where it may be today—Central Intelligence does not say."

Other factors also helped keep things in a constant state of flux and turmoil. One was Congress. Various members made a practice of baiting and ridiculing the officials of the Voice of America program. William Benton, now Democratic Senator from Connecticut, was MacLeish's successor as Assistant Secretary in charge of public relations. Some of Benton's future Senate colleagues virtually nailed him to a cross while he was in the Department.

When General George C. Marshall succeeded Byrnes as Secretary of State in January, 1947, another wave of resignations swept the Department. Once again, a tide of rumors of drastic changes and reorganization swirled high.

Marshall did make changes both in personnel and in organization.

But, as with Byrnes, this was not reform. It was the old game of musical chairs.

Marshall is an example of a great man who did not make a great Secretary of State. He never really caught hold of the reins tightly and ran things. One reason was that he was out of the country attending international conferences for long stretches at a time. But another more fundamental reason was the way in which he operated.

Marshall deliberately kept himself remote from the day-to-day operations of the Department. He laid down the rule that, as in the Army, all decisions should be made at the proper points in the chain of command and that the top official would determine only over-all objectives. Whenever a ruling was needed from him, someone in the lower echelons drew up a report on the questions involved. The report would consist of three sections: Facts, Conclusions, and Recommendations. At the bottom of the report would be two small boxes, one marked Yes, the other No. Marshall read the report and indicated his decision by putting a check in either of the two boxes.

This system, on paper an admirably concise and efficient method of procedure, was a glaring flop in practice. Diplomacy is a political art, and the important factors are the intangible ones which cannot be measured or readily detailed in a table or a summary. As a result of his system, Marshall was virtually the prisoner of his staff and, particularly, of the Foreign Service officers who drew up the memoranda. It also meant that Marshall often went to foreign conferences badly briefed, because he was not informed about the complex factors which had been boiled down to a compact digest for his consideration.

Marshall was also cursed by his understandable weakness for surrounding himself with men of military background. Many were not professional officers but civilians who had entered the services during the war. But almost invariably they were conservative in their background and inclined toward the military viewpoint.

This strong drift to the right was accentuated by Marshall's unfortunate choice of Robert Lovett as Undersecretary when Acheson returned to private life. Lovett, a bald, dapper, man-of-distinction type, was a Wall Street banker who had made a record speeding up heavy-bomber production when he was Assistant Secretary of War for Air. Lovett, again understandably, selected like-minded associates, such as

General Charles Saltzman, West Point graduate and a former vice-president of the New York Stock Exchange, who became Assistant Secretary in charge of occupied areas.

Byrnes had started the practice of tapping military brass for key Department jobs, but it was Lovett who was largely responsible for the heavy influx of old-line conservatives to a Department which had always suffered from excessive conservatism. This infusion from the right had disastrous effects on our denazification and decartelization programs in Germany, hampered our relations with Britain and our other Western European Allies, which, almost without exception, are led by left-of-center governments, and—worst of all—served to inhibit a more daring and enlightened approach to the foreign problems which oppress us.

So many Republican bigwigs, bankers, business tycoons, generals, and ex-generals crowded into Foggy Bottom that Paul Porter, the witty lawyer and ex-OPA director, wisecracked that a new section would have to be added to the government loyalty oath, "Do you solemnly swear that you are not now and never have been a member of the Democratic Party?"

Meanwhile, however, the Foreign Service began to develop signs of a schizoid or "split" personality. Unlike an ordinary neurosis, this was a healthy manifestation.

It indicated that at least part of the Service recognized that the twentieth century had arrived, and was struggling to face up honestly to the grave social problems which exist in the world. Marshall installed three experienced career diplomats on his staff. One of them represented the old school and two the new.

The oldest of the three was Norman Armour, who was coaxed from retirement to take the job of Assistant Secretary for Political Affairs. Armour, before his retirement, had served in the Department for over thirty years. He had been Minister to Canada, Ambassador to Chile, Spain, and Argentina, and had held many lesser posts. He was the very epitome of the old-fashioned, old-school-tie career diplomat.

Armour had all the virtues and most of the defects of the type. He was handsome, well educated, well bred, and well meaning. He had a well-trained and well-stocked second-rate mind. He was friendly and courteous. He was sufficiently well to do to entertain as becomes a representative of the U.S. government. All he lacked was imagination, ideas, and personal force. He had the velvet glove, but it covered a fist of putty.

The other two career men Marshall promoted to top rank were men of the generation following Armour's. They were both in their early forties. Both entered the Foreign Service on the eve of the great depression and the rise of Hitler to power. Both knew scarcely any other age but the recent present, scarred with social strife and shadowed by totalitarian threat. Both were schooled in the ways of the Russian dictatorship and anxious to devise methods to combat it.

These two men were George Kennan and Charles Bohlen. Kennan became chairman of a new unit to map out long-range policy; "Chip" Bohlen became Counselor of the Department.

George Kennan, when upped to chief of the newly created Policy Planning Staff in the spring of 1947, was forty-three years old. His selection was the climax of a brilliant twenty-year career in the Foreign Service, which had three times brought him within the iron-gray walls of the Kremlin. He first went there in 1933 when diplomatic relations with Russia were re-established, and he was last there as embassy counselor at the height of the war. In the two crucial years preceding Pearl Harbor, Kennan put in a tour of duty at another center of modern totalitarianism—Nazi Germany. Thus, few men have a more intimate knowledge than Kennan of the workings of the modern police state. Able to speak and read Russian, he has an equally keen insight into the murky depths of the Soviet mind.

The task of the Policy Planning Staff is to consider the long-range problems of American foreign policy and to anticipate problems before they arise. The members of the staff have nothing to do with day-to-day operations.

The policy planners meet in the room adjoining the Secretary's office. No anteroom or corridor separates them. There is only the connecting door. There are no telephones, no baskets for incoming and outgoing mail, no individual desks. Nothing but a long, highly polished table surrounded by eight leather chairs. Kennan and Carlton Savage, Hull's old handy man who serves as permanent secretary, are the only fixed members of the group. The rest of the staff is made up of four or five departmental members who vary from time to time.

Such a group is unprecedented for a Department which had always puttered along from one crisis to another on the Micawberish hope that "something will turn up" tomorrow. The saying in the Department used to be: "America's foreign policy is made on the [daily] cables." Now, at long last, a quarterback was calling the plays.

Charles Bohlen, a New Yorker whose family is related distantly to the famous German Krupp munitions-making clan, had long been an imperturbable fly in the Russian borsch when Marshall promoted him to Counselor. The late Russian Ambassador Oumansky once bitterly characterized him as an "unfriendly contact." "He is a faithful servant of the United States Department of State," Oumansky snapped. "That is very, very unfortunate."

The recipient of this unintentional compliment is a slender, brown-haired, gray-eyed, ruggedly good-looking six-footer who has the easy-going manners and wears the rather baggy attire of a campus undergraduate. He has changed little in outward appearance since he graduated from Harvard back in 1927. But the intervening years have been crowded and highly eventful. He began his preparation for a diplomatic career in a characteristically paradoxical fashion. He got on a tramp steamer after graduation and spent eighteen months going around the world. In 1929, he joined the Foreign Service and was sent to Prague as vice-consul. Later he was shifted to Paris, where he had an opportunity to learn Russian at the Institute of Oriental Languages.

Just as he completed his course, a big break came his way. The U.S. re-established relations with Russia. Bohlen was assigned to Ambassador Bill Bullitt's staff. He was subsequently shuttled back home and briefly to other foreign spots, but in the course of the next eight years Bohlen put in three tours of duty in the Russian capital.

In 1941, he was shifted to Tokyo, where he was stationed when the war broke out. He had just arrived in America from Japan on the Swedish exchange ship, S.S. "Gripsholm," when he received a hurry-up order to report to the White House to act as President Roosevelt's interpreter in the coming conversations with Russian Foreign Minister Molotov. Roosevelt liked Bohlen's fluency and came to rely on his wide background knowledge of Russia and the Russians. Harry Hopkins, impressed with his quick mind, took him up as a personal protégé. In this double role of presidential interpreter and political confidant, Bohlen attended all the Big Three conferences during the war. He continued to perform this dual role when the team of Truman and Byrnes took over.

Truman has the honor of being the only man ever to stump Chip Bohlen as an interpreter. In the middle of one of the sessions at the 1945 Potsdam Conference, Truman remarked, "Let's take a seventh-inning stretch." Chip had a little difficulty explaining to Joe Stalin what a "stretch" was.

Notwithstanding the acclaim over the Marshall Plan and the program for the containment of Russia, the State Department was in a disorganized condition when Dean Acheson became Secretary.

The Department had grown to five times its prewar size. The European Division alone had more employees than the whole Department in 1939. But new bureaus and divisions and added personnel were not integrated into the departmental structure; they had just been piled on top of existing offices. Practically nothing had been abolished or thrown away.

The standard response to every new problem was the creation of a new committee to "study" it. (One wag suggested that the Foggy Bottom theme song should be "Set Up Another Committee," sung to the tune of "Give Us Another Old Fashioned.") Many incompetents in the Foreign Service were still entrenched in key places. The Department was not yet functioning as a coherent organization under capable and inspiring leadership.

Acheson was extraordinarily well equipped to take the helm. His six years as Assistant Secretary and Undersecretary and his months with the Hoover task force on reorganization gave him unparalleled insight into the Department.

His career as a subordinate officer had also given him experiences which were still vivid in his mind, and some equally strong opinions on certain subjects. One of these was the inertia and stodginess of too many of the careerists. Another was the danger of divided authority. Still another was the need for strong leadership from the top.

Acheson's first move was to implement many of the Hoover Commission recommendations, which called for a reassignment of authority and the expansion of the top staff.

Under the new setup, Acheson has two special advisers, an Under-secretary, two Deputy Undersecretaries, eight Assistant Secretaries, a counselor, a legal adviser, an Intelligence chief, a German adviser, and a long-range policy adviser. These officers are neatly grouped into three blocs: Functional (public relations, congressional relations, economic affairs, and legal affairs); Policy (Intelligence chief and the Policy Planning Staff); and Operating (the four "geographic" Assistant Secretaries—Europe, Latin America, Far East, Africa and Near East, plus the German adviser and the Assistant Secretary for United Nations Affairs).

Acheson has built up the following "team" to man this imposing array of offices:

Special Advisers: John Foster Dulles and John Sherman Cooper. Both
    served briefly in the Senate. Cooper rose from obscurity to fame
    as a senator; Dulles rose from fame to notoriety.

Cooper, a well-to-do lawyer, served as Republican senator from Kentucky from 1946 to 1948 to fill out the balance of "Happy" Chandler's term. He became noted as one of the more liberal and intelligent members of the Republican Eightieth Congress, which was not noted for either of these qualities. Perhaps sensing this unhappy contrast, the Kentucky voters decided, in 1948, to give the seat to a Democrat named Virgil Chapman, with whom nobody could suffer by comparison.

Dulles is the well-known international lawyer of Sullivan & Cromwell and Nazi-cartel fame. During the war, he wangled himself a job to study peace plans for the highly respectable Federal Council of Churches of Christ and zoomed across the political heavens as a self-propelled "expert" on international affairs. He immediately struck up a working arrangement with Governor Thomas E. Dewey as a "mentor" on foreign affairs.

It was a case, apparently, of one cold, pompous, desperately ambitious man recognizing another. But Dulles was not too good at masterminding; his man lost twice in a row, and he never did get to be Secretary of State.

In 1949, Dewey gave Dulles an interim appointment to the Senate—after former Secretary of War Robert Patterson turned it down. Dulles firmly announced that under no circumstances would he run for the job in an election. But once he got to Washington, the chance to upstage Vandenberg and crib his lines about "bipartisanship" seemed so good that Dulles let his vanity get the better of his previous common sense. He did become a candidate, waging one of the shabbiest campaigns in years.

Dulles made unsupported charges of communism, saw spooks under Truman's desk, attacked social-welfare measures as "totalitarianism," and wound up insulting the voters of New York City by telling an upstate audience that they would surely vote for him "if you could only see the faces of those people down there." Later, he lamely explained he had meant Communists. He was defeated overwhelmingly by former Democratic Governor Herbert Lehman.

The administration for several years had been toting Dulles around to international conferences as "bipartisan" window dressing. After his bawdy campaign conduct, Truman and Acheson resolved to have nothing more to do with him and his sanctimonious mouthings. The President disclosed this in a talk with former Interior Secretary Harold Ickes. As Ickes was leaving, the President remarked that he was worried about the New York election.

Turning from the door, Ickes said, "In my opinion, John Foster Dulles is a son of a bitch."

Truman nodded and agreed that he didn't like Dulles either.

"John Foster Dulles is a falsie on Dewey's chest," Ickes said, "a falsie that's slipped down."

But it was a measure of the administration's desperation that in April, 1950, at the height of the McCarthy frenzy, Dulles was recalled and once more became a State Department "bipartisan" adviser.

Undersecretary: James Webb. A forty-three-year-old lawyer from
    North Carolina, Webb knows little about foreign policy, but he
    is a high-powered efficiency expert who draws up all of Acheson's
    organization and personnel plans.

Webb is a protégé of the late O. Max Gardner, Governor of the Tarheel State in the late '20's and Truman's first Undersecretary of the Treasury. Webb left Gardner's law firm for the Sperry Gyroscope Company. He rose to vice-president by the time he was thirty-six and supervised the corporation's wartime expansion from eight hundred employees to over thirty thousand. In 1944-45, he served in Marine

Corps aviation. He then rejoined Gardner's law firm and, in 1946, became Director of the Budget when his boss recommended him to Harry Truman. The President, who has an insatiable penchant for neat paper schemes and a great admiration for "order" and "efficiency," took a warm liking to Webb. He made him his personal choice for Undersecretary when Acheson became Secretary in 1949. There is no friction, however, between Acheson and Webb because the latter has no desire to meddle in matters of high policy.

Deputy Undersecretary in charge of Administration: Carlisle H. Humelsine.

Humelsine is one of the youngest men in high office in the government. He is only thirty-five. Humelsine represents that new type of fixture on the Washington scene—the professional administrator. Humelsine worked after his graduation from the University of Maryland as administrative assistant to the president of his alma mater. When the war came, he entered the Army and landed the assignment of organizing the central secretariat for Chief of Staff George Marshall. As assistant secretary for the General Staff, Humelsine attended the Yalta and Potsdam conferences. In 1946, Byrnes brought him into the State Department as an administrative aide. The next year, when his old boss, George Marshall, took over, Humelsine received the assignment of organizing an executive secretariat comparable to that in the Pentagon. This organization supervises the flow of paper work and provides for the proper coordination and review of decisions taken in all areas of the department. In 1949, Humelsine moved up to be righthand man to his predecessor, John E. Peurifoy. When the latter was named envoy to Greece in the summer of 1950, Humelsine succeeded to the top position.

Humelsine is a bureaucrat by profession; he is not a policy maker. Like advertising men who think they can "merchandise" anything, Humelsine is an administrator who presumably is willing and able to administer (and coordinate and integrate) anything from the sale of goat's milk in Somaliland to the selling of lemons in California.

His predecessor, John Peurifoy, was the epitome of the non-Foreign Service type who has made good in Foggy Bottom in recent years. A stocky, black-haired, genial fellow, he has brains and energy and a keen interest in politics. He was the only State Department official to campaign for Truman in 1948. Peurifoy says frankly, "To tell the truth, the State Department was ripe for guys like me."

Deputy Undersecretary in charge of Political Affairs: H. Freeman Matthews. One of the abler and more liberal of the career diplomats.

Matthews, fifty-one, was brought back from his post as Ambassador to Sweden to head the political affairs setup in the early summer of 1950. A Maryland native and a graduate of Princeton, he has been in the Department since 1924. He served for a time as assistant to Ambassador John Winant in London during the war. He was later head of the Office of European Affairs, the area on which he concentrates in his present job, and has attended all of the major postwar conferences.

Assistant Secretary for Public Affairs: Edward W. Barrett. A former associate editor of *Newsweek* magazine, Barrett is the latest in a long succession brought in to handle the Voice of America and the public information program. Like Archibald MacLeish and William Benton and other predecessors, Barrett is highly capable and experienced in his field, but it is too early to tell whether he will succeed in a job which has traditionally been a graveyard for ambitious men.

Assistant Secretary for Congressional Relations: Jack K. McFall. He came to Washington in 1924 to study at Georgetown Foreign Service School, but it took him twenty years to get around to joining the State Department.

His first job was as secretary to Senator Arthur Robinson, militant champion of the Ku Klux Klan. In the book, *More Merry-Go-Round* (1932), Robinson was described as a "little, sly, ferret-faced, oily-mannered Republican who rocketed out of obscurity in the bigoted depths of Indiana backwoods politics." McFall stuck with Robinson for three years, until he came up for re-election in 1928. McFall then got an Indiana Republican congressman to wangle him a more secure job on the staff of the House Appropriations Committee.

But, to everyone's surprise, the resurgent bigotry of the 1928 Al Smith campaign caused Indiana voters to perpetrate the re-election of Senator Robinson. However, McFall stayed with the House Committee. For the next eighteen years, except for shore duty with the

Navy in Africa during the war, he was a denizen of Capitol Hill. He handled the budgets of the State and Justice Departments and was generally regarded as a harmless and amiable hack.

In 1946, McFall joined the Foreign Service and was sent overseas to Greece. He was there in 1949, when Acheson elevated him to his present job.

When McFall's appointment was announced, one congressional newsman quipped, "He ought to be able to do a good job. He certainly knows all the s.o.b.'s up here." There is little doubt that McFall is well acquainted in Congress, but he has made it clear that just "knowing all the s.o.b.'s" is not enough.

A good salesman has to know what he is selling and to have confidence in his wares. McFall, tall, heavy-set, with slick black hair, dark eyes, lush baritone voice, and a slinky black mustache, has all the sincerity and conviction of a real-estate promoter. Totally devoid of ideas and ideals, he has bungled and sold short much of the Department's congressional program by his insistent instinct for "compromises" and "deals."

He has to be practically chained to the wall to prevent him from jumping into bed with the Dixiecrats and Republican isolationists every time they cast a come-hither look in his direction.

One earnest and conscientious liberal congressman remarked, "Dean Acheson must think all congressmen are either fools or knaves or both to have picked a man like McFall to represent him up here."

Assistant Secretary for Economic Affairs: Willard L. Thorp. A fifty-one-year-old former professor, Thorp is not a member of the "new" Acheson team. He joined the Department in 1945 and has been Assistant Secretary since 1946. A New Yorker with a Columbia Ph.D. in economics, Thorp taught at Amherst College, put in a whirl with the old NRA, and wound up in 1935 as vice-president and director of research for Dun & Bradstreet. Tall, dignified, full-faced, Thorp looks like a prosperous business executive.

Legal Adviser: Adrian Fisher. When Fisher graduated from Harvard Law School back in the late '30's, Felix Frankfurter, one of his professors, said of him, "He is right now better qualified to sit on the Supreme Court than the majority on it."

Fisher promptly came to Washington to give the Court a closer inspection; he served as Justice Brandeis' law clerk and, when the latter retired, switched to Frankfurter, who was appointed in that period. Fisher has spent his whole career in government.

After leaving the clerkship at the Court, he went to work for David Lilienthal as an assistant legal counsel for the TVA. Fisher's father had been Senator Kenneth McKellar's law partner, but Fisher was not influenced by the coincidence. He had practically to blast his way into the "shooting war" because of the insistence of his superiors that he was more valuable where he was. Fisher finally got his chance and became a bomber navigator overseas.

When the war ended, Averell Harriman asked him to come to the Commerce Department as Solicitor. Fisher left in 1948 when Harriman did, and then went over to the Atomic Energy Commission under his old boss Lilienthal. In the fall of 1949, Acheson brought him into the State Department. Fisher is the son of an All-American football player and was captain of the Princeton team in his own undergraduate days. He has the towering height and physical build of a football hero, but his high forehead, wide mouth, keen eyes behind rimmed spectacles, and sober demeanor are a better gauge of his serious and scholarly nature.

Director, Policy Planning Staff: Acheson retained George Kennan, who took a temporary leave of absence in 1950 and was replaced by Paul Nitze, youthful alumnus of the Dillon-Read investment banking house.

Assistant Secretary for European Affairs: George W. Perkins. He is the son and namesake of the Morgan partner who financed Theodore Roosevelt's Bull Moose campaign in 1912.

Perkins' only previous public service was as a young man, in 1921-22, when he was Postmaster General Will Hays's secretary. The next twenty years he spent with Merck & Co., a big New Jersey chemical firm. In 1942, he joined the Army as a colonel in the Chemical Engineers. Perkins was personally drafted by Acheson to serve as head of the European Division. This cool, reserved, fifty-five-year-old millionaire is a man of strong conservative leanings. He is an active Republican and once served as assistant treasurer of the GOP State Committee in New York.

Assistant Secretary for Latin America: Edward G. Miller is a young lawyer who was one of the fledgling attorneys who served as Acheson's assistants early in the war.

Miller idolizes his chief. He was a junior member of Sullivan & Cromwell, John Foster Dulles' firm of international lawyers, when he rejoined the Department in 1949. Born in Puerto Rico and raised in Cuba, Miller speaks Spanish and Portuguese fluently. His idea of dealing successfully with Perón was to give that strutting, tinhorn Argentine dictator a $125,000,000 loan to bail him out of the hands of New York and Boston bankers.

Assistant Secretary for Far East: Dean Rusk. He was formerly in the slot now occupied by Deputy Undersecretary Matthews.

In the spring of 1950, when the collapse of China and the growing fight for Indo-China made the Far East post critical, Acheson shifted Rusk to this assignment, with a technical drop in rank but no real loss in power and influence. Rusk is a former professor of government at Mills College in California. He was born in Georgia in 1909, earned his A.B. at Davidson College in North Carolina, and studied at Oxford as a Rhodes scholar.

Joining the Army when the war broke out, Rusk served in the China-Burma-India theater and rose to be a colonel and deputy chief of staff to General Stilwell. He was later brought home and put in the Operations Planning Division of the General Staff at the Pentagon. Here he caught General Marshall's eye, and Marshall took him along when he became head of the State Department. Rusk's first top-level job in Foggy Bottom was as director of United Nations Affairs.

Assistant Secretary for Africa and Near East: George McGhee. A Texan, McGhee is a veteran of twenty-five years in the international oil business. He entered the government during the war and later helped run the Greek-Turkish aid program.

Assistant Secretary for United Nations Affairs: John D. Hickerson. Another Texan, Hickerson graduated from the State University in 1920 but long ago left the Texas plains for Eastern drawing rooms. He entered the consular service and put in time in Mexico, Canada, and Brazil. In 1930, he was made assistant chief of the Western European Affairs Division and spent the next nineteen years there. Acheson switched him to the UN field in 1949.

In defending his associates during the course of his talk to the American Society of Newspaper Editors in April, 1950, Acheson declared proudly:

"Here in this top command, I say to you, we have men as distinguished, as able, as powerful, and as vigorous as any of my great predecessors, from John Marshall to George Marshall, ever had in the Department of State. . . . Today, as rarely before in the State Department, there is no backbiting, there is no jealousy, there is no undercutting. You have an organization of people which is loyal to those within it, which is loyal to the President of the United States, and which is loyal to the United States of America."

There is no doubt that Acheson has assembled a better balanced and a more united team than any of his immediate predecessors. Also, that conniving and intrigue are at an all-time low.

It is a young staff. Most of the members are in their early forties; Miller and Fisher are still in their thirties; Perkins, at fifty-five, is the oldest of the group. Two of them, Fisher and Miller, are personal protégés of Acheson. The rest all owe their appointment or advancement directly to him. With the possible exception of Undersecretary Webb, none has sufficient standing with the White House or the public to go over Acheson's head.

Another significant fact about Acheson's team is that eight of the thirteen are Southerners; of the remainder, three are from New York, and two are Midwesterners. Five are men from big business and corporation law—or, as in Webb's case, from both. With the exception of Legal Adviser Fisher, none is a liberal.

Disregarding the inept Jack McFall, each man in Acheson's baker's dozen is at least competent to perform the job he holds. But this raises the question, is competence enough?

The answer is obvious. Only the very best can be adequate to do the job that has to be done for the United States in the world today.

When Acheson was recruiting his staff in early 1949, he could have had the very best men in the country. Despite Truman's constant yammering on the subject, there is no shortage of good men to serve in government. It is only his own uninspired leadership and the clammy sterility of the Snyders and Sawyers and McGraths which have created an artificial shortage. Government salaries have nothing to do with it. They are now adequate. Acheson, a man who has proved that he can inspire devotion and enthusiasm in his associates, and who had the challenge of exciting work and responsibilities to offer, could easily have attracted men of highest caliber for every post he had to fill.

He failed to do so.

Only in the case of Kennan, Rusk, and Fisher did he select men of genuine attainments. And of these, the first two were inherited and the other is an old personal friend. Most of the others are not top-drawer quality.

George Perkins, in charge of the vital European Division, is a thoroughly uninspired figure. The talents which caused Acheson to "draft" him—whatever they may be—have never been exposed to public view. John Hickerson, chief of the UN Division, is a routine bureaucrat of the red-tape variety. He is operating beyond his level. George McGhee, the veteran oilman, is in charge of the Africa-Near East Division. The Near East, rich in oil and poor in all other resources, is an ancient, poverty-stricken region which has a highly unstable society. At present, it is a power vacuum into which Russian power may at any time begin to flow and make of it a new China. The situation there is not critical, but it may soon be. McGhee, wedded to the intellectual stereotypes of old-time oil-company policy in the area, has produced no program to meet the potential threat. His chosen subordinates are equally bankrupt intellectually. As for Webb and Humelsine, while both are capable executives, it seems strange that two of the three highest positions in the Department should be monopolized by nonpolicy-making "efficiency" men who contribute nothing in the way of constructive ideas.

And it is ideas that are precisely the urgent, vital things which Acheson's assistants sorely lack. They are generally capable, but they do not toss off many intellectual sparks to light the way into the future.

There are few among them of the caliber of the New Dealers, who were always bubbling over with ideas, projects, suggestions, and enthusiasms. Some of their schemes were not sound, and others were not politically feasible; but, in the final reckoning, it cannot be denied that a lot of their ideas did work. The country did move forward.

There is not that intellectual ferment around Acheson, and there is desperate need that there should be. His men see the problems and are conscientious in trying to meet them as best they can. But they do not range far enough afield. Their imaginations and creative impulses lack motive power.

It is not that Acheson didn't want to get subordinates of first-rank stature. He did. His intentions were the best.

It is simply that Acheson is not a superman, and administration and the organization of a staff are not spheres in which he excels. That is a frequent failing of lawyers. In fact, often the better the lawyer, the worse the weakness. They tend to run a bureau or a department in the same way they run their own law firms, which is an unsound analogy. Winning one case at a time, or even hopping around successfully among eight or ten cases simultaneously, is not the same as formulating and administering policies continuously over a long pull.

Another factor that has seriously handicapped Acheson on personnel has been lack of time. From the moment he became Secretary, he has been under punishing pressures from all sides. Not the least of these has been the viciously irresponsible attacks of Wisconsin's know-nothing Joe McCarthy. Acheson has had utterly no opportunity to proceed in a slow and deliberate manner. He has had to function literally under constant heavy shelling.

In view of these and other handicapping circumstances, Acheson, on the whole, has done very well as regards his staff. If it isn't the best that it should be, it is the best in the history of the State Department.

And that in itself is a titanic achievement.

In addition to the shortcomings of his staff, Acheson has still another serious personnel problem. This is the many weaklings in the corps of ministers and ambassadors who represent us abroad. In some instances the fault is not Acheson's. But in others it is, and with no credit to him.

An example of this is in England, where Acheson has let old friendship cloud his judgment. He has kept in office Ambassador Lewis Douglas, whom Truman would like to fire because of Douglas' fraternizing with the Republicans during the 1948 campaign. Whatever his political defections, however, Douglas should be ousted for another reason.

He has been a wholly unsatisfactory representative of the American people.

He is hostile and cold to the British Labour government and has let his private reactionary predilections sway his official judgment. Several times, Anglo-American relations have fallen to dangerous lows. Only their desperate predicament has prevented the British from becoming altogether sour on America. Much of this is Douglas' fault. It is a common saying in London that the closest the American Ambassador ever comes to mixing with the British people is when daughter Sharman dances with a British playboy.

Ambassador James Dunn in Italy is another Old Guardsman who is meddling in the affairs of a country in the throes of social upheaval, while he himself has nothing to offer but high-button-shoe philosophy.

In Latin America, the level is even lower.

In Argentina, we are represented by Stanton Griffis, a New York investment banker who owns the Brentano bookstore chain, plus Madison Square Garden and a chunk of Paramount Pictures. Griffis since the war has been—in quick succession—envoy to Poland, Egypt, and Argentina. This could indicate he was a very versatile and talented man. Or it could indicate what is really the case: Griffis comes across when the plate is passed at campaign time.

The same is true of Richard C. Patterson, former United States Ambassador to Yugoslavia and now nominally Ambassador to Guatemala. Patterson got into diplomacy by first becoming a Tammany contractor and then sharing some of his gains with the party as treasurer of the Democratic National Committee. He knew so little about Yugoslavia when he was appointed Ambassador that, when someone asked him if he knew anybody in Yugoslavia, he replied, "Oh, yes, I know Beneš very well."

Beneš, of course, was a Czech. He was just about as much a Yugoslav as Patterson.

In Guatemala, Patterson tangled with the left-wing government. The situation was admittedly difficult, since the regime is to some extent infiltrated by Communists. It is "halfway to Poland," as one observer remarked. But Patterson was so blatant and crude in his tactics that, in the end, the State Department had to call him home indefinitely. What country he will be inflicted on next is conjectural.

In India, Loy Henderson holds forth. He is the veteran Near East "expert" who consistently knifed President Truman's Palestine policy in 1947-48, in a desperate effort to protect his old Arab friends. Henderson was not on the payroll of the Arab League; he only acted that way.

When Acheson took over, he was anxious to oust Henderson from his strategic job as chief of the Near East Division. The problem was how to do that, as Henderson was strongly entrenched. Acheson finally hit upon India as a good place to junk him. There, this aging careerist, who is the champion among the now passé striped-pants clique as a wirepuller and inside manipulator extraordinary, has been something less than a howling success.

Prior to Prime Minister Nehru's visit to this country in 1950, Henderson completely misled the administration on the extent of Nehru's pro-American sentiment.

Acheson and Truman expected the Indian leader to come out openly on our side against Russia and to lead the way in the formation of an anti-Communist, pro-American bloc in Asia. When he got to Washington, they discovered that, while sympathetic to us, Nehru was very much a fence-sitter and was determined to keep his country neutral in the cold war. The disappointment in Foggy Bottom was intense, and the big build-up for Nehru's visit, including the speech to Congress and all the rest, fell embarrassingly flat.

Henderson had been blathering through his hat again.

The United States Ambassador to Turkey is George Wadsworth, another career man and pasha of the Arab cult within the State Department's Near East Division. Wadsworth was Henderson's hatchet man when both were striving mightily to commit mayhem on the infant Republic of Israel.

In the fall of 1947, after the President and Secretary Marshall had both come out officially for "partition" (that is, the creation of an independent Jewish state in Palestine), Henderson brought Wadsworth home from the Near East and gave him orders to go to the UN meetings in New York and spread the word around that the President was only talking for home consumption, and that the United States did not "really" favor the Jews. As a result, Liberia and several Latin American countries, which usually follow our lead in UN matters, voted contrary to our position when the Palestine question came to a ballot. This was a product of Mr. Wadsworth's ardent and intensive lobbying.

Since the failure of his mission against the Israeli, Wadsworth has decided to take life easy. In Ankara, where he now holds forth, he is best known for his monumental laziness and his weakness for playing cards, especially bridge. Bridge is Wadsworth's passion. He plays not only in the evenings but in the afternoons as well. Next to Arabs, our discriminating Ambassador loves "Blackwood" best of all.

Top-flight ministers and ambassadors are not easy to find, in or out of the State Department. So Acheson is doing the next best thing. He is trying to integrate the Foreign Service into the Department and eventually hopes to make it possible for experts, now outside the Foreign Service and consequently chained to Washington, to go abroad on alternating assignments with the career men. Meanwhile, he has taken several preparatory steps which diminish the "caste" nature of the Foreign Service.

No longer can the Service hire and train its own employees, make and spend its own budget, and control its own promotions. All that was handled by Deputy Undersecretary Peurifoy in the same way he performed these functions for the rest of the Department, and his successor, Humelsine, is continuing that policy.

In the past year, the career diplomats, like the Navy admirals, have had to rejoin the American Union. Acheson inherited an array of difficult problems in various fields. For example:

Latin American affairs under Marshall were in the feeble hands of Assistant Secretary Norman Armour and the bunglers who surrounded and manipulated him. Never in the past twenty years did American policy in this hemisphere sink so low as during 1947-48.

The ultimate and crushing debacle came at the Ninth Inter-American Conference at Bogotá, Colombia, in May, 1948.

The man chosen to be president of the Conference was Dr. Laureano Gómez, a friend of Hitler, twice decorated by Franco, a long-standing enemy of the United States, and who was detested by the mass of people in his native Colombia. But that wasn't all. The president of the Commission on Human Rights was none other than the delegate from the Dominican Republic, a despotism where no one has any rights except Dictator Trujillo and his corrupt friends. Moreover, in the opinion of experienced observers, "the United States sent to Bogotá the least impressive delegation it has sent to any recent Hemisphere meetings."

In the midst of the deliberations, a fierce riot erupted, which stalled the Conference for days and highlighted the desperate poverty, misery, and decay which exist behind much of the façade of Latin American society. As the Department lamely explained, the riots were fostered in part by local Communists. But there was ample unrest for them to exploit, and the State Department took no steps to deal with a probable explosion. Nor, indeed, did they even anticipate one.

When the parley was resumed, the Argentine delegation promptly objected to including any statement about the "rights of man" in the Conference report. It also opposed any attack on Russia or communism.

At this point, Assistant Secretary Armour stepped in and made a characteristic deal. The "rights of man" pronouncement was scrapped in return for Argentine acceptance of a hypocritical and meaningless statement against "subversive action."

Once again, "we bargained away our democratic principles in order to keep the 'good will' of the Gaucho of the Pampas."

Marshall had only two aims in his Latin American policy. One was to line up the South American countries into a solid phalanx against Russia, and the other to get an agreement to standardize South American armaments with those of our own military forces. This second project was a pet scheme of the late Defense Secretary James Forrestal. In order to put it across, Marshall yielded not only to Perón but to all the other Latin American dictators and would-be dictators.

The Bogotá Conference, therefore, adopted the shameful doctrine that whenever a new government took over in the Western Hemisphere, no matter how bloody or fraudulent its seizure of power, it should be recognized immediately. This was supposed to "consolidate" the anti-Communist front.

Meanwhile, back in the United States, Congress failed to warm up to the idea of arms standardization, and nothing came of the matter.

Youthful Edward G. Miller took over this mess under Acheson.

The main fruit of his policy so far has been the granting of the $125,000,000 loan to Perón in the spring of 1950.

In a way, this marks a return to the Welles-Duggan policy of talking in a "soft" tone: a combination of shrewd, realistic bargaining and friendly cultivation. Miller has no illusions about what a phony blowhard and posturing bully Perón is. But, at the same time, Miller does not feel that the mailed fist is feasible. Like Duggan and Welles, he feels that forcing Perón out is too difficult and dangerous. Perón is to be brought within the family—but kept at arm's length.

Unquestionably, it was a grievous blow to Perón's prestige that his gross mismanagement of Argentina's economy should become so grave that he had to come crawling to Washington for a handout. It spiked, for all to see, his noisy pretensions of being the dominant power in the Western Hemisphere.

If Miller follows up this score effectively, then the loan may bring political advantages in other parts of South America that will be worth the price.

The greatest dilemma which Acheson took over when he became Secretary of State is our relationship with Russia.

On this, Acheson's position is firm and consistent. He outlined it clearly in a press conference discussion following the speeches of Senators Brien McMahon and Millard Tydings in the spring of 1950. Acheson told the reporters:

"If we could reach our goal by agreement, of course that would be highly desirable and the simplest and easiest way to do it. But I think four years of experience have brought us the realization that that is not possible.

"The Soviet government," he continued, "is purposeful and determined but also highly realistic. We have seen time after time that it can adjust itself to facts when facts exist. We have seen also that agreements reached with the Soviet government are useful when those agreements register facts or a situation which exists, and that they are not useful when they are merely agreements which do not register the existing facts.

"Wherever a situation of weakness exists in Asia or Europe, it is not only an invitation but an irresistible invitation for the Soviet government to fish in those troubled waters. To ask them not to fish, and to say that we will have an agreement that you won't fish, is like trying to deal with a force of nature.

"You can't argue with a river; it is going to flow. You can dam it up, you can put it to useful purposes, you can deflect it, but you can't argue with it.

"Therefore we go to work to change these situations of weakness so that they won't create opportunities for fishing and opportunities for trouble."

It is this policy of creating "situations of strength" in critical areas that is the core of Acheson's program. Upon this will depend his historical reputation—and America's safety. The returns are not yet in.

Already, however, his battle lines have been under attack from many sides on different issues and under many pretexts.

First, there was the effort to pin the disaster in China on the State Department. This charge was politically inspired from the first. Acheson's firm stand on the South Korea invasion, whatever long-range results it may have, buried forever the myth that he favors appeasement in Asia.

Another attack on Acheson took the form of McCarthy's smear campaign. This got under way with the advantage of a lapse of judgment by Acheson. Questioned on the conviction of Alger Hiss, he declared simply, "I shall not turn my back on Alger Hiss." He referred his hearers to an appropriate section in the Bible which explained his position. Acheson's stand was a beautiful Christian gesture. But it was very bad politics.

Acheson's defense of Hiss had a lot of precedents in American history. President Grant, while in office, took the stand and testified on behalf of his secretary, who was charged with bribery. But, as Drew Pearson pointed out, "Roosevelt undoubtedly would have used a different strategy from Acheson's. He operated on the theory that . . . a good field commander must remain behind the lines while his troops —and friends—were necessary casualties in battle."

As McCarthy's bombast began to collapse from lack of evidence and its multitude of contradictions, Herbert Hoover opened an attack on a different level. The ex-President came out for scuttling the United Nations and abandoning our allies in Western Europe. This brought him the sound bashing on the head he so richly deserved. The proposal lapsed into oblivion for a while.

And, of course, all the while the old-time hatchet men such as Representatives John Taber, Clare Hoffman, and Joe Martin did their isolationist utmost to cut foreign aid appropriations and sabotage our foreign policy by indirection.

Others raised the cry that the Department is full of homosexuals and other perverts.

This endless clamor on so many side issues all swirls about Acheson's head. Some say he is much to blame personally, because he high-hats Congress. Others argue that he fails to get his message across to the public. Neither allegation is correct, though each has an element of truth.

It is true that Acheson sometimes seems to be looking down his nose at certain members of Congress. That is scarcely something for which he can be blamed. Who doesn't! It doesn't take a bishop's son who went to Groton to look down one's nose at a political hoodlum like Joe McCarthy or a political hillbilly like Joe Martin. It is the natural reaction of every decent human being who knows them at close range.

Nor is it correct to say that Acheson cannot get his message across to the public. His prepared speeches do often read better than they sound. But no one can surpass Acheson as an off-the-cuff speaker. No one in this administration, and few men outside it, could have put on the brilliant extemporaneous defense of his staff which he made before the American Society of Newspaper Editors in the spring of 1950. And in personal conversation, Acheson is regarded by many who knew Franklin Roosevelt well, as the most persuasive talker since the late President.

The trouble is that speech making and barnstorming are activities for which the Secretary of State has no time these days. Acheson might do it superbly if he had the leisure, but he doesn't have it. This is something he must leave to the President.

Here, the difficulty is that Truman is not sufficiently versed in foreign affairs to be able to sell the Acheson program very well. The President never gets beyond broad generalities and vague aspirations.

The real tragedy is that the constant sniping and mudslinging at Acheson have inhibited him. He is capable of big and daring things.

He might be able to outgeneral the Russians even better than he has done, if he had the time to reflect. But he is hampered and hobbled by the constant savage onslaughts of his detractors. Whatever thinking he does, he has to do while on the run.

He suffers as a result. But his country is the real loser.

But despite Acheson's occasional failures, the variegated quality of his staff, the weakness of his political position, and his own defects of temper, he is essentially on the right road. It is not an easy or clearly defined road. Back in 1946, when he was Undersecretary, Acheson made a speech to the Associated Harvard Clubs in Boston in which he defined the way ahead as cogently as he could. What he said then applies just as pertinently now.

"For a long time we have gone along," Acheson said, "with some well-tested principles of conduct: That it was better to tell the truth than falsehoods; that a half-truth was no truth at all; that duties were older than and as fundamental as rights; that, as Justice Holmes put it, the mode by which the inevitable came to pass was effort; that to perpetrate a harm was always wrong, no matter how many joined in it, but to perpetrate it on a weaker person or people was particularly detestable. . . . Our institutions are founded on the assumption that most people will follow these principles most of the time because they want to, and the institutions work pretty well when this assumption is true.

"It seems to me," Acheson continued, "the path of hope is toward the concrete, the manageable. . . . But it is a long and tough job, and one for which we as a people are not particularly suited. We believe that any problem can be solved with a little ingenuity and without inconvenience to the folks at large. . . .

"And our name for problems is significant. We call them headaches. You take a powder and they are gone. These pains about which we have been talking are not like that. They are like the pain of earning a living. They will stay with us until death. We have got to understand that all our lives the danger, the uncertainty, the need for alertness, for effort, for discipline will be upon us.

"This is new to us. It will be hard for us. But we are in for it, and the only real question is whether we shall know it soon enough."

THE PENTAGON BRASS

On a rolling stretch of intricately paved and landscaped Virginia countryside directly across the Potomac from Washington squats the huge building that is the intellectual center and administrative core of the nation's far-flung military forces.

This plain, unadorned structural giant is the famed Pentagon.

Its aloof location is symbolic of the place the Armed Services hold in the country's mind today.

That place is a no man's land between the traditional attitude toward the military in time of peace and the traditional attitude in time of war. In peacetime, the military man is a neglected figure, regarded by himself as a drudge and by the country as a drone; in time of war he is the idolized hero, regarded by the country—and by himself—as the peerless savior of the republic, humanity, and democracy.

In the past, the average serviceman fought one war in his lifetime and spent the other thirty years going to seed. Drinking, sex, and aimless chores filled his arid days. Military life was not intellectually demanding or stimulating.

Army and Navy librarians during the war reported almost unanimously that it was not the Regulars—either officer or enlisted man—who patronized the libraries; it was the inductees from civilian life. General Eisenhower freely admits that his favorite reading is Wild West pulp stories. When he became head of Columbia University in 1948, a friend gave him a book and "Ike" replied, "Thanks, I appreciate this very much and I'll try to read it. To tell you the truth, I haven't read a book in nine years." Eisenhower is well above the mental level of the average regular officer.

The old peacetime American attitude toward the soldier was accurately summed up by a Russian. In his epic novel *War and Peace,* Leo Tolstoi wrote:

"A secret voice tells us that we must be to blame for being idle. If a man could find a state in which while being idle he could feel himself to be of use and to be doing his duty, he would have attained to one side of primitive blessedness. And such a state of obligatory and irreproachable idleness is enjoyed by a whole class—the military class. It is in that obligatory and irreproachable idleness that the chief attraction of military service has always consisted and will always consist."

But in time of war, the nation's attitude changes overnight. Yesterday's lazy, posturing nonproducer becomes the prototype of all that is fine and noble in society. "Our boy," "our hero," "our savior."

He is glorified in the movies, in public speeches, and on the front page of every newspaper. His sacrifices are extolled and his virtues acclaimed. Even his defects, such as moss-bound traditionalism, lack of initiative, and instinct for rigid conformity, are transformed into attributes and labeled prudence, discipline, and national unity. His long, empty, dreary years at remote and inbred posts and stations, which have eroded and stultified many a capable officer, are glossed over as a valuable period of education and preparation. The soldier becomes the hero, his desires commands, his needs primary, his qualities peerless.

The Truman administration came to power in 1945 just as World War II was ending, and throughout the administration's span the military has dangled in an uneasy state between peacetime indifference and wartime adulation.

To the public, and especially the large economy and isolationist elements, the military has been at once an onerous burden and a prized bulwark. Similarly, the tremendous and unprecedented power of the military has been deeply distrusted and resented at home yet hailed as a comforting shield abroad.

These endless paradoxes have been confusing and disquieting both to the country and to the military.

Neither has had a chance, in the agonized peaceless, warless world we are living in, to decide just what is the role of the military in our nation of today.

The military establishment is fabulously large in size and inexorably strident in its demands on the national economy.

More than 2,100,000 are in uniform. In addition, the military has another million civilian employees, a number greater than the total that worked for all government agencies in 1933. Since 1947, the military has never had less than one-third of the federal budget. Today, the ratio is more than fifty per cent.

Both to improve the combat effectiveness and administrative efficiency of the three Armed Services, Congress in 1947 finally enacted the so-called "unification" law. What precisely is meant by "unification" is still a smolderingly bitter issue. The fierce controversy killed the first Secretary of Defense, and the fate of his grimly embattled successor has still to be written.

The struggle over unification is the crimson thread running through the whole pattern of the military establishment in the Truman regime.

At the vortex of this struggle is Secretary of Defense Louis Johnson, who has very definite ideas of what unification should mean and the guts and savage determination to put them over. Whatever else he may or may not do, Louis Johnson will leave an imprint on the Armed Services that they will bear for a long time to come.

That is one reason why a lot of the high brass secretly hate him. They know things will never be the same again. Johnson persistently makes them uncomfortable.

Illustrative of this attitude is the following story going the rounds in Navy circles. A young lieutenant did not show up at his Pentagon desk one day, and his colleagues became concerned. One recalled that the lieutenant had expressed the intention to stand outside the Russian Embassy and tell the Soviet Ambassador to go to hell and take Joe Stalin with him.

"If he really did that, it could be serious," an officer said. A hurried check disclosed that, sure enough, the young lieutenant was in the hospital. His friends rushed over to see him. They asked if he had gone through with his daring plan.

"I sure did," he replied. "I waited till the Ambassador came out and then I yelled, 'To hell with Stalin,' and the Ambassador shouted, 'To hell with Louis Johnson.' We were embracing each other in the middle of the street when a taxi hit me."

The anecdote graphically expresses the general Navy opinion of Johnson, whose name has become a cuss word at Annapolis. That does not perturb him in the least. He is used to being sworn at. Big, two-fisted, and tough-skinned, Johnson has been hitting hard and getting his way for most of his life.

He was born in 1891, in Roanoke, Virginia. His maternal grandfather had been one of Robert E. Lee's more dashing Confederate lieutenants. His father was a smalltime grocer. Johnson early showed his get-up-and-go spirit. He still has the first fifty-cent piece he earned selling beans he had grown himself.

In high school, he was top man in his class and played a slashing game as guard on the football team. Even in Sunday School, his restless energy displayed itself. At fifteen, he became head of the local Epworth Methodist League and soon built a whole network of Leagues under his control. At the University of Virginia and subsequently at its law school, he continued to manifest his passion for running things. He was president of his class three times running, set up an alliance of small fraternities and "independents" which dominated campus politics and made him kingpin, was the top student in his class, and won the wrestling and heavyweight boxing championships.

Finishing law school, Johnson cagily decided to begin practice in Clarksburg, West Virginia, a small town then enjoying a boom in natural gas and oil. Both law and politics were wide open, and Johnson moved right in. He went up fast. He scarcely had his hat off and his suitcase open before he ran for mayor as a Democrat and lost by only thirty votes in what had always been an overwhelmingly Republican stronghold. Two years later, he won a seat in the legislature and promptly took the whole State Capitol by storm. At twenty-six, he was Democratic Floor Leader and chairman of the Judiciary Committee.

That was 1917. Johnson interrupted his career to join the Army; he went overseas and fought in the Meuse-Argonne offensive.

In 1919, when he returned, Johnson married the wealthiest girl in Clarksburg and began specializing in big-time clients. In a few years he was in the $50,000-a-year class and more active than ever in politics and the American Legion. In 1930, he became State Commander and for two years was National Commander.

Johnson first strode onto the Washington stage in the same sphere in which he is now officiating—the military. Roosevelt named him Assistant Secretary of War, and Johnson immediately turned loose his driving energies to revitalize the comatose Army. He had a tough time because Roosevelt's interest was centered on the Navy, and Johnson's immediate superior was Harry Woodring, a small-bore, reactionary, isolationist politico from Kansas.

The feud between the two men steadily worsened until by 1939 they did not speak to each other unless business demanded it. Finally, in June, 1940, Roosevelt kicked Woodring out, but instead of elevating Johnson, he appointed Republican Henry Stimson, at the instigation of Felix Frankfurter.

Johnson swallowed his disappointment and campaigned for Roosevelt. When war came, the President sent him to India as chief of Lend-Lease. There he tangled with Henry Grady, senior American envoy, and even more with the British. This warmly endeared him to Gandhi and Nehru. In Johnson's office today is a photograph of Nehru signed, "To Louis, in friendship." In 1949, when Nehru visited Washington, the one American he wanted to see besides the President was Johnson.

The years immediately after the war Johnson spent shuttling back and forth between his law offices in Washington and Charleston, West Virginia. His business grew to factory proportions. He employed fifty attorneys, had clients like Montgomery Ward and the New York Life Insurance Company, and made more than $300,000 annually. In addition, he drew a $50,000 salary as president of the General Dyestuff Corporation, a German firm seized by the Alien Property Custodian during the war and subsequently "Americanized."

In 1948, Johnson took over the financial end of Truman's campaign when others wouldn't touch it with a ten-foot pole. Johnson produced in a big way and frankly expected to be rewarded the same way. He was—with the Defense portfolio. It was his greatest ambition. For nine years he had waited and hoped to return to the cabinet in the military field, and he finally made it.

Johnson is a curious man. He loves to have responsibilities thrust on him and to exercise authority. That in itself is not unique in a power-seeking city where ambition is as common as rain. But what is different about Johnson is that he does not mask his ambition with coy disclaimers or hypocritical dodges. He is frank and aboveboard about it.

He eschews the social racket, does not play cards, and rarely attends a cocktail party. His private life is austere and aloof. His visitors, and they are many, label him cold, self-seeking, and hard-driving. His partisans swear by him fervently as a forthright square-shooter and a loyal and unwavering friend. One thing is certain:

Johnson is one of the Capital's most controversial big shots, and he likes it.

Possessed of great drive and energy, he is iron-willed, self-confident, and self-sufficient. He had to be to take on singlehandedly the arrogant and rebellious admirals and their press and congressional satellites and kick them resoundingly in the pants. That took raw courage and steely resolution.

Johnson is the first civilian since the late great Josephus Daniels who had the guts to do that. It is no small achievement.

When Johnson took over in 1949, he assumed command of a Defense establishment riddled with conflict, intrigue, and spiteful and vicious disunity. Chief reasons for that, aside from the carefully nurtured and perpetuated rivalries and jealousies of the services, were the defects of the unification law of 1947 and the administrative failings of Johnson's predecessor, James V. Forrestal.

Never did a man turn a more misleading countenance toward the world than the late James Forrestal.

His grim, taut expression, flat, broken nose, thin, almost nonexistent lips, and the jaunty, compact set of his body all indicated a man who was tough, quick, self-possessed, and resolutely effective. But that was not the case. Forrestal was far from being what his outward appearance implied.

The son of an immigrant Irish politician in New York, Forrestal worked his way through Princeton, had to quit in his senior year because of lack of funds, entered the investment banking business, and worked his way up slowly through the hierarchy of Dillon, Read and Company. By 1940, he had amassed a considerable fortune and turned to public service. Roosevelt gave him a chance as one of the "passion-for-anonymity" assistants and then shifted him to Assistant Secretary of the Navy. Upon Secretary Frank Knox's death in 1944, Forrestal was upped to the top post.

But throughout his whole career Forrestal was not the firm, decisive administrative leader he so strikingly seemed to be. Actually, he never tackled problems or conflicts head on and foursquare. He approached them in a cautious, tentative manner. His instincts and methods were those of the wary banker rather than the bold executive. Also, Forrestal was at heart a bookish man with strong leanings toward the life of the intellectual. He frequently talked of retiring from public life and becoming a newspaper or magazine editor.

The one indispensable prerequisite for the job of Secretary of Defense is the capacity to make tough decisions, fast and firmly. This quality was tragically lacking in Forrestal.

His weakness was gravely magnified by the nature of the Unification Act. It did not provide for unification at all.

True unification was first proposed during the war by the Army, but actual work on the plan was postponed until the emergency was over. In 1945, President Truman directed Clark Clifford, then his Assistant Naval Aide, to get the military services together on a unification measure. The Army promptly offered an expanded and detailed version of its wartime proposal.

This called for merging the Armed Services into a single Department of Defense headed by a Secretary and three Assistant Secretaries who would be in charge of procurement, research, legislative liaison, public relations, and all the other common activities of the services. The Joint Chiefs of Staff, set up as a temporary organization by Roosevelt during the war, would be made permanent. But instead of each service being represented by a Chief who would be an equal partner with a veto, one Chief of Staff was to be named for all three services. He, in turn, would have a staff made up of an assistant, or deputy, Chief from each of the services.

The Navy went into paroxysms of rage. It howled, bit, clawed, and lobbied frenziedly against the proposal.

The official spokesman of the Navy in this jeremiad was Navy Secretary James Forrestal.

He demanded that any consolidating be limited to a "form" of unification, politely termed "coordination." As Forrestal expressed it, the Secretary of Defense would be a "persuader and mediator," not a ruling executive with power to make final decisions.

Truman strongly favored the Army concept but did not actively intervene in the fierce melee.

Much of Forrestal's opposition was the undercover inspiration of Ferdinand Eberstadt, a fellow alumnus of Dillon, Read, and a wartime civilian aide of the Secretary of the Navy. Finally, under Eberstadt's prompting, Forrestal agreed to accept some concessions. A two-man military team, consisting of Admiral Forrest Sherman, now Chief of Naval Operations, and Air General Lauris Norstad, then head of Plans and Operations for the Army, was appointed to work out the details. Their plan, reshuffled to some extent by Congress, finally became what is known as the Unification Act of 1947.

This provided for a Secretary of Defense and three "Secretaries" without cabinet rank to head the Army, Navy, and Air Force. Each of these service Secretaries had the authority to go over the Defense Secretary's head and appeal directly to the President on budgetary and other questions. Further, there was no direct line of authority from the Defense Secretary down. He worked only through the three service Secretaries whom he could not dismiss or overrule. They were responsible only to the President who appointed them.

The Joint Chiefs of Staff were retained, but each member continued on a par with the others, and all decisions had to be unanimous. Each Chief had an absolute veto, like that of the Russians on the UN Security Council.

Finding someone to take over this nebulous new job of Secretary of Defense did not prove easy. Finally, Truman offered it to the most adamant foe of unification, Navy Secretary Forrestal. This was a gesture to the Navy to reassure it that Navy interests would be protected and that the other two services could not "gang up" on it. Forrestal accepted.

Then the long agony of indecision began.

Asked to agree on a budget, the Chiefs came up with a combined request of $32,000,000,000. What that amounted to, in effect, was a demand for nothing less than a separate and complete Defense establishment for each of the services, each to have its own Army, Navy, and Air Force. The rest of the country, the burden-bearing civilians, would have to get along with the scraps left over by the military.

At the heart of this whole bewildering but ferocious conflict is a deep-seated difference over the basic mission of each service and strategy.

In the past, it was the national policy to keep the Navy at near full strength in time of peace, as the main "defense force in being." The Army and subordinate Air Force were allowed to deteriorate, to be built up by emergency efforts in time of war. Reason for this traditional system was geographic. The only way an enemy could reach us was across two great oceans. The Atlantic and Pacific were our mighty defenses in depth. Therefore, as long as we had a Navy to ward off attack, we could afford to get along with only a skeleton Army and Air Force.

World War II changed all that. Science, in the form of long-range bombers and the cataclysmic A-bomb, wiped out the oceans that for more than one hundred and fifty years had been our national bulwark.

The youthful, cocky Air Force strode forward and stridently demanded that it—and it alone—henceforth be the main "defense force in being." It now was the possessor of the answer to averting enemy assault on the homeland. Through its mighty bombers, the Air Force would atom-bomb the enemy and smash his offensive power before he got started.

That is the concept of the "strategic counteroffensive" and was summed up by the Finletter Commission on Air Power as follows: "We . . . must have in being and ready for immediate action a counteroffensive force built around a fleet of bombers, accompanying planes, and long-range missiles which will serve notice on any nation which may think of attacking us that, if it does, it will see its factories and cities destroyed and its war machine crushed."

The Army does not dispute the basic thesis of this concept. But it does emphatically reject the corollary, implicit in it, that strategic bombing alone can subdue an enemy. General Eisenhower, in his final report as Chief of Staff, declared, "Today the only element of the military establishment that can hold a defensive position, seize for exploitation a major offensive base, exercise direct complete control over an enemy population—three fundamental purposes of armed effort—is, as always, the foot soldier."

The Navy goes much further. It repudiates the Air Force theory *in toto*.

The seagoing admirals cling unyieldingly to their ancient contention that control of the seas is the primary essential for sound national security. Therefore a big Navy is absolutely indispensable.

The fact that Russia—sole threat to the peace of the world—is notoriously weak in naval strength is blandly disregarded by the choleric admirals. Similarly, they suffer from a pronounced "Bikini complex." That A-bomb test proved beyond refutation that planes carrying this fearful weapon can sink the biggest and best ships afloat, while those that do not directly suffer that fate become untenable through ineradicable lethal radiation.

The air admirals have a stronger and more appealing case.

They came into their own in World War II and they desperately —and rightly—fear that the Air Force is bent on gobbling up their newly won power and prestige. In their furious resistance, the flying admirals center their fire on the so-called "polar concept." This is the idea publicized by Air General George Kenney that the next war will be fought via the North Pole. The Great Circle offers the shortest and quickest flying route to Russian targets—and vice versa, of course. The air admirals caustically deride the polar concept. They point out that storms in the polar region are so numerous and fierce that losses due to weather alone would be prohibitive. Also, that electromagnetic disturbances jam sensitive flying instruments and would cause havoc for any closely planned expedition.

The air admirals propound a theory of their own concerning the next war. They contend that if the Russians overrun Europe, they will become virtually invulnerable. With no European land bases and beachheads available to us, we will be unable to get at them. The only answer, therefore, is to build huge floating bases, specifically 65,000-ton super-aircraft carriers.

This, in broad outlines, is the pattern of the three-cornered struggle which raged from September, 1947, when Forrestal took over as Secretary of Defense, until March, 1949, when he was succeeded by Johnson. Within six months after assuming command, Forrestal confessed to the President that he could not do the job successfully without some of the very powers which he had vehemently opposed granting the Secretary of Defense.

Belatedly, Forrestal discovered what he had been warned against by Secretary of War Robert Patterson and other able and veteran administrators of military affairs—that it would be impossible to control the brass without cudgels in the form of a real mandate. That is all they understand and all that works with them. Voluntary give-and-take, restraint, moderation mean utterly nothing to them where their jealous service interests are involved. No entrenched monopoly or vested interest fights more violently than does the military for its "empires."

In an effort to resolve the grave double impasse that confronted him —preparing the 1949 budget and, even more important, deciding on strategic planning—Forrestal finally began a round of anguished conferences. Endless, weary weeks were spent in wrangling at the Pentagon, all without result. In the hope that a change of scene would help, he shifted the parleys to Key West and then to Newport. But still no lasting accord. General Bradley kept voting resolutely for the Army, Admiral Louis Denfeld for the Navy, and General Hoyt Vandenberg for the Air Force.

Meanwhile, the presidential election was drawing near, and the view became general that, since Dewey was going to win, everyone might as well mark time and see what he wanted done. Forrestal shared this attitude. Unfortunately for him, his job—unlike that of the generals and admirals—was not permanent. When Truman won, Forrestal lost.

When, a few months later, Johnson became Secretary of Defense, it quickly became clear that if anyone was going to have a nervous breakdown in the Pentagon, it was not going to be Louis Johnson.

His first and prompt major move was to wield the ax on the 65,000-ton super-aircraft carrier which the Navy had started building without express authorization of Congress. As Brigadier General Robert Ginsburgh, one of Johnson's aides, explains, "The Secretary believes that strategy is a matter of common sense. He has as much common sense as the next man. If the generals and admirals can't convince him of the merits of a project, then he decides it is not sound." Ginsburgh also has on his wall a drawing of a turtle with the boldface inscription, "Consider the turtle; he makes progress only when his neck is out."

Johnson continued to move rapidly on other fronts. Unification, efficiency, and economy became the watchwords, and Johnson wasn't fooling. He never does. The fact that his hard-boiled prodding and driving was bitterly resented by most of the brass and was slowly driving the frustrated admirals berserk didn't disturb him at all. He kept right on hammering away. When his new budget slashed more "fat" from the Navy, the admirals really blew their tops and broke out into open revolt.

This rebellion was, of course, not called that. The admirals and their subordinate me-tooers had not yet reached the stage of their Latin-American counterparts who, when miffed, resort to shooting up the government. The admirals confined themselves to shooting off their mouths—with unrestrained indecency and shamelessness.

These iron-handed demanders of discipline and unquestioning obedience from others had no hesitancy themselves in violating every tenet of the military code and credo. They literally ran amuck.

The admirals cloaked their insubordination in a rash of phony issues and charges, such as that there was something smelly about B-36 procurement and that the value of the giant bomber as an offensive weapon was highly questionable. They even went to the astonishing hypocritical length of shedding crocodile tears over the wholesale slaughter of civilians by A-bombs. This was the grisliest farce of all.

Admiral Ralph Ofstie, who put on this sanctimonious act, was the very same warrior who, some months before, had thundered at a New York audience, "The A-bomb is the main shot in our armament locker. The delivery of the atomic bomb both should be and probably is a major consideration today in the war plans of the Air Force and of Naval Aviation."

Probably the most acute commentary on the whole shambles was made by Edwin A. Lahey, forthright correspondent of the *Chicago Daily News,* who wrote: "The odd part of the present struggle is that the school-tie admirals should in desperation try to appeal to the public which keeps them. It is the first time that I can recall that they even recognized the public."

The admirals launched their offensive in a manner in keeping with its nature and their conduct. They pulled a sneak smear attack.

A mysterious, unsigned letter was sent to members of the House and Senate charging that the Air Force's vaunted B-36 was a much overrated weapon and that it would never have been built at all if it were not for the fact that Louis Johnson wished to throw a lush contract to the Consolidated Vultee Aircraft Corporation, of which he is a former director and of which Floyd Odlum, a Wall Street financier and heavy Democratic contributor, is chairman of the board. Playing a big role in this undercover job was Representative James Van Zandt, Pennsylvania Republican and a truckling Naval Reservist who wants passionately to be an admiral.

Van Zandt is the same brass-galled politico whose idea of helping the desperate struggle in Korea, early last July, was to announce in a hoopla speech that U.S. troops would be forced to abandon the peninsula in seventy-two hours. Van Zandt gave the impression he had inside information—which was utterly false. He knew so little about what was going on that he didn't know that at that very time two divisions were on the verge of debarking in the battle area and other much greater reinforcements were rapidly approaching. But with Van Zandt, like his fellow Republican Joe McCarthy, anything goes that will produce a headline.

After a thorough investigation of the anonymous accusation, the House Armed Services Committee officially declared it had found not "one iota, not one scintilla of evidence" to substantiate the charge.

After the collapse of this poison-pen attack, a new figure entered the fray. Admiral Louis Denfeld, Chief of Naval Operations, began to play a peculiarly equivocal role.

A stodgy, conservative, easygoing Navy politician, Denfeld had spent many years in the Bureau of Personnel. There he got to know practically every officer in the Navy. He also became adept at inside politicking. Ambitious in an amiable, good-natured way, he was very fond of being referred to as "Uncle Louie."

Although he was clearly totally unaware of the fact, the revolt of the admirals was actually a damning reflection on Denfeld. It branded him a failure on two counts: he was so weak as a commander that he was incapable of controlling his subordinates; and they felt they had to accomplish in an underhanded way what he had failed to do with the Joint Chiefs.

When the storm first began to blow up, Denfeld showed a disposition to play along with his civilian bosses. As the October deadline for resumption of House Committee hearings approached, Denfeld and Navy Secretary Francis Matthews conferred with Representative Carl Vinson. They all agreed it would be wisest to postpone any further investigating until Congress reconvened the following January. Any more fulminating in public would seriously damage the prestige of the military in the eyes of the nation and might give away valuable information to the Russians.

Matthews and Denfeld summoned a group of top-flight admirals to explain this and win a pledge of support. The majority acquiesced. But a minority, headed by Admiral John Price, Vice Chief of Naval Operations, balked at a postponement unless Admiral Arthur Radford, commander of the Pacific Fleet and the spiritual leader of the Air clique, should agree. Radford was not in Washington. Matthews insisted, and the group seemed to back him up. The revolt appeared to have been nipped in the bud.

But the next day the full story of the meeting was published in the *Washington Post.*

"It was," Matthews later remarked bitterly, "as if the reporter had taken notes under my desk." The reporter had not been present, but one of the rebels was. As soon as the meeting ended, the story was deliberately leaked to the *Post* in such a manner as to give the impression the admirals were being gagged.

On the afternoon of October 3, another conference was held in Matthews' office. This time Radford was present. After he had made his argument for an immediate and public probe, Vinson reiterated his stand for postponement. Once again the rebels appeared to have lost.

That evening a Navy officer, lurking in a dark, shadowy corner of a building, passed out copies of a document to summoned reporters, giving them permission to use it in full as long as he was not identified.

The "mysterious officer" was Captain John G. Crommelin, who was just dying to be a martyr. The document he distributed was a blistering letter which charged that unification was destroying Navy morale. The letter had been written by Vice Admiral Gerald Bogan, commander of the First Task Fleet, and approved by Radford. But most sensational of all, it also bore the signature of Denfeld.

It later developed that Denfeld had been pressured by the admirals into signing a blank sheet of paper which Bogan filled in!

The disclosure of this letter had the desired effect. It forced Vinson to reverse himself, and the Armed Forces Committee voted by a margin of one to hold public hearings immediately.

That was the opportunity for which the rebels had been conniving desperately for months, and now there was no stopping them. They stormed in like raging tornadoes to destroy Johnson, Matthews, unification, the Air Force, the B-36, strategic bombing, the polar concept, and everything else to which they objected. That they should seriously have thought they could execute this mass scuttling illustrates graphically their brazen insolence, gross insubordination, and glaring lack of perspective. It showed them up as a herd of exigent bulls who functioned by feel instead of reason.

After the admirals got their long-sought chance to yak in public, their testimony was a laughable anticlimax. They had no concrete facts and few specific grievances.

Admiral Radford, for example, led off with an astoundingly incongruous lecture on the need for loyalty and then drearily rehashed the stale facts of the B-36 controversy. Others attempted to propound the theory that the atomic bomb would do little damage a short distance from its target. A year and a half earlier, Admiral Dan Gallery had written a secret memorandum in which he said, "It seems obvious that the next time our Sunday punch will be an atomic bomb." Of course, nothing was said about that now.

How Denfeld would testify was in doubt almost to the end. He at first agreed to confer with Secretary Matthews on the scope of his testimony. But at the last moment he capitulated to the rebels and read a ringing pro-Radford declaration which Matthews never got a chance to examine until he saw it in a press release.

Denfeld, trapped in his own tortuous game of pussyfooting, won the resounding applause of his nominal subordinates. But that is all he won. Matthews told him, "Your usefulness as Chief of Operations is at an end."

For the remainder of the hearings, "Uncle Louie" was at the beck and call of the rebels. On the afternoon on which General J. Lawton Collins, Army Chief of Staff, concluded his rebuttal testimony, Radford stepped outside the hearing rooms and telephoned Denfeld at the Pentagon.

"Louis," Radford said, "I thought you were going to be here today." Denfeld explained he had been tied up with budget matters.

"Well, you should have come over," retorted Radford. "Now you take Collins's statement and go over it thoroughly tonight. There are parts in it that we must refute. We can't let them go unanswered." Denfeld said he would read the statement.

The counterattack of the other Armed Services was devastating.

General Hoyt Vandenberg stated the Air Force's case in a restrained but crushing manner. General Omar Bradley, chairman of the Joint Chiefs of Staff, delivered a paralyzing knockout. In a flat, unemotional voice, Bradley recalled the Pearl Harbor disaster and pointed out that it could have been avoided by "complete understanding, cooperation, and trust" among all the services. "That fatal day," he said, "should have taught all military men that our forces are one team, in the game to win regardless of who carries the ball."

"This is no time," Bradley continued, "for 'Fancy Dans' who won't hit the line with all they have on every play unless they can call the signals. Each player on this team—whether he shines in the spotlight of the backfield or eats dirt in the line—must be an 'All-American.' "

General Collins, speaking for the Army, delivered the *coup de grâce*. His concluding statement put the whole issue in its simplest terms. Paraphrasing a Navy spokesman who had said, "What is good for the Navy is good for the country," Collins declared, "What's good for the country is good for the Army, the Navy, and all the other Armed Services of the United States."

The peevish revolt of the admirals was not a pretty spectacle. It was a disgrace to them as officers, to their service, and to the country. For despite all their pious objections to unification, strategic bombing, etc., etc., what the admirals were really up to was far deeper and more sinister.

This affair at its core was a brass-hat rebellion against civil authority.

It was a defiant attempt to overthrow civilian control of the Navy and to make the admirals the masters not only of their own service but, in effect, the rulers of the entire military establishment. Like the Russians in the UN Security Council, the admirals proposed either to rule or ruin.

To the everlasting credit of Secretaries Matthews and Johnson, the admirals did not get away with their rebellion. The honor, morale, and efficiency of the Navy is all the better for that.

The admirals lost, but the Navy won.

This tumult was only one of the many problems which Louis Johnson faced in his first year as head of the Defense establishment.

One of the main claims made for unification was that it would result in tremendous savings in money and, even more important, in human skills, matériel, facilities, time, and lives. The savings that might have been made during World War II and were not, and the incredible inconsistencies and confusion which resulted both at home and overseas are innumerable. Some of them were detailed in a confidential G-4 report in 1947 by Lieutenant General LeRoy Lutes, Army Procurement Director. Generally known as "Lutes No. 2," this penetrating study was later suppressed by President Truman.

The U.S. government, Lutes noted, spent in excess of $160,000,000,-000 during World War II for equipment and supplies—more than $4,000 for every family in the country.

In spending this vast sum, Lutes pointed out, competition between the services was "stiff" and procedures were chaotic. Apparently it was unthinkable for the top brass of the Army and Navy to get together and formulate a common set of procurement regulations. Instead, each issued its own, the Navy publishing frequent and lengthy directives while the Army produced a 5,000-page opus in two volumes. But this was only the beginning.

Lutes reported the following divergencies and conflicts in policy:

"One department purchased component parts of needed items and furnished them to contractors to perform final assembly; the other service required that the assembler . . . subcontract similar items. One department permitted contractors to include reserves for contingencies in contract prices but did not permit subsequent inclusion of reserves for contingencies, but instead permitted contractors to negotiate price increases resulting from unexpected events beyond their control. One department was willing to exempt certain contracts from renegotiation if it could be determined in advance that a close price had been set; the other department did not generally allow such exemptions. One department required the contractor to send notice of shipment; the other did not. One department provided for upward adjustments of prices if state or local taxes increased; the other had no similar provision.

"Such differences are unavoidable unless policies and procedures are jointly worked out and uniformly administered."

Many other indefensible practices prevailed. One was the "freeze-out." Under this wasteful and obstructive tactic, one service tied up a company's facilities for years with a big backload of orders. When another service attempted to get quick emergency deliveries of the same or some other product, it found itself frozen out.

In many instances, differences in specifications between the two services were so minor as to be ridiculous. Both, for example, bought ten-ton bridge trestles from the Michaels Art Bronze Company, Covington, Kentucky. The Army and the Navy each furnished the concern with separate drawings, and the manufacture of the trestles was carried on as entirely separate operations. Yet the only difference in specifications was in the spacing of the drilled holes. But this utterly stupid and incomprehensible difference was just enough so that in an emergency only a small portion of the costly equipment was interchangeable.

Other tremendous wastes occurred in the field because of lack of unification. On one occasion, 250,000 rations were lost on Guam because covered storage space was not available for one service, while at the very same time a lot of *non*perishable supplies were being stored under cover by the other service.

Morale suffered repeatedly for this reason. "Time after time," declared Lutes, "in outfits side by side, soldiers would receive one kind of treatment and sailors another kind." Many times near mutinies occurred when soldiers were ordered to unload cases of beer or Coke to be drunk not by themselves but by sailors. Reverse incidents were equally numerous.

In England, the Army and Navy used identical trucks; yet the speed limit for one was 25 miles per hour and for the other, 40 miles per hour. Throughout the war and everywhere, the record of the Army and Navy was one of divided responsibilities, reduced efficiency, increased over-all requirements, and fierce competition.

Lutes's report put its finger on the central issue of the heatedly controversial "Johnson economy program":

"We are certain that the matériel demands of any future war will not be less than those of the last," said Lutes. "It may become, then, a simple matter of survival. Whether we use our resources efficiently or not may very well be the determining factor between victory and defeat."

That, in a few words, is what Johnson tried to do. His primary purpose was to put into effect the savings of men, money, and matériel which are possible if unification is honestly and effectively applied.

Ex-President Hoover told Congress that savings up to $1,500,000,000 could be made in the 1949 military budget. "And by savings, I mean attaining the same ends for less expenditures," he added tartly.

It was deeply ironic that the man who headed the Hoover Commission "task force" that chronicled the failures of unification was the same Ferdinand Eberstadt who, during the 1945-46 controversy, had masterminded the Navy's successful fight against unification. Eberstadt had much to do with writing the 1947 Unification Act which neither unified nor coordinated the three services but only established a liaison among them.

One high Pentagon official who was in on the whole struggle from the outset remarked, "If ever there was a man who was asked to act as coroner at his own autopsy, it was Ferdinand Eberstadt."

Johnson tackled this situation from two directions at the same time.

He led a vigorous drive that put through Congress a number of changes strengthening the Unification Act as recommended both by the Hoover Commission and by Forrestal in his last report. Simultaneously, Johnson introduced the brusque, direct method of knocking heads together whether or not he always had the power to do so and, in effect, daring the doubting parties to do anything about it. Anguished howls went up, but, of course, nobody did anything about it.

Three weeks after he took office, he abolished twenty-one military boards and committees. A month later, he wiped out twenty-seven other commissions and agencies. And, within the following month, he deposited seventy-five more interdepartmental committees in the ash can. In July, 1949, he changed the boundaries of Naval Districts so they would conform with those of the Army and Air Force. He also set up a unified Military Sea Transportation Service and a Joint Army-Air Force clemency and parole board.

Johnson also endeavored to introduce some order and consistency into the budgetary and bookkeeping procedures of the three services. An example of their chaotic methods is the way they handle the accounting of research and development work.

In 1949, the Army spent $112,000,000 on this vital activity, the Navy $203,000,000, and the Air Force $215,000,000. Actually, the Navy spent closer to $300,000,000 and the Air Force probably only $150,000,000. These differences were due to the deceptive nature of their respective bookkeeping systems. The Navy lumps a great deal of the cost of its research into the cost of each ship it builds. It charges to "research" only the salaries of scientists and the materials they use. Clerical help is charged to another account entirely. The Air Force, on the other hand, includes under the heading of "research" the cost of buildings, heating, office help, janitors, guards, and a host of other miscellaneous items.

The result is, as one expert pointed out, that the Research and Development Board, which is supposed to coordinate military research, is trying to coordinate the uncoordinatable.

"The Board," declared this authority, "cannot tell within fifty per cent what the several services are spending on research, or how they are apportioning such funds as they are known or suspected to be spending. The Board would like to come within ten per cent to maintain an effective control on emphasis. As it stands, if the Board decided that guided missiles were the thing to concentrate on, and the Navy thought Anti-Submarine Warfare, the chances are that the Navy would stress ASW anyway—and there would be no way for any civilian authority to find out about it or control it before it was all over."

This effort to bring some sense and coherence to the crucial field of military research is only one example of the incredibly difficult and complex problems which Johnson faced. It also demonstrates the falsity of the highly prejudiced clatter that attacked Johnson's budget reforms as penny pinching. The crux of the whole matter is whether the constituted civilian executives of the country shall exercise effective control over the military or whether, because of defective knowledge or lack of courage, they continue as prisoners in the hands of their military subordinates.

That was and still is the issue among the Pentagon brass.

In riding herd on this vast military organization, Johnson relies heavily on his staff of right-hand men.

These include Undersecretary Steve Early, the canny newspaperman who served as Roosevelt's press secretary and who gave up a $50,000-a-year job with the Pullman Company to return to public service; and three special assistants: Wilfred J. McNeil, who acts as the comptroller; Paul H. Griffith, Pennsylvania Republican and ex-National Commander of the American Legion, who handles personnel and public relations; and Marx Leva, in charge of legal and legislative affairs.

This is a high-powered team. Early, tireless, profoundly hep and experienced, and widely popular, has saved Johnson from many blunders. It is no exaggeration to say that Early is Johnson's smartest appointment and has been worth his weight in gold to Johnson and to the Defense Department. It will never have a better man than Steve Early. McNeil is efficient and hard-driving. Leva is a brilliant, highly personable young Southerner who served as Justice Hugo Black's secretary before the war and was Forrestal's adviser on legislative matters. Griffith isn't up to the caliber of this group, but he serves his purpose. He is an old crony of Johnson's and a fellow kingmaker in the Legion. Griffith has an imposing roster of duties on paper, but his chief job is to serve as buffer between Johnson and various political and other nuisances.

Johnson also set up a top Management Committee to centralize the procurement of all supplies. There has been some criticism of the fact that the head of this key unit is a military man, General Joseph T. McNarney, who is thus in a position to overrule civilian executives like the Secretary of the Army. This is a legitimate complaint, particularly if the practice becomes widespread in the Pentagon. But of immediate moment is the question of McNarney's capabilities. Unless he has improved since his far from outstanding days on General George Marshall's wartime staff, McNarney's record in his present position will be something less than brilliant.

Johnson has put great stress on the role of the Munitions Board, an agency which was almost defunct under Forrestal. Johnson's attitude is a carry-over from his prewar experience as Assistant Secretary of War.

In those days, he shouted from the housetops about the need for industrial preparedness. Now he has an agency whose express function is to think and work along those lines, in conjunction with Stuart Symington's National Security Resources Board. The Munitions Board is deep in the monumental task of preparing a common catalogue covering the five million different items of equipment used by the services. This catalogue will replace fifteen systems and parts of systems and will, it is hoped, eliminate at least some of the confusion and waste spotlighted by the Lutes Report. The Board is also consolidating individual service regulations into a single Armed Forces procurement system.

Much of the waste in the military services, however, is due to human or historical causes which Johnson has been unable to get at readily.

There is the traditional, and often intense, rivalry among the services which leads them to try to outdo one another in everything from airplanes to uniforms and officers' clubs. There is the matter of retaining on the active lists many proven incompetent and unfit senior officers solely because they "belong." But the most basic reason for waste is the attitude inbred in the services that if you want two things, you ask for five in the hope of getting three.

Generals invariably ask for an army when they need a regiment, or for a million blankets when they need a hundred thousand.

This tradition has developed partly because most military officers have little sense of responsibility in spending money, and partly because Congress and the civilian chiefs have never been able to get together on any consistent long-range planning. Appropriations run only from year to year; everything is on a feast-or-famine basis. Military men ask for everything they can get this year, for fear that next year Congress may not be so sympathetic.

The responsibility of Congress for this wasteful and chaotic budget situation cannot be minimized. It is very largely to blame for much of the "fat" in the military appropriations.

It is Congress, for example, that has insisted on coddling and pampering the semiautonomous Army Engineers—one of the most powerful, arrogant, and pernicious lobbies in Washington. Talk about power-hungry and self-perpetuating bureaucracies—this is it, in person! The Engineers squander hundreds of millions of dollars on boondoggling river and harbor projects which Congress eagerly approves solely because of their local pap and patronage appeal.

When Johnson took over the Defense Department, he inherited a full complement of civilian administrators, including Secretaries of the Army, Navy, and Air Force, plus the usual roster of undersecretaries, assistant secretaries, etc. Even under the newly revised Unification Act signed in September, 1949, these officials retain considerable autonomy and independence. Forrestal found this hobbled him at every turn. Johnson has not allowed these restrictions to bother him too much. He bypasses and overrules them with little hesitation and no qualms.

Further, he short-circuited the law by "packing" the top civilian jobs with men who will be loyal to him first and to their particular service second. From Forrestal he inherited Army Secretary Kenneth Royall; Navy Secretary John L. Sullivan, an admiral-controlled Forrestal henchman; and Air Secretary Symington. It was an open secret that Johnson was not enthusiastic about them and vice versa. Royall soon left. Sullivan resigned over the super-aircraft carrier cancellation. Symington finally departed in the spring of 1950 for the National Security Resources Board. He, too, left with no tears from Johnson.

To replace this trio, he brought in Francis Matthews, Omaha lawyer, to head the Navy Department; Gordon Gray and subsequently Frank Pace to head the Army; and Thomas Finletter to replace Symington. Matthews and Pace are strongly beholden to Johnson. Finletter is different.

He is the author of the famed Finletter report that first advocated seventy combat Groups and is the Bible of the Air Force. His experience and intimate knowledge made him the logical choice to succeed Symington, and President Truman was strong for him. That clinched it, and the appointment has worked out very well. He and Johnson get along smoothly and effectively.

Secretary of the Army Frank Pace is a young man of a non-Fair Deal background and non-Fair Deal views. His meteoric career is proof that, in the Truman administration, the less liberal you are, the farther you get.

Pace's father was the leading lawyer in Little Rock, Arkansas. Pace graduated from the local high school at fourteen, attended the fashionable Hill School at Pottstown, Pennsylvania, for two years, then went to Princeton and Harvard Law School. In college, Pace was a good student, but he was better known as a crack poker player and a bridge fiend who played with experts such as Oswald Jacoby and Eli Culbertson.

In law school, Pace was one of Felix Frankfurter's students, but he is not a typical member of the "happy hot dogs" clique. He did not become a Frankfurter protégé. As a student, Pace developed a penchant for the almost mathematical intricacies of tax law and after graduation took a job with the Arkansas Tax Bureau. This gave him very useful appellate experience; Pace argued his first case before the U.S. Supreme Court in 1939 when he was only twenty-seven.

After the war, Pace came to Washington as a tax specialist on Attorney General Tom Clark's staff, but he soon moved to the Post Office Department as administrative aide to Bob Hannegan. In 1949, he succeeded James Webb as Budget Director. In this job, he won Truman's admiration and complete support by his hard work, quiet affability, and flattering air of youthful deference. When Gordon Gray resigned as Army Secretary in 1950, Pace was Truman's personal choice for the post.

Pace is a tall, relaxed, athletic-looking young man with black, curly hair (which, like his last budget, is rapidly showing a deficit), and a soft Arkansas twang. He talks in flaccid, lawyerlike language. He professes to have no political ambitions and approaches his succession of top-drawer jobs with the mathematical mind of an accountant and the tireless capacity for work and indomitable good spirits of a young hound dog. Pace thoroughly enjoys life, and his only regret is that he cannot get out to the golf links and tennis courts more often. He is a two-time golf champion of the National Press Club and tennis champion of the Congressional Club. His social horizons are sharply delimited by the business and country-club set he has always moved in. Today's means and not tomorrow's ends are what interest him.

Pace's only preparation for the job of Secretary of the Army consisted of some work on the revision of the Unification Act while he was Budget Director. Like his predecessor in that office, James Webb, whom the President personally made Undersecretary of State, Pace was shifted to the Pentagon as an efficiency man to bring a traditionally moss-bound and managerially inept service into better working order. How he will make out in these pressing times is a grave question. His knowledge of the Army and of military matters is desperately thin.

But Pace started out better equipped than many of his top-echelon colleagues in the Truman administration. He has an alert mind and a fund of youthful energy. The brass may put something over on him once but not twice. Pace learns fast.

Air Secretary Thomas Finletter is a wealthy New York lawyer who has been in and out of the Washington scene for almost a decade.

During the war, he served as an aide to Cordell Hull. He stayed on under Stettinius and helped arrange the San Francisco United Nations Conference in 1945. Next, Truman named him chairman of the special Commission on Air Power. It was this group which formally promulgated the Air Force's demand for seventy combat Groups. Following this, he spent eighteen months in England as special Ambassador in charge of ECA. Returning to private life, he wrote a provocative study on the defects of the congressional system called *Can Representative Government Do the Job?*

Finletter is bald, dignified, and has a pleasant, dry wit. He is married to the daughter of Walter Damrosch, the famous conductor. He is friendly with and moves in the same social and intellectual orbit as Lewis Douglas, Ambassador to England, and John McCloy, U.S. High Commissioner for Germany. Like them, he is an able, high-minded conservative with a yen for public life. He is a serious, well-read man who has plowed through books like the six-volume *Study of History* by Arnold Toynbee—a feat which testifies to his perseverance if nothing else.

Finletter will need all his ability and perseverance as Air Force Secretary. The "fly boys" are wild and woolly and, in their way, just as insatiable, high-handed, and incorrigible as the admirals.

Secretary of the Navy Francis Matthews is also a wealthy lawyer and businessman.

Before coming to Washington, he was active in Catholic charities, in the Chamber of Commerce, and, in a modest way, in Nebraska Democratic politics. He readily admits he then knew nothing about the Navy. He views his job as an administrative one; he lets the admirals handle the military problems.

Matthews is a cheerful, friendly, sentimental man who likes to show people pictures of his grandchildren and to reminisce about his early days as a struggling lawyer. His candid, old-hat manner is most refreshing in Washington, where stuffed shirts and eager beavers are the two dominant species. In his casual, informal way, Matthews sometimes forgets that others are not as well to do as he is. A friend tells the story of talking with Matthews one day about a log cabin the latter was building. "I have a log cabin, too," the friend remarked, "my place has two rooms."

"Oh," replied Matthews, "you're only talking about a place to take shelter in a storm. My cabin has twenty-six bedrooms and a private chapel."

The friend agreed that wasn't exactly the kind of cabin he had in mind.

It is to Matthews' great credit that he is strongly disliked in certain diehard Navy circles because he had the guts and integrity to bring the rebellious admirals to book. He knows this full well. As he remarked, "Because I fought, certain officers will always hate my name as they hate that of Josephus Daniels, the last Secretary who openly tangled with them."

For decades the Navy has been the spoiled brat of the military. Two strong-willed Presidents, Theodore and Franklin Roosevelt, personally espoused the service. Two great industries—steel and shipbuilding—back it powerfully. The Navy League ferociously fights its propaganda battles. Any Secretary who tries, like Josephus Daniels or Charles Edison, to control the admirals is knifed and obstructed at every turn.

Even Forrestal had his troubles. He was far from a foe of the admirals. He carried his affection for the Navy to the point where he had his office painted blue and outfitted with ship's clocks and portholes. Yet the admirals did not always trust him. In the end he had personally to go to the communications room and read messages which his subordinates kept from him.

Moreover, the Secretary of the Navy is hobbled by laws, put through by the admirals, giving semi-independent status to the heads of various bureaus, such as Ordnance. Also, he is weighed down by overpowering tradition and institutional custom which make the Navy almost a closed corporation impossible for a newcomer to master and effectively control. Ferdinand Eberstadt, although a staunch Navy man, wrote a fascinating memorandum for Forrestal in 1945 explaining, in effect, why the Secretary of the Navy cannot be Secretary of the Navy. Said Eberstadt:

> "There is, always has been, and always will be as long as the principle of individual responsibility and exclusive authority [of the bureaus] is continued, a centrifugal force in the Department of the Navy that the usual Secretary possessed of fragmentary knowledge cannot withstand. What all this means superficially is that the Navy Department is a defective administrative mechanism—it provides no adequate device by which subordinate agencies may be made immediately responsive to the will of a central intelligence. . . .
>
> "Under such conditions it is inevitable that the administration of the Navy has been entrusted primarily to the indi-

vidual bureaus. The supreme civil authority in ordinary times is, in practice, isolated from the real activity of the organization over which he presides. . . . At the best, as one Secretary recently pointed out, he has acted ordinarily as an umpire between the bureau chiefs when they disagree; but it should be added, he has perforce to act as an umpire with no very certain grasp of the rules of the game.

"It is interesting," Eberstadt continued, "to investigate the reasons why the Navy Department has been held on an administrative dead center; to discover the sources of the tremendous inertia that has opposed successfully the centralization of authority in the Department for a century."

One of the reasons Eberstadt pointed to was the attitude of the officers themselves:

"Those men associated with the bureaus have traditionally and naturally found it desirable to preserve the integrity of their vested interests. . . . [The officer] knows, almost by instinct, where sources of authority can be found; where roads to promotion lie, where he fits in the scheme of things. Within this rigid framework all officers know how to deal with each other, with Secretaries, with congressmen, and with the public."

Matthews, forthright, honorable, and well intentioned, took over the Navy and readily acknowledged he had never skippered anything bigger than a rowboat before and that he had doubts about his ability to run the Navy. He didn't have to wait long to learn how tough his job was.

He was quickly confronted with all the service's "tremendous inertia" that Eberstadt outlined so clearly, plus the bitter shock of outright insubordination and treachery. Matthews soon discovered what other conscientious and patriotic executives had found out before him, that he was dealing with men who had baffled the most eminent statesmen of our time. Henry L. Stimson, once Secretary of State and twice Secretary of War, was one such great public servant. His experiences with the admirals were related in the book *On Active Service in Peace and War,* by Stimson and McGeorge Bundy, in a passage which is destined to become a classic:

> "Some of the Army-Navy troubles grew mainly from the peculiar psychology of the Navy Department, which frequently seemed to retire from the realm of logic into a dim religious world in which Neptune was God, Mahan his prophet, and the United States Navy the only true Church. The high priests of this Church were a group of men to whom Stimson always referred as 'the admirals.' These gentlemen were to him anonymous and continuous; he had met them in 1930 in discussions of the London Naval Treaty; in 1940 and afterwards he found them still active and still uncontrolled by either their Secretary or the President. This was not Knox's fault, or the President's, as Stimson saw it. It was simply that the Navy Department had never had an Elihu Root. 'The admirals' had never been given their comeuppance."

Matthews may not have as profound and lasting effect on the Navy as Elihu Root had on the Army when he was Secretary of War fifty years ago. But there is little doubt he is the first iconoclast in a long time to get a foothold within the dim, mysterious church that is the Navy. It will be to the eternal credit of the homespun prairie lawyer that he gave "the admirals" their comeuppance—for a little while, anyway.

Army Chief of Staff J. Lawton Collins is in the unenviable position of the player in an All-Star game who comes to the plate after Tommy Henrich, Ted Williams, and Joe DiMaggio have batted. He may be a very good hitter but he is sure to suffer by contrast with those who preceded him. Collins became Chief of Staff of the Army after the post had been filled successively by Generals Marshall, Eisenhower, and Bradley. Anyone would be hard put to it to equal their performances.

"Lightnin' Joe" Collins is the man to match their record if anyone can do it. He is an exceedingly able officer who ranks high by any computation.

Collins first came to prominence during the Normandy invasion when he was a Corps commander. In the early, difficult weeks he held his assigned position despite fierce German counterattacks. Like General "Rock of Chickamauga" Thomas of Civil War fame, Collins displayed the same tough, stubborn, bulldog determination to hold on till hell froze over.

In the kaleidoscopic campaigns that followed, Collins displayed other qualities in addition to those of the fighting gamecock. He showed he could think under pressure and move with lightning swiftness when necessary. There was little doubt by V-E Day that Collins was the outstanding Corps commander in the ETO and one of the coming men in the Army.

Thereafter, he held a variety of assignments, including Director of Army Public Relations. He revealed that he can talk just as effectively as he can fight. He is unusually articulate as a speaker, in contrast to the average tongue-tied military man. Collins is fluent, vigorous, and absorbing.

In the summer of 1948, General Bradley created the new post of Vice Chief of Staff and promoted Collins to the job. The next year, Collins succeeded him in the top spot. Here he has set some kind of record as an astute diplomat.

Collins has won the cordial esteem of the other services. In fact, a leading Navy officer rates him higher than Marshall and Eisenhower. In the Navy's view, Marshall was too academic and Eisenhower too parochial. (An added reason is that the Navy has always resented the fact that during the war Marshall and Eisenhower were elevated in the popular mind to a point where they could not be sniped at by the Navy. In this same period, the Navy was saddled with Admiral Ernest J. King, a mediocre stuffed shirt who could not hold a candle to either Marshall or Eisenhower and who was generally—to the Navy's dismay—widely recognized for precisely what he was.)

Collins has essentially a political temperament in the best sense of that expression: he is frank, warm-hearted, ingratiating, and ambitious.

A handsome, square-shouldered Irishman of medium height, he cuts a trim and dapper figure in his natty battle jacket, which is tailored to be form-fitting and suitable for youth and not for a general in his fifties. Few officers of any age can wear this type of uniform as dashingly as Collins. Also, unlike many of his West Point comrades, he has not frozen into a pompous brass hat. He remains as genial and pleasant as he was thirty years ago as a "shavetail."

Collins knows his way around in the game of Army politics. He has to. No man ever reaches the top without learning those ropes. Army politics is as hectic as any in civilian life.

Every time a new Chief of Staff is to be appointed, the whole upper echelon of the Army is arrayed in contending camps. Friends of the outgoing Chief strive furiously to put over one of their crowd, so that their chances for promotions, choice assignments, and other perquisites will not be endangered. At the same time, various other aspiring cliques are just as active trying to put their champions over. Illustrative is what happened when General MacArthur's term as Chief of Staff expired in 1935, and he angled for a reappointment. But Roosevelt named the late General Malin Craig, an old Cavalry protégé of General Pershing.

Immediately, heads rolled. MacArthur partisans were eliminated from top jobs and members of the Pershing-Craig faction installed in their places. One of the beneficiaries of this shake-up was a Colonel George Marshall, a crack Pershing staff officer in World War I whom MacArthur had exiled to duty with the Illinois National Guard. Marshall was soon promoted to Brigadier General, and three years later became Craig's Deputy Chief of Staff. In 1939, Marshall succeeded to the top command.

The war shook up Army politics drastically because a number of unknowns made big reputations and others had "palace" reputations unmade—by the Germans. But the intriguing, conniving, and scrambling for advancement and self-perpetuation continued as before.

The Eisenhower-Bradley partisans generally played ball with one another and formed one group. Marshall protected the interests of certain protégés and old friends such as General Joseph McNarney and General Wade Haislip. In passing, it may be noted that Marshall's War Department staff during the war was one of the least competent in history—a curious fact in view of his own indubitable high caliber. But his right-hand assistants were practically all third-rate and worse. It can be truthfully said that the war was won in spite of them. Collins' staff is head and shoulders above its predecessor.

The history of the postwar period has been one of unsuccessful struggle by the other factions to oust the Eisenhower-Bradley bloc and of constant shifting alliances which occurred in the effort to bring that about.

Eisenhower was the inevitable choice to succeed Marshall, and when Ike retired to academic life, he strongly recommended Bradley. This choice was heartily approved by Truman. But if Roosevelt had lived, it is probable that General Mark Clark would have been given the post. He was a personal friend of both the late President and Mrs. Roosevelt. In fact, Clark was FDR's fair-haired boy, and he skyrocketed to high command once the war began. Roosevelt steadfastly supported Clark, despite a number of grievous blunders which Clark and his notoriously hack staff committed in Italy. If Clark had succeeded Eisenhower as Chief of Staff, there would have been sweeping changes and a whole new setup brought in. But Truman passed him over in favor of Bradley. When the latter was promoted to chairman of the Joint Chiefs in 1949, Clark was again passed over in favor of Collins, a relatively young Eisenhower man.

Clark is now rusticating as head of the Army Field Forces. This is a virtually useless command that the Army retains for the sole purpose of providing a handy pigeonhole for discarded four-star generals who are not old enough to be compulsorily retired and won't do so voluntarily.

Meanwhile, however, General Alfred Gruenther, who was Clark's Chief of Staff throughout the Italian campaign, deftly untangled himself from Clark's aegis. This is a tribute to Gruenther's agility and ability, which are very real. Gruenther had served under Eisenhower when the latter was with the Third Army before the war. It was a friendship that paid off nicely years later. In 1947, Gruenther was named staff director of the Joint Chiefs and later was moved up to his present job, Deputy Chief of Staff for Plans and Operations. Here he serves just below Collins and General Haislip, Marshall's old friend who has survived his mentor's departure and is now Vice Chief of Staff for the Army.

Gruenther is much more than an adroit politician. He has a keen, incisive mind, an extraordinarily retentive memory, tremendous capacity for hard work, and a suave, ingratiating personality. He graduated from West Point in 1918, fourth in his class, and spent most of the '20's as an instructor there. At that time he gained a national reputation as a bridge player and both played in and refereed national tournaments.

Like practically everyone else in the Pentagon, Gruenther is ambitious. He is well thought of by Louis Johnson and by congressional leaders. He may well be Collins' successor as Chief of Staff. In any case, he is a good bet for the job some time in the next ten years.

General Hoyt Vandenberg is "Mister Air Force" himself. He has all the *élan,* dash, and good looks the public romantically associates with Air Force men. That Vandenberg is a proud grandfather does not detract from his glamour one bit.

Some critics have sniffily attributed Vandenberg's rise to the claim that he is a glad-handing playboy and the nephew of powerful Senator Arthur Vandenberg of Michigan. Neither aspersion is true.

Vandenberg won his four stars on his own—plus a lot of luck in surviving many years of military flying.

Vandenberg rose steadily during the 1930's, throughout which period his uncle was in the political ash can and carried no weight with the War Department or any other part of the Roosevelt administration, for that matter. It is true the General enjoys the Washington social whirl, but that does not prevent his putting in long hours at work. Vandenberg made the grade strictly on his merits; every promotion he received, he earned by his brains and courage.

He has an enviable combat record. Throughout the war, he flew dangerous fighter and bomber missions. He has been flying all his life. He started with the Air Force when all it had were canvas-covered crates that a Hollywood stunt man would not fly today. The Air Force in those days had only a few hundred men, and the rate of attrition was high. It is frequently forgotten that while Army and Navy men rarely die in line of duty in peacetime, Air Force personnel risk—and lose—their lives every day. Vandenberg survived those dangerous years. That took considerable luck, but also skill and courage as well.

During the admirals' revolt, Vandenberg handled himself exceed-

ingly well. The Air Force followed the smart strategy of saying nothing and letting the admirals hang themselves.

These were wildly spoiling for a fight with their hated rivals.
Nothing would have suited the admirals better than to bait their foes
into a roaring brawl. And there were a number of Air Force firebrands
who were itching to slug it out. They were as eager to tangle with the
admirals as the latter were to fight. But Vandenberg clamped down
on them. He not only ordered them to say nothing but took precau-
tionary measures to ensure that they would keep silent.

General Curtis LeMay, the daredevil who instituted the spectacular
low-level bombing raids over Tokyo, and General George Kenney, the
fierce protagonist of the polar concept, were actually assigned special
press officers who had instructions to keep them from sounding off and
causing an incident.

Vandenberg is an old hand at coping with Congress. During budget
hearings, he is adept at singing the old Army blues,

> "We ain't got enough
> You're doing us wrong."

On one occasion, however, he was caught short. The Air Force's
"Pacusan Dreamboat" had made its record flight, and the Navy, in an
effort to steal the thunder, had its plane, the "Truculent Turtle," make
a distance flight. Several days later, Vandenberg went before the House
Armed Services Committee to testify on a pending bill. Representative
Dewey Short, (Rep, Mo.), who was feeling a little under the weather
that day, asked, during a lull and apropos of nothing at all, "Say, General, what do you think about the 'Mock Turtle'?"

Vandenberg stared in puzzled silence.

Another committee member broke in, "I think you mean the 'Truculent Turtle.'"

"That's right," said Short. "I guess I had soup on my mind."

When Admiral Forrest Sherman was a boy of twelve, he spent the
summer sailing with his grandfather in a small boat off New Bedford.
On one of those excursions the old man dropped dead. The youngster
coolly brought the craft back by himself.

Forty years later, Sherman was summoned home from the Mediterranean to take command as Chief of Naval Operations. This time he
faced heavy squalls of opposition and the bitter charge that he was
taking over to scuttle the ship and not to save it. But Sherman showed
in this crisis the same deliberate calm and self-control he had displayed
as a boy.

Sherman at fifty-three is the youngest CNO in the Navy's history.
He is the first aviator to hold the post in peacetime. This twin accomplishment is the product of steadfast ambition, cool-headed calculation,
and the intellectual and temperamental capacity for high command.

Envious Navy critics of Sherman are fond of carping, "He was born
an admiral."

He was certainly born for the sea. At the age of seven he decided
to make it his career. He never swerved from that early enthusiasm.
He spent his childhood summers sailing with his grandfather, a retired
whaling captain. The old sailor filled him with the lore of ships and
the men who sailed them. Sherman graduated from Annapolis in 1917,
just in time to serve in World War I. He came out of the Naval Academy second in a class of 203. During his days there, he acquired the
nickname "Joe," but it did not stick. He is not a man to be nicknamed
or back-slapped.

Sherman turned to aviation after the war, because he had the vision
to grasp that air power was the coming thing in warfare. He won his
wings at Pensacola in 1922 and rose steadily during the peacetime
years. When World War II came, he went to sea in command of the
"Wasp." A Jap submarine torpedoed the carrier off the Solomons in
September, 1942. Sherman fulfilled the Navy tradition; he was the last
man to leave his sinking ship.

But his grateful crew will always remember him for another quality
just as precious as bravery but not so common—presence of mind
under fire. As the "Wasp" began to go down, its forward section was
swept by fires from the fuel and ammunition stores. A strong wind
blew the flames back over the carrier. Sherman, standing on the burning bridge, ordered the ship's course reversed. But remembering that
there might still be men left in the forward section, he had the presence of mind not to order the "Wasp" brought fully around but only
part way, to a position where the wind swept the flames over the side.

This action saved the lives of one hundred and thirty men who otherwise would have been trapped in the bow.

Wartime comrades also recall Sherman as a great champion of chief petty officers; he was always stressing the importance of these noncoms. One friend laughingly relates, "I swear I think that some time in his career Forrest Sherman must have been about to pull some awful boner and a grizzled old petty officer grabbed him by the arm and set him straight. Sherman's been grateful to all petty officers ever since."

After losing his ship in combat, Sherman became chief of staff to Admiral John Towers, one of the earliest and greatest of Navy champions of air power and wartime commander of Naval Aviation in the Pacific. Later, Sherman became war plans officer for Admiral Chester Nimitz. He excelled in these two staff jobs. By the end of the war, he was marked as destined some day to be Chief of Naval Operations. What was surprising was that the appointment came so soon and under such stormy circumstances.

After the war, Nimitz brought his brilliant protégé to Washington and made him his Deputy Chief of Naval Operations. Sherman was the principal Navy negotiator who sat through all the early struggles over unification. In 1946-47, he negotiated with General "Larry" Norstad the basis of the original unification law. It was at this time that Sherman first became a target for criticism from the more frenetic of his colleagues. Radford and his clique opposed the separation of the Air Force from the Army and felt it marked the permanent setting of the sun for Naval Aviation. Sherman dissented from these gloomy tirades and went ahead with his work.

Sherman's next assignment was the command of the Sixth Task Fleet in the Mediterranean. In the next two years, he sailed the rim of the cold war and watched closely the deterrent effect that the presence of the American fleet had on Russian moves in that ancient cockpit. Sherman is a man whose mind turns instinctively to large concepts and broad perspectives. He is a master geopolitician and has steeped himself in the writings of authorities on that subject. His return to Washington brought one of the nation's few top-flight politico-military intellects to the inner council rooms of the Pentagon.

Sherman took over a Navy seething with dark, confused resentments and frustrations. He was viewed by the more rebellious partisans as another Judas degrading himself and betraying the Navy's "cause" by taking the thirty silver pieces of power. Momentary resentments, however, inevitably spend themselves; rancor ebbs away. But Sherman moved into "a dim religious world" catacombed with old rivalries, ancient hatreds, and complex intrigues that had histories far older than the revolt over unification.

The Navy is like a giant spiral: there are factions within factions, cliques within cliques that wind their way inward as far as one can see. Annapolis graduates (the "trade-school boys") look down on officers who have risen from the ranks (the "Mustangs"). Seagoing Navy men (the "black-shoe Navy") look down on the naval aviators (the "fly boys"). The latter, in turn, are always careful to distinguish themselves from aviation personnel which does not fly (the "Airedales"). The surface fleet looks down on the submarine men in more ways than one. And, of course, no one looks down on a "damnmarine" (also known as "gyrene" or "seagoing bellhop") more than their half brothers in the Navy—a distaste which the haughty Marines return with more than equal intensity.

Further, within each of these segments there is an endless web of factions and coteries. The Navy itself moved to break up one of these —at least on paper—when it forbade the "Green Bowlers," a secret fraternity at Annapolis, to "tap" any more recruits. It had long been felt in Navy circles, despite facile statistical demonstrations to the contrary, that all the plushy jobs in the service were monopolized by Green Bowlers, who always play ball with one another.

Particularly acute today is the tension between the aviators and the seagoing black-shoe Navy. The aviators have had to wage a long and rugged battle for recognition. Even before the Wright brothers had successfully flown an airplane, a Navy board investigated the subject and reported, "The Board is . . . of the opinion that such an apparatus as is referred to pertains strictly to the land services and not to the Navy." For forty years, Navy air enthusiasts struggled to smash this persistent prejudice. Not until 1940-41 did they begin to get wide acceptance of their views among the top brass. The island-hopping campaigns of the Pacific war brought them at last into their own.

Then came unification.

The aviators feared that if the Air Force were made an independent service, it would soon overshadow the Navy air arm and absorb most of its functions. Sherman, charged with the task of conducting the actual negotiations with the Army, insisted that an equitable arrangement could be worked out, and ignored these shortsighted fears. But the tension continues to exist.

The conflict is unofficially recognized, in that it is now the fixed custom that if the Chief of Naval Operations is of one branch, the Vice Chief must be from the other. Thus when Sherman became CNO, Admiral John Price, another air admiral, was replaced by Admiral L. D. McCormick as Vice Chief.

Sherman moved into this fratricidal orgy with deft decisiveness. As a matter of deliberate policy, he did not punish the ringleaders of the revolt. Some were transferred out of Washington to less crucial spots but at the same time were given attractive assignments. This is characteristic in the world of the military brass.

Occasionally when a feud or flare-up occurs, there are dark hints of retribution and wholesale purges, but nothing ever happens. This is due to the fact that while the military brass may knife one another savagely to advance their own careers or that of their friends, they never do so simply to advance the public's interest.

Sherman even championed the cause of Navy Captain Arleigh Burke who, when he was in charge of "OP-23," used that post to pump out a steady stream of virulent antiunification propaganda. The President first removed Burke's name from the promotion list, but Sherman later persuaded him to reinstate Burke, and in June, 1950, the latter got his star.

At the same time, Sherman re-established something approaching normal discipline. This sometimes required extraordinary measures.

One amazing incident prompted him to issue a special memorandum warning all officers that it was incumbent upon them to salute the President, their commander in chief. Sherman noted: "Recently, President Truman, on his morning stroll, greeted a Lieutenant with 'hello.' The officer, instead of returning the greeting or saluting, turned on his heel and walked the other way. This should not happen again."

Sherman also went to work mending the Navy's fences on Capitol Hill. In the old days, the Navy had the most efficient lobby in Washington, bar none. But in 1947, when the Congressional Reorganization Act went into effect, the more politically conscious admirals began to pay assiduous court to the late Representative Walter "Ham" Andrews, New York Republican who became chairman of the combined Armed Services Committee. The Air Force, on the other hand, shrewdly cultivated Representative Carl Vinson, the demoted Democratic chairman of the old Naval Affairs Committee, whom the admirals now ignored. This more than paid off later when Vinson, in the Democratic Eighty-first Congress, became the foremost champion of the seventy-Group program. This was quite a change from the days when Vinson used to speak of "my Navy" and of various Navy Secretaries as "the best (or the worst) Secretary I ever had."

Sherman decided it was time to restore the *status quo ante*. He began in a deliberate, subtle fashion to play up to the "old man." It doesn't require too much subtlety with Vinson, because he is ludicrously vain.

On one occasion, during budget hearings in the spring of 1950, Representative Paul Kilday, Texas Democrat, in a solemn tone said to Sherman, "I want to ask you a very serious question, Admiral."

"Go ahead, sir."

"Is the Navy aware of the fact that twelve o'clock noon last Saturday was the last time to file for election in our Chairman's district, and no one had the temerity to file?"

Momentarily surprised, Sherman replied quickly, "That is good news, very good news, indeed, sir."

Vinson added with a broad smile, "Yes, even I was glad to hear that."

Within six months after taking office, Sherman had won the respect of the Navy which distrusted him, of the President and the Navy Secretary who did not know him, and of Congress which did not know what to think. But respect is all Sherman will ever win. He is not a man who kindles warm personal attachments.

"Uncle Louie" Denfeld was affectionately regarded by men who did not respect him as a commander; Sherman is respected by many who will never love him.

He is the epitome of the reserved, highly disciplined military man. He knows what he wants and how to go after it. Early in his career he decided he was going to be Chief of Naval Operations and planned accordingly.

He was a champion fencer at Annapolis; today, his favorite recreation is riding, which he approaches in the same orderly manner he does everything. He does not play golf or tennis and spends most of his spare hours reading serious political and economic books and articles.

Sherman is not as appealing a speaker as General Collins, but he is perfectly at ease on his feet and always cogent and competent. Had he become a lawyer, he would have made a distinguished solicitor general. It was largely due to his persuasiveness that the Joint Chiefs reversed themselves on a number of decisions affecting the Navy. These included a renewed emphasis on tactical bombing, the building of a flush-deck, super-aircraft carrier, the strengthening of the Pacific fleet, and concentration on antisubmarine warfare.

All these gains were won by Sherman before the Korean war broke out. Subsequent events proved the wisdom of Sherman's contentions and still further enhanced his stature and repute.

Sherman still has his enemies. The eight admirals who were passed over when he was selected will never really forgive him for usurping the prize each expected would be his. But the country knows that in Forrest Sherman it has a leader with a forward-looking, alert brain who will not falter when the chips are down.

Sherman is one admiral who intends to do all his fighting against foreign enemies.

General Omar Bradley is the first to hold the newly created post of permanent chairman of the Joint Chiefs of Staff.

He came out of the war justly esteemed in and out of the Army as a gentleman and an officer in the finest sense of the American tradition. He won that popular accolade because he is a man of great simplicity and profound decency. He is utterly devoid of ambition. He is not a glad-hander or a schemer or a martinet—three of the more common and less attractive military species. It is inconceivable to think of Bradley's leading anything comparable to the admirals' revolt.

He recognizes and abides by the canons of American military

practice. One of these is that the military does not meddle in politics. Another is that orders are obeyed whether or not they are liked. A third is that the civilian branch of the government is supreme.

Bradley is keenly aware of the Army's proper place in the body politic and the body economic. He recognizes there is an over-all federal budget and a national economy which is supporting the stupendous burden of military expenditures. Too many of his Pentagon colleagues act as if the military were living in a financial vacuum. Bradley always emphasizes that total security is impossible, that we can have only "reasonable security." (He also recognizes that there are factors other than the purely military that are important in the world today.) On one occasion, Representative Jack Javits of New York asked him at a committee hearing whether he favored rearming the Germans. Bradley replied that, from the purely military point of view, the entrance of Western Germany into the Allied security system certainly would strengthen the West, but there were other factors and other nations to be considered.

Bradley brings to his job as head of the Joint Chiefs a lifetime devoted to preparation for this service. He has wide battle experience, far more than Marshall and Eisenhower, who spent almost all of their careers as staff officers. Bradley's only weakness as a commander was his dislike for firing bungling subordinates. But on the whole he had competent staffs. His great virtue was that when he had a good man, he recognized the fact and let him have his head. Bradley thus used the enormous talents of field commanders like the brilliant George Patton to maximum advantage.

As chairman of the Joint Chiefs, Bradley has no administrative or command responsibilities. His work involves solely the consideration of strategic problems. This consists largely of reconciling conflicting points of view.

The measure of Bradley's high eminence as a military leader, a citizen, and as a person is the simple fact that he never indulges in warmongering or scare talk. He agrees with Winston Churchill, who wrote in *The Gathering Storm:* "How many wars have been averted by patience and persisting good-will! . . . How many wars have been precipitated by firebrands!"

On Memorial Day, 1948, Bradley spoke at Longmeadow, Massachusetts, to a group honoring a Medal of Honor winner, and he said, "It is easy for us who are living to honor the sacrifices of those who are dead. For it helps us assuage the guilt we should feel in their presence. Wars can be prevented just as surely as they are provoked, and therefore we who fail to prevent them must share in guilt for the dead."

INDEX

485